John SANDFORD

THE TRANSFORMATION OF THE INNER MAN

From

Jack & Barbara

11/96

VICTORY HOUSE, INC.
Tulsa, OK

All Scripture quotations are taken from
the New American Standard Bible
(NAS), unless otherwise indicated.

To our dad,
George O. Sandford,
whose constant prayers
were for this book,
and who died October 18, 1980,
when sixteen chapters
had been completed.

Acknowledgments

Our thanks to all who so faithfully supported us in prayer, and often supported us financially, so we could write. Especially to Bill and Rachel Johnson (he is the head of the psychology department of Whitworth College, and both of them are counselors par excellence) who stand by us as our own friends and advisors.

To Joyce Poland and Tony Lincoln who deciphered many of John's impossible chicken scratchings and typed them onto legible sheets; to Tony for editing a number of the chapters.

To Janet Wilcox, our in-house counselor, who continually ran interference against the telephone and who so often kept the household running while we were immersed in the book.

To our children and grandchildren, relatives and friends who so frequently had to repeat questions and statements while we swam back from deep pools of thought to say, "What?—What? Er—oh, yes, would you say that again?"

There are so many whose foibles, successes and sins are narrated in this volume whose names are *not* changed to protect them, especially our own parents, children and other relatives. In each case, permission has been granted, and we are grateful for their willingness to be exposed before all the world.

As we prepared final copies, Leanne Payne's new book about homosexuality, *The Broken Image*, came off the presses. We want to commend her book with unreserved praise for those who want further study after reading our chapter sixteen, "Archetypes and Homosexuality."

Special thanks to our friend Marcia Tiffany for patiently and perseveringly typing the final copy while wading through multiple inserts, deletions, and cryptic markings.

Our thanks to all our board and members in Elijah House who persistently fought our overworking natures to try to hold us to the task of keeping a Sabbath for ourselves, and who tried, often without success, to preserve our first priority for book writing from the constant inroads of requests and demands from so many in the Body of Christ for help from us.

Of course no list of acknowledgments could be complete in a book concerning the healing of the inner man which does not give thanks for the pioneering work of Agnes Sanford. Not only was she for all of us the forerunner in the field of inner healing by prayer, but she was also our own first mentor in the Lord, our friend and advisor. It was her solid common sense which first hauled our soaring mysticism to safe moorings in sound theology, the Word of God, and earthiness.

Above all we want to praise and thank the Lord for His refreshing, steadfast love and His humorous ability to withstand our capacity to make complex His simple ways!

All biblical quotes are taken from the New American Standard Bible (NAS), unless otherwise indicated.

Preface

This book does not flow like a novel. It is designed for study. Our hope is that lay readers, pastors, teachers, college professors, periodicals, and journals can lift out and use any chapter, because each is able to stand by itself. That requires constant repetition of basic themes. Therefore, the book is more like a symphony. Each movement repeats the grand motif in new ways and tempos. We ask the reader to understand, perhaps to skim the familiar, to light like a bee upon each new flower of thought and take home whatever nectar seems best for his particular brand of honey, (wisdom).

This book is not designed to be an essay, nor is it an intellectual exercise. It is not written to act as a purely impersonal, objective teaching device, but to involve the reader's heart. Reading is intended to be experiential, not detached. It may be slow reading. No one should feel guilty if he cannot get through much of it at a time. Many will have to put the book down and ponder awhile. It may require many return readings, as the heart becomes more fertile soil.

Much may upset some readers. That is not part of the plan but we know it probably will happen. We trust the reader's "bounce-ability" and God's grace. Whoever reads may be less nice to be around for a while if thoughts and emotions are stirred. First fruits may seem bad, tempting one to put the book down and go celebrate the joys of faith. But wait. New seeds burst open in death in the ground. It may seem nothing but loss so long as new shoots have not yet appeared. Wait yet another while; first blades aren't ready to bear fruit. Stall a while longer; flowers are not for eating. Hold on with patience; unripe fruit usually tastes sour. Don't hurry even then, most ripe foods taste better when cooked slowly. Good fruits will come.

Reading is an individual experience. Results are not. Seeing is solitary; comprehension requires friends and sharing. Don't do too much reading without friends to talk with.

Isolation resulted in Jonestown. Share who you are as you read.

The church may not have been where you were when you started reading. It most certainly won't be when you finish! Be a leaven. Keep a few about you who understand. Don't expect others to. Don't rush out to tell everybody what's wrong with them. The church can easily do without that. Especially don't beleaguer the pastor. He will get there soon enough without your help. Most likely he has been sitting on the front porch waiting for the prodigal son to come home.

You survived this long with all the mess intact. Let's not try to straighten it all up at once. God knows the way through the wilderness.

Contents

John & Paula
SANDFORD

THE
TRANSFORMATION
OF THE INNER MAN

Section I

Foundations

1

Sanctification and Transformation

*And the very God of peace sanctify you wholly;
and I pray God your whole spirit and soul and
body be preserved blameless unto the coming of
our Lord Jesus Christ. (I Thess. 5:23 KJV)*

During World War II Agnes Sanford was a volunteer aide
in a hospital. There she found Harry, a young Jewish-
American soldier from whose leg three inches of bone had
been blown away. Agnes prayed for him, taught him to pray,
and rejoiced with him in the following weeks as those three
inches grew back! During that time he received Jesus as his
Lord and Savior. Later, he wrote to Agnes saying that he was
just fine, studying to be a Christian psychiatrist, but could not
understand why every once in a while he would fly into
unaccountable rages and do awful things, like throwing his
typewriter across the room. That drove Agnes to the Lord,
who showed her a vision of Harry as a little boy being taunted
and beaten by Gentile ragamuffins. The Holy Spirit revealed
to her that the problem was not in the grown Harry but in a
festering sore in his heart that had never been healed. Agnes
prayed for the little boy to be eased and comforted and helped
to forgive his tormentors. Harry wrote back amazed. What
had she done? He felt lighter and freer than he ever had, and
the rages seemed to be gone—and have been ever since.

The Lord soon began to reveal to Agnes many other such
inner, forgotten traumas in many people. Psychologists had
long known and taught such things. The new fact was the
power of present prayer to touch past events.

Agnes began then to teach what was soon called "the
healing of memories." Agnes never liked that term. It was not
her idea. To her the work was that of the confessional, as in
James 5:13-16, "Confess your faults one to another, and pray

3

for one another, that ye may be healed" (KJV). She saw and taught that ancient, unforgiven, forgotten sins buried in the heart could be manifested in unwanted, unseemly behavior, which could be changed if such sins were forgiven and the heart were cleansed.

A sound church woman, she saw this ministry as a work of the church, specifically to teach professional people concerning the relationship of faith and healing, to better equip pastors and elders to care for their people (Eph. 4:11). With her husband, Ted, an Episcopalian rector, she founded the School of Pastoral Care, which still today conducts occasional teaching seminars for doctors, nurses, clergymen, and others who minister. Healing of the inner man became, in the beginning, a small part of the Holy Spirit's curriculum for most such seminars.

Many pastors, doctors, nurses, and others came and learned; among them were Francis MacNutt, Barbara Shlemon, Tommy Tyson, Herman Riffel, Paula and myself, and others who have since written or become noted concerning the healing of the inner man. None of us at the time, I am sure, caught the full vision of what the Holy Spirit had begun to reveal. Agnes's interest had always been in the area of healing. To her, and throughout her teaching, this knowledge remained simply a tool for the healing of mankind. So it has continued for most others in her track.

I (John) met Agnes Sanford in 1961 in Springfield, Missouri, where she prayed for the healing of my back by asking the Lord to enable me to forgive my mother. (Until I was thirteen, my relationship with my mother had been terrible. But then I forgave her and was forgiven, and since that time we have enjoyed a good, if imperfect relationship.) I knew by my psychological training that Agnes was praying for the inner boy from conception to thirteen whom I could not reach. It worked. I was healed.

Subsequently I had a dream in which Agnes came through my front door (without bothering to open it) and tackled me. We wrestled all over my living room floor

(Gen. 32:24-32). I was then a 165-pound weight lifter who stood six feet tall. That five-foot-four-inch woman beat me! She then went out the door beckoning me to follow, and went through the night to a tall tower of a building and raced from floor to floor turning on lights. Ever since then the Lord has been turning on lights in my "tower of knowledge."

In 1963 I joined Agnes as a teacher in many seminars conducted by the School of Pastoral Care. Together for several years we taught the healing of the inner man in schools and missions across the country. Though at first I saw the ministry mainly as an extension of the confessional into the priesthood of all believers, the Lord gradually opened my eyes to His larger intentions. I came to understand a vast difference between the original events, the *sins* of resentment and judgment which lie behind present behaviors, and sinful *practices* in the old nature. *Sins* need forgiveness. But our *sin nature* can only be dealt with by our own death on the cross. Forgiveness is done for us totally by Jesus. Death on the cross requires our participation. I saw then that many who had come into inner healing were rightly praying for forgiveness but frequently failed to call the sin nature to death on the cross. On the other hand, many pastors, who rightly called their people to daily death of self on the cross, had little awareness of the formation of those practices in early childhood, nor how to reach to the inner child to accomplish that death and rebirth. These ministers seemed to me like gardeners continually lopping off weeds which just as persistently regrew from the roots. None seemed to comprehend the whole job, to lay the ax to the roots. Roots lie hidden, beneath the surface. Neither healers nor pastors seemed to know how to transform our carnal natures at the deep level of *causes*, dealing both with sins and the sin nature. That I saw, was the great lack in the Church, and therefore one explanation for the continuing lack of maturity through lack of true sanctification and transformation in the Body of Christ.

I saw then that we had all been like little children, fumbling unwittingly with the key to the door of sanctification.

Agnes had begun to reveal it. Many had learned to reach to the inner child, "See to it that no one comes short of the grace of God; that no *root* of bitterness springing up causes trouble, and by it many be defiled. . ." (Heb. 12:15, italics mine). But none seemed yet to have comprehended the full vision of inner transformation by *continual* death and rebirth. Being healers, they thought only to restore men to the abundant life, whereas God wants to raise perfected sons. Thus, many were only patching old garments rather than slaying the old to replace with the new.

None seemed yet to know that ministry to the inner man is not merely a tool to heal a *few troubled* ones; it is a vital key to the transformation of *every* heart of *every normal* Christian! Since the efficacy of applying the cross by counsel and prayer to every moment of life from conception to the present, in order to mature in Christ, had not been fully grasped, not only by the pioneers but by all of Christendom, "once done always done" had become a magic motto for born-anew people. All one had to do was to accept Christ as Lord and Savior. That falsely became the magic which was to have accomplished everything to fit us for life here and in heaven. Rightly grasping that every sinful deed was fully washed away, the Body failed to realize that every part of the heart had not fully appropriated the good news of that fact. Rightly believing that positionally the old man is fully dead and a totally new creature is present, the Body failed to grasp that in fact many areas of the inner man have refused even to be seen, much less to lie down and accept that death. So Christians proclaimed, "I'm born anew; I'm a totally changed man; I'm a new creature; the past is all gone," while the testimony of their lives all too often proclaimed the opposite. And the good news of Jesus was blasphemed to unbelievers. Healing of the inner man seemed to these believers a denial of their salvation, and still does to many today.

I saw then that one reason so many born-anew people turned from inner healing (except for simple basic flight from the pain of continual death by claiming it was once and for all accomplished) was that so many who entered the field were too unaware of sound biblical and evangelical understanding of our sin nature, thus also tending too much to think in a psychological way. Psychology, insofar as it follows its founders' teachings, believes that life writes on us who we are, that we are conditioned by what happens *to* us. It tends to overlook sin and talk about conditioning, thus minimizing guilt. Whereas sound theology maintains that many practices in us stem from our sin nature itself, quite apart causally from events in this life. As Christians, we believe that what is already in us, by inheritance from Adam, colors our interpretation of all that happens to us, and influences drastically our choices in responding. Further, Adamic sin often initiates many wrongs done by us before events happen to form us wrongly. It is not merely that life does things to us; we first do some things to life. Therefore, as Christian counselors we are always dealing *first* with guilt, then with conditioning.

Psychologists want to restore the individual ʼu a functioning level; Christians want to forgive and bring to death and rebirth. For us, the counselee's difficulty is not first something only to deplore and overcome, but something as well to appreciate as the context in which God matures a soul. We look to the entire life, especially to the transformation of the sin nature. Unfortunately, wherever men were not grounded theologically in a biblical doctrine of sin, the field of healing was becoming problem-centered rather than cross and sanctification-centered. That meant that forgiveness and comforting, wonderful as they are, were all too often being applied apart from the call to our sin nature to die on the cross; thus causing men as we said, to "fall short of the grace of God." True and lasting change was not happening. Band-Aids were being applied to gaping wounds. Events had been dealt with by the blood, but death of inner structures on the cross had not been accomplished. It was not that to forgive and comfort was wrong, but that it was incomplete. Something was yet lacking. That something, that key to sanctification, turned out to be the knowledge of *how* to reach to the depths of the heart with the power of the cross and resurrection to effect lasting change, by continual death and rebirth.

For many years I had pondered the question of the Church's continuing perversity and weakness despite the presence of the Word, the Holy Spirit, and the gifts. I saw then that one major missing element in the Church's life and ministry is its lack of comprehension of the necessity and ways of inner sanctification and transformation. In short, the heart has never yet been effectively dealt with. "They have healed the wound of my people lightly, saying 'peace, peace' when there is no peace" (Jer. 6:14; 8:11 RSV).

Scripture passages began to leap out at me: "The Spirit of the Lord is upon Me, because He anointed Me to preach the gospel to the poor. He has sent Me to proclaim release to the captives, And *recovery of sight* to the blind, *To set free* those who are downtrodden, To proclaim the favorable year of the Lord" (Luke 4:18-19). "And do not be *conformed* to this world, but be *transformed* by the renewing of your mind, that you may prove what the will of God is, that which is good and acceptable and perfect" (Rom. 12:2, italics mine). *"Put to death* therefore what is earthly in you: fornication, impurity, passion, evil desire, and covetousness, which is idolatry. . . . Do not lie to one another, seeing that you have *put off* the old nature with its practices. . ." (Col. 3:5, 9 RSV, italics mine). *"Put on* then, as God's chosen ones, holy and beloved, compassion, kindness, lowliness, meekness, and patience. . ." (Col. 3:12 RSV, italics mine). *"See to it* that no one fail to obtain the grace of God; that no *root of bitterness* spring up and cause trouble, and by it the many become defiled. . ." (Heb. 12:15 RSV, italics mine). "Woe to you, scribes and Pharisees, hypocrites! For you clean the *outside* of the cup and of the dish, but *inside* they are full of robbery and self-indulgence. You blind Pharisee, first *clean the inside* of the cup and of the dish, so that the outside of it may become clean also" (Matt. 23:25-26, italics mine). "And like living stones *be yourselves built* into a spiritual house, to be a holy priesthood, to offer spiritual sacrifices acceptable to God through Jesus Christ. For it stands in Scripture: 'Behold, I am

laying in Zion a stone, a cornerstone chosen and precious, and he who believes in him will not be put to shame' " (1 Pet. 2:5-6 RSV, italics mine).
I understood then that the Holy Spirit intended to open a door to ministry for the whole Body of Christ. It was not merely for a few superstars to heal the few troubled ones, but for the sanctification and maturation of every member of the entire Body, done by Him, *by all for all.* He did not want only to heal specific memories, nor merely to forgive particular sins. He purposed to raise up a John-the-Baptist ministry to lay the ax to *every* root of *every* tree (Luke 3:9). He is raising up His "messenger" to purify the entire Church, and through it the world, "And He will sit as a smelter and purifier of silver, and He will purify the sons of Levi and refine them like gold and silver, so that they may present to the Lord offerings in righteousness" (Mal. 3:3).

> To me, the very least of all saints, this grace was given, to preach to the Gentiles the unfathomable riches of Christ, and to bring to light what is the administration of the mystery which for ages has been hidden in God, who created all things; in order that the manifold *wisdom of God might now be made known through the church* to the rulers and the authorities in the heavenly places. (Eph. 3:8-10, italics mine)

Overeager and overzealous, I tried to write this vision for the Body of Christ. That was in the winter of 1968-69 in Wallace, Idaho. November to March, snow lay more than six feet deep! I was writing on sheets of paper laid out on a table in our camper. Returning from a speaking mission, I discovered that the weight of melting snow had sprung a leak in the camper roof, in only one place—directly over my work table! Everything was soaked. The lines of writing were blurred on every page, and all the pages were stuck together. How much better could the Lord have proclaimed, "John, you're all wet!" Then came the "seven years eating grass" of which we wrote in *The Elijah Task,* chapter four, "The Call of a Prophet," pages 51-57. During that time I was to see a major correction in my thinking—like turning the world upside down (Acts 17:6)! My picture of transformation could then have been represented by the frame of a man in which crosses could be superimposed upon sores here and there until the entire man was cleansed and became whole. I thought that as the Lord transformed one area of trouble after another, we would become better and better and holier and holier, and so at last we would arrive at the perfect man I thought Ephesians 4:15-16 promised.

I was to see in those seven years of suffering that the Holy Spirit does *not* intend to improve us or make us better and better! He intends to bring us to fullness of death and make us new. I learned also that transformation of the inner man does not once and for all fully reform our flesh this side of physical death, *but rather slays its power to control us*, while clothing us with the righteousness of Jesus. *"He* is the source of your life in Christ Jesus, whom God made our wisdom, our righteousness and sanctification and redemption. . ."* (1 Cor. 1:30 RSV, italics mine). If, on this side of mankind's ultimate perfection, the Holy Spirit were to so transform any area of a man's flesh that he could always rely on that dimension of his character, that man would inevitably cease to lean on Jesus and begin to trust in his own flesh. His perfection would thus have to be total, or he could not escape the corruption of pride. He would lose gratitude for Jesus' continuing salvation. (Perhaps for this reason the Lord took Enoch—Gen. 5:24—lest he be corrupted among us.) Therefore, the Lord so heals that we may have confidence and rest, but only in *His ability* to keep us, not in the strength of *our* character or *our* will to do right. Paradoxically, we are healed by being taught to put no confidence whatsoever in our own flesh, simply to rest in Him. The permanence of our change is in His steadfastness, not something supposedly solidly built or changed in us except a fresh ability to trust in Him. "For we are the true circumcision, who worship God in spirit, and glory in Christ Jesus, *and put no confidence in the flesh"* (Phil. 3:3 RSV, italics mine).

It became clear to me that since many Christian counselors, rightly using psychological insights, had wrongly taken their stand there, much confusion was resulting. Psychologists would mend our self-images so that we could have confidence *in our selves.* Christ would slay all our fleshly self-confidence so that our only self-image becomes, "I can do all things *through Him* who strengthens me" (Phil. 4:13). A self-image is something *we* build, in which we falsely learn to trust. A self-image necessarily sets us into self-centered striving—to live up to it, to make sure others see and reward it; we must defend it, build and rebuild, etc. But a Christian's identity is a gift, something God builds in us, not having to be seen, rewarded or defended.

Christian healing comes then not by making a broken thing good enough to work, but by delivering us from the power of that broken thing so that it can no longer rule us, and by teaching us to trust His righteousness to shine in and through that very thing. Those who were healing by restoring the self-image were causing people to trust in something repaired in the flesh, a practice reshaped in their old carnal natures, doomed sooner or later to failure. Whereas the Lord heals by leaving the broken part right there in place, overcoming it by His nature. Our trust as Christians can only always be solely in His righteousness in us as us for us!

Thus the world is turned upside down! The world would fix the broken thing and rebuild personal pride and confidence. The Lord says, "We'll fix it by not mending it at all! We'll use that broken thing to give glory to God, and from that awareness of sin we will build a trust every day anew in God's Holy Spirit to sing the beauty of Christ's nature through us for all to see." We do not have to say, "We'll be careful to give you all the glory." Once we fully understand our death in sin, He already has it all! *We* do no good thing. *He* accomplishes all. For the soul, there is in that sense no healing—only death and rebirth. The Old Testament does speak of restoring the soul (Ps. 23:3, 19:7, etc.), but Christians need continually to translate that to mean by death and rebirth in Jesus' righteousness:

> Therefore we have been buried with Him through baptism into death, in order that as Christ was raised from the

11

dead through the glory of the Father, so we too might walk in newness of life. For if we have become united with Him in the likeness of His death, certainly we shall be also in the likeness of His resurrection, knowing this, that our old self was crucified with Him, that our body of sin might be done away with, that we should no longer be slaves to sin; for he who has died is freed from sin. Now if we have died with Christ, we believe that we shall also live with Him. . . . (Rom. 6:4-8)

At precisely this theological turning point many Christian counselors have driven their counselees' ships upon the rocks. Whoever seeks to rebuild another's self-image (apart from Christ in us) works against the cross.

Those who desire to make a good showing in the flesh try to compel you to be circumcised, simply that they may not be persecuted for the cross of Christ. . . . But may it never be that I should boast, except in the cross of our Lord Jesus Christ, through which the world has been crucified to me, and I to the world. (Gal. 6:12-14)

We suggest the reader substitute for "circumcised," "compel you to find and live for your own self-image," rereading these verses in that light.

All this could sound as though we ought not, in the world or in Christ, to attempt to build good character. "It's all doomed to fail anyway, so why try?" Though God may destroy that which we have built apart from Him, He never discourages our own character-building attempts. He wants us to try. He wants us, as in Oliver Wendell Holmes's "The Chambered Nautilus," to "Build thee more stately mansions, O my soul." "First the blade, then the head, then the mature grain in the head" (Mark 4:28). God knows that the sooner and the harder we try, the earlier we shall discover our need of a Savior. He knows that when what *we* have built ripens to disgust, it and we will fall to death, and then whatever was of wood, hay or stubble will be burnt up in the fire—leaving in the process the trace of wisdom which will enable Him to build us anew with stone and silver and gold (1 Cor. 3:11-15). So God loves a stable home, which builds solidly in the soul. Though He can and does turn failure to glory, how much more He prefers to turn a beautifully formed character to death and rebirth, for then it has not only the glory of wisdom but the beauty of the ages in its inheritance.

Good or bad, whatever of character is built in us must come to death and reformation in Christ. Sanctification is not a process of removing each spot of corrupt practices until the whole nature shines as something beautiful (as I had thought). Far from knowing ourselves to be perfectly formed, we know ourselves to be perfectly corrupted and have come to rest about that in Jesus.

At the end of his ministry, when men took handkerchiefs from his body and laid them on the sick and they recovered (Acts 19:12), St. Paul wrote, "It is a trustworthy statement, deserving full acceptance, that Christ Jesus came into the world to save sinners, among whom *I am foremost of all*" (1 Tim. 1:15, italics mine). It was not that St. Paul had been a sinner and was now an innocent saint. Maturity had meant instead an increasing awareness of *present sin* until he knew himself to be the chief of sinners! In effect, he was saying, "I haven't arrived yet. I still think I'm better than *some* people!" His was a progression from knowing himself as having sinned worthy of death to realizing that his death was already a *fact* because of his sins, "Even when we were *dead* in our transgressions, [God] made us alive together with Christ (by grace you have been saved)" (Eph. 2:5, italics mine). St. Paul saw that Jesus Christ did not merely die for *sins*, but for *sin*. We are not merely sinners. We have become sin! As Pogo said so eloquently, "We have met the enemy—and they is us!" "For I know that *nothing good* dwells within me, that is, in my flesh. I can will what is right, but I cannot do it" (Rom. 7:18 RSV, italics mine). "He made Him who knew no sin to be sin on our behalf, that we might become the righteousness of God in Him" (2 Cor. 5:21). The result of such comprehension of total depravity is that His nature overshines and glories through all our brokennesses.

Jesus became not only the perfect sacrifice for our *sins.* He became like us in every respect (Heb. 2:17). He took on himself our nature (Heb. 2:14-16). Since the fall of Adam and Eve, sin is our very nature. That is what Jesus became and what He died for. His was not merely a physical death on the cross. Having become our sin in all that He was, He died in all that He was—heart, mind, soul, and body. It is from that fullness of death that Jesus raises us to be new creatures in Him. Truly we *are* new creatures. "Therefore if any man is in Christ, he is a new creature; the old things passed away; behold, new things have come" (2 Cor. 5:17).

Nevertheless, a danger remains: we may forget that underneath the shiny, new paint of Jesus, the rust of our own corruption waits to reassert itself if we turn away from Him.

We would like to feel after all that we are pretty good people. To be sure, we did some awful things. But Jesus paid the price for that, and now we can be the "good guys" God created us to be. Not that way, folks! You can't peel it off and get down to the good. The whole thing got corrupted, and now it's "Leave it there, and put on Him" (Col. 3). That is how we have the new nature, by wearing it.

What the Church has lacked is day-by-day death and rebirth in Christ. We have smugly sung that death and rebirth have been accomplished, when the process has only begun! The very saint who wrote that salvation is a free gift not of works (Eph. 2:8-9), also wrote, ". . . *work* out your salvation with fear and trembling" (Phil. 2:12). The *blood* of Jesus washes away sins, and the *cross* redeems, justifies, and atones, while His *resurrection* restores and gives new life. But it is our own personal daily taking up of *our own cross* which continues the necessary slaughter of our old man. Only as that daily work of continuing sanctification happens to the fullest does the mature man of faith appear, whether that be an individual or the corporate Body of Christ (Eph. 4:16). From birth on, each of us is trying to build a self we can accept. It is the same striving whether we want to be like God, gentle and good, or powerful, or evil. The attempt is to build a character structure which works the way we want it to. All too many Christians, without being aware of it, are still trying to *use* the Lord to build that good self. Their prayers and deeds are to that end. But that is not the Lord's design. He does not want us to build a successful self (1 Cor. 2:8). That whole search to build something we can accept and rest in is the very thing which was to have died on the cross. Continuing to try to build ourselves is actually based on flight from accepting what we are—as though if we could just build something powerful or lovely enough, we might come to peace about ourselves and forget the search to overcome the hidden rotten core. But the simple good news is that the search is already ended. We are already accepted, right where we are, as we are. The Lord's love is unconditional. *He* will build us.

The Lord wants us to accept ourselves as we are, rotten and unchanged, and then let Him express His goodness and righteousness in us through His Holy Spirit. "Come to him, to that living stone, rejected by men but in God's sight chosen and precious; and like living stones *be yourselves built* into a spiritual house, to be a holy priesthood, to offer spiritual sacrifices acceptable to God through Jesus Christ" (1 Pet. 2:4-5 RSV, italics mine). Note the passive voice, "be built," not "build yourselves." The call is not to build; the call is to die.

> I urge you therefore, brethren, by the mercies of God, to present your bodies a living and holy sacrifice, acceptable to God, which is your spiritual service of worship. And do not be conformed to this world, but be transformed by the renewing of your mind, that you may prove what the will of God is, that which is good and acceptable and perfect. (Rom. 12:1-2)

> And He was saying to them all, "If anyone wishes to come after Me, let him deny himself, and take up his cross daily, and follow Me!" (Luke 9:23)

> I have been crucified with Christ; and it is no longer I who live, but Christ lives in me: and the life which I now live in the flesh I live by faith in the Son of God, who loved me, and delivered Himself up for me. (Gal. 2:20)

> Now those who belong to Christ Jesus have crucified the flesh with its passions and desires. (Gal. 5:24)

The tragedy is that all too many Christians are still trying to build, rather than to rest in Him. Sanctification is the process by which we come to rest in Him. Sanctification is daily death and rebirth. Sanctification is that part of the maturation of the sons of God which proceeds by the Holy Spirit solely through the cross of Christ, borne individually! The end product of sanctification is not only a new person but a clean one. "Now in a large house there are not only gold and silver vessels, but also vessels of wood and earthenware, and some to honor and some to dishonor. Therefore, if a man cleanses himself from these things, he will be a vessel for honor, sanctified, useful to the Master, and prepared for every good work" (2 Tim. 2:20-21).

Before the Fall, sanctification and maturation were one and the same—steady, simple growth in humility, into the holy wisdom of God, as Jesus "increased in wisdom and stature, and in favour with God and man" (Luke 2:52 KJV), without sin. The Fall of man, descending from generation to generation (Deut. 5:9), demanded death and rebirth.

In every age, God's work has been to raise His sons. Sin being what it is, ever since Adam and Eve, He has always been about the business of changing hearts. Healing of the inner man is not new, we only call the process by new names. The new fact is that today God is calling the entire indwelt Body of Christ to ministry and maturity. Maturity comes by the Word and sanctification. Sanctification happens as Christians learn to speak the truth to one another in love (Eph. 4:15).

Transformation

Transformation is that process of death and rebirth whereby what was our weakness becomes our strength. Sanctification overcomes the power of canceled sin, but transformation turns the mess to glory. As is true for the work of inner healing, so transformation of the inner man is not the work of a few superstars. It is the labor of the entire body, in labor pains for the continual birth of the body, "and she cried out, being in labor and in pain to give birth. . . ." "And she gave birth to a son, a male child, who is to rule all the nations with a rod of iron. . ." (Rev. 12:2 and 5—see also Isa. 66). Transformation is the work of the total Body of Christ, to prepare us all as a bride adorned for her husband.

Transformation proceeds by brokenness. "The Lord is near to the brokenhearted, And saves those who are crushed in spirit" (Ps. 34:18). Wherein we still trust in our own righteousness, His grace has little room to express His righteousness. But wherein we are acutely aware of our sin and brokenness, His life is most set free to be resurrection Life in us. Truly our "strength is made perfect in weakness" (2 Cor. 12:9).

The good news of the gospel is not merely pardon, which leaves the record of sin, and of itself says nothing of change in the sinner. (In legal terms, pardon only says that the sinner will no longer be punished, whereas forgiveness erases the record of sin.) The good news is justification, but not merely that (that in Christ the debt ledger is paid and we are even with the board again). The good news is also, but not merely, redemption, that in Christ Jesus we are bought back from the hand of death. The good news is victorious fullfillment! We do not only get out of jail free, we go past GO and collect $200 with all our mortgages paid and houses and hotels collecting rent again!

It is not as though we started from ground zero on a scale of one to ten, arrived at point two and fell, being subsequently returned by grace to point two to begin again. It is as though having fallen at two, we have returned as the prodigal son at point seven or more to put on the ring and robe of authority, having gained by what we have been through, wiser and richer than we would have been had we never fallen!—even as the heart of the prodigal son knew more of his father's love than his elder brother did (Luke 15:11-32). It is not merely that our waste places are comforted. Every wilderness in our personal life becomes a part of the tree of Life of Rev. 22:2, "For the healing of the nations." Our deserts are turned to glorious gardens for the feeding of others. That is the joy of the gospel and the meaning of transformation, not merely return, but fullness of victory for ministry to others.

Grace never says that we should run out to sin in order to become wiser. Rather, as awful as sin is and as much as it is to be deplored, the latter side of it by the foolishness of the gospel is the grace of God to turn every worst degradation into our highest glory! Some have naively said what is not in God's Word, "If you haven't forgotten, you haven't forgiven," and "You should forget you ever sinned." Far from forgetting our sins, we are to remember them with sweet gratitude and joy. God forgets our sin, but it is not wisdom or fullness if we do. Having fallen, remembering means we cannot justify blaming another; and we are prepared by our "misbeings" and "misdoings" to help others from the same holes and traps.

Therein is the specific meaning of the word "transformation." Death and rebirth alone could seem to connote that the old was all a waste and had best not been at all, and that the new creature has no relation to it whatsoever. But transformation rises out of "For since He Himself was tempted in that which He has suffered, He is able to come to the aid of those who are tempted" (Heb. 2:18). Because of what we have been, we are able to minister. The new creature in Christ now treasures the old. If he does not, and yet shudders, transformation is not yet complete, for in the failures and corruptions of the old the gold of wisdom was formed, "tried in a furnace on the earth, refined seven times" (Ps. 12:6).

> Blessed be the God and Father of our Lord Jesus Christ, the Father of mercies and God of all comfort; who comforts us in all our affliction so that we may be able to comfort those who are in any affliction with the comfort with which we ourselves are comforted by God. For just as the sufferings of Christ are ours in abundance, so also our comfort is abundant through Christ. But if we are afflicted, it is for your comfort and salvation; or if we are comforted, it is for your comfort, which is effective in the patient enduring of the same sufferings which we also suffer; and our hope for you is firmly grounded, knowing that as you are sharers of our sufferings, so also you are sharers of our comfort. (2 Cor. 1:3-7)

A pearl is one of the symbols of wisdom because wisdom is formed in the same way a pearl is formed. A grain of sand becomes an irritant, forcing the oyster to wrap layers of pearl around it. Likewise the irritant of sin, crucified and coated with the blood and righteousness of Jesus, writes into our hearts a wisdom priceless beyond rubies (Jer. 31:33, Prov. 3:15 and 8:11).

Healing of memories as taught by some seems to say that we should erase the old. Neither healing nor transformation ever erases what is past. That would be to invalidate rather than to celebrate. Transformation says, "For this reason we have lived and sinned and have been redeemed, that out of the ashes of what we have been and have done has grown the ministry we are."

Transformation holds implicit that nothing in our lives is ever wasted. The prevenient grace of God is so complete that there is no event in our lives without which we would be better off, no structure in our souls which ought to be excised (cut out, as by surgery). Transformation, therefore, confirms that Satan has won no victories whatsoever among the saved, for from the ground plan of creation, even as God planned to turn the lowly cross to highest victory, so He has turned *every* aspect of our (seemingly) defeated lives to glory!

Transformation celebrates that the lizard which rode our backs is the very thing which will become the noble steed to carry us to victory in the battle for others (C.S. Lewis, *The Great Divorce*). Transformed alcoholics minister best to alcoholics. The formerly depressed know by their own desert experiences how to feed the downtrodden the only kind of manna they can receive. The judgmental become tenderhearted extenders of mercy. Hearts of stone become warm hearts of flesh to melt wintry souls (Ezek. 36:26).

Transformation is, therefore, not synonymous with healing (unless we mean by "healing" what transformation is). The word "healing" seems to imply that something got broken, so we fix it. In our carnal minds formed in the world, healing may yet mean "to restore something formerly good to working order again"—like a good car with some hidden flaw which creates a malfunction until a mechanic discovers and fixes it. That's fine. Good things need to be mended. But that analogy cannot be applied to the human soul. To the body, yes. Our bodies are good and clean, washed by the blood of Jesus (Acts 10:15), and often need to be mended. A wounded spirit may also need that kind of healing. But no structure in our carnal nature is to be patched up; every part is to be slain and reborn. The human soul is not in that sense to be mended. "But no one puts a patch of unshrunk cloth on an old garment; for the patch pulls away from the garment, and a worse tear results. Nor do men put new wine into old wineskins; otherwise the wineskins burst, and the wine pours out, and the wineskins are ruined; but they put new wine into fresh wineskins, and both are preserved" (Matt. 9:16-17). The inner being is not good, that it should be restored, "For I know that nothing good dwells in me, that is, in my flesh; for the wishing is present in me, but the doing of the good is not" (Rom. 7:18).

We died, and were made perfect, positionally, in every part of us, when we first received Jesus as Lord and Savior. "For by one offering He has perfected for all time those who are sanctified" (Heb. 10:14). Abraham was given the land of Canaan when he first came there (Gen. 15:7-21), but it took centuries of suffering, imprisonment, exodus, trial, wilderness-walking and conquering before the Israelites did in fact possess what was already positionally theirs. Just so, our total being received its death blow at the moment of our conversion. That innermost salvation must become manifest in our lives in entirety (Phil. 2:12). But our entire selves are not always aware of or ready for death and rebirth! By common sense, this side of death, we simply could not stand to be completely transformed all in one moment. The Lord intends to *put* His law in our minds and to *write* it on our hearts (Jer. 31:33 and Heb. 8:10). That *writing* lasts a painful while (1 Pet. 5:6-10). It requires a slow process, for "precept [must be] upon precept, precept upon precept; line upon line, line upon line, here a little, [and] there a little" (Isa. 28:10 RSV). That slow process is one reason for the Church, and within the Church, for the ministry of a counselor. As we were not naturally born and raised by ourselves, without fathers and mothers, so spiritually we are not slain and reborn without the ministry of the Body of Christ. Though the Body may err, Christ will use those very errors to inscribe lessons on our hearts, and He will not fail.

This book is written to inform the Church for ministry. God has placed us within the Church for this reason, that through the Church He may transform our nature,

> . . . for the equipping of the saints for the work of service, to the building up of the body of Christ; until we all attain to the unity of the faith, and of the knowledge of the Son of God, to a mature man, to the measure of the stature which belongs to the fulness of Christ. As a result, we are no longer to be children, tossed here and there by waves, and carried about by every wind of doctrine, by the trickery of men, by craftiness in deceitful scheming; but speaking the truth in love, we are to grow up in all aspects into Him, who is the head, even Christ, from whom the whole body, being fitted and held together by that which every joint supplies, according to the proper working of each individual part, causes the growth of the body for the building up of itself in love. (Eph. 4:12-16)

2

The Evangelical Base of Transformation, Parts 1 and 2

*Take heed, brethren, lest there be in any of you
an evil heart of unbelief, in departing from the
living God. (Heb. 3:12 KJV)*

Part One: The Unbelieving Heart of a Believer

The problem of God with man has never been solely to convince the conscious mind. If it were, He would need only to raise up forensic debaters or brilliant apologists, rather than pastors and churches who nurture. "For with the *heart* man believeth unto righteousness; and with the mouth confession is made unto salvation" (Rom. 10:10 KJV, italics mine). It seems to me we have all too often mentally mistranslated that passage, "For with the *mind* man comes to believe, and confesses with his mouth. . . ." It is easy to confuse deep, heartfelt conviction with mere intellectual assent and to think salvation is thereby accomplished. I do not mean to say that anyone's conversion experience is thereby invalid, but that it did not go far enough. We have been too easily convinced of completion.

When belief in the heart, to whatever degree, opens the floodgates of understanding to the mind and conviction to the spirit and we respond in the sinner's prayer to invite Jesus in, we *are* redeemed. That is an eternally accomplished fact. In that moment, we *are* justified, a thing needing never to be repeated, by us or by the Lord. Our sins are washed away in the blood of the Lamb. Our destiny is changed from hell to heaven. We are once and for all time fully "saved."

But that experience of conversion is not all there is to being saved. Christians use the word "salvation" too loosely. Salvation is a far larger word than justification or redemption, or being born anew, or going to heaven, or all these and more put together. Redemption and justification are entrances to the process of growing into salvation (1 Pet. 2). So also is being born anew. Going to heaven is the end product. All of what happens in between, the process of sanctification and transformation, is the major part of salvation, which means etymologically from its root, "to become whole," "to be healed."

When we ask, "Have you been saved, brother?", we mean "redeemed," "justified," "born anew," and "going to heaven." Well and good. Perhaps there isn't a better word to use. But the question is confusing. If we mean, "Has the Lord gotten hold of you, paid the price, and set your face toward heaven?", every born-anew Christian ought to answer with an unqualified, "Yes, I'm saved, and I'm going to heaven." But concerning the *process in this life* of *being* saved, none ought ever reply that it is all done. Each one should answer, "I'm saved, and I'm being saved every day."

The question is further confounded by the fact that though every believer is in process, he knows by faith (as we said earlier) that *positionally* he has already been made perfect (Heb. 10:14), already been raised up to sit with Him in heavenly places (Eph. 2:6), "It is finished" (John 19:30). Perhaps we will have to continue using "saved" and "salvation" when we actually mean only "converted." But for our purpose here (to reveal the process of sanctification and transformation and our part in it) whatever *further* conversions of the heart we explore ought never to be taken to imply that our first conversion was invalid or insufficient for entrance to heaven. On the other hand, no matter how dramatic or conclusive that conversion was, we run the risk of crippling our abundant life and further salvation the moment we "build a tabernacle" as though it once and for all finished the process it in fact only began. The heart needs to be converted anew in far more reaching inner areas every day, or we fail to grow in Jesus. Indeed, that is our primary definition of growth in Christ— further and further death and rebirth through *continuing* inner conversion.

One might ask, "Isn't it confusing to insist that we need to be converted anew when we have already been converted?" It may be, but we don't know a better way to say it.

From that fact of the unconverted heart of a believer emerges the crucial calling of a Christian counselor. He is not first a teacher, though he may teach. Secular teaching is primarily an impartation of knowledge from intellect to intellect. Christian teaching to Christians builds a structure of knowledge and character upon the foundation already laid (Rom. 15:20 and 1 Cor. 3:14). But there can be no such teaching in those hidden areas in the believer where the heart has not in fact been born anew; the heart and mind can not retain and actualize the teaching in life. Nor is a Christian counselor initially a guide or spiritual director, both of which imply that a foundation is to be built on. The Scriptures do not say, "Take care. . . lest there be an *ignorant* heart," but to beware of "an *unbelieving* heart." God's answer for unbelief is not teaching or guidance but the preaching of faith for repentance and conversion. Therefore, He works through Christian counselors to convict the heart of sin, to convert anew. Counselors must first "plow" the heart, breaking up the stubborn clods of self-righteousness, weeding out the old in mind and heart, plucking up the seeds of the enemy, and preparing the heart for the seed of faith so it may produce good fruit, sixty to a hundredfold (Matt. 13:3-8).

Another image we might use is that the Christian counselor is called of God to lay the ax to the root of the trees (Matt. 3:10). That means to cut, not at the visible stump but at its hidden source. To teach or direct is to build. A counselor may later do that too. To convert means to haul to death on the cross through belief, repentance, death, and rebirth. It is the sword of truth which pierces to that task, "even to the dividing asunder of soul and spirit, and of the joints and marrow, and is a discerner of the thoughts and intents of the heart" (Heb. 4:12b KJV). Note carefully: "the thoughts and intents *of the heart*," not the conscious mind. Thus the *primary* task of a Christian counselor is that of an evangelist, bringing the gospel by circumstance and counsel to the unbelieving heart of the already believing. Evangelism of the unbelieving heart of believers is the continuing and constant work of Christian counselors; indeed, evangelism is the primary way of all sanctification and transformation.

In the first and second great awakenings in America, many evangelists arose, and Congregationalists in New England were converted by the thousands. The converted then asked, "What's next?" and began to say, "We need to grow up." The results of their pioneering efforts in Christian education were the founding of Sunday schools, public schools, and many of our great colleges—Harvard, Yale, Dartmouth, Oberlin, Yankton, Drury, etc. But Congregationalists lacked sufficient awareness of the need for the heart to be continually converted. After a while, the denomination (John's own) lost sight of the need for conversion altogether! Other evangelists appeared, crying for repentance and rebirth. Many who responded to their preaching never heard the call to mature, or like the Congregationalists, tried to mature, but missed the essential element of continual death and rebirth in the inner man.

Therefore, historically in America, sanctification came to mean striving to live up to the law, upon the base of a supposedly clean heart. That struggle all too often led to judgmentalism and hypocrisy rather than the gentle nature of Jesus. It led to Phariseeism, thus "Puritanism," against which many Americans still rebel today. Part of the tragedy was that the *heart* had never been *that* clean. Our *spirits* are washed clean at the moment of conversion (though they may need it again and again). And so are our consciences sprinkled (Heb. 9:14). But not all the heart has yet agreed or received. Why else should the Psalmist cry, "And *all* that is *within* me bless his holy name. . ." (Ps. 103:1 KJV, italics mine)? Obviously there were parts of the Psalmist's inner being that did not yet bless the Lord, or the cry would have been redundant. It is the same for a Christian.

It is not only that the task of a counselor is to lay the ax to the root and so convert the unbelieving hearts of believers, it is historical fact that the maturation of the entire Church waits upon this single missing ingredient. Nothing can be securely built because the laying of foundations is incomplete. Jesus is not yet that firmly seated as Lord in the inner depths of most Christians. It must hurt the Lord deeply that in the churches which are most sound doctrinally and evangelically, even in those churches most filled with the Holy Spirit, sin so often still runs rampant, even among the leaders! Or even where obvious sin has not reared its head, so little fruit of the Spirit is seen. Or if His fruits are there, battles and dissensions seem never far away. In such churches the work may be complete in the mind, but in the *heart* (from which comes evil) the fields remain "white already to harvest"—and almost untouched!

Pulpit preaching of God's word penetrates to the heart, for that is the sword of the Spirit at work. But how often have we all remarked that the ones who needed it most either were not there or even if they were present, seemed to hear it least? In that fact is the call and necessity for the total Body to apply the spoken word in counsel one to another. The one-on-one interplay of two hearts and minds is the most effective model of "preaching," the extension of God's Word. Every member ought to be a counselor with at least some training, whose primary function in counsel is to convert anew, area by area, here a little, there a little, in ever-increasing sections of the human heart, until all with the Psalmist can sing out as an accomplished fact, "Bless the Lord, O my soul: and *all* that is *within* me, bless his holy name" (Ps. 103:1 KJV, italics mine).

To enable the Lord to occupy the "land" of inner space is the work of the counselor. His weapon is the Word of God, not psychological cleverness or analysis. His method is conversion by prayer with the other, until the other takes up the battle cry against the flesh and makes it his own joy to plunge daily to inner death and rebirth.

Part Two: How We See God

Blessed are the pure in heart: for they shall see God. (Matt. 5:8, KJV)

Mark again those words, "pure *in heart.*" I (John) used to think that since I had received Jesus I would someday (when I died) be allowed to see God the Father and be unafraid when that time came. Of course that is true, but the Lord has been revealing that to "see" God does not refer so much to physical sight as to come to know and comprehend His nature. In conversation we say, "Oh, I see," when we really mean, "I understand." Jesus was saying that those whose hearts are purified come to understand and embrace God for who He actually is. The inference is that because our hearts are not pure, we impute to God motives and ways which are not His. We do not see God, but only our projection of Him.

"We love, because He first loved us. If some one says, 'I love God,' and hates his brother, he is a liar; for the one who does not love his brother whom he has seen, cannot love God whom he has not seen. And this commandment we have from Him, that the one who loves God should love his brother also" (1 John 4:19-21). Here we see that the impurity is hate. Hate blinds the eyes. We are told further that our hatred of fellow human beings colors what we see of God—or prevents it altogether; we do not love or see God. That is one of the primary facts which necessitate continual conversion of the heart. Our hidden and forgotten judgments, especially against our fathers and mothers, prevent us from seeing God as He is.

"He who curses his father or his mother, his lamp will go out in time of darkness" (Prov. 20:20). We call this our twenty-twenty-vision Scripture. Our judgments made against our parents in childhood, usually long forgotten, have darkened our spiritual eyes. We do not see ourselves, others, life, or God with twenty-twenty vision. "The spirit of man is the lamp of the Lord, searching all the innermost parts of his being" (Prov. 20:27). Our lamp fails to discern our own hidden ways, or those of others, to the degree and in the areas in which judgments have been made and our spirits have been consequently darkened.

People have many times come to us saying, "Don't talk to me about a loving God. Why doesn't He stop all the wars, or at least prevent some of the bestial things men do to men, sometimes in the very name of religion? Or doesn't He care?" We have all heard statements like that. Being counselors, Paula and I never try to defend God. We avoid theological debates (1 Tim. 6:20). We know the answer is not a mental one, but it is a matter of an impure heart. We merely ask, "What was your father like?" Invariably we uncover a history similar to what the counselee has imputed to God—cruelty, insensitivity, desertion, criticism, etc. No matter what the *mind* may learn in Sunday school of a gentle and loving God who "so loved the world, that He gave His only begotten Son. . ." (John 3:16), the *heart* has been scarred and shaped by reactions to the earthly father, and projects that onto God. Not until such people forgive their natural fathers can they in fact see God as gentle and kind, lovingly present for them.

In our church (United Church of Christ, Congregational, in Wallace, Idaho, 1965-1973), we used to take a team of lay people with us when we taught about inner healing. They counseled, and led groups in counseling and prayer. One was Johnnie, a beautiful lady who became our best evangelist. If someone needed a solid, first-time conversion experience, we sent that person to Johnnie. Each returned believing the free gift of salvation, knowing his sins were washed away, sure that he'd been born anew and that Jesus was living in his heart. Nevertheless, every time Johnnie had a problem, and we got down to it in counseling, she would say, "Oh yeah, if I don't do right, God isn't going to love me!" At the heart level, she could not believe in a God who loves unconditionally, though her *mind* was fully convinced and she preached it to others. Johnnie was not a hypocrite. Unbeknownst to her, she had not forgiven her father, who again and again conveyed the message that if she didn't live up to his demands, he couldn't and wouldn't love her. Our Holy Spirit-filled evangelist had an unbelieving, impure heart, until the Lord revealed, by insight and prayer, that her inner child could forgive and be forgiven. Her own heart had remained unregenerate in that hard and stubborn section. But afterwards, born anew in that area, she was able to believe God could and would love her, even if she failed. Until that happened, she could not see God—an unconverted evangelist.

Paula has a wonderful father who is kind and strong, witty and sensitive. But he was a traveling salesman, on the road two or three weeks at a time. The mind of the little girl thought, "I love my daddy; I'm proud of him. He goes to work for us." But her hidden heart was not that magnanimous. It was saying, "Why isn't he ever here for me, and why is everything more important than I am?" Her heart was angrily making resolves: "I'll have to do everything for myself. No one will be here to defend me." Paula received the Lord when she was eleven and thereafter knew God as a loving, heavenly Father (perhaps more easily because her father was). Secretly, however, part of her was cherishing bitterness and could not believe that God would be there for her twenty-four hours a day, three hundred and sixty-five days a year. On weekends, because her father had been home and had gone to church with the family, she could feel close to God, especially in the fellowship of worship. But during the week despite what her mind grasped of Psalms 91 and 121, she could not sense as reality that God was there for her. Because of her sinful hidden reactions to her weekend father, hers was a "weekend God." Finally, at my insistence, though she never had nor ever has felt any resentment towards her father, she gambled that something must be there (1 Cor. 4:4), and repented solely by faith. God answered by immediate changes in many of her mental attitudes, especially toward me, and then wrote upon her heart His capacity to protect her in a most dramatic way. But let Paula tell it herself.

John and I were on our way to Seattle, Washington, to minister to a group of Christian counselors. It was a beautiful day, and I was at the wheel of our new car. I had often been very critical of John's reluctance to give up the driver's seat even when he was drowsy, but this day he had relinquished his position with admirable grace and trust. The cruise control was set at fifty-five miles per hour, the car radio was playing quietly, John was nodding toward a nap, and I was relaxed and confident as we headed west on the highway.

The next thing I knew, I was being jostled awake by John's elbow in my ribs. I looked out the left window and saw the road going by level with the top of the window! On the right, I could see nothing but a rocky hillside at close range. Stretching ahead of us was a gravel-filled ditch, and we were running through it! But in that instant all my awarenesses and responses seemed to be in a great calm, quiet, unbelievable slow motion. No butterflies. No panic. Just profound silence.

"We have gone off the road into a deep ditch," I thought. I could see two posts down the way a bit, one of them a light post, and the other some kind of road sign. I thought, "If I try to get back onto the road before we come to those posts, I'll run the risk of wiping out on this loose gravel. I'll tap the brake, steer between the posts, and then turn onto the road." I proceeded to do just that.

When we had skinned our way between the posts (which John says were hardly wide enough to permit our passage), and had regained the road, I stopped tapping the "brake" and found the car returning to the fifty-five miles per hour still registered on the cruise control. I had been tapping the accelerator!

John looked at me and said quietly, "That was a humbling experience, wasn't it?"

As we continued our trip, these words began to rise from within me as from a deep bubbling fountain, "He loves me— God loves me—He really loves me!" I had always known that, in my mind, and to some degree with my heart. But this new *knowing* included the brand-new dimension of assurance that God is on the *throne* of my life. I had been asleep at the wheel, out of control, and He was alert on my behalf, defending, guiding, delivering me from the results of my own error! To this day we cannot understand what kept the car from plummeting straight into the rocky hillside. Somehow that car turned itself, or was turned by God. The greatest miracle of deliverance had happened while I was still asleep!

When we arrived home after the weekend conference, a phone call came from a friend, Marian Stilkey.

"What were you doing last Thursday about 10:00 in the morning? I was typing and suddenly the Lord called me to pray for you. And I did—fervently—for about ten or fifteen minutes!" That was the exact time of our trip through the gravel ditch. I *knew* that not only is the Lord aware of my predicaments—He is able to call others across space to pray for me when I'm totally helpless.

From that day on my "weekend God" has become more and more an ever-present, live-in Father who is never more than a breath away.

O Lord, Thou hast searched me and known me.
Thou dost know when I sit down and when I rise up;
Thou dost understand my thought from afar.
Thou dost scrutinize my path and my lying down,
And art intimately acquainted with all my ways. . . .

Where can I go from Thy Spirit?
Or where can I flee from Thy presence? . . .

If I take the wings of the dawn,
If I dwell in the remotest part of the sea,
Even there Thy hand will lead me,
And Thy right hand will lay hold of me.
(Ps. 139:1-12)

Before this I had had an unbelieving heart; I could not believe God would be there for *me*, though I had taught His faithfulness to others across the country!

I (John) also had a gentle and kindly father who was also a traveling salesman, gone much of the time. During the summer of 1979 I found myself puzzling over why thoughts of unbelief so often trooped through my mind. In airports, or while driving on busy freeways, I would find myself thinking, "How can God really be concerned about every detail of all these people's lives?" Or, "How can He actually know every hair that falls from every one of these teeming millions of heads (Matt. 10:30, Luke 12:7)?" My mind insisted, "This is purely a logical matter. After all, that's a reasonable question to ask." But my spirit was not at rest. I knew something else was involved. Finally I thought to ask the Lord, whose reply was instant, *"Your father had little time to notice what you were doing."* That revealed my inner world of judgments! Dad wouldn't see, compliment, affirm, or care. Never mind that in fact he did when he was home. My bitter root grew because he wasn't always there. So of course God wouldn't be there for me. And I worked so hard for Him! Then I saw that those thoughts plagued my mind most especially whenever Paula and I were busy serving the Lord. The little boy had been hurt because he worked so hard and received so little notice for it, and the grown one subconsciously expected God to treat him like that too. It wasn't noble or very self-flattering to admit to that kind of peevish anger, so the place where that steam happened to vent was in pesky wonderings disguished as cool, clear logic. The heart could not believe. God would be too busy elsewhere to be there for me. Following the revelation, repentance was easy and joyous. The result has been that I have never since been bothered by such nagging doubts. Now I have not merely belief but *surety* of knowing and feeling that my Father sees and approves of my service to Him. Now I have abiding rather than occasional fellowship with Him, in heart as well as spirit (1 John 1:3).

How many of us have come to our parents for something, and they said, "We'll see," and then forgot about it? Or we pleaded with dad to come home early and take us to the movie or ball game or something, and he promised—but didn't come? Or our parents made a promise to buy us something (a bike, fishing equipment, new coat. . .); we waited and waited, and either it never arrived or came so late the joy of it was gone? Covertly, that colored our faith in God. What kind of angers did we push down and forget, because "It's not good to be angry with dad and mom"! What kind of resentful judgments did our hearts cherish, and our minds forget?

God's Merciful Answer

In February, 1979, the Lord had been teaching Paula and me about Psalm 62:5, "My soul, wait thou only upon God; for my expectation is from him" (KJV). And "He will give you the desires of your heart" (Ps. 37:4 RSV). He had been showing us that the word "wait" is not primarily a reference to time, as we had thought, but speaks of a quality of faith. Unknown to us, "wait" hooked into bitter disappointments about absent fathers, and to the childish agonies of waiting hour after hour for some hoped-for moment which sometimes never arrived at all.

On February 14, snow lay two feet deep. That evening Paula and I and Janet Wilcox (who was then visiting us) decided to take a walk around the block. For the first time I noticed how the neighbors' driveways and sidewalks looked. Snow blowers had done neat, effective work. We were still in the "make-do" mentality of our upbringing in depression days—a coal shovel would do fine. But we often ran out of time and energy, having a huge area to clear. I thought, "Lord, I ought to have a snow blower, but those things cost a small fortune. Well, forget it. I can't afford one. Praise you, Lord, anyway." That was my "faithful, fervent, and earnest" prayer (James 5:16). We said nothing else to anyone. At the time, a man who had flown in from Colorado for counseling was in town. The next day an appliance dealer delivered a five-horsepower snow blower—a gift from that counselee! The Lord was beginning to reach another area of our unbelieving hearts.

That same evening we were packing to speak in a city in Montana. I thought, "Styles have changed. I ought to have a vested suit. My two old suits are both blue. I need a brown vested suit. Well, those cost money, and I don't have any. Forget that. Thank you, Lord, anyway." The next evening after our first talk, a man introduced himself and said, "I own the local clothing store. One way I pay my tithe is to outfit the Lord's servants who come to speak in our town. Come on down in the morning—better yet, I'll pick you up, and we'll see what we can do." The next morning he walked up to a rack and pulled out an expensive, gold-colored jacket. It was a good fit. He said, "It's yours." Then he grabbed a very expensive, brown vested suit which also fit me perfectly (I hadn't mentioned a word of what I needed). "What else do you need, John?"

I spluttered, and finally blurted out, "Some shorts. I need some shorts." He handed me six pairs of shorts, six undershirts, ten pairs of socks, and two pairs of shoes, two pairs of sports pants to go with the jacket, two dress shirts, two sports shirts, and two ties! Humbled and grateful, I knew the Lord was expansively and delightedly writing on my heart, "It is your Father's *good pleasure* to give you the kingdom" (Luke 12:32 KJV), and that right away, not after long delays. My heart had been impure. I couldn't see His faithfulness, and had often ruefully called Him "the 11:59 God." How little that sanctified His nature (Num. 20:12). Now Paula and I know more than just intellectually that He will supply our need even before we know we have one, ". . . for your Father knows what you need, *before* you ask Him" (Matt. 6:8, italics mine). He moved, in delightful ways, to convert our unbelieving hearts—and we repented of our judgments on our fathers.

We have all lived with criticism; some have experienced it worse than others. For most of us, it came from our parents, and that hurt deeply. Or it came from brothers, sisters, aunts, grandparents, peers, or teachers. Our responses, whether expressed or repressed, were often angry. Consequently, bitter-root judgments lodged in our hearts. We expected people to criticize us from then on—and dutifully, they usually did. Unbeknownst to us, that also dimmed our view of God. How many of us who have learned to listen to God have imagined we heard Him pointing out our failings, after a sincere attempt to serve Him? I (John) used to think, after presenting some thought or idea to a group, that it was the Lord who was criticizing me for things I had said or done wrong, or things I *ought* to have done but had forgotten. Then one day I heard Tommy Tyson teach on the difference between the Lord's *correction* and Satan's *accusation!* I began to ponder this in my heart. Shortly thereafter, the Lord caused James 1:5 to leap off the page at me, "If any of you lack wisdom, let him ask of God, that giveth to all men liberally, *and upbraideth not;* and it shall be given him" (KJV, italics mine). The Word pierced my heart. That criticizing voice had never belonged to the Holy Spirit! God the Father would have waited until the right moment and then gently and kindly talked it out with me: "Come now, and let us reason together, saith the Lord: though your sins be as scarlet, they shall be as white as snow; though they be red like crimson, they shall be as wool" (Isa. 1:18 KJV). I repented then of my judgments on my parents and God, and of my denial of God's nature by believing that Satan's accusations were His. I could not see God's gentle, affirming nature. My heart had remained unconverted in that stony area due to my unconfessed sin. Praise God for His holy and gentle conviction! I have never again felt attacked or criticized by the Lord. He only affirms and comforts—and later sits down to reason, considerately calling me to account; and I like it.

Perhaps the most important way we all fail to see God is in the most basic—love. Few of us had parents who could and did take the initiative regularly to comfort and to give affection when we needed it. Some had parents who hugged and kissed only in front of company or when they felt expansive, but not at times that were appropriate to the signals we gave. We learned to detest that kind of offer; it exploited us instead of blessing us. Most counselees insist that their parents did not initiate action appropriate to their needs in childhood, and many complain that their parents never showed affection at all. So we learned to define love not as a sacrificial, steadfast, daily giving, with sensitivity to what others want, but as some kind of vague sense of being half-wanted, when someone feels like touching us. That clouded our heart's picture of God, no matter what our minds learned to think of Him.

The entire Bible is the history of God taking the initiative to come to deliver all mankind and us personally. We see that basic fact, if we have eyes at all to read. But in the daily practice of devotional life, we strive to reach a God who we think may not be listening after all. We feel alone (when we never could be). We don't expect God to be sending His angels to rescue and His servants to heal before we cry out. Never mind the Scriptures about His leaving the ninety-nine in the fold (Luke 15:4-7), "He wouldn't come after me unless I do something first, or deserve it." Our dirty heart sees God clothed in our parents' mannerisms. In that area too we are unconverted in heart.

Goethe wrote of history, "Here at the roaring loom of time I ply, weaving for God the garment thou seest Him by." How fantastically true! All mankind's history teaches us at our heart's level that God is created in our image instead of the other way around. Our own personal history, every moment of it, is a fabric by which we see God. All our hurts and judgments are colored glasses which darken the face of God. No wonder He says, "For My thoughts are not your thoughts, Neither are your ways My ways, declares the Lord. For as the heavens are higher than the earth, So are My ways higher than your ways, And My thoughts than your thoughts" (Isa. 55:8-9).

From the moment of our first conversion, the Holy Spirit is given license to work upon our hearts, to reveal and convict. The Christian life of sanctification and transformation is therefore,

> Beloved, now we are children of God, and it has not appeared as yet what we shall be. We know that, when He appears, we shall be like Him, because we shall see Him just as He is. And *every one who has this hope fixed on Him purifies himself*, just as He is pure. (1 John 3:2, 3)

Counselors are meant to be God's sharpest tool for that purification.

As God raises some priests to be ordained among the priesthood of all believers, and some prophets to be recognized as such, though we all are, so there are counselors especially gifted to perceive the practices of the flesh, though this work of taking captive such areas of the imagination (2 Cor. 10:4-5) is the work of every brother and sister for every other brother and sister. How many countless ways do our forgotten judgments prevent us from seeing the true life of God manifested among us? Parental adulteries, carousings and lies, the fear of hearing loud voices in the night, violence in our parents' lives, how do all these picture God? Consider how the inability of a father or mother to sympathize or understand portrays God's nature to the heart: "God wouldn't or couldn't understand me." Or how God may appear to a child who is always controlled and told that what he thinks is not really what he thinks, or that his talent is worthless. There is no way he could feel free to assert who and what he is and expect that God would be delighted and would cherish him for his own talents. So it goes, in myriads of inner darknesses. After eighteen years of counseling others, Paula and I are still discovering, as we have related here, more and more areas in which our own forgotten childhood judgments of our parents have blinded our eyes to God. And we had good, loving, well-intentioned parents. What of the many who have been so fiercely wounded? St. Paul said, "I press on to know Him. . ." (Phil. 3:8-12). Our first conversion has resurrected our inner Lazarus. Now let us be members of that fellowship of Bethany called by Christ to take the grave clothes off one another's hands, feet, and faces (John 11:44), so we may behold life himself and walk with him and hold his hand.

Perhaps the following poem, written by a Holy Spirit-filled friend in a moment of inspiration in a Christian camp, expresses better than all in prose:

> I'm not the same on the outside
> as I am on the inside.
> I smile, I laugh.
> But I don't know joy.
> Where is my joy, O my God?
> Why have you forsaken me?
> Everything was once so free. . . .
> Once grass was green,

and hills were pretty.
Now I seem to see them through
a veil of gray.
Inside is cold and tight and sad.
I cry and ache. Most days
I long for eyes to see me.
But I hide so well, none can see.
I know it's me but then I think,
They don't care—He must not care.
But too long I have known His love,
and I know this is not true.
Yet, I am unable to get above
and I am sinking slowly in the sands.
"Help," I say—inside I scream—
but on my face, I smile.
Only my eyes express—the well
of pain in me.
I'm careful not to look at those
who might strip away my mask.
But I want it to come down, at last
Reality to grasp.
I cannot do this for myself.
Am I ready for You at last?

"Honesty," we cry,
"transparency," and the like.
But who will brave this scary turf?
I've been brave, I've tried.
But from openness came pain, from
those who want to close my door,
who trample my little girl.
So light and gay is she, but oh, so sensitive,
and too many times others have driven
her in.
"Come out, little girl," I coax,
But she just sits and mopes,
No longer can I coax her out.
Are you sleeping, little girl?
Lord, send someone to love her to
life, once more.

Amen to that prayer. Lord, send laborers into the harvest.
Send counselors to the blind in heart.

3

The Evangelical Base of Transformation, Part 3

You foolish Galatians! Who has bewitched you?
Before your very eyes Jesus Christ was clearly
portrayed as crucified. I would like to learn just
one thing from you: Did you receive the Spirit by
observing the law, or by believing what you
heard? Are you so foolish? After beginning with
the Spirit, are you now trying to attain your goal
by human effort? (Gal. 3:1-3 NIV)

Part Three: Performance Orientation

The constant propensity of the born anew is to fall back to striving by human effort. Our minds and spirits know the free gift of salvation, but our hearts retain their habit to earn love by performing. Most commonly we who are "saved" are unaware ("bewitched") that other motives than God's love have begun to corrupt our serving into striving, tension, and fear; or suspecting, we fail to know which, why, or what wrong motive.

Performance orientation is a term which refers not to the service we perform but to the false motives which impel us. Having brought performance orientation to death, we may do exactly the same works, in much the same ways, but from an entirely different intent in the heart. In bringing performance to death we are not saying to stop serving and doing, but to die to the wrong hidden intents in the heart.

As little children we all in some degree accept lies and build them into our nature. The most pervasive, destructive lie corroding all our actions is, "If I don't do right, I won't be loved." "If I can't be like mommy and daddy want, I won't belong." Sometimes even the conscious mind believes that error; more commonly it lodges like a snake hidden in the grass slithering through all our efforts. Unseen, unknown enemies have far more cogency than the known. The base of all life for the performance oriented is not restful acceptance and consequent confidence but constant anxiety, fear, and striving.

The lie becomes part of us through common daily acts, such as potty training. "Oh, you did good. Mommy loves you." Of course mommy would have loved us no matter how many times we messed our pants, but in our childish minds we connect performing with love, and soon arrive at the inverse, "If I don't do right (on the potty or anywhere else), mommy won't love me." Performing may soon so intertwine falsely with love that we cannot conceive of being loved unless we have performed rightly. Or worse, we come to believe that not performing earns rejection, so even if someone gives us love, we think we didn't deserve it and either won't receive love offered, or false guilt assails.

Mothers normally don't intend to teach wrong things. It just happens, again and again. "Oh, you look great in your new dress; Mommy loves you"—the child may take home the message that good appearances earn love (and sloppiness or ugliness lose it). "You slept *all* night and didn't cry once. I'm proud of you, son; I love you"—right there we may slip the hand of love into the prickly glove of striving to please. So simply and easily our heart laminates what ought to be separated—behaving well and being loved. We learn to fish for love, every action a lure; no action, no fish (equals no love), and to our minds deservedly so. It all becomes a delusion.

Now let us add the many mistaken forms of correction most of us have endured. "Where did my little boy go? He was here a moment ago. This can't be my little boy who acts like this." We are directly told that what we actually are is unacceptable; only the doll image, someone else's picture for us to act out, can be our identity. Fear strikes the heart lest we fail to be that identity. We dread becoming lost, from others and ourselves, and so lock ourselves into performing. Ironically, to the degree that we succeed in acting out what is wanted, we do in fact become lost from what would have been us.

Children need to be nasty. That's what we are, rascals with angelic eyes and dirty skin. "Foolishness is bound up in the heart of a child; The rod of discipline will remove it far from him" (Prov. 22:15). We need to be stopped by firm hands, and given our parameters, while being warmly held and accepted just when we have been our worst. That says love is unconditional. It writes into the heart that love is a gift fully given and unlosable. It creates security.

But the temptation so easily succumbed to by most of us parents is to use a child's need for love to try to control—"I can't love you when you act like that." How dreadfully damaging to a child! "Help! I must remember what I am supposed to be! What if I can't? Or won't do it? Oh, nobody can love me. I don't deserve it." If he could voice it, the child would say, "I'm angry. Why can't they just love me as I am?" So, out of dread, he sets himself to earn love.

"Now you go to your room, and when you can act like you, you can come out again." Translation: "Only the performer is acceptable here; not performing up to our standards earns rejection."

"Leave the table! When you can come out wearing a smile, you can be part of us. We're not going to have an old grump around here." Real message: "Love is not unconditional around here. You are not free to express honestly. Lie, and put on a hypocritical face. Then we can accept you." Our spirit knows better than that, but fear and the need to belong master us, so we make ourselves act out what we are not.

Not only are we told in many ways that letting the real one live earns rejection, we add to it after a while that the real one ought not to exist at all. From then on, honest impulses of anger, or sometimes of frivolity or spontaneity, are identified as "not us," something to be suppressed or avoided, until at last the inner being quits trying, and dies, and the hollow shell performs, devoid of real abundant life. Until that kind of wrong death, the inner being keeps trying to live. Duality of personality is thus basic to all of us.

"A Sandford man never hits a girl." That was a fine teaching. To this day I am grateful for it, and still live by it. But what was I to do with the part of me that wanted to wallop my sister, Martha Jane? To have to learn to check my feelings and make appropriate choices was good. But on what basis did I make such choices? Was it from love in my heart and respect for my father and mother, and brothers and sister, or because I was afraid I wouldn't be a Sandford? Perhaps a mixture of both? Was fear not to belong more the ruling factor than love? Which motive actually governs me?

The simple rule is this: Where much laughter and affection are present, children learn they are accepted no matter how well or poorly they perform. They are free to be. When children who have just goofed badly can leap into their parents' arms, and all can laugh and learn (even if discipline has to be applied), children learn that the nasty side is also me and is loved and lovable too. "Love covers a multitude of sins" (1 Pet. 4:8). Nowhere is that more true than in the helter-skelter of children's emotions. Unconditional love, not taken for granted, but often expressed, grants security to venture all sides of the "me" a child is discovering; and freedom to choose which modes to settle into, from an altogether different base than fear.

Conversely, uptight, rigid demands for behavior, without affection, clamp upon children the manacles of control, "You will not be loved unless you can deserve it." Once that lie is grafted in, it becomes the governing trunk to all our fruit. All our actions flow through that stem.

Even in the warmest, most secure families, anxiety normally tinges freedom with fear. Have we not all seen how our infant can play peek-a-boo for hours, and giggle afresh every time daddy or mommy comes out from behind the covering? Children, perhaps from birth trauma into a sinful world, have great inner fear of being left or rejected. The game acts out that fear, and assures again and again, because mommy and daddy are still there. Even in warm, loving families, we can fear blowing the good life, fear dishonoring the family, fear that after all we might be unacceptable if we prove to be too different from everybody else.

Therefore, the rule is: *anxiety is augmented to dread and compliant performance to the degree of coldness and rigidity in the family behavioral pattern.* To that degree, fear binds all life, ". . . who through fear of death were subject to slavery all their lives" (Heb. 2:15). The death we fear is not physical death. To the performance-oriented believer, physical death would mean release. Rather, we fear dying to that world of control we have falsely come to believe guarantees us belonging and love. That fear of death prevents even the born anew from change—until love reaches frozen corners, and death of self sets us free.

Performance orientation does not mean one who works hard, but one who works hard for the wrong reasons. A free person may work harder, in the same works—impelled only by love. Performance-oriented people require constant affirmation (unconsciously demanding it, sometimes verbally). They cannot handle criticism well. Their security is not first in God and themselves but in what people think of them. They are dependent upon the reactions of others. They have little center of decision in themselves. They must become whatever it takes to gain approval for themselves. They have become what Erich Fromm calls "market-oriented personalities," who sell themselves to be or do whatever purchases them signs of acceptance. Reproofs are taken defensively, not as signs of acceptance and love, but as rejection. Guilt cannot easily be admitted because that is translated into, "I didn't try," and "I don't belong," and "I must keep trying to belong or I am lost." Give a rebuke to a performance-oriented person and you may be astonished to hear, "You're telling me I don't love you." Secure persons living with performance-oriented people often marvel, "How did he/she get that out of what I said?" Emotional outbursts can erupt from the slightest or even unintended sleights, and we are amazed to hear, "How could you ever doubt that I love you!", usually followed by, "After all I've *done* for you." Or, "You don't appreciate me. You never do."

Performance-oriented people dole out affection by measure according to how well the primary people around them have behaved. Love is not given when others haven't done well. "They don't deserve it." Having been dealt with that way, they do it to others. How many husbands have been chagrined to discover that their wives' ability to cherish them sexually is connected to how well they themselves have behaved—according to *her* standards. Sex becomes a weapon of control. Or how often do we give each other the cold shoulder or the silent treatment, intending by that to control the other, to drive him to what we want?

Christian love ought to be opposite to performance-oriented behavior. The Word-become-flesh is love given unconditionally, unvaried by the good and bad behavior of the other. Christian love is born in the unfailing heart of Christ in us for the other. How we act out that love may vary according to the other's behavior, to be appropriate to the needs of the moment. Rebuke may be the action love requires. Or tenderness. Or withdrawal. We are governed not by insecurity but by the flow of Christ's love in wisdom. Unfortunately, however, we have been conditioned in a pre-Christian life. Performance orientation has been built in. It is the warp and woof of us. The Holy Spirit must find ways to pour love out from the center of that tangled bramble bush we have become—and many people get stuck on the undead points of us. We still use love to control, until death of self proceeds to that deliverance.

Performance-oriented people are sometimes afraid to try new things. It isn't okay to fail. Not that they don't sometimes try new things. Performance orientation may drive them to venture wildly, or cause them not to be strong enough to prevent innate creature drives. But the point is fear. All normal people fear. But in performance-oriented people fear of failure rises more out of what loved ones and others will think of them than how failure may hurt another. Security which makes fun of trial and error is gone. The performance-oriented person wants to know what the rules are, beforehand. The subliminal messages are: "Tell me how to do it so I can feel secure." "I want to know before I venture so I can feel good about myself." "I need to be in control." Therefore performance-oriented people cannot be spontaneous—unless they can play act it as a part of doing what acts out the roles of the party. Self control is a virtue for them to the point of idolatry and rigidity. They are always poised and correct—in public.

Sometimes the burden becomes too heavy. The more people and new circumstances such a person encounters, the more subliminally he must work to find out the rules and roles. Thrown under too much pressure, he may crack up, or fall into depression. He cannot conceive that he is accepted just because he exists, but only if he conforms to prevailing patterns.

If a performance-oriented person belongs to groups whose mores conflict with his own, he is nearly torn apart trying to shift gears. For example, the husband who works for a demanding, obscene, burly, macho boss who then comes home to live with a demure, righteous Christian wife finds that all day he must act tough and speak obscenely, and share dirty jokes, only to come home and act like a saint. Putting the two together at the annual Christmas party spells torture. The burden of trying to find out and act whatever buys such a person the love he needs may become so heavy that he will flip out in fright or rebellion—drunken sprees, being spaced out on drugs, gambling, having an affair, whatever blows the role of the good guy, or vents the hidden anger that comes from having to perform.

Since performance-oriented people have little center of their own, and must act out whatever the group model is, this goes far to explain why so many "good" boys seem to have so little resistance to doing wrong when in bad company. They were never that moral from a base of love but only by virtue of performing according to their parents' standards. Present temptations pull together two powerful drives: one, to break out of the mold and do something to blow the whole role, and two, to belong to the gang which presents the temptation.

Performance-oriented people may lose their true identities.

A child faces choices, hundreds of times a week, whether to act out the doll image the parents require, or to express his real feelings. A person developing performance orientation must repress the actual again and again. Several things begin to result: One, the inner being finally gives up sending messages until the person feels he really is what he is acting out. Two, below the level of consciousness, the performance-oriented person feels prostituted. He resents having to sell himself for the reward "money" of love. Three, mounting anger causes him to develop a "loser"—a need to lose. He wants to do something drastic enough to destroy the whole spurious game. He wants no longer simply to have to believe that he is loved. He wants to discover as fact, expressed and experienced, that he is still loved if he does everything wrong and becomes what is to him totally unlovable. Four, he therefore becomes a powder keg, looking for a match to give him an excuse to blow up.

Many times Paula and I have counseled people who have become successes in their chosen fields, only to have "exploded" and lost it all. Precisely at the moment when they could have enjoyed rest (Luke 12:19), they themselves blew the whole thing. They fell to alcoholism, or gambled, or had an affair, or developed some excruciatingly obvious psychosomatic illness— anything to lose! They can't understand why. It's all a mystery to them, and unfair! The reasons are simple. First, during all their striving to succeed, their inner being had to be told, "Lie down, we've got work to do." Normal interior needs for alternation, rest, expression of angers, wild impulses, fantasies, etc., had to be sacrificed to the outer drive to succeed, or so it seemed. That is like holding a ball under water; the moment exterior demands slacken, inner drives shoot up, exploding great splashes in every direction. Like an impatient child throwing a temper tantrum, the inner self screams through the losing circumstances for its chance to be heard. Two, during all the striving, the outer man tells the inner, "When we get there (million dollars, stardom, acclaim, whatever) then we'll be able to rest." Arrival threatened to reveal delusion—the person felt no more approved of, loved, or secure. Success was the wrong answer for the wrong question. Another million, another pinnacle had to be achieved, else we have to admit the whole game was hollow—but we can't do that because performing has been our whole definition of what it is to have life and be loved! The alternative *seems* to be laziness or worse, rejection, and emptiness of all purpose in life. Money, or success, never was actually the performance-oriented person's goal, even if he thought it was, but the power to feel good and acceptable—to himself and others. So the Marilyn Monroes commit suicide and the Morgans go on to try to own the whole world.

One midwest pastor felt the pressure of performing so keenly that he projected his own inner demand, created mainly by his relation to his mother, onto his wife. He just couldn't live with that woman another minute. She made life a prison house for him (he thought), demanding that he live up to her expectations. She came for counseling and changed. It made no difference whatsoever; to him she was the problem. (If he could have located his anger at his mother, he could have stopped projecting, but he had her too well protected from himself—it's not nice to hate mommies.)

This pastor was an evangelical, born-again preacher; saving souls was his business, and he was good at it. But his own heart had not yet heard what he preached. He was no hypocrite, merely a man caught in undead flesh. He felt prostituted, by and for his wife and the whole church. He had a desperate need to do something drastic enough to escape the treadmill. I (John) saw this and warned him. "Oh, no, John. I'm saved. Christ died for all that in me. I've claimed it. That's all dead. How could a born-again, Holy Spirit-filled man have all that in him?" The problem was "out there." If I couldn't help him "shape up his wife," he would have no further part of any counseling with me.

The inevitable adulterous affair was not only unconsciously, purposefully not hidden, it was especially crude and carnal—further, he *had* to blab about it. Why? To make sure the entire good-guy image was sufficiently destroyed. Fortunately, the wife and the elders to whom he blabbed both forgave, received and cherished, and today he is still the pastor of that church and is on his way to wholeness! (Confession to elders is good; his was not confession, however, but childish self-tattling.)

One of our dear friends, raised as an only child, born late to cold and distant parents, had no awareness at all of love without earning it. He would perform well, but every so often would go on a drinking spree. After one such spree, in a rare moment of truth, he told his wife, "I'm going to test you again and again, until I know for sure you really love me." Sure enough, he did, again and again, including not-too-hidden adulteries. She forgave at increasing cost, persistently. Love had to be given unconditionally until she found she no longer could give love, and in despair, she discovered that only Jesus in her could give this kind of love. At last his heart believed, and he turned around.

At what seems to me (John) the worst level, performance orientation can produce "shrikes." A shrike is a bird which tears its victims apart muscle by muscle. In humans a shrike is a person who so gathers all the righteousness to herself/himself (more commonly a woman) that the other (usually the mate, often the husband) has no room to express righteousness, and acts out the role of the villain. Usually in such persons, performance orientation is combined with sibling rivalry (the child learned to ace out the other siblings by out-performing for whatever scraps of parental praise were available) and with bitter-root expectancy that others will fail to serve as well, or do right at all. (See chapter 14 in this book, and chapter 11 in *Restoring the Christian Family*.) Bitter-root expectancy in a shrike broadcasts to the mate twenty-four hours a day, "Do wrong. Do me in. I know you will. Make me into a noble martyr. That's the way I expect life to go. That's the role I play (without admitting it)."

One lady came to me (John) wanting to know why her husband was such a weakling, falling again and again into drunken binges. She was a paragon of virtue—in dress, morals, posture, church attendance, prayer life. You name it, she was it, the "saintess" of the church. Beneath all her behavior was not pure love for others but a self-serving need to be perfect, coupled with bitter-root expectancy that the man (her father had been a drunkard) would be weak. I sat and watched as they entered into a spat. Everything but her actual words screamed at her husband her demand that he be the weakling she needed. Understandably, the more secure he became and the less he drank, the more upset rather than glad she became. Her whipping post was deserting her. Her ability to feel good about herself depended upon being able to contrast the failure of others against her own supposed virtue. This made her the perpetual noble martyr, supported in all those feelings by her Job's comforters in the church—"Isn't she a wonderful Christian living with that awful man?" Tragically she is far from an isolated case; the pattern is almost endemic. One man, not fully understanding the truth he was shouting, screamed at his wife as he beat her, "You're so damn perfect! You're so damn perfect!" His inner being knew what he hated, though his mind didn't. He had never yet had a real wife, only the performing shell.

Shrikism happens to women more than men not because men are better, (they aren't), but because women are built by God to want more to please than men, and so they fall more naturally into performance orientation than men do. Lacking physical power, women learn as girls to use emotional wiles, and forgetting that, may unconsciously use performance to ace out the husband and play the noble martyr. Men with other men tend to rebellion more often than to compliance, but having been raised with controlling mothers, they are more susceptible to performance for a wife, though less apt to be shrikes.

In the church performance orientation becomes a religious spirit rather than Christian. Religion is defined (in my big Oxford dictionary) as: "action or conduct indicating a belief in, reverence for, and a *desire to please*, a divine ruling power. . . ." Theologically, religion is defined as man's search for God, man using Bible study, church attendance, good works and devotion to try to find and *please* God. Christian faith is the opposite. It is God finding man, giving to mankind out of His unfailing heart of love. In religion, man hangs onto God. In faith God hangs onto man. In religion there is striving, fear, and false guilt—we're never good enough, we can never quite make it. In faith there is rest and peace, because the enterprise of us has been released into the Father's hands, and He will do a better job with us than we can. In faith all striving (Col. 2:1, 1 Tim. 4:10, Heb. 4:11, and 12:4) is undergirded with peace. God has us. We are loved and chosen. We may fall out of fellowship temporarily but not out of love, and when we do, He will come and get us. So we are secure. We are free to goof, and because we are, we need to less often.

Religious people have transferred performance orientation to God. Now they most emphatically have a Father whose "demands" *have* to be lived up to! Never mind that God the Father isn't at all like that. He wears the overlay of our life with our earthly parents (see chapter 2: "How We See God"). Therefore, as soon as the original relief of redemption passes, and the Holy Spirit comes, performance-oriented people think in their hearts, below the level of conscious thought, "Now I really ought to be able to live up to it!," and set themselves to strive to be perfect, not actually for love of Jesus, but out of the same old carnal fear of parental rejection. Unfortunately, all too many sermons scold and exhort for performance, building the same fearful striving, instead of preaching the simple good news of God's grace to little children peering out of adult eyes.

Religious people (P.O.s* born anew) become centers of dissension in the church. They cannot relax—nor can anyone around them. They criticize others and cannot receive rebuke in return. It was the religious leaders who crucified Jesus, and who have persecuted the faithful ever since. (In this sense, communists, being performance oriented, are religious fanatics.)

---

*An abbreviation which will be used henceforth in place of the term "performance orientation," or "performance oriented."

Religious people are the Pharisees of today.

> And the Pharisees and some of the scribes gathered together around Him when they had come from Jerusalem, and had seen that some of His disciples were eating their bread with impure hands, that is, unwashed. (For the Pharisees and all the Jews do not eat unless they carefully wash their hands, thus observing the traditions of the elders; and when they come from the market place, they do not eat unless they cleanse themselves; and there are many other things which they have received in order to observe, such as the washing of cups and pitchers and copper pots.) (Mark 7:1-4)

Their security depended upon doing the "right" things—ritual washings and ceremonial rites, not on knowing His love for them or in doing acts of love. He upset their world. They had carefully built that system of proper behaviors to insure righteousness for themselves, and to ace out all the siblings who failed to perform as well as they. (The same is often true in the church today.) Along came Jesus and by His love and merciful flaunting of their Sabbath laws, told them that all their work-righteousness was to no avail. In no way could they feel His love—apart from rites and rituals. The alternative seemed emptiness. He was a menace. He undid them. Therefore they hated Him—and they still do today, even though they are born anew and naming His name in worship every Sunday in His Church!

The great tragedy is not that P.O. people persecute those of restful faith, but that the faithful have not known how to minister to them to set them free. Believers must learn how to love strivers to rest. Nowhere else in all society can a P.O. person find rest, for only after he has again and again tested love offered can he settle it in his heart that he is okay just because he exists in Christ. The world will not so continue to accept and forgive. *In Christ* is the key, for any man's spirit will be open to the accusation of Satan until he knows in the depths of his heart that imperfect as he is, he is okay just as he is, because the Lord Jesus Christ has become his strength, his salvation and his song.

Satan seeks a prey whom he *can* devour! (1 Pet. 5:8). Paradoxically the one he *can* devour is the one who is sure of his righteousness, or thinks he must have some or be undone. In whatever area, and to whatever degree a man has accepted the P.O. lie that he must do right in order to be loved, Satan has a playing field. He can always come along and point out some area of failure. The one he cannot touch is the one who knows he remains a sinner, though redeemed, without any righteousness of his own, needing none, because Jesus is his righteousness.

Behavior still needs to be in accordance with the standards set by our Lord Jesus Christ. Being without righteousness does not mean freedom as a pretext for evil (1 Pet. 2:6). Behavior will follow as an outcome of His love in us. But success or failure in behavior is not the mark of our righteousness; Jesus is.

One does not escape P.O. or a religious spirit by leaving the Church. Nor by abandoning moral laws, which may seem to the P.O. person to be the prison. The structure of P.O. is internal; we take it with us wherever we go, like the old saw, "You can take the boy off the farm but you can't take the farm out of the boy." Wherever one is in society, performance is demanded. Nowhere is performance more fearsomely controlled by peers than in criminal society! We suggest reading *Tell It to the Mafia* by Joe Donato. Criminal societies admit people in or cancel people out solely according to how well they perform. I (John) used to answer the dispatcher in Yellow Cab days and find myself transporting call girls to "work." (By law a taxi driver must take passengers where they want to go.) I was continually surprised listening to these prostitutes complaining bitterly about other call girls who "didn't do it right." They "give our whole profession a bad name"—as though it didn't have one already! Businesses, clubs, friends, even chance acquaintanceships all contain imperious demands for behavior and penalties for noncompliance. The only *emotional* difference outside or inside the Church is that in the Church the Lord Jesus Christ has a chance to bring us to death and consequent rest in the relaxing grace of God.

The internal structure of performance orientation forms a most obstinate area of unbelief in the heart among born-anew Christians. The mind hears the message of the free gift and the spirit sighs in relief, but the heart has long been trained to strive to please for wrong reasons. As said earlier, soon after the glow of conversion dies down, performance resurrects with a vengeance, and now the Christian in dead earnest has a Father and demanding standards to live up to! Many come into the fullness of the Holy Spirit only subsequently to crack up because that undead area of the flesh throws them into an inner striving no one can live up to! Johnnie, referred to in the last chapter, had learned P.O. from her father. Now that she had a heavenly Father, the flesh grandly transferred onto the Father God all her striving to earn her natural father's love, and heaped the whole weight of Christ's example on her. Life quickly became impossible. She often slumped into depressions.

It is not that we should give up trying to live for Christ. What needs to happen is death of old motives and birth of the new. Before we are crucified, behind all our serving is that striving of the flesh. We obey law in whatever degree we are able to do so in order to win brownie points, or for fear of punishment, or to earn the Father's love, or out of duty because we were trained to, or for fear we can't live with our false and accusing conscience, or for threat of what others will think of us, or that we won't belong—all wrong motives for a Christian. *All of that needs to die.* What should impel us, singly and purely, is the flow of Jesus' love through us. What we do doesn't earn us anything, put anyone in our debt to respond in kind, ensure that we will belong or be loved, or stave off fear. Those things have all been answered by the only true answer— the gift of Jesus. But until our *unbelieving heart* comes *in truth* to apprehend that fact, we will keep on keeping on. We may, having finally died to performance, return to do exactly the same works for the Lord in identical words and ways, but what flows through us will now be Jesus' love, not our flesh, and others will quickly read and take note.

In one church we visited there was a deacon who was "Mr. Everything." He took up the collections each Sunday, sang in the choir, sold the tickets for the men's banquets, drove shut-ins to church, and volunteered for every job that came along. But he was also "Mr. Thorn-in-the-Side" for the pastor, and "Mr. Dissension" in the church. On his face and in his walk was a little boy saying, "Don't you see I'm doing it right; I'm being a good boy. Now you have to love me." In his voice, raised often, was condemnation and criticism. He just couldn't see why "others can't serve the Lord like I do." No way could he hear what was infecting all his serving. He had no awareness of his inner motives. He could not see that his criticisms were not born of love for the Lord but from his child's need to outperform sibling rivals. Since his full-flowered P.O. could not take the slightest rebuke, he could never hear the kindest explanations of what actually was happening. He has since left the church, thoroughly disappointed with those "back-sliders." The church has since become warm, unified and loving. This deacon was a born-again man on fire for the Lord. What a tragedy and a repentance for us all that we have not understood ministry to the heart, to be the kind of body that could have saved him—an unbelieving believer.

Peggy came to us because her husband had left, and she couldn't understand why. She had "done everything for him." Listening to her, I (John) couldn't see what was the real reason for the separation. Then it happened that Peggy was the guest host for a house meeting at which I spoke. The moment I entered, Peggy busied herself, blustering here and there, overserving. On her face and in her manner, even in her walk she was saying, "I'm performing well for you. Tell me that I am. Don't you feel guilty if you don't?" I knew why her husband left. The poor man could never rest in his own home. Every service she did laid a demand on him to respond, to appreciate, to notice. A man gets tired having to prove over and over that he loves and appreciates. She could never simply believe she is loved, and rest beside him. She *had* to serve and he *had* to affirm. "It is better to live in a corner of the housetop than in a house shared with a *contentious woman*" (Prov. 21:9 RSV, italics mine). "It is better to live in a desert land than with a contentious and *fretful* woman" (Prov. 21:19 RSV, italics mine). "Better is a dry morsel with quiet than a house full of feasting with strife" (Prov. 17:1 RSV).

I tried to tell her. She couldn't hear. She too was a born-again, Holy Spirit-filled, believing, churchgoing woman. She knew salvation. But her heart could not receive it and rest. "An evil man seeks only rebellion, and a cruel messenger will be sent against him" (Prov. 17:11 RSV). It was not long in coming.

Her husband returned home, but lost his job. Now he lay on the couch and demanded service. She had to go out and find a job. Not only would he not help straighten up the house or do dishes, he would not even drive her to work or let her take the car! She had to pedal her bicycle, work all day, pump home, clean up the house and his day's dishes, prepare supper, do dishes, wash clothes, and get ready to do it all over again the next day.

Whenever we continue in our own stubborn way, the kind, seeming-unkindness of the Lord is to pile on more and more until we reach the end and become disgusted enough to quit. Finally there came a morning in which, still a half mile from work, Peggy turned to churn against a forty-mile gale! That did it. There on the bike, pumping for all she was worth, she blew up at God, screaming at the top of her lungs, "Here I'm trying to get to work, I'm trying to serve you, I'm loving that no-good husband *you gave me*, I'm doing all that work at home and he won't help me—and you have to send a storm against me!" That outburst opened the doors and broke her control, and out of Peggy poured all of her pent-up feelings. She cursed, raved, and ranted, and wound up shouting obscenities at God! And what happened? No lightning bolts hurtled out of heaven to strike her down. No cars came along to crush and punish. Instead, there came an overwhelming peace. Anointing and blessing and love poured out of heaven all over her! Right there in the middle of the road she stopped and cried like a baby. For the first time in her life she *knew* someone would love her—even if she didn't do it all right. Her unbelieving heart had finally been evangelized.

A few months later, Peggy came to see me, not for counsel but to say "thanks." Always before, she had sat on the edge of her chair, knees together, hands folded in the lap, overly prim and proper. Now she lounged comfortably in the deep chair, laughed and joked, and admitted easily and honestly what she actually felt. Incidentally, finding out that it was okay to goof had not caused her to lose her moral nature. (Peggy happens to be one of the most gloriously beautiful blondes a man could wish for.) Now, being moral had become easier, originating from a base of love for God, not from compulsion. She had finally learned the true meaning of grace—undeserved, unmerited favor.

I have to confess that often, while counseling overachievers, in my flesh I have wished they would go out and do something thoroughly prodigal so they could truly learn what it is to have and need a Savior. Martin Luther used to so overconfess to his confessor that finally Spatina shouted at him, "Martin, will you quit wearing me out confessing all these little peccadilloes and go out and do some mighty sin? Then come in here and confess!" Of course the answer is not to do what Martin Luther said, in exasperation for the same reason as a counselor, "If you must sin, sin mightily!" We don't all, like that pastor mentioned earlier, have to have an affair to discover love and salvation in the heart.

Paula was like that beautiful blonde, thoroughly moral and nearly as performance oriented. In the beginning of our marriage, I could rarely tell her anything that contained rebuke; it would be thrown back on me, with defensive rancor. I had my own faults, much more grevious, but that was one of Paula's. I tried again and again to talk with her about it, but could never get through to real reception and comprehension. Finally, after sixteen years, I said to the Lord, "I give up.

58

You'll have to get through to her."

At the same time, I (Paula) was saying much the same thing to the Lord, "I give up. I don't know what he's talking about. I don't know how to change. I can't live with this impasse. Do whatever you can, Lord, to break through." Even at the time as I prayed I couldn't identify the problems as something in myself. From my point of view I was working hard to fulfill and coordinate efforts in multiple roles: mother of six, high school teacher with preparation to do in four subjects, plus being a minister's wife active in the life of the church. I was striving to succeed in all of this, and John's conversation came as an accusation and burden to suggest that I was not doing enough. Of course that was not the message he intended. But that was what I heard. I was exhausted. I wanted him to just love me for me and couldn't see that my striving and my defensive walls were preventing him from doing so. Performance-oriented people usually work hard to love by serving others but cannot let others close enough to give them love in return. We have talked to many charismatic Christian leaders since who have become isolated and lonely at the top of the stairs because no one dared to break through their P.O. to minister to them. Some friends had spoken to John, "Why can't I get close to Paula?" He had replied, "I don't know. Ask her." But I carried such a poise and control that no one seemed willing or able to tackle me head on. It seemed that each time I asked for prayer from others, the words my heart longed for never came. Instead it was, "Praise God for this wonderful strong woman." That missed me totally. I was lonely, and angry, and all I knew to do was to try harder. The defensive walls were so thick that if John had been an angel he would have had difficulty passing through. And he was lonely for me and hurting. "Sometimes I wish I'd married a dumb, talentless blonde," he once said. And I thought, "What an unappreciative nerd."

God knows that walls too high to leap over and too sturdy to pass through need dismantling. When the two of us finally "gave up," He ignored even the martyr strain in our cry and answered in a magnificent way.

I was teaching school in Mullan, Idaho, a small town about six miles toward Lookout Pass from Wallace where we lived. It was October and though the snow had not yet begun to fall, sometimes there were patches of black ice on shaded curves of the road. In the middle of the day I expected the roads to be clear as I drove home in our VW van. Suddenly at sixty miles-per-hour I hit ice (the speed limit was seventy in those days). The weight of the rear engine spun the van like a tilt-a-whirl. The microbus hit the guardrail, rolled two and a half times, and I flew through the front windshield some time before the van came to rest on its top. I woke up lying on my back in the middle of the concrete freeway looking into the face of a man I had only met once before. I thought I must be hurt, but I felt no pain, and was unbelievably peaceful. Calmly I told the young man to have the ambulance take me to the Kellogg Hospital (fourteen miles from the scene of the accident) because that was where our doctor practiced. Inquiring about involvement with any other vehicles, I was assured that there were none, and I felt tremendously relieved. Words of the twenty-third Psalm ran through my mind over and over all the way to the hospital, but the sense of peace continued. At Kellogg, as the doctor removed volumes of gravel from my underclothes, I became aware that my eye was swelling shut and requested that we pause a moment to remove my contact lenses while we could. A friend cried hysterically in the waiting room, but still a sense of quiet and calm hovered all about me.

I received a number of injuries. The top of my head felt like a water balloon. My neck and shoulders developed a lovely shade of navy blue. I must have had a swollen, fat face for a time because many days later an orderly put his head through my door with a friendly—"Well, good morning *skinny* face!" My thighs and legs were bruised and lacerated, several stitches were taken in my left knee. And when my back continued to go into spasm, X-rays discovered four broken transverse crosses. I slept a great deal of the time for two and a half weeks. I was aware of a constant stream of visitors. Church members, fellow teachers, and administrators, family, neighbors, and students all came. Their love and concern ministered deeply to me. Mail flooded in. John reported that he had received phone calls from all over the country with the message, "What's the matter up there? The Lord has been calling me to intercede for you." At home parishioners volunteered to do baskets of ironing for me (including some clothes that they had no way of knowing I had earmarked for the rummage sale!). They sent food to my family and cared for the children. The community prayed. One friend brought our youngest child, Andrea, then two, to the hospital almost every night to tuck me in. Loren, our son, came home from college to sing and play his guitar for me. I was literally inundated by love and prayer and there was nothing I could do but lie there and learn to receive.

Even the company of heaven attended me, and I wonder now that I was not startled at the time, nor did I question what I saw. But as real as the flesh-and-blood-people coming and going, there were rows of faceless figures lined up on either side of the door of my room and out into the hall. They bordered a tunnel of light that extended all the way to my bed. For a time my bed itself seemed to be covered with roses, and then the roses changed to lilies. And on the wall I could see like a penciled progress report—a sketch of myself looking down, looking ahead, then looking up as the days passed. And finally no more mystical realities. But the embracing peace remained. And I was warm inside. My walls had been smashed. I *knew* the love of the Lord as healer. I was fitted with a therapeutic back brace and told I would need to wear it from six weeks to four months. I was discharged two and a half weeks after the accident, returned to school several days after that, took on an extra class, and wore the brace for only one week.

We (John writing again) share this story to follow it with others in order to show from our own lives how stubborn the heart is, how very really unconverted it is among Holy Spirit-filled, Bible-believing people, and how many ways God must move heaven and earth to reach the many-faceted diamond of our heart. Paula now for the first time could, as she said, let people minister to her, and for the first time she could hear rebuke from me and we could have open-hearted, give-and-take, real conversations. But a still-unconverted level of her heart could not believe that God would be there for her. So God touched her again through the off-the-road incident as told in the previous chapter. But she still remained an elder sister suffering from the elder-brother syndrome (Luke 15:11-32). Paula had never known outright, purposeful sin. She had always been a "good girl."

In the Third Baptist Church of St. Louis in which I, Paula, grew up, there was none of the judgementalism and legalism for which some fundamentalists have come to be known. Dr. C. Oscar Johnson preached a very loving Jesus who gave himself and died for me because He loved me. I gave myself to Him at eleven because I *knew* He loved me. I went to the altar to receive Him, solely because of love. I loved Him so much I couldn't sit through a communion service without crying. It never dawned on me that I had never known myself as a sinner needing a Savior.

Long after Elijah House was formed and John and I were traveling all across the country to teach the love of Jesus in daily life, two Roman Catholic members of Elijah House began to confront me with a stunning, impossible word. "Paula, you don't know what it is to have a Savior."

"What do you mean, I don't know Him? I've known Him since I was eleven and I've taught about Him for years."

"You don't know Him *as Savior*. You've never known yourself as a sinner. Only sinners can know a Savior. We feel sorry for you." (Imagine, this was coming from Catholics who were speaking to an evangelical, born-anew Baptist, no less!)

I went with this to John, and he said (doubtless heaving a sigh of relief), "Ask God to show you. Ask Him to reveal your sin nature to you. He will." So I did.

Then one day a pastor brought a parishioner to see John, and while they were in counseling the pastor visited with me. I had difficulty believing my ears. I knew this man to be a very fine Spirit-filled pastor. And he was telling me in great detail about his early life as a male prostitute! I had never even heard of such a thing. But I had long practiced an unshockable manner of listening. I kept handing my reactions to the Lord, silently. But I wondered why he was telling me all this. He must have repented long ago, and knew himself to be completely forgiven and made new, so why was he talking about it? The subject changed, he left, and in the hours following I was overwhelmed with the most confusing feelings. We never lock our doors. Yet I felt a compelling urge to lock all the doors and windows. I felt silly. "There's nothing threatening me. Why am I afraid?" Then the Holy Spirit let me know that I was trying to lock out awareness of my own sinful *nature*. His sharing had not at all excited me sexually. I am too locked into John for that. But what the Lord then made me aware of was that what his sharing did was to make me aware somehow that that same capacity to sin is in all of us—and therefore also in me! That word registered as truth. For the first time I knew it was not because I had succeeded in being good enough that I had not fallen into gross sin. It was rather that the Lord had saved me by His grace, blessed me with family and upbringing and circumstance so totally unmerited that the baser part of my nature, as black as that man's or anyone else's, had not been so greatly tempted by opportunity to express the sinful nature in me. Given the same conditions, I *could* have done the same or worse as my pastor friend. I saw myself as sin, and from that base we express sin, not as someone good who occasionally sins and so is called a sinner. That realization was truly humbling.

Now that I know myself as sin, I have nothing left to defend. Every once in a while, when I get into too much work and not enough devotion, my motive base subtly swings back from love to performance. God has left us a barometer. We can tell our distance from the Lord by the resurgence of striving, control, and defensiveness. Presumably He will never take performance orientation away altogether, this side of heaven, and undoubtedly there are many more facets to the heart's diamond, still hard, rough, and unpolished. But note the continuum; as the heart is softened, God has been able to deal with me more and more gently, from near death in a physically damaging accident, to a near accident, to words of reproof, followed by a parable in the testimony of another's life. Could that say something revealing about the change from God's ways in the Old Testament with backsliding Israel to the New Testament with a loving Jesus? Can it say something explanatory about our own lives? How much easier might life go if our stubborn, unbelieving hearts could hear?

That is the work of transformation, and its base in evangelization, to reach anew and afresh to the countless inner unconverted areas of believers' hearts.

How do we transform the performance-oriented individual? It is not easy. The evil practices of the flesh are stubborn. "Therefore, since we have so great a cloud of witnesses surrounding us, let us also *lay aside every encumbrance, and the sin which so easily entangles us,* (RSV says "which *clings so closely")* and let us run *with endurance* the race that is set before us" (Heb. 12:1, italics mine). We are not accustomed to thinking of performance orientation, by which we strive to do so many *good* things, as sin, but it is desperately so.

First we must help the person to see it. Talk with him about it. Use this book. Give him tapes to listen to. (We in Elijah House use two by John and Paula, "Performance Orientation" and "Dying to Performance Orientation," and one by Loren entitled, "Freedom From Performance.")

The person must come to see performance orientation not as some little series of events nor as a tiny, peculiar segment of his nature but much as a metastatic cancer extending tentacles into everything he is and does. He must see it not as some isolated little flaw but as the very warp and woof of his entire life, and he must come to hate it. "Hate that which is evil" (Rom. 12:9 NIV). P.O. is the central structure of our kingdom of self!

Repentance, from *metanoia* (Greek), means change, to turn around and go the other way. All such structures as performance orientation have a life of their own in us. We are created in God's image, and whatever we create within us has a life of its own and does not want to die. That evil practice in us will throw smoke screens and alibis, "Oh yeah, well, you do the same thing," or "You're not so neat yourself." Loren used to come home feeling guilty, and knowing we had discovered some of the reasons, he would confess two or three of the maybe ten things he had done. He felt better, and so he was able to gloss over in his own conscience the other seven or eight. We thought of him as a most honest and dutifully repentant son—until we caught on. Just so, our own inner being will throw out golden apples for us to chase while the real nature of sin runs on unchecked (a parable of our inner psyche from Greek mythology). Counselors must have the tenacity of a bulldog and the penetrating power of a steel chisel. ". . . Surely the whole house of Israel is stubborn and obstinate. Behold, I have made your face as hard as their faces, and your forehead as hard as their foreheads. Like emery harder than flint I have made your forehead. Do not be afraid of them or be dismayed before them, though they are a rebellious house" (Ezek. 3:7-9).

All such structures as performance orientation carry a reward system with them. So long as we prefer the rewards, we will not change. One time I (John) kept trying and trying not to do a particular sin, praying about it over and over, only to do it again. Finally I got mad at God and cried out, "Why don't you help me with this?"

He answered quickly and succinctly, *"You aren't disgusted enough yet!"* Hate had not yet become fully ripe. God then told me, "You are still enjoying that thing."

"I do not. I hate it," I protested.

"Son, if you hated it enough, you'd quit it. You enjoy it."

That led me to ask myself in what hidden ways I might in fact be enjoying sin. The Lord began to reveal mazes of subterranean lines carrying hidden delights from one pocket of pus to another. If the sin was, for example, to turn silent, cold and inattentive around Paula, behind that single, simple happening were: the delights of punishing a critical mother; feelings of power in getting another's goat; the wicked fascination of making another suffer; fantasies of being the noble martyr keeping his cool while Paula—poor thing— blows her control and becomes furious, not as able to be as "Christian and controlled" as I am; inadmissable feelings of getting even with Paula; dominance and control; male superiority; and so we could catalogue a nearly endless list of delights behind one simple sin. I am not likely to give up such rewards so long as they mean more to the hidden control centers *of my heart* than Paula or God mean to me. To come to a proper and sufficiently intense hatred of the self we have built in opposition to God is a distinct gift from the Lord. I soon discovered I couldn't hate sin enough by the power of my fleshly will to come to a true repentance. I stood helpless in corruption. "The heart is more deceitful than all else and is desperately sick; Who can understand it?" (Jer. 17:9). The Latin derivation of "desperate" means "without hope," helpless.

Repentance is born of a gift of love which reaches an unrepentant, unconverted segment of our hearts. Until true love is allowed, or somehow finally touches that guarded area, we cannot change. We may set the sails of our wills determinedly again and again, but usually the first change in the winds of life find us unable to tack—and so we *attack*. Paula and I, feeling overly responsible, have carried thousands of people in our hearts (Phil. 1:7) and worn ourselves out trying to touch that needed depth, only to discover when we let go that God could use the most unlikely circumstance (like a bike in a forty-mile-per-hour wind) or impossible person (like a mongoloid to touch a brilliant professor). We learned finally to believe for the other that God would touch his heart (1 Cor.13:7, "love *believes* all things"), and offer to be there in case the Lord wanted to touch the other through us.

A counselor must be willing to bear and endure (1 Cor. 13:7 "love bears all things") in patience, for the counselee, like the drunken husband mentioned earlier, may test again and again. One lovely young lady to whom we had become father-

and-mother-in-Christ wrenched our hearts again and again. One day she came for counsel to me (John) and watched my face with a twinkle in her eye as this erstwhile, thoroughly moral girl told in livid detail her recent sexual experience in her first adulterous relationship. There was no way I could keep the grief out of my eyes and off of my face. But I could extend forgiveness and show her that I could still love her and would still be her "father." The grief told her more than all else that I do love her. That love and grief gave her understanding for the first time concerning how our sins grieve Jesus, and that it is not the Law, but our unwillingness to wound our loving Lord which keeps us from sinning. My acceptance and continued unconditional love broke through her performance orientation and told her she could rip and tear, sin and wound, and she would still be loved. The twinkle in her eye was there because she was testing me (and because of the same perverse delights I catalogued earlier in punishing Paula). Whether or not all that sin was necessary, the Lord used it to touch her heart and transform her. From that moment on she began to mature from a twenty-seven year old, who was like an early adolescent, to the lovely young woman she is today, still a "daughter," but now a grown friend.

The counselor should pray *with* the performance-oriented person, reaching the inner child with love and forgiveness. In such persons are hidden resentments stemming from a feeling that their parents did not give the kind of love which could have enabled them to find their true identity and security. The counselor should ask the person to renounce aloud the whole pattern of performance. There is no magic about this. The prayer will most likely not do away with it right then and there. But it *will* give the Lord permission to send forty-mile-an-hour winds, or whatever is needed, to get to the heart.

As the counseling relationship continues, and the counselee admits the counselor more and more into a primary relationship, increasing trust and familiarity can begin to allow some surprising forms of treatment. A performance-oriented person is overserious. Humor and comedy are not full and free. About the only jokes the performer allows are rueful quips about inability to perform. He may have, as Paula did, what our small group called a "gallows laugh"—a way of laughing with embarrassment to cover feelings of failure. P.O. people are noted for their lack of ability to comprehend a joke, and are apt to respond with belly laughs only when authority is humbled, as in "Keystone Cops" movies. Repressed anxiety and anger at authority for demanding performance is released by such comedies. A wise counselor begins to use teasing and banter as soon as the traffic can bear it. He invites the performer to laugh at himself, to learn not to take life and himself so seriously.

A Christian counselor may purposely say something crude, to shock the "niceness" out of the other—not as though recommending that style of life but as an occasional medicine. God sent me, a very proper theological student, onto the streets of Chicago driving a Yellow Cab at night. It was very good medicine for my uptight nature. College fraternity was good for me. It did not take the Lambda Chis long to discover my too rigid moral nature. God used their banter and teasing for my good. I still remember the night they were razzing me about my supposed amorous adventures the night before. I protested, "I did not. I was in bed by 9:30." And some wag retorted, "Yeah, and by 12:30 he was up again and on his way home." The whole house roared with glee, and even I had to laugh. How good that form of God's medicine was for me, to be forced to laugh at myself and recognize sin in my heart just as the brothers knew it was in theirs. That began to transfer my security from uptight behavior to God's grace. Counselors should take note, and use banter and teasing with the performance-oriented individual.

As trust increases, and the counselee accepts that the counselor really loves him, sarcasm and scorn can become a healthy tool. As the counselee relates the week's events, I (John) may cut in with, "My, wasn't that noble of you," or "My, what a martyr!", or play an imaginary violin. My smile and presence assure and answer his inquiring look, or I may explain in detail why I did that. The next time it takes no more than a look or a word before the counselee giggles and says, "Oh, I did it again, didn't I?" After a while it takes only a raised eyebrow or a smile, and the counselee checks himself. Finally, I do nothing, and watch as his own mirror reflects and he catches himself again and again in his own tricks.

Gradually the counseling relationship changes. It moves from dependence to independence, from confessor and coach to friends visiting; it moves from superior to equal. That pattern is true of all counseling relationships, but specifically in relation to performance-oriented people it is most indicative of progress. The performer may want unconsciously to turn the counselor into an imperious dictator; if the counselor will only tell him what to do, he can feel comfortable performing for the counselor, and he won't have to change and grow up.

The counselor must look for ways to affirm when the person has done something real, or independently expressed his own choice, or acted out of right motives of love rather than control or duty. It was that which made the confession of the girl with the twinkling eyes so poignantly painful for me. Not only did it hurt me that she had committed adultery, it hurt that the very first thing she had done on her own, apart from performance, I not only could not compliment and affirm, I had to rebuke. When she saw the hurt in my eyes, and asked, we talked about this very crossover in my own emotions. She needed me to be real with her, as her father should have been.

A lady called me (John) recently who had years ago been in deep depression. Through counseling and prayer she had come out of it. I hadn't seen her for several years. She called to tell me her daughter had recently been diagnosed as having a peculiar disease inherited solely through Italian bloodlines. She remarked with wonder that the doctors even warned never to let her daughter date an Italian. She went on to relate that the disease can cause the kind of deep depression she had suffered so many years. She was calling to ask me to pray, knowing I knew how in Christ to stop generational sin. In her report and in her voice I heard confidence and faith and was happy to point out to her how the whole thing was not throwing her into fits of fear and depression as it would have in years past, and how well in faith she was meeting this test. She was delighted, and strengthened in her faith by my affirmation.

Counselors do need to be aware that performance-oriented people have been conditioned to being controlled by compliments. We must not use flattery to manipulate them. That throws them into anger or disbelief. They don't want that from us. What they need is celebration of real change. They need that affirmation and support.

At last the counselor becomes a friend, visiting, laughing, and joking. He must cut the other free. The counseling relationship must die so that the new can come. A counselor must be sensitive, not to cut the other free too soon, but also not to let the counselee "return to Egypt." If he gives enough freeing love and acceptance, usually the other will cut free on his or her own, even as Olivia de Havilland in "Snake Pit" finally said to her psychiatrist, "I don't love you any more, do I?" And he said (in meaning if not in actual words), "No, but we are friends."

4

The Base of Law

The law of the Lord is perfect, restoring the soul;
The testimony of the Lord is sure, making wise
the simple. The precepts of the Lord are right,
rejoicing the heart; The commandment of the
Lord is pure, enlightening the eyes. The fear of
the Lord is clean, enduring forever; The judgments
of the Lord are true; they are righteous altogether.
They are more desirable than gold, yes, than
much fine gold; Sweeter also than honey and
the drippings of the honeycomb. Moreover, by
them Thy servant is warned; In keeping them
there is great reward. (Ps. 19:7-11)

In chapter three we wrote about how we impute to God
motives which are not His. Nowhere is that more true than in
our fears relative to God and the Law. "There is no fear in love;
but perfect love casts out fear, because fear involves punishment, and the one who fears is not perfected in love" (1 John
4:18). From our fear of discipline as children, and our hidden
resentments of authority, we may be unable to think of
impersonal laws, the law of serving and reaping, discipline,
and retribution without confusing these with personal punishment or vindictiveness. A counselor must settle it in his heart
that every law of God is the most loving gift (other than Jesus)
God could give to mankind. Law describes the way love must
act, or action ceases to be love. The reaping of evil seeds sown is
impersonal, not personal punishment, having nothing to do
with vindictiveness or vengeance (see chapters 8, 9, and 10 in
our first book, *The Elijah Task*). If a man does not have a pure
heart concerning childhood discipline, being unable to understand God, he cannot truly appreciate that all law is given by

the Father so that man may live in blessedness.

God wants us to be happy. The "thou shalt nots" have that aim behind them, to keep us happy in the way of blessedness. It is not that God is uptight and rigid, standing in heaven with a heavy fly swatter, waiting for someone to get out of line so He can swat him to a pulp. He had to create an orderly universe for all men and nature. The universe necessarily operates on unbending principles. When we sin we set in motion irrevocable forces. God, seeing that, "so loved the world, that He gave His only begotten son" (John 3:16) that we might not perish.

Forgiveness does not mean that God looked the other way. It does mean that the just requirements of the Law are fulfilled in pain upon the precious body of the Lord Jesus Christ. That is how He came not to abolish the Law but to fulfill it (Matt. 5:17). He became as us in Gethsemane so that on Golgotha He could take onto himself the full legal demands of all we set in motion (Col. 2:14 RSV). Nevertheless, the effect of that salvation often waits upon our confession, else we reap the full weight of what we have sown. That is the precise need of a counselor, for most often we cannot see to confess our sin without someone to help the Holy Spirit reveal it to us (James 5:13-16).

If a counselor knows with unwavering certainty the laws of retribution, he will know with equal certainty the power of the blood and the cross to deliver. When he pronounces a forgiveness according to the Word of God, he will not have one wisp of fear that it might not happen. He knows with absolute certainty that the blood of Jesus has in that moment washed the other clean. There is not one flicker of unrest or wondering if it will happen. It is done, finished, and unchangeable, both here and in eternity.

> My little children, I am writing these things to you that you may not sin. And if anyone sins, we have an Advocate with the Father, Jesus Christ the righteous; and He Himself is the propitiation for our sins; and not for ours only, but also for those of the whole world. (1 John 2:1-2)

If you forgive the sins of any, their sins have been forgiven them; if you retain the sins of any, they have been retained. (John 20:23)

What blessed and holy power the Lord has placed in every Christian. Each one is an ambassador plenipotentiary (2 Cor. 5:20). If such an ambassador commits his nation by word or treaty, the whole nation proceeds to war or peace. Heaven moves in response to the prayer of forgiveness said by the least Christian. Results are not a matter of having enough faith to make it happen. God's Word cannot lie or fail. Success is not up to the one who says the prayer. Accomplishment belongs to God, and He has declared once for all, "It is finished" (John 19:30). It makes no difference whether a giant of healing or a newborn babe in Christ responds to pronounce forgiveness. God does not respect the person (Rom. 2:11), but the work and merits of His Son on the cross. Nothing in heaven or on earth could be more sure than the accomplished forgiveness of God for sin upon the cross of His Son.

However, one of the strangest paradoxes in twentieth-century culture is our attitude toward scientific and moral law, and therefore, our attitude towards the absoluteness of the laws foundational to Christian counseling. More scientists are alive today than in the sum total of all known history. So many inventions, new appliances, and space flights have happened since World War II; we have moved in thirty-five years through changes several previous centuries could not have hoped to see. Knowledge has not only increased as prophesied (Dan. 12:4), it has rocketed far out of sight. Whereas a man in Milton's day could lament that he had learned everything in every field available to know, now a professional man in only one limited field may find he is out of touch and his knowledge is outdated in less than ten years, especially if he does not take constant renewal courses! Our airplanes are obsolete before they leave the drafting boards. All this has come about as mankind has gained the humility to investigate natural things and admit that some things are forever bound by natural law. "Thou hast established all the boundaries of the earth" (Ps. 74:17). All mankind, and most certainly every scientist, knows we can project rockets with precision past Jupiter solely by most circumspect obedience to natural laws—with computers to help us keep on track.

If a pilot were to say, "I'm a free thinker. I think we ought to be able to land this plane upside down over there on the grass," we would not only not honor his "free thinking," no one would ride in anything piloted by him, and most likely if he persisted, we would send him to a mental hospital. Scientifically, freedom cannot be allowed to mean license. We rightly demand that every car be engineered and built within sound principles. The construction of every house we intend to live in must stringently obey architectural laws. It is a fair statement to assert that every technological advance we celebrate in our day owes its existence to the discovery of and obedience to precise, immutable natural laws. This most scientific of all ages is, *ipso facto*, the most law-abiding; obedience to natural law is the *sine qua non* of all science. Without obedience, nothing!

Yet the paradox is that in this most humble and obedient age, relative to natural science, we have become most arrogant and deluded concerning laws which govern our hearts and spirits! We could trace historically in philosophy and semantics how such a confusion has happened but the heart's cry would be the same, "How could we ever have become so foolish!"

> For even though they knew God, they did not honor Him as God, or give thanks; but they became futile in their speculations, and their foolish heart was darkened. Professing to be wise, they became fools. (Rom. 1:21-22)

Mankind, outside limited circles in the Church, has cast off restraint. "The kings of the earth take their stand, And the rulers take counsel together Against the Lord and against His Anointed: 'Let us tear their fetters apart, And cast away their cords from us!' " (Ps. 2:2-3). Many men think that all acknowledged moral laws are the fictions of men's minds, or at least only relative. Relativity, scientifically, never has meant what some have done with it in disregarding moral law. Relativity only means that each law is relative or relevant to operate within its own sphere, not that that law is not fully to be obeyed in context. The greatest scientific relativists would not dare to say that the law of gravity is not effective upon them in high places, only that it is affected relative to various conditions. But we in our foolishness have come to believe that "Thou shalt not commit adultery" is only relative, meaning "not needing to be observed." When in every other sphere of natural intercourse, we recognize the operation of compelling laws, how could we fail to see that, for example, in human sexual intercourse, there are laws just as immutable, just as severe, just as irrevocable!

This is a legal universe. Every physicist knows for every action there must be an equal and opposite reaction. Every chemist knows every formula must balance. Even the most addled sexual aberrant knows life must begin with a sperm and an ovum. We see natural laws operative all about us in relation to human beings, working invincibly, unceasingly, brooking no question. A man who does not breathe cannot live beyond physical endurance. We must eat. We must sleep. That is absolute law. Nothing changes it. We have sense enough to know that.

Nevertheless Paula and I have ministered even to hundreds of preachers of God's Word who think they can occasionally lie, cheat, steal, or hop in bed with anyone, and nothing will come of it! Agnes Sanford used to be fond of saying, "If you step off a cliff, you do not break the law of gravity, you illustrate it." No law of God can ever be broken! His laws work to exact retribution no matter whether we know them, mentally ignore them, choose not to observe them, feel good or bad about them, want them or hate them, believe in them and in God or not. "Do not be deceived, God is not mocked; for whatever a man sows, this he will also reap" (Gal. 6:7).

Let men question the wisdom of our forefathers. Let men wonder whether God really said the Ten Commandments or not. Forget if you will the entire religious history of mankind.

Discount all the Bibles, Korans, and Rig Vedas. Does it not appall the mind that men could (apart from all these) see the controlling nature of law all around them in every sphere of human and natural existence, and not see at least by inference that the same immutability of law could pertain in spiritual and moral matters? "For the wrath of God is revealed from heaven against all ungodliness and unrighteousness of men, who suppress the truth in unrighteousness, because that which is known about God is evident within them; for God made it evident to them. For since the creation of the world His invisible attributes, His eternal power and divine nature, have been clearly seen, *being understood through what has been made*, so that they are without excuse" (Rom. 1:18-20, italics mine). Incidentally, every major religion on the face of the globe contains the same basic laws we find in the Ten Commandments. God has not left himself without witness in any age anywhere (Acts 14:17).

Is it not reasonable to assume that if I see rain falling down by the law of gravity, and the sun and moon swinging with all the planets and stars through the universe with such precision that even ancient mankind could build a Stonehenge centuries ago so precise it still predicts the operation of the sun with unwavering precision, that God would take care to build the life of the spirit, and consequent moral and ethical relationships, with equal care for precision and law? What a strange paradox that with firm obedience to chemical law, we fill our tanks and swallow our drugs—and think we can lie, steal, or commit adultery with impunity! It fails to make sense either scientifically or philosophically; or forget the big words—it doesn't even make common sense the way we sometimes act!

A man with an iota of consistency to his thinking ought to be able to make a simple comparison: if a plane must fly by natural laws, so ought a marriage to "fly" solely by ethical and moral laws. Can anyone tell me how modern man can have become so paradoxical and foolish as not to know these things? The simple, horrible fact is, we have. "In whose case the god of this world has blinded the minds of the unbelieving, that they might not see the light of the gospel of the glory of Christ, who is the image of God" (2 Cor. 4:4). We are not only blinded to the gospel, millions no longer can see the laws of God! There is surely an enemy. Notwithstanding, lest we blame our foolishnesses out there somewhere, our flesh alone, without Lucifer's aid, is foolish enough, "They became futile in their speculations, and their foolish heart was darkened" (Rom. 1:21). "And just as they did not see fit to acknowledge God any longer, God gave them over to a *depraved mind,* to do those things which are not proper" (Rom. 1:28). "The mind set on the flesh is hostile toward God; for it *does not subject itself to the Law of God,* for it is not even able to do so" (Rom. 8:7). *You see, we obey those laws of the natural order which build our creature comforts and insure the mammon-good life, but those moral laws which haul us to account and chain our rebellious passions we want to call irrelevant, relative, man-made or old-fashioned, anything to excuse our lusts and give them full vent!* So we reap the consequences—and wonder, in an age of knowing scientific, mechanical laws, why life doesn't go right!

All of this is to say to counselors an irrevocable, unbendable maxim: Whoever would call himself a Christian counselor, must know, without a flicker of a doubt (James 1:6-8), that God's moral laws are absolutely inflexible. *Sin is sin! Law is law!* Shades of compassion and understanding relate to our comprehension of the motives for which men sin, not to the Law itself. Condemnation has no place in Christ, but that fact arrives by the mercy of the cross, never by the relaxing of any law of God.

> For truly I say to you, until heaven and earth pass away, not the smallest letter or stroke shall pass away from the Law, until all is accomplished. (Matt. 5:18)
>
> Heaven and earth will pass away, but My words shall not pass away. (Matt 24:35)
>
> Whoever then annuls one of the least of these commandments, and so teaches others, shall be called least in the kingdom of heaven; but whoever keeps and teaches them, he shall be called great in the kingdom of heaven. (Matt. 5:19)

A counselor does not become kind and non-judgmental by lessening or doing away with the surety of law; he only becomes inept. Judgmentalism dies only as a man sees his own sin and dies in Christ to all blame, not by developing a supposed "liberal" mind.

There will come a day when men have returned to venerate the laws of God. This is an age of fleshly rationality, in which the *avant-garde* have wanted to appear magnanimous and liberal, somehow thinking man's foolish fleshly wisdom could be more kind than God's law. But "Has not God made foolish the wisdom of the world?" (1 Cor. 1:20). When the light of Christ arises (Isa. 60:1-2) and the more than 2,000 pigs of men's mentality have been chased into the sea, and mankind has been returned to sit fully clothed in his right mind at the feet of Jesus (Luke 8:26-39), then:

> Behold, a king shall reign in righteousness, and princes shall rule in judgment. And a man shall be as an hiding place from the wind, and a covert from the tempest; as rivers of water in a dry place, as the shadow of a great rock in a weary land. And the eyes of them that see shall not be dim, and the ears of them that hear shall hearken. The heart also of the rash shall understand knowledge, and the tongue of the stammerers shall be no more called *liberal*, nor the *churl* said to be bountiful. For the vile person will speak villainy, and his heart will work iniquity, to practise hypocrisy, and to utter error against the Lord, to make empty the soul of the hungry, and he will cause the drink of the thirsty to fail. The instruments also of the *churl* are evil; he deviseth wicked devices to destroy the poor with lying words, even when the needy speaketh right. But the *liberal* deviseth liberal things; and by *liberal* things shall he stand. (Isa. 32:1-8 KJV)

In this deluded world the philanderer and the homosexual can yet parade upon the ground of supposed rationality and magnanimity. The day will come when men have awakened to the truth of God's shining principles ribbing all of life with sure pillars to live by. Counselors must never be daunted or intimidated by the minds of men or by those who parade their own silly speculations. Like little children who have matured beyond asking the unanswerable—"Who made God?" and "Who was before Him?", counselors must come to sufficient humility to know that some things are forever fixed, no matter what our puny minds may be tempted to think. The mind of a counselor must be at rest, firmly settled in every word of God. Psalm 119 should be a counselor's constant song of covenant. He must be passionately in love with the law of God, meditating on it day and night (Ps. 1:2).

Whoever would enter Christian counseling not sure that God's Word is absolute, not fully settled that His laws are by revelation, and that He meant what He said, I (John) beg of that person to get out of counseling before you do any more harm! I mean that with every fibre of my being! Countless times Paula and I have listened with great grief to troubled souls whose lives were even more wrecked by the foolish counsel of some to "have an affair" or "don't feel so guilty," or "that's just old-fashioned nonsense," or "surely you don't believe that stuff any more, do you?" What judgment such counselors are heaping up for the day of reckoning: "Let not many of you become teachers, my brethren, knowing that as such we shall incur a stricter judgment" (James 3:1). "But whoever causes one of these little ones who believe in Me to stumble, it is better for him that a heavy millstone be hung around his neck, and that he be drowned in the depth of the sea. Woe to the world because of its stumbling-blocks! For it is inevitable that stumbling-blocks come; but woe to that man through whom the stumbling-block comes!" (Matt. 18:6-7).

The personal life of a Christian counselor must be impeccable. Perhaps no other office in the Church is more subject to temptation. Those who enter the inner chambers of people's secret hearts, to yearn and wrestle for them, can not help becoming contaminated by their counselees' emotions, and sometimes somewhat overburdened with their cares and sorrows. A Christian counselor must know by the Word of God how to detach himself and cut himself free from burdens (see chapter 18, "Renunciation or Cutting Free" in our book *Restoring the Christian Family*). "For wisdom is protection just as money is protection. But the advantage of knowledge is that wisdom preserves the lives of its possessors" (Eccles. 7:12). Whatever counselor (indeed—whoever) does not cherish and wed himself eternally to God's law in Christ is described by Proverbs 25:28 (KJV), "He that hath no rule over his own spirit is like a city that is broken down, and without walls."

A counselor's personal devotional life is his salvation. Only the Lord can cleanse the gunk and lift the load of people out of his heart and spirit. Only love, often refreshed at the fountain of life (Ps. 36:9), can cause his love for obedience to the law to be born continually from the love of Jesus flowing through him to others. The love which flows from the throne of God is like a river (Rev. 22:1, Ps. 46:4). A counselor loves the Law because it provides sure banks for the river of that love to flow in its own channel. If a counselor does not keep up his own devotional life, the river will run dry, his heart will become barren and brittle, and law will become a whip to scourge a counselee rather than banks for the river of God's love.

A Christian counselor's personal moral life must be above reproach, not only for his own sake but for the security of his counselees. Paula and I have ground our teeth in anger and shame when we have heard as I did not half an hour ago (February, 1980) when a counselee reported she had learned that the counselor she had been seeing had been sleeping with his women counselees all the previous summer. She would not return to him; that was why she would come only to us. I thought of an erstwhile pastor of whom I had learned earlier who was doing the same; it turned out to be another Christian counselor whom I had trusted that he knew better. It broke my heart—in grief for him and them. If that so wounds my human heart, how deep must be the grief in the heart of our gentle Lord? How can we in His service love Him so little as that? If we do not grasp the eternal reality of law and the grievous price Jesus pays for us on the cross, Satan can use the melee of the battle to put blinkers on our eyes until we no longer see the consequences of what we do nor have a conscience that works as it should. These men, who began well, became lost from the Lord in the midst of the battle—and they became blinded.

Many may be frightened by the thesis of this book that the entire Body of Christ is called to be counselors. They rightly retort that the common man is not trained in psychology. Let us therefore distinguish carefully. We are not calling any Christian to be a psychologist. Any of us may use psychological insights, and be grateful for them. But our base is not the same.

Psychology takes its origin from Descartes, a French philosopher (1596-1650), who said, *"Cogito, ergo sum"* or "I think, therefore I am." That makes our life dependent on what we have been trained to think rather than on the fact that we have an immortal spirit and soul. He maintained that we are as a *tabula rasa*, a grained but blank sheet, on which experience writes our character and personality. Exactly oppositely, Christian faith takes its origin in revelation, according to the Word of God, which means we say, *"Sum, ergo cogito"* or "I am, therefore I think." Faith maintains that we have a spirit, which by personal choices form a soul, in which are character and personality.

Auguste Comte (1798-1857) another French philosopher, classified the sciences and began to examine the psychological evolution of thought, and to press for a religion of humanity. From this base primarily originated the movement now called "humanism"—which espouses human rights causes today.

Herbert Spencer, an English philosopher and exponent of evolution (1820-1903), pressed for understanding of natural law and processes of evolution as the *only* viable bases for discovering the "knowable." Christian faith (among some) agrees that following creation, nature does evolve, but disagrees with Spencer to insist that we are not confined to the empirical as the *only* viable means to knowledge. Faith says, "God speaks, and we can hear." And adds that our spirits can intuitively grasp knowledge far beyond the mind even without God's help.

All this means that ever since that beginning with Comte and Spencer, social sciences measure, examine by test tubes, and in psychology count statistical noses to arrive at truth, and call that "discipline" and "science." We do not disrespect that approach. It is a valid way insofar as it goes, and a good counterbalance and checkpoint for Christian intuition. We can glean much insight from psychological fields. But faith refuses to allow the claim of those based (unknowingly perhaps) on Spencer that *only* that way is scientific, disciplined or practical for the discovery of truth. Faith maintains that revelation contains its own discipline, and contains a more primal access to truth through the Holy Spirit. Christians maintain that faith, properly disciplined, is not any less "scientific," though not based in or confined to worldly science.

The purview (area of sight) of psychology has always been a dichotomy, examining only the conscious and subconscious or unconscious mind. Even parapsychology still regards extrasensory perception, kinesis, clairaudience, clairvoyance, psychometry and other related phenomena as functions of the psyche. Thus psychology examines only two levels of human existence. Faith embraces a trichotomy of mind, heart or unconscious, and spirit. Faith says it is our spirit who is the child, who is the father of the man, that the conscious mind and heart are informed, guided, sometimes controlled and surely greatly influenced by the deep mind and heart of our spirit.

Since the advent of Emile Durkheim (1858-1917), psychology has tended toward cultural determinism, which holds that man is determined by his circumstances. Russian "theology" of communism is based upon the belief that man can be improved by changing his environment, thus the Marxist contention that the state can crush the masses forward into perfection in the "dictatorship of the proletariat." It is this concept of exterior determinism which is behind attempts to "brainwash," both in communism and extremist cults such as that created by the Jonestown fiasco. The millions of Christians who defy communist brainwashing, even to the point of martyrdom, and the many who walked away from Jonestown before doomsday despite threats and coercion, disprove the theory that all men can be totally conditioned and controlled. Faith maintains that the spirit of man is indomitable and free. The brainwashed in cults today, and those who died at Jonestown, give evidence of what happens when we no longer listen to the promptings of our inmost being. "For in my *inner being* I delight in God's law. . ." (Rom. 7:22a).

Psychologists who are Skinnerian behaviorists (based on determinism) attempt to change people by giving them "modes" or ways of changing the way they behave. Social actionists, based (often unknowingly) on Durkheim, think that if they can lobby to change laws to improve society and thus spread a good environment to every person, they will have effected change to bring about the brotherhood of mankind. Christians may lend support to some social actions, and Christian counselors may employ some Skinnerian modes for self-discipline, but Christians see no lasting change by any other means than changing the *inner* heart by reaching the spirit with conviction of guilt, confession, and forgiveness. We are not changed from outside in but from the inside out.

Psychological method is enlightenment, to know one's *self*. Christian method is "enlightenment," to know one's self *as sin*. Psychologists attempt to encourage change by intention or will power to make a better person. Christian power is first the Holy Spirit, secondly prayer, to make a *converted* person. Psychologists try to change the environment, the way the family behaves, or the circumstances (like the way the house is kept, or job stresses, or the companions around us). A Christian counselor, seeing such actions as somewhat helpful, seeks first to change inner attitudes and motives towards persons and circumstances by forgiveness and the indwelling, loving nature of Jesus. A Christian counselor may not attempt to change the circumstances at all, seeing those as the milieu in which the Lord intends to write on the counselee's heart whatever lessons God knows he needs to learn.

A psychologist has his eyes on function, attempting to restore the counselee to capacity to act. Whereas a Christian counselor, though eventually wanting the counselee to be able to function, seeks first to enable the counselee to be convicted in his heart. If a counselee returns to ability to function too soon, that may be for the Christian counselor a defeat rather than a victory. He knows the Lord will have to put the counselee between some other "rock and hard place" for him to be changed in the heart.

Thus the Christian counselor works to establish guilt. He is not afraid of it, and unless he perceives false guilt, never tells the counselee, "don't feel so guilty." Unless one recognizes guilt, his sin cannot find its way to the cross, and freedom cannot happen.

Some psychologists, relying too much on the deterministic approach, too often look upon persons as victims rather than perpetrators. Life has happened to them. Cultural determinism means that life has done to us what we are. Thus criminals are "not responsible." We (society) have created them. Consequently, some psychologists have become soft-headed about crime and the reasons for its existence. In counseling, such counselors all too often produce self-pitying persons, sure that life has done upon them all their troubles. Karl Menninger, a great contemporary psychiatrist, has hauled secular psychology to account for its failure in this area, in his book *Whatever Became of Sin?*, from which we quote: *"The message is simple. It is that concern is the touchstone. Caring. Relinquishing the sin of indifference. This recognizes acedia as the Great Sin; the heart of all sin. Some call it selfishness. Some call it alienation. Some call it schizophrenia. Some call it egocentricity. Some call it separation."*

" 'Have the men of our time lost a feeling of the meaning of sin?' asked Paul Tillich. 'Do they realize that sin does not mean an immoral act, that "sin" should never be used in the plural, and that not our sins, but rather our sin is the great, all-pervading problem of our life? *To be in the state of sin is to be in the state of separation.*'

" 'Separation,' he continued, 'may be from one's fellowmen, from one's own true self and/or from his God.' [Tillich used "Ground of Being"; the reader can choose his own word.]

"Separation is another word not only for sin, but for mental illness, for crime, for nonfunctioning, for aggression, for alienation, for death. Some prefer one or the other, but all these words describe the same thing.

"But now that the idea of sin has been reconsidered theologically and ethically, the time has come for scientists to reconsider it also and to give it an appropriate place in their work."

Power for change for psychologists is found in natural desire and human will power, plus counsel and the support of friends and relatives. Power for change for Christian psychologists is first faith in the power and intentions of God as expressed through His Son, our Lord Jesus Christ upon the cross, through His blood and resurrection life, followed by other helps the Holy Spirit inspires.

Thus we are not calling members of the Body of Christ to be psychologists; rather to be confessors, midwives and fathers and mothers in Christ to one another in the Body of Christ. We are calling the body to deal with the common daily problems of life in a biblical, concrete manner of counsel and prayer.

If one truly grasps the few simple laws on which God has constructed the operation of human nature, that single key is enough to begin to unlock the myriad mysteries of the human heart! Human nature, like car engines, operates on absolute mechanical principles. Once one understands the base of law behind all human relationships, he has the foundation on which to build and plumb perceptions into every problem. The genius of Einstein was to discover the simplicity of law behind the seemingly complex construction of all nature. The genius of the Word of God is to lay bare the simplicity of life. It is as though all life, like fractions, is built on simple common denominators upon which operate multivarious numerators. If a counselor is sufficiently gripped by the simple statutes of

God, his eyes will never be blinded by the kaleidoscopic variations of human complexities. Beneath all he will see and return to the simple keys. The numerators (how we see and act) vary as often as there are individuals who mess up. The denominators (the laws of God) are few, basic, universal, and simple.

God gives us the single basic key to life in the Ten Commandments and the Sermon on the Mount. Those moral laws are not somebody's guess as to how life ought to run. They are not mankind's invention. We did not learn them by trial and error. They are not merely a bunch of rules which if only everybody would obey, this would be a better world. They are *God's description of the way reality works.* The Ten Commandments and the Sermon on the Mount are the architect's blueprint for building the house of family life. They are the chemist's formula for brewing safe mixtures of men and women. They are the engineer's principles for construction and operation of all relationships. They are the cook's recipe for nurture, not poison. They are not inert, negligible things. If a man leaves his car in the garage, the only harm is that he hitches rides or walks and pays his car bills for nothing. But if a man parks the Ten Commandments in the garage of forgetfulness, he will sooner or later reap a whirlwind of destruction.

Many people think that the Ten Commandments and the Sermon on the Mount are some nice idealists' list of "shoulds" but of course the practically minded macho man knows better. Many think that not to know a commandment or to neglect or disregard one is of no more consequence than a liberating philosophical exercise, affecting nothing other than an over-active conscience. A strange fact is that not one of these same "practically minded" people would ever think he could walk in a room full of tear gas and expect that his ignorance of it or neglect to wear a mask could have no effect! God's laws are like a thousand-mile-an-hour gale; given time they will sweep everything before them, even as a thousand-mile-an-hour wind will eventually wear down a mountain. Anyone who has watched a mighty flood uproot a tree or hurl a house like a toothpick has a tiny approximation of the power of God's laws. A wind will stop and a flood will cease, but God's laws will continue to operate beyond the pale of death throughout eternity.

The truth is that the "practically minded" man is blinded and deluded.

> Because sentence against an evil deed is not executed speedily, the heart of the sons of men is fully set to do evil. (Eccles. 8:11 RSV)

The mills of God's justice grind slowly, but they grind exceedingly fine. Because the "practical man" does not see immediate retribution, he fails to believe. That unbelief has no effect whatsoever upon the operation of God's law; he and his descendants will reap without fail no matter what he thinks or disbelieves, is aware of or rejects. Note again, even in Christians of long standing, we are dealing with unbelief in the heart. Millions upon millions of Christians have never yet become so grounded in God's Word that His law is written indelibly into their hearts (Jer. 31:31). In the heart they still believe they can do whatever they want with no effect. It is as though the strands of consistency are all snapped, swaying in the scattering winds of fleshly lusts and desires. They do not and cannot effectively connect cause and effect, sowing and reaping, sin and result. Or good deed and blessing.

Every Christian counselor must consequently never let himself assume that the other effectively holds to the laws of God, or right and wrong. The counselee's mind may give lip service, but "This people honors me with their lips, but their heart is far from me" (Matt. 16:8). Every Christian counselor is therefore constantly an evangelist and teacher *to the heart.* Men simply do not connect sin and retribution *in the heart and life* in real and practical terms.

> And when he drew near and saw the city he wept over it, saying, "Would that even today you knew the things that make for peace! But now they are hid from your eyes." (Luke 19:41-42 RSV)

The fundamental, simple and single key to all Christian counseling is found in the fifth commandment, "Honor your father and your mother, as the Lord your God has commanded you, that your days may be prolonged, and that it may go well with you on the land which the Lord your God gives you" (Deut. 5:16). That single principle, that life will go well with those who honor their parents, and that life will not go well with those who do not, is sufficient to explain *the root* of every marital problem, every child-raising dilemma, every moral and immoral inclination. That single fifth commandment is a description in all human life of the way reality works. In every area consciously or unconsciously in which we could in fact honor our parents, life will go well with us! In every area consciously or unconsciously that we judged or dishonored our parents, in that very area life will not go well with us!

Life is that fundamentally simple.

> Even so, every good tree bears good fruit; but the rotten tree bears bad fruit. A good tree cannot produce bad fruit, nor can a rotten tree produce good fruit. Every tree that does not bear good fruit is cut down and thrown into the fire. So then, you will know them by their fruits. (Matt. 7:17-20)

> Do not judge lest you be judged yourselves. For in the way you judge, you will be judged; and by your standard of measure, it shall be measured to you. (Matt. 7:1-2)

> Do not be deceived, God is not mocked; for whatever a man sows, this he will also reap. (Gal. 6:7)

Those few simple laws encompass every human relationship. There is no escape. There are no exceptions. Life will absolutely without fail go the way of our good deeds, sins, judgments and sowings, unless the grace of Christ intervenes.

Once a counselor settles it in his mind that we are not dealing with fantasy or myth but with eternal, unchangeable reality which will outlast all the universe, he cannot be carried away into suppositions and fallacies (Ps. 119:89). He has the unfailing key to truth. For example, a counselee says, "Oh, I couldn't help doing this or that wrong thing to the mate," for example, when over-correcting, scolding and criticizing he may rationalize it by saying, "I just learned from my parents that there is a right way to do things, and if a thing is worth doing, it's worth doing right. And I love him (her) so, I just want him (her) to do the best he (she) can, so everything will go right for us." A good tree cannot produce bad fruit. To demand and control is bad fruit; it is impossible for that to arise from love. Love is good. Control is bad. That bad fruit had to have come from some bad root in the counselee's life. Perhaps the father or mother was a critical, nagging, controlling person. The child hated that, but it is not acceptable to judge and hate parents, so the child repressed such feelings. Now the law (Rom. 2:1) compels the adult to nag and criticize in the same manner as it was done to him (her).

So much of the time we want to ascribe our rotten behavior to good things in us. Understanding of the pristine clarity of God's laws reveals man's lies to himself. The purity of law threads the eye of every needle and unties the Gordian knots of human character. The Law of God pierces webs of deception. "The commandment of the Lord is pure, enlightening the eyes" (Ps. 19:8). "The unfolding of Thy words gives light; It gives understanding to the simple" (Ps. 119:130).

There are plenty of maybes in our understanding of problems, and every counselor ought to be clothed with humility and willingness to admit error. "The first to plead his case seems just, Until another comes and examines him" (Prov. 18:17). "Iron sharpens iron, so one man sharpens another" (Prov. 27:17). But there are no maybes in the operation of law. Our understandings are faulty, but the swing of retribution in the realities we examine is without elasticity or change. Only the grace of Christ on the cross stops the swing of inevitable retribution.

Therefore when God reveals, we need to believe and act with prayer to deliver. We cannot do that if we are "tossed here and there by waves, and carried about by every wind of doctrine, by the trickery of men, by craftiness in deceitful scheming" (Eph. 4:14). It is firm belief in the Law of God which pinions our mind to the secure foundations of life.

"No, if you can't release your child to go to college, it is not because 'you love him too much'." Possession is bad fruit. Love is good. Good trees can't produce bad fruit. Now let's find out the real reason why you can't let him go."

"You love your wife too much; therefore, you say you couldn't help beating up on that guy who looked at her at the party? No, my friend. Love, being good, produces no bad fruit. Bad fruit has to come from bad roots in a bad tree. Now who left who in your childhood, or who kept taking something away that was yours? What happened between your father and mother, or with your brothers and sisters? Somewhere there's a bad root. Let's find it."

"He would have left me. I had to go to bed with him. I love him too much, I guess." Never allow a noble reason behind an ignoble thing. That is impossible. Good trees don't produce bad fruit. "Not so, honey. Love, being good, doesn't produce sin. We try to use love to cloak sin, but something else produced it. What were you afraid of? Let's look at your relation to your father. What kind of a job did he have? Was he home at night? Was he 'home' when he was home? Did he stay with your mother? How did they get along?"

Do we begin to see how the Word of God is a protection to the mind of a counselor—or anyone else? "How can a young man keep his way pure? By keeping it according to Thy word" (Ps. 119:9). "Thy word I have *treasured in my heart*, That I may not sin against Thee" (Ps. 119:11, italics mine). "Every word of God is tested; He is a shield to those who take refuge in Him" (Prov. 30:5).

The Word of God is the counselor's sure sword of analysis, not psychological tests or gimmicks. That is what the Holy Spirit himself says it is,

> For the word of God is living and active and sharper than any two-edged sword, and piercing as far as the division of soul and spirit, of both joints and marrow, and *able to judge the thoughts and intentions of the heart*. (Heb. 4:12)

Then you will discern righteousness and justice And equity and every good course. For wisdom will enter your heart, And knowledge will be pleasant to your soul; Discretion will guard you, Understanding will watch over you, To deliver you from the way of evil, From the man who speaks perverse things; From those who leave the path of uprightness, To walk in the ways of darkness; Who delight in doing evil, And rejoice in the perversity of evil; Whose paths are crooked, And who are devious in their ways; (Prov. 2:9-15)

A counselor is like a detective, seeking for the real "who-done-its" in each circumstance. The Word of God is his sure magnifying glass, and just as every fingerprint uniquely nails the culprit, so the Law reveals precisely the stamp of each man's nature. If he has a problem with his wife, his half of it has to be located in his judgments and sins relative to his parents (or other childhood primary people), not first in her. For those who fear oversimplicity, remember that within the limits of law life is immeasurably complex and varied. We plead here for every counselor not to be bedazzled, and to root his mentality in the singleness of God's Word. "The lamp of the body is the eye; if therefore your eye is clear, your whole body will be full of light" (Matt. 6:22). The "eye" is the way we interpret life—a counselor's eye must be single, captive to the Word of God (2 Cor. 10:5).

Therefore, having this ministry by the mercy of God, we do not lose heart. We have renounced disgraceful, under-handed ways; we refuse to practice cunning or to tamper with God's word, but by the open statement of the truth we would commend ourselves to every man's conscience in the sight of God. (2 Cor. 4:1-2 RSV)

Our life with our parents, or whoever raised us, is the root and trunk of our life. Whatever manifests in the present derives from those roots. After twenty years of counseling as many as 1,200 hours in each year, Paula and I can confidently and restfully say that counseling is at root that simple, and the Law of God is that basic.

It is not that parents are to blame. Whatever parents were, saints or hellions, normal people or psychos, what is important is the child's reactions. We have seen cases of children hellishly abused who nevertheless became loving and gentle adults. As said earlier, we are not dealing with cultural determinism, or behaviorism, which believe that man is formed by his circumstances, by environment, and people. We are comprehending by the Word of God, which proclaims that by our spirit we have chosen how we react. In every way we have reacted sinfully, we have set in motion forces that must be reaped, unless mercy prevails. We do not blame parents by seeing that the root and trunk of all life is formed with them. It is always the counselee who must bear his own load of guilt (Gal. 6:5).

Placing guilt on a two-year-old does not place blame or condemnation. In Christ that is ruled out (Rom. 8:1). We see the facts of the operation of law in order to deliver by the cross. We are not interested in finding out whose fault (whose blame) anything is. We *are* interested in seeing what events and what reactions happened, and what resultant character structures were built, so that we can take the result of sin to the cross. Once we see that every human being is sin by inheritance, blame dies. We might justly attach blame to someone who as Paul says has already been cleansed and filled by the Holy Spirit and who then purposely chooses evil, and thus chooses to crucify Jesus anew (Heb. 6:6). But in dealing with the normal sinfulness of us all, blame is not a part of the game, totally irrelevant like a player who never got into the ballpark, much less up to bat. All of us have been born with sinful hearts into a sinful world.

> He has not dealt with us according to our sins, Nor rewarded us according to our iniquities.
>
> Just as a father has compassion on his children, So the Lord has compassion on those who fear Him.
>
> For He Himself knows our frame; He is mindful that we are but dust. (Ps. 103:10, 13, 14)

If it seems that we have said on the one hand that every man is responsible for choosing wrongly, and that now we say that every man is born sinful, thus inferring he had no chance, that may not be far from the truth! Every man's wisdom stops at this great theological dilemma and impasse. We say "both—and." Every man is responsible for his choices. We are guilty. But compassion says that although every man is held accountable, the compassion of the Lord does not blame and condemn him; it only loves and delivers.

The absoluteness of the Law of God also becomes the surety of healing.

> For when God made the promise to Abraham, since He could swear by no one greater, He swore by Himself, saying, "I will surely bless you, and I will surely multiply you." And thus, having patiently waited, he obtained the promise. For men swear by one greater than themselves, and with them an oath given as confirmation is an end of every dispute. In the same way God, desiring even more to *show to the heirs of the promise the unchangeableness of His purpose,* interposed with an oath, in order that *by two unchangeable things, in which it is impossible for God to lie, we may have strong encouragement,* we who have fled for refuge in *laying hold of the hope* set before us. This hope we have *as an anchor* of the soul, a hope both sure and *steadfast* and one which enters within the veil, where Jesus has entered as a forerunner for us, having become a high priest forever according to the order of Melchizedek. (Heb. 6:13-20)

One final word of clarification and comfort for all those, whether or not they yet know themselves called to be counselors, who would venture to stand upon the absoluteness of God's Word, but fear to do so for threat of being called narrow, bigoted, arrogant, opinionated or foolish. Satan and our confused modern mentality have completely turned things backwards, making crooked the straight paths of God (Acts 13:10). Men in the world call that arrogant which is humility and vice versa. For example, in the face of all the amassed evidence of scientific endeavor, if a man were to stubbornly insist that the world is flat, we would not call that man anything but arrogant or foolish, would we? Considering the evidence, to admit that the earth is round is humility. To believe that fact unreservedly is not arrogance or narrowness, it is to have a sound mind (2 Tim. 1:7 KJV). To settle the roundness of earth as something proven beyond doubt is to possess the flexibility to change any erstwhile contrary opinions, and the sense to lock the mind firmly onto reality. It is the same concerning the absoluteness of God's Word.

In the beginning, to accept the finality of God's Word may have to be taken as one would a scientific hypothesis. One tests it, and wonders if he has taken leave of his senses. Whoever so puts God to the test (Mal. 3:10) and obeys His statutes, will soon discover that God confirms by signs and wonders (Mark 16:17). And that "In the mouth of two or three witnesses shall every word be established" (2 Cor. 13:1 KJV). The confirmation of God will soon become such a mountain of evidence that not to believe and settle it once for all would be the height (or nadir as it were) of mental arrogance, narrowness, and foolishness.

Once it is seen that in His revealed and written Word, God has indeed spoken once for all, that sight so overturns the world's way of thinking, that it becomes humility to admit His absolutes to the core of all our thinking, and arrogance to continue to parade upon the ground of man's fleshly speculations. Christians who *know* the absoluteness of God's laws need not fear; it takes a humble mind to be settled honestly upon the truth of God's Word, and an arrogant mind not to be so settled.

5

The Central Power
and Necessity of Forgiveness

And whenever you stand praying, forgive, if you have anything against anyone; so that your Father also who is in heaven may forgive you your transgressions. But if you do not forgive, neither will your Father who is in heaven forgive your transgressions. (Mark 11:25-26)

The first necessity of forgiveness derives from the Law. Until forgiveness is effected in the heart, the law of retribution swings to its inevitable conclusion. "Let no one say when he is tempted, 'I am being tempted by God'; for God cannot be tempted by evil, and He Himself does not tempt anyone. But each one is tempted when he is carried away and enticed by his own lust. Then when lust has conceived, it gives birth to sin; and when sin is accomplished, it brings forth death" (James 1:13-15). The legality of the universe demands resolution.

Every anger in a family is a stimulus. Every stimulus engenders response, whether we acknowledge consciously or repress. Each response becomes stimulus to the other, in turn demanding response, which becomes stimulus, demanding further response, and so arguments incite to fights, group hassles to riots, and national tensions to wars. "What is the source of quarrels and conflicts among you? Is not the source your pleasures that wage war in your members? You lust and do not have; so you commit murder. And you are envious and cannot obtain; so you fight and quarrel" (James 4:1-2).

Emotional stimuli operate as legally as the laws of electricity. We may try to control our passions, break the stimulus-response arc by will power or kindly character, or withhold further stimuli by suppressing our own responses, but we only delay, for there are lawful impetuses which cannot be denied. We *will* reap what is sown (Gal. 6:7). God's laws (His Word) cannot be broken (John 10:35).

That fact of immutability of law, and irretrievability of stimulus and response is the truth of what the Holy Spirit said in Malachi 3:6, "For I, the Lord, do not change; therefore you, O sons of Jacob, are *not consumed.*" If God changed, we *would* be consumed. If He changed what? "Hence also He is able to save forever those who draw near to God through Him, since He *always lives to make intercession for them* (Heb. 7:25, italics mine). The logic is inescapable—if Jesus changed and thus stopped interceding before the Father, the result would be, "This tape will self destruct in five seconds!"

Our stimuli demand increasing response. The laws of sowing and reaping and of increase ensure that all our human relationships, indeed all of human life, by dint of our continually sinning nature, must be ever accelerating to war and destruction! Nothing can stop that swing, save the cross of Christ. That is the centrality of forgiveness. "And according to the Law, one may almost say, all things are cleansed with blood, and without shedding of blood there is no forgiveness" (Heb. 9:22). Hate murders. "Every one who hates his brother is a murderer; and you know that no murderer has eternal life abiding in him" (1 John 3:15). All anger, resentment, and bitterness are born of hate; no matter how we may want to euphemize and claim we don't hate, we do. Our emotions murder (or bless) the other. Murder destroys life. Life is in the blood (Gen. 9:4). Stimulus demands response, seed sown requires reaping; therefore every hatred requires blood. Only the blood of Jesus can stop the increasing cycle of human hate. The blood of forgiveness is thus central even to the possibility of continuance of human life.

When Mary Jones feels slighted by her husband, Sam, that stimulus demands a response. If she vents it, he responds. Angers increase, and battle ensues. If he suppresses, that stimulus does not die. It foments a ferment in his heart. Somewhere, somehow, it *will* express, even if only by silent rejection, while subliminally Sam's emotional nature is unknowingly murdering his wife. Sam may, by fleshly determination, or even by the power of the Holy Spirit, give back a loving answer, and that stimulus may evoke a loving response, and so the evening may spiral to joy. Nevertheless, that original hurt cannot be denied. It lives, repressed and forgotten. But the universe is legal, and that hurt must yet find a response. If we multiply that event by the thousands that normally occur in any relationship, we see that if Jesus failed to intercede continually, death of happiness, or even physical destruction is unavoidable for all of us.

"But if we walk in the light as He Himself is in the light, we have fellowship with one another, and the blood of Jesus His Son cleanses us from all sin" (1 John 1:7). Sam's choice to love was an invitation, by choosing to walk in light, to allow the blood of Jesus to cleanse the heart. No one can know how many billions of instances flow every day in human relationships by His blood, all unseen and unknown to wholeness. How overwhelmingly gracious our Lord's mercy is no one can ever know!

Nor can anyone know why so many billions of incidents can wash unknown in the blood, and yet sometimes conscious recognition and confession is required, else we suffer the full consequences. Surely God, in His wisdom, knows. Most sins apparently are cleansed without our ever knowing. Suffice it to say that the command, "Do this in remembrance of me" (Luke 22:19-20), is probably based on Jesus' knowledge of continuous need of washing. How often does God forgive and cleanse us as we worship and we are not aware of it? Choices to walk in love cleanse, but the most effective choices are worship and prayer. We need to pray for one another regularly, as did St. Paul, "May the God of peace *sanctify* you entirely; and may your spirit and soul and body be *preserved* complete, *without blame* at the coming of the Lord Jesus Christ" (1 Thess. 5:23). What a prayer!

Having been privileged as perhaps few others to see daily into the inner workings of the human heart, Paula and I both rejoice and grieve over the Scriptures,

> Let us hold fast the confession of our hope without wavering, for He who promised is faithful; and let us consider how to stimulate one another to love and good deeds, *not forsaking our own assembling together,* as is the habit of some, but encouraging one another; and all the more, as you see the day drawing near. For if we go on sinning willfully after receiving the knowledge of the truth, there *no longer remains a sacrifice for sins,* but a certain terrifying expectation of judgment, and the fury of a fire *which will consume* the adversaries. (Heb. 10:23-27)

We rejoice because we know that those who do attend worship, whether communion is served or not, will be cleansed by walking in the light, and their marriages and families will be blessed whether or not they know it. Families may battle upon exit from the church doors, but much of that prior week's accumulation of seeds sown to hate has been reaped by our Lord. People may remember angers, and call them into new battles, but the necessary legal retribution of the past was effectually ended at the cross in worship.

We weep as we see the grayness of death come over the faces of those who never darken His door; we know what horrendous accumulations of evil rebound to resolution in reaping because they have failed that opportunity to choose life in Him, and thus gave Him little opportunity to cleanse.

The power of forgiveness is the blood of Jesus. And the blood of Jesus is sufficient (Heb. 10:19-29). We doubt that the Church could get "bloody" enough. Menno Simons (1496-1561), from whom the Mennonites were spawned, was noted both for his piety and for his emphasis upon the blood of Jesus—an emphasis which was inherited by his followers. While on board a ship bound for America in 1735, John Wesley was so influenced by the gracious piety of a party of Moravians, who sang of the blood of Jesus, that from that beginning many believe came his impetus into revival, and from that experience early Methodism was filled with piety and songs of celebration of the blood of Jesus. A cursory check through American church history reveals that wherever piety and celebration of the blood of Jesus have *preceded,* so also has *proceeded* revival and true loving life in our Lord Jesus Christ. It is the blood of Jesus which sprinkles the heart, the arena of inner space we need to conquer. "And since we have a great priest over the house of God, let us draw near with a sincere heart in full assurance of faith, having our *hearts sprinkled clean from an evil conscience* and our body washed with pure water" (Heb. 10:21-22). How often have we sung "Draw me nearer, nearer, nearer, blessed Lord, to Thy precious bleeding side," (Hymn, "Draw Me Nearer") and did not know the power of what we sang?

May every Christian counselor never forget the greatest tool of power God has placed in his hands—the blood of Jesus. The Word of God is given the counselor for a mighty tool, for it is "the power of God for salvation" (Rom. 1:16). But for the cleansing of the heart, which is the most incisive task of a counselor, the blood is his foremost power, "And to Jesus, the mediator of a new covenant, and to the sprinkled blood, which speaks better than the blood of Abel [which cried to the Father from the ground]" (Gen. 4:10, Heb. 12:24).

Therefore even the first covenant was not inaugurated without blood. For when every commandment had been spoken by Moses to all the people according to the Law, he took the blood of the calves and the goats, with water and scarlet wool and hyssop, and sprinkled both the book itself and all the people, saying, *"This is the blood of the covenant which God commanded you."* And in the same way he sprinkled both the tabernacle and all the vessels of the ministry with the blood. And according to the Law, one may almost say, all things are cleansed with blood, and without shedding of blood there is no forgiveness. Therefore it was necessary for the copies of the things in the heavens to be cleansed with these, but the heavenly things themselves with better sacrifices than these. For Christ did not enter a holy place made with hands, a mere copy of the true one, but into heaven itself, now to appear in the presence of God for us; nor was it that he should offer Himself often, as the high priest enters the holy place year by year with blood not his own. Otherwise, He would have needed to suffer often since the foundation of the world; but now once at the consummation He has been manifested to put away sin by the sacrifice of Himself. And inasmuch as it is appointed for men to die once, and after this comes judgment; so Christ also, having been offered once to bear the sins of many, shall appear a second time, not to bear sin, to those who eagerly await Him, for salvation. (Heb. 9:18-28, italics mine)

Central then to the healing of the human heart is the blood of Jesus. The Word corrects *the mind* and *pierces to the heart* (Heb. 4:12), but it is the blood that heals the heart. The paradox is that though that blood once offered need never be offered again, its application is daily required or the heart sickens and sours anew. We cannot by logic or will power change the heart. No matter how clearly we see what lodges there, there it remains. Here is where the secular psychological counselor stands bankrupt, for he cannot cleanse what he sees. But the Christian can. Where the secular leaves off, the Christian has only begun. He has but to call for the blood of the Lamb. "Behold, the Lamb of God [our perfect blood sacrifice] who *takes away the sin of the world!*" (John 1:29, italics mine).

The prayer takes no measure of faith, only enough to voice the asking. The least Christian wields the fullness of its power. It can never be exhausted. Barbara Shlemon (author of *Healing Prayer*) once attended a charismatic Catholic conference at which it was decided to serve Mass in both elements. So many attended that just as she arrived at the altar rail to receive, a priest stepped up to bawl out in a loud voice, "We have exhausted the blood of Jesus!" Barbara nearly fainted! How indescribably great that though sins multiply as darkness increases, we can never exhaust the blood of Jesus! His faithfulness guarantees that it is always there, at the merest asking, to cleanse the heart thoroughly and completely.

We urge every counselor to pray aloud with those who come, that the blood of our Lord may cleanse their hearts at each confession. The prayer is not a magical incantation.

There are not certain words which must be said, in just certain orders. Any stumbling, halting, confused cry is enough. We need only to mention the blood and ask for its application. The greatest difficulty concerning forgiveness is that most often we do not know we still cherish resentment, or have lied to ourselves and forgotten. We plead with every Christian counselor not to believe what the counselee says about his feelings. We must not base conviction, or lack of it, on the counselee's feelings. Feelings are inveterate liars at best. Our thoughts and memories are glossed over with euphemisms and lies. The key was given in the last chapter; if a bad fruit exists, a hidden unforgiveness must lie at the root. We counsel on the basis of the clean logic of the Word of God, not man's confused notions and feelings about himself.

Pilots must go through intensive training to retrain the mind not to adhere to their own senses of up and down, light and dark, but to believe the instruments, and lock coordination into flying "blind." "Who is blind but My servant, Or so deaf as My messenger whom I send? Who is so blind as he that is at peace with Me, Or so blind as the servant of the Lord?" (Isa. 42:19). "And He will *not judge by what His eyes see, Nor make a decision by what His ears hear*" (Isa. 11:3, italics mine). Christian counselors must learn to fly blind, trusting only the instrument of God's Word, not men's senses or feelings. "The law of the Lord is perfect, *restoring the soul;* The testimony of the Lord is sure, *making wise* the *simple*" (Ps. 19:7, italics mine). Though we laid down these understandings as basic in the last chapter, let us now see that nowhere are they more true and incisive in application than in the matter of forgiveness. People almost invariably think they have forgiven when they haven't. And how shall we know? By simple, pure logic according to God's Word. If the problem is still there, forgiveness is incomplete.

For the counselor to see the problem is one thing; it is another thing altogether for the counselee's heart, as well as his mind, to do so. Though the Law is absolute, there are no certainties in comprehension. We must watch never to say,

"Aha, you've got this or that problem." Rather, we need to remember to invite the other, by question, parables, stories, etc. Perhaps for this reason, to reach the heart of the other, "All these things Jesus spoke to the multitides in parables, and He was not talking to them without a parable" (Matt. 13:34). We need to remember carefully to search out the whole history of the person, and not to leap to premature conclusions, and to invite the other by that searching to see and connect things within himself.

Many people confusedly think they have to go back and find whoever the person was and talk it out, and since the person may have died, there is no way. We are not ministering merely to the grown person, but to the child yet living in the heart. It may not only be unnecessary to talk to the person in question, but hurtful. Whoever hurt us may be unaware, or if aware, thought it long ago forgiven and done with. The counselor can pray for the forgiveness to be accomplished purely within the hidden heart of the counselee. If the Holy Spirit later prompts a possible present talk and reconciliation, let it be done with wisdom and with tact. But seldom is it necessary. And of course not when those involved have passed on.

When parents were normal and good, it is strangely more difficult to get at roots than when parents were recognizably evil. Resentments in the latter case are easily seen and admitted consciously. But loyalty masks the other, both in childhood and in counseling sessions. Here again, the straight clean logic of the Word enables us to act on faith, disregarding feelings, as Paula and I have testified earlier.

Frequently, resentments lie totally beneath both the heart and mind, having originated either in the spirit in the womb or at birth, or from reactions to things left undone by those who ought to have done them for us. Sometimes parents have almost never done anything demonstrably evil, and yet have almost totally failed as parents. One instance occurs in homes in which parents were God-fearing, moral, upstanding, dutiful people, but never touched the children with affection.

The children's minds and hearts could not know what was lacking, and remembered only the good things the parents did. But their spirits ached for touch, and resented its lack. Now the adult cannot give love, and the family is starving. Perhaps the mate is unfaithful. Bad fruit evidences the bitter root. Prayer for forgiveness delivers where no resentment has ever been felt.

Another example is most tragic. We have often counseled people whose parents not only did almost everything correctly, they also gave copious affection, and yet they failed miserably as parents. Why? Because they did not know how to give the child space to be his own person. They so overdid things that they snuffed out the budding life of the child. Such children as adults may have extreme difficulty seeing resentment as a base in their hearts in their present difficulties. Again the presence of the fruit of a fearful, squashed life reveals the presence of a bad root of resentment in the spirit of the child. Repentance, confession, and absolution must be solely by faith according to the Word of God. Truly a counselor must learn to trust such diagnosis and treatment, solely by faith.

Events are not what we are primarily concerned about. Horrendous events may not score deeply in the heart at all, depending on God's grace. Slightest happenings may leave scars and resultant practices which wreck relationships from then on. What is important is the heart's reaction. Sometimes reactions are not apparent immediately, exploding later, much like a bomb with a delayed fuse.

Forgiveness concerning events may not yet accomplish deliverance. Reactions to events in childhood cause behavior adaptations which become habits or practices in the old nature. Those behavior patterns, once firmly structured into the soul, are not easily dealt with. For example, coldness on the part of parents may initially be touched by forgiveness. More crucial, however, are the patterns of withdrawal, the stony heart, the habits of vengeance-taking, and all the other writhing tentacles of the octopus of self. Counselors should be more concerned about the practices in the old nature (Col. 3:9) than the events from which they were built.

We said earlier that if bad fruit persists, forgiveness is not yet accomplished. A person may, however, fully forgive the one who initially wounded, and yet retain a destructive resulting practice. That practice is also dismantled (or transformed) by the cross—and forgiveness. When a person has forgiven another, he yet has himself to forgive. We cannot allow the destruction of our inner practices until forgiveness of self restores capacity to trust and to let go. Death of self is predicated upon, and made possible, only by the fullness of forgiveness. We cannot stand to be crucified with Him so long as we continue to blame and chastise ourselves and try to be different. Death of that striving to set things straight is predicated upon fullness of forgiveness, in which we cease to attack ourselves.

Forgiveness brings us to rest. The blood of Jesus washes away the strivings of guilt precisely so that the structures of habit can be let go to death. If prayer for death on the cross has been expressed many times, and yet that old pattern continues to operate, counselor and counselee need to return to base one, and examine whether fullness or forgiveness of self and God has in fact been accomplished.

We cannot get to the cross save by the route through Gethsemane—which is when we identify our sin, and wrestle our emotions away from attachment to the old way, otherwise we will in effect snatch our old way off the cross before He cries out "It is finished." Forgiveness happens *before* death even as Jesus first petitioned, "Father, forgive them," hours before He was ready to proclaim once for all "It is finished." Fullness of forgiveness prepares us for happy, easy death-like letting go a feather in a gentle wind. Without fullness of forgiveness, we put a practice on the cross, only to discover it still stuck on the hand, glued there by unforgiveness of self and God. Without fullness of forgiveness, the work of sanctification and transformation is heavy, and sweaty. But forgiveness makes it light and easy.

Transformation thus has two parts. The blood of Jesus washes the heart clean, but the blood will not destroy the works of darkness in the soul (1 John 3:8). Only the cross can do that. Forgiveness is central, but it only begins the process. The work of transformation is a daily struggle from then on, to crucify the self.

Nevertheless, some ongoing aspects of forgiveness can continue to influence and enhance that transformation. Chapter 19, "Forgiveness," in *Restoring the Christian Family*, develops those aspects more fully. Suffice it here to say that the counselee needs to be encouraged to pray blessing for those who wounded or failed (Rom. 12:14-21, 1 Pet. 3:8-14). The counselee should be exhorted to minister to others in like difficulties; as he does he will see himself more clearly, and love will overflow his own deserts.

Most especially the counselee should be urged to pray in thanksgiving for everything in the past, so that the heart is changed from a stance of self-pity and anger to glorying in what God has accomplished in and through all.

Forgiveness is not complete until God the Father is included. Scripture says, "When a man's folly brings his way to ruin, his heart rages against the Lord" (Prov. 19:3 RSV). Note again that word "heart." The mind protests, "How could I ever be angry at God? He's so perfect. He never did anything to me." But that's not what the heart says. The heart perversely cries out, "Oh yeah, if you were a good Father, you wouldn't have let me fall this far!" Or in the case of people wounded in early childhood, in the womb, or at birth, "You sent me to serve you and then you let me get so messed up by these people. Now how do you expect me to serve you? It isn't fair!" Or, "Where were you when I needed you?" Or, "Why me, God?" And so on, the heart's cries being as infinite as the problems we get into.

For that reason Job cried out, "Neither is there any daysman betwixt us, that might lay his hand upon us both" (Job 9:33 KJV). A daysman was the same as a counselor in Bible times. Men went to such a man to settle disputes, as when the two women made King Solomon their daysman in their dispute over whose baby was whose (1 Kings 3:16-28). Such a counselor, or daysman, talked to both parties, reasoned with them, and having settled the dispute, laid his hands on both their shoulders and drew them together for forgiveness. Job's cry calls for our Lord Jesus Christ to become our daysman betwixt God and man. And that is what 2 Cor. 5:18-20 says He is, namely, that "God was in Christ reconciling the world to Himself." Observe in the last phrase of the quote, St. Paul speaks of our being reconciled to God, not the other way around. We need to be reconciled to God because we are angry at Him. In the next phrase the Holy Spirit speaks of His forgiving us, "not counting their trespasses against them." That is the function of the daysman, to lay his hand on each, and so make mutual forgiveness and peace.

Jesus is our daysman. Counselors should not stop short; we are to enable forgiveness between God and man, both ways.

6

Breaking the Cycle

For as many as are of the works of the law are under the curse: for it is written, Cursed is every one that continueth not in all things which are written in the book of the law to do them. But that no man is justified by the law in the sight of God, it is evident: for, The just shall live by faith. And the law is not of faith: but, The man that doeth them shall live in them. Christ hath redeemed us from the curse of the law, being made a curse for us: for it is written, Cursed is every one that hangeth on a tree: That the blessing of Abraham might come on the Gentiles through Jesus Christ; that we might receive the promise of the Spirit through faith.
(Gal. 3:10-14 KJV)

And they that are Christ's have crucified the flesh with the affections and lusts. (Gal. 5:24 KJV)

It is not enough merely to forgive. The existence of our undead, carnal nature guarantees that we will repeat many of our offenses far more than four hundred and ninety times (Matt. 18:21-22). If one were to picture a prizefighter deftly warding blows through countless rounds, defending against a relentless attacker, that might begin to portray the incessant need of forgiveness in a family so long as the flesh is not dealt with. Don't we all at times feel like martyrs who seem to have to do all the forgiving in the family and become dreadfully impatient for God to change everyone else? Habitual structures inflict so continually that they may eventually wear out the most patient saint. Therefore the cross is central to survival, for the blood does not break the cycle of hate. It only washes away results in the heart. Only the cross stops the ravages of the flesh.

Repentance is not a feeling; it is action. It will not effect much change to feel sorry. Change happens in relationships only as the cycle of hatred is broken and transformed by the stimuli of love. Change can happen only in individuals, one by one, in relationships. Change happens in individuals only as those structures which stimulate wrong actions and which respond to them are crucified on the cross. Without that crucifixion, battle scenes will be repeated in endlessly varied forms.

Many counselors and counselees attempt to heal relationships by changing the surface ways people say things or act. Since all words and actions have behind them rivers of inner intention and hidden structures in the carnal nature, that is much like sticking a finger in a dike, only to discover another break and then another until one gets the picture of a man splayed over a wall with every finger and toe engaged while emotions and incidents pour like a sieve all around him until the whole relationship bursts open.

By becoming as us in Gethsemane, our Lord Jesus Christ gained the right (necessitated by our free will) to die for us *as us* on the cross. That death crumbles the structures of self. The moment our physical body dies, the vacated spirit no longer has access to sustain its structures, and collapse and decay set in. The moment the attitude of our hearts finds its death knell on the cross, the structures it sustained begin to find their death on the cross. In each such successive inner death, we go through a process. We may find ourselves going through stages foretyped by the forerunner and pioneer of our faith even as He died and arose again. Like Jesus, after a while (three days in the belly of the earth), a new and resurrected spirit in us fills that old, newly dead structure with a new and transformed intention which can move through "locked doors and windows" (John 20:19-26) to meet and heal the hearts of others.

When death of a character structure happens, that portion of our inner being figuratively sinks "into the heart of the earth." "For just as Jonah was three days and three nights in the belly of the sea monster, so shall the Son of Man be three days and three nights in the heart of the earth" (Matt. 12:40). In biblical symbolism, the belly is the repository of thoughts and feelings. "He that believeth on me, as the scripture hath said, out of his belly* shall flow rivers of living water" (John 7:38 KJV). "But Mary kept all these things, and pondered them in her heart" (Luke 2:19 KJV). Death of a portion of our self initiates a convulsion or deep shudder throughout our interior being. We undergo sadness, confusion, disorientation, despondency, heaviness, sleepiness, or turmoil. In that time, death is happening throughout the subterranean regions of our motives and practices. Truly we also, like Jesus, spend our three days in the belly of the earth.

The "three days" may be but a moment, or hours, days or months, depending on who knows what within the complexity of us. Paula and I have visited with many counselees during their "three days." They may say any number of the following:

"I don't know what's happening to me."

"I'm so tired all the time."

"I feel so heavy I feel like I'm drugged."

"I don't seem to want to do anything."

"I don't seem to have my normal usual feelings."

"I'm walking about like a zombie."

"I feel like a bowl of jelly inside."

"I'm all scrambled."

"I feel like an inner earthquake rumbling around somewhere and I can't get hold of it."

"I just want to sleep all the time."

"You never told me it would be like this. How long does this go on? Is this normal?"

The most common experience is extremely heavy fatigue.

---

* "Belly" is rendered "from within Him" (ASV and NIV), "heart" (RSV), "innermost being" (NAS, footnote, "literally, *out of his belly*").

Actually what has happened is akin to what occurs in the first days of a much-needed vacation. When we let down, our fatigue catches up with us. The weariness is not actually new. It was there all along. Our letting down causes us to feel accumulated past fatigue in the present.

Jesus came to call the weary, "Come to Me, all who are weary and heavy-laden, and I will give you rest. Take My yoke upon you, and learn from Me, for I am gentle and humble in heart; and *you shall find rest for your souls*. For My yoke is easy, and My load is light" (Matt. 11:28-30). Every structure in the old nature is marked by unrest. Whatever in us which has been built by God is at rest, even as He rested (Heb. 4:10). Whatever we built in us has no rest; it must be constantly examined, reworked, defended, appreciated, and approved of. Thus, each practice demands energy to sustain itself. That is why sometimes our conscious mind forgets what it was doing. Our inner struggles rob the surface mind of its ability to concentrate by draining off its energy for more demanding inner battles. So when we come to death with Jesus on the cross, our inner being goes into the tomb with Him, and we let down into that emotional, mental, and spiritual fatigue which was there all along.

That time of inner death cannot be hastened. Like Jesus, we need our "three days in the belly of the earth," however long or short that may be. Oh, that every counselor would hear us now: *we must not haul the counselee up too soon!* We also need our Joseph of Arimathea and Nicodemus to be there as we come off the cross of death, to lay us lovingly to rest. (Matt. 27:58-59). That means practically that we need people who can stand for us to change, people who are not threatened if we act differently, or fail to act. People who stand by us, not forcing us to return to the old ways of acting, people who do nothing but stand there, accepting us, as we stop doing what is familiar to them. Who are not upset because we don't play the old games any more. We need people who do not demand that we respond out of an erstwhile emotional center which is no longer there, who are not hurt, accusing, or controlling.

People who let us be a dead mess, and love us anyway.

We too need a Roman centurion and his soldiers, people who stand guard about us through the long night of our death. We cannot take the full clamor of new events and challenges during that time of inner death. We need people to pick up the slack for us, to handle details, and not criticize when we flub a detail we used to do easily by rote. We need a pocket, like a quarterback depending on his guards to pick off the blitzers long enough for the play of life to unfold in a new way before us. There is an inner night of death we need to have time to go through.

We may not be ready quickly to be touched, like Jesus with Mary in the garden (John 20:17). As Jesus needed to go yet to His Father, so we may need quiet confirmations of the new life until it settles in, and "after you have suffered for a little, the God of all grace, who called you to His eternal glory in Christ, will Himself perfect, confirm, strengthen, and establish you" (1 Pet. 5:10). And people may not recognize us (John 20:14, Luke 24:16). They are not used to the new us, and neither are we. So the old familiar demands upon us need to be held off for a while. Another analogy might be that we are like a newly overhauled motor which ought not to be run full bore until the new piston rings are well seated. We need to ease into the new old body of us.

Counselors need wisdom and perception to stand by and let us go through the process. If hurried, we may not come into the fullness of rest and new identity we are meant to become.

There is a hiddenness which ought to be respected. No one knows what happened to Jesus during those three days in the tomb. We know what He *did*, "For Christ also died for sins once for all, the just for the unjust, in order that He might bring us to God, having been put to death in the flesh, but made alive in the spirit; in which also He went and made proclamation to the spirits now in prison" (1 Pet. 3:18-19). But we do *not* know what kind of *metamorphosis*, if any, was happening in Him, or how. We know that He was made perfect through what He suffered (Heb. 2:10). Perhaps that

111

perfection was continuing to be accomplished there, in the depths of suffering our death, unless "It is finished" referred as well to that process. Whether or not anything was continuing to happen *to* Jesus, it certainly does happen *in us* in our "three days in the belly of the earth." For that time, counselors must protect that secretness. That means that *introspection needs to stop.* Paula and I in counseling have often felt the check of the Holy Spirit, prompting us to tell people to quit "looking in" for that time period. The Lord at such times would reveal nothing further concerning the inner nature of the counselee, and would make it apparent to us that this was not the time to deal with anything else already seen inside the person. Other things might later come to a time of death, but right then so much death and deep hidden reformation was going on that we only wanted to sit and celebrate, seeing nothing. We have often had to say, "Will you quit digging up the seed to see how well it's doing, and let well enough alone?" Our holy and ghostly counsel then is to read a dime-store western, or watch a comedy, or play a game— anything to busy the mind outwardly—distracting it from interior speculations, so as to let the inner being alone.

How significant it is that Jesus came back into the same physically wounded body. Apart from all the theological significances, which could never be overstated, there lies an import to the inner being which is the essence of transformation. Our own new nature likewise arises within the very structure of what we have been. It is not that we would be okay if we could just get away from us, and move over there somewhere else and become some other personality. Maybe we would all like to be like that friend or neighbor whose character seems so ideal to us, or like some favorite saint. But God didn't call us to be like them. He called us to be us, and to become that new us within the very mess we have been, now transformed by the resurrection life of Jesus in us.

When Jesus replaces us, He does not superimpose His own being in such a way that we are type-stamped, like cookie-cutter gingerbread creatures. Rather, His nature is still such a death of himself for us, that He fills out what we are to be, which is uniquely and gloriously us. We are not robbed of anything we have been by our own personal crucifixion. We are fulfilled. His life fills our life's structure with His resurrection power to be the glory He intended from the first that we should be. "There are also heavenly bodies and earthly bodies, but the glory of the heavenly is one, and the glory of the earthly is another. There is one glory of the sun, and another glory of the moon, and another glory of the stars; for star differs from star in glory. So also is the resurrection of the dead" (1 Cor. 15:40-42).

Our delightful God revels in variety. "How lovely are Thy dwelling places, O Lord of hosts!" (Ps. 84:1). "Or do you not know that your body is a temple of the Holy Spirit who is in you, whom you have from God, and that you are not your own?" (1 Cor. 6:19). "In whom you also are being built together into a dwelling of God in the Spirit" (Eph. 2:22). God will never turn out one individual like another. No one can be replaced. Every child of God is unique, glorious in his own right, and needful to the whole. Therefore a counselor does not build into another what the counselor thinks he ought to be. The greatest loss on earth would be a bunch of John and Paula Sandfords all acting identically. We fail if we produce clones. Every counselor stands by to watch as Jesus resurrects the other into that unique wonder of creation God intended for him/her to be. That is the joy of a counselor, to watch the unique beauty of each butterfly emerge.

As we said earlier, until inner death happens, and the new creatures we are to be emerge, the cycle of hate is not broken. Our old habit patterns continue to create stimuli to anger, both in us and others. And the battle is on again and again. Now we add that even if we are in process of catching the deceptive games of the self in some areas, in other areas we are but beginning or have not even started the labor of catching ourselves, checking our responses, and hauling them to the cross. There are no easy-to-come-by saints. There is only perseverance (Heb. 3:14, Heb. 12:1). Let but a moment's off-guardedness happen and we are back into outward battles. How tired of it we become. Peace does not fully come until the whole structure has been dealt with. Though full in the inmost spirit the moment of *conversion*, peace does not settle into all our living until the entire inner being has been dealt with, and the self is transformed.

Even so, that transformation depends upon the continued grace of our Lord's presence in us. If we walk dry, apart from prayer, that arid condition becomes the ground of resurrection, not of the new but of the carnal old. "Thou wilt keep him in perfect peace, whose mind is stayed on thee: because he trusteth in thee" (Isa. 26:3 KJV). Mark carefully, not that *we stay* the mind on him, by determination or whatever power of the flesh we could beckon to the task; ". . .*is stayed*,"is kept by the Lord. So the one who *abides* in Him bears much fruit (John 15:1-5). "And He was saying to them all, 'If anyone wishes to come after Me, let him deny himself, and take up *his cross daily*, and follow Me" (Luke 9:23). The most common factor we deal with in counseling is the fact of undead flesh in bornanew Christians. Comprehension of crucifixion is crucial to the maturation of the body in Christ. Note therefore a difference: Physical death is apt to be something easy and quick, but crucifixion is slow and painful. Evolvement is even more slow and painful. As there are no instant saints, neither are there sudden transformations.

Al Durrance, an Episcopal rector friend of ours, likes to wear a T-shirt which reads, "The trouble with living sacrifices is, they keep crawling off the altar." How true! We may have to suffer the embarrassment of failures numbers of times and so deeply that we can't stand what we are more than we fear death—until we can't stand not dying.

We cannot very successfully put ourselves on the cross. We have to be impelled to it by the process He puts us through. If we could do it ourselves, we would never be able to escape pride that we managed to become deader than the next fellow. "Well, my friend, you will be as holy as I am when you have just managed to die enough." The Lord so engineers our salvation that though we have a part in it, we can never take credit for our own crucifixion. In Christ all boasting is excluded. "That no man should boast before God. But by His doing you are in Christ Jesus, who became to us wisdom from God, and righteousness and sanctification, and redemption, that, just as it is written, *let him who boasts, boast in the Lord"* (1 Cor. 1:29-31).

Only so does death and resurrection happen, by the providence of God. Now let us see whether every counselor, indeed every Christian, can hear what follows from that fact: If it is the Holy Spirit who moves us by the grace of God's planning, at the right time and way, to our own personal crucifixion, what have we to do with judging any brother for being when and where he is? We are tempted to anger by the stubborn slowness, even tardiness of others and us, but when we come to understand the way we all must come to crucifixion solely by His timing, all hustle and demand die. For we see that God in His wisdom knows how to move us on the checkerboard of life. Can we blame a brother for being immature? Had God not persisted, despite our stubbornness, there we would be also. Maybe it is not that fellow's time yet. Let God judge whether he is tardy and rebellious or not. The task of a counselor is therefore not to prod and push or pull. Perhaps the Holy Spirit will prompt the counselor to exhort and urge the other, but our flesh will accomplish nothing.

"Truly, truly, I say to you, when you were younger, you used to gird yourself, and walk wherever you wished; but when you grow old, you will stretch out your hands, and someone else will gird you, and bring you where you do not wish to go" (John 21:18). When Jesus spoke to Peter, he referred specifically to the time when men would carry Peter to be crucified upside down. But notice, the context is crucifixion, and that text can be taken as a parable for us. When we were first born anew and filled with the Spirit, we steamed ourselves up (girded ourselves) in our own emotions and by our own individual prayer life. We rushed here and there sharing this word and that, trying this and that gift, to get our own ministry going. We "went where we would." Maturity in Jesus meant crucifixion. The point being that He accomplishes that crucifixion through the means of where others *take us*. We "put forth our hands," both to minister and to be ministered to. But others take hold of us, and carry us where we would not—to death of self.

The lesson for counselors is, we need to encourage others to stop fighting the people and circumstances God puts in our way. It may be those very incidents and people who carry us to our death (which is most likely precisely why we *do* fight them). We may not be able to stop fighting. We may not like the whole process. But at least we can understand it. And praise God for it (with gritted teeth, perhaps). "Though he slay me, yet will I trust in him" (Job 13:15 KJV). We sing so often these days, "For He is Lord." Do we really mean it? Or believe it? Does the unbelieving heart of a believer actually expect that His Lordship means that He *will* put us through the process? Perhaps we can learn nothing more valuable in all of life than to trust that He really is who He is, and will accomplish what He has purposed to do. "That He might present to Himself the church in all her glory, having no spot or wrinkle or any such thing; but that she should be holy and blameless" (Eph. 5:27). "Now to Him who is able to keep you from stumbling, and to make you stand in the presence of His glory blameless with great joy . . ." (Jude 1:24).

We cannot close this chapter without teaching how to keep one's healing. There is a necessity to stand on faith. Once crucifixion is in process, or being completed, we need to claim that fact by what we allow ourselves to feel, think, say, or do. We need to continue to reckon as dead that thing we prayed about. Many people go directly from healing prayer to a testing, and feeling that same old emotion they conclude, "Oh, it didn't work." They may then plunge right back into all the same old feelings. Old habits will continue to sound off, like chime stones swinging in the wind. But if we have taken a thing to the cross, that is all they are, mere sounds in the wind, having no force of reality behind them any more. They are truly dead, and we are made new. But, if we will believe they still have life, and plunge into struggling with them, we can impart false life to those old crucified structures, and wrestle unnecessarily all over again.

A habit of jealousy, or temper, or being critical, whatever, will keep on flaring up, having been prayed for. But if we have laid the ax to the root, and prayed, that thing is in fact dead. If we let the continued recurrence of the old habit bother us, we can be stampeded only by ghosts and old empty haunted houses in our nature. It is often merely because of that fact of unbelief, and lack of self-discipline, that counselees fall back until "the last state has become worse for them than the first" (1 Pet. 2:20).

If the counselee believes that old thing still has reality, he will either give it energy by grappling with it, or give in and flop back into the old habit. Neither is necessary. All he has to do is reject the old feeling, not fighting with it, merely saying, "I don't have to have that any more. That is dead," and then go on with the life he wants, ignoring contrary feelings from that point on. Or if it's a thought or an action, he needs only to reject the old thought or deed, from that point on ignoring that thought and making himself act in a new way, without bothering to question or quarrel with himself or even concern himself that that old thing still exists. Thus he gives it no reality.

The old form in the nature, once dealt with, can be likened to a swinging pendulum in a grandfather clock, the main spring of which is broken. If we will let it alone, and not hit the pendulum again, pretty soon it will wind down and quit. Or as with a bouncing ball, if we will quit dribbling it, it will eventually stop bouncing and roll to a stop. We must learn not to pay attention to dead symptoms. All our feelings have a life of their own, and do not want to die. Our thoughts likewise fight not to perish. If we will just get in and fight with them again, the feelings and thoughts can have a grand time plunging us into problem after problem, just to keep themselves alive and on center stage.

Therefore do not *let* sin reign in your mortal body that you should obey its lusts, and do not go on presenting the members of your body to sin as instruments of unrighteousness; but present yourselves to God as those alive from the dead, and your members as instruments of righteousness to God. For sin shall not be master over you, for you are not under law, but under grace. (Rom. 6:12-14)

Our mind and heart do not want us to be whole. They want to cook up crisis after crisis. "Because the mind set on the flesh is hostile toward God; for it does not subject itself to the Law of God, for it is not even able to do so" (Rom 8:7). We haul such habits of mind and heart *daily* to death after prayer by acting the new life and ignoring the old signals.

A woman came who could not give herself to her husband sexually. After we found the roots and brought all the old self structures to the cross, she still found herself tensing at her husband's approach. Her mind and feelings ran scattered like rebellious children. She learned not to fight her feelings or her mind, or get mad at her continued failures. Rather, she said silently, "I reject that" and turned her attention to opening to her husband's touch and spirit. She was soon warm and loving and having a ball, and so was he.

A woman came oppressed by feelings of worthlessness, loneliness, and self-pity. Having gotten at the roots, she had to learn not to let herself be tyrannized by continued recurrence of the old feelings, and made herself do things which distracted her mind from the symptoms. In a few weeks she couldn't remember what she used to feel.

A man came who could not spend time with his children and enjoy it. The roots being taken care of, he found the desired new life no automatic gift. He had to take hold, and make himself be with his children, play games, take walks, go fishing, and read stories to them, ignoring the pull of TV and all the old feelings and non-feelings. After a while he was having so much fun with his children he wondered why he never had discovered such joy before.

A final point. We have found it to be a law that those who merely want pain removed do not get well. Those who want to go on enjoying their own selfish, self-centered life never become free and happy. They only want to escape trouble (the very thing God would use to wake them up) so they can go on serving their own selfish god of mammon pleasure. But those whose joy it is to lay their lives down in service for others are soon well and happy. The secret of life is in fact to lose it (Luke 17:33).

7

The Role of a Christian Counselor

Before she travailed, she brought forth;
Before her pain came, she gave birth to a boy.
Who has heard such a thing? Who has seen
such things?
Can a land be born in one day?
Can a nation be brought forth all at once?
As soon as Zion travailed, she also brought forth
her sons.
"Shall I bring to the point of birth, and not give
delivery?" says the Lord.
"Or shall I who gives delivery shut the womb?"
says your God.
"Be joyful with Jerusalem and rejoice for her, all
you who love her;
Be exceedingly glad with her, all you who
mourn over her;
That you may nurse and be satisfied with her
comforting breasts;
That you may suck and be delighted with her
bountiful bosom."
For thus says the Lord, "Behold I extend peace to
her like a river,
And the glory of the nations like an overflowing
stream;
And you shall be nursed, you shall be carried on
the hip and fondled on the knees.
As one whom his mother comforts, so I will
comfort you;
And you shall be comforted in Jerusalem."
(Isa. 66:7-13)

God intends to give daily rebirth and nurture to us through the Church. It is the Church which now is called to give birth anew, more and more, to the Church. That, we believe, is the primary calling upon the Body today.

"And do not be conformed to this world, but be transformed by the renewing of your mind, that you may prove what the will of God is, that which is good and acceptable and perfect" (Rom. 12:2). Note the little word "by." We have wondered why sometimes we are simply healed by the Lord, and why at other times it seems we must obtain just the right bit of knowledge in order to be sanctified in a given area. Some have made such an issue of *mental* comprehension and confession for people to come into the fullness of redemption and maturity, it seems to us they have enthroned the conscious mind! To be transformed *by* the renewal of the mind does not mean that we must all become auto-analysts, excavating every moment of our history into the light (or confusion) of mental awareness. Some things may be better left unseen and unsaid. Sometimes the Lord renews our deep mind without our ever having consciously understood. We simply find ourselves thinking differently, for ". . . out of the heart come evil thoughts . . ." (Matt. 15:19). If the *heart* is changed by the Lord, the mind, both conscious and subconscious, *is renewed*. Sometimes we simply grow out of a childish way. We have thought as children and reasoned so, but when we became adults in Christ, we put that away (1 Cor. 13:11).

Many counselors have erred by driving the counselee to see and examine everything, as though we are saved by right thinking. That is gnosticism. Rather, we are saved by the person of our Lord Jesus Christ, and counselor and counselee alike must be open to His Holy Spirit to see what only *He* knows is pertinent to our transformation.

For the transformation which goes on without our conscious awareness, the general Body of Christ is easily both our womb and our midwife. But for those instances in which the Holy Spirit requires that we understand ourselves, the priesthood of all believers may or may not be sufficient. Those who are our compatriots in Christ should be our first counselors. Sometimes, however, a person of special insight is needed. "A plan ('purpose' in RSV) in the heart of a man is like deep water, But a man of understanding draws it out" (Prov. 20:5).

The scriptural base for every counselor in Christ is found in what Jesus was and is as expressed in Isaiah 11:1-3:

> Then a shoot will spring up from the stem of Jesse,
> And a branch from his roots will bear fruit.
> And the Spirit of the Lord will rest on Him,
> The spirit of wisdom and understanding,
> The spirit of counsel and strength,
> The spirit of knowledge and the fear of the Lord.
> And He will delight in the fear of the Lord,
> And He will not judge by what His eyes see,
> Nor make a decision by what His ears hear;

A Christian counselor must not judge by what his eyes see or his ears hear. He must see beyond events and circumstances with the gift of insight. A counselor must look, as God does, upon the heart. ". . . For God sees not as man sees, for man looks at the outward appearance, but the Lord looks at the heart" (1 Sam. 16:1). Sight alone endangers the beholder with judgment. "Do not judge lest you be judged yourselves. For in the way you judge, you will be judged; and by your standard of measure, it shall be measured to you" (Matt. 7:1-2). It is not that we must never judge. We cannot live without making appraisals and acting accordingly. We judge whether a bridge is safe to cross, whether a piece of merchandise is worth its cost, or whether we ought to entrust our life to a particular doctor's skill. More pertinently, we decide whether we ought to risk our confidences with a man, or trust our emotions with his temperament, or our confessions to his confidentiality or to his concepts of authority and forgiveness. It is the stance of the heart that matters. The above Scripture passage concerns blaming and condemning. Christian counselors must hold firm the knowledge that in Christ there is no condemnation (Rom. 8:1). We stand together at the foot of the cross, seeing we are all under sin. No one is better than another, however well some may have performed. Otherwise, seeing another's fault, we become self-elevated. A counselor sees and judges, but never with blame. He attempts to see not the surface but the intent of the heart, and so judges not the *context* but the true *content* of what is happening.

"Woe is me, for I am ruined! Because I am a man of unclean lips, *And I live among a people of unclean lips;*" (Isa. 6:5). A Christian counselor must consider his brother's sin as his own. It is of no consequence that we dwell *among* sinners unless we know their sins as ours. We are one, whether we want it so or not. The fact that a counselor may not have succumbed to that particular sin is not to his credit, but to the Lord's grace. If he does not know these things, he cannot help but feel himself better than the one he counsels.

Further, to the extent that a Christian counselor thinks the blood has washed him lily white, remaining unaware that his sin nature yet runs rampant, his ministry will also put down rather than set free. He will look down on those he counsels. Every ministry (preaching, teaching, evangelism) stands in danger of this, but it is most likely to happen in the close confines of the counseling office. Counselors more than all others wade the sewers of human hearts. If a counselor does not know he belongs there (in the sewer), and deserves no better than any life he sees, he cannot help but become puffed up like the Pharisee, and send not only himself but the counselee home unjustified (Luke 18:9-14). Such a counselor may try to appear understanding but will come across as condescending, for the counselee will sooner or later read his heart. If he cannot see himself to be as rotten as any other sinner, accepting himself as finite and broken, he cannot bring another into rest nor give Jesus all the glory. He will scold and scald, or palliate sin, and whitewash walls (Ezek. 13:10-15). To know himself as sin is the *sine qua non* qualification of every counselor in the Lord Jesus Christ!

> Is any among you sick? Let him call for the elders of the church, and let them pray over him, anointing him with oil in the name of the Lord; and the prayer offered in faith will

restore the one who is sick, and the Lord will raise him up, and if he has committed sins, they will be forgiven him. Therefore, confess your sins to one another, and pray for one another, so that you may be healed. The effective prayer of a righteous man can accomplish much. (James 5:14-16)

Iron sharpens iron, So one man sharpens another. (Prov. 27:17)

Where there is no guidance, the people fall, But in abundance of counselors there is victory. (Prov. 11:14)

In the beginning when people sat down in front of me (John) for counseling, fright would threaten to undo me. I felt like I had to perfect them, all at once—and who was I to do that! Wisdom soon revealed that was not my task, only to do the thing the Holy Spirit prompted that day. But then fear assailed in another direction. How was I to know what was needful just then? That fear is long overcome, but still residual. The prayer should always ascend from every Christian counselor, "Lord, make me appropriate to where he is." "Cause me to catch the clues." "Make me sensitive to what you are doing in the other. Give me wisdom to help, not to interfere or throw off the track."

Unlike a psychological counselor, a Christian counselor most likely will not use psychological tests to discover what is in the other. If he does, it is in order to obtain a general picture of the other. He still must rely on the Holy Spirit to reveal the details to be dealt with on a particular day. So also does a psychological counselor (though he might not give credit to the Holy Spirit) with this difference, that whatever is seen is not viewed as the problem to be attacked and overcome but as the context for the Holy Spirit to "perfect, confirm, strengthen, and establish" (1 Pet. 5:10).

Consequently, a Christian counselor can be described by several models. First, he is a father-confessor, as in James 5:16. Hearing the confession of another, he probes for causes, admonishes and teaches as a father, and pronounces forgiveness as a part of his priesthood in the priesthood of all believers.

Secondly, he is a shepherd, pouring on oil and providing still water. The thick wool of sheep prevents ticks from all parts of the body except the face and ears. A shepherd carefully examines each sheep each night, and if a tick is found, pours on oil until the tick backs out. "A tick of the mind" is an oriental idiom to describe a way of thinking that drains energy, which "sucks the blood of life," such as hate or vengeance or resentment. The oil is of course the Holy Spirit's anointing.

Sheep cannot drink fast water. It will bloat them. They must have still water. If he cannot find naturally still water, the shepherd digs a small hole by a stream and then a channel to it. Fast waters are the racing and troubled thoughts and emotions of the soul. The shepherd-counselor becomes a quiet and calm pool of listening acceptance and counsel.

Third, a counselor is a midwife. People frequently dream of struggling to give birth, or not to miscarry, or some other such birth or baby dream or nightmare. By that our inner being is portraying to the surface mind an inner trauma of something being born in us—a new idea, a realization, a new talent, or on the other side some evil thought or resurrection of the carnal nature. Some such births need to happen, some to be prevented. A counselor is sometimes called on to be the Lord's midwife, to assist the other in the birth process.

Fourth, he is also an executioner, slaying the little monsters born of sinful wombs of the mind, heart, and soul. He assists the other to the cross, and helps him to hold himself there till the job is done.

Fifth, he is a spiritual director, one who hears the whole life and calls for balance, or helps to set direction and pace. He may say, "You've been working at it too hard. It would be a good idea to take your wife out to dinner and a show." Or, "Try reading this (or that)." Or, "Have you considered praying this way?" Or, "Don't read so much for a while." He suggests whatever he sees is the needed next step in the counselee's life, or whichever counterbalancing thing needs to be done.

Finally, he may become as a father or mother in Christ (chapter 21, "Fathers and Mothers in Christ").

A Christian counselor is a friend who ministers. He is not merely a Christian who happens to counsel. Every Christian occasionally counsels and should improve his skills. People have come to us wounded and in increased confusion because they have been advised by many and counseled by some, sincere in their desire to help, but untrained and unskilled. Too often the one who counsels tends to project his own experience or problems onto the one he counsels, whether it fits him or not. A Christian counselor daily must call his own knowledge and experience to death on the cross so that he may be appropriate to the counselee, fresh and open to him and to the Holy Spirit. That requires a learned discipline. Our hope is to be a part of that training of the entire Body of Christ to minister. But some in the Body are especially called to counsel. When we speak of Christian counselors in this book, we have in mind those Christians who have been distinctly called, gifted by the Holy Spirit to counsel, and who hopefully are being recognized, anointed and given that office by their pastors and churches.

Christian counselors of that sort make no charge for their services. They must not unless happening to be psychologically trained and credentialed through whatever federal, state, county, or local agencies, they are required to do so. There are professional counselors who happen to be Christian, and counsel as such. Though our material may be helpful to them, we write primarily to non-professional counselors within the Body of Christ.

(We want to make it as clear as possible that we have no quarrel with psychology or psychological counseling. One of our best friends and advisors is Dr. William Johnson, head of the psychology department of Whitworth College. We check with him to make sure that whatever we say is psychologically sound. We treasure the insights of psychology. But we do not counsel as psychologists. We counsel as Christians, according to the Word of God. In that context, biblically sound psychological perceptions are helpful.)

On the other hand, a church may follow the principle that the "laborer is worthy of his wages" and "You shall not muzzle the ox while he is threshing . . ." (1 Tim. 5:18). The church or other organization may provide a salary or other form of compensation. It is our belief that if a church or organization does this, and we know some who do, neither the counselor, the organization nor the church ought initially to make a charge for services offered. A church in Spokane called me to teach and counsel there every Tuesday for several years. The church secretary set up appointments for counselees to come to me and to the several counselors I trained, but never was money mentioned. The church paid me for that day's services, but they paid nothing to any of the counselors trained within that body. Elijah House pays a salary to Paula and me, and to Janet Wilcox who counsels regularly for us, but the ministry never charges for counseling. Some counselees leave a gift, or mail one. For approximately nine years gifts related to counseling have amounted to only about nine percent of Elijah House's income. We *give* His ministry, and believe it should be so. The Christian counseling of which we write is intended first for the transformation of Christians, only secondarily for unbelievers. It belongs in the Church, supported in every way by the Church.

Some counselors and organizations have found that most people will be more willing to face their inner problems and put into practice what they learn if each counseling session costs them *something*. Human nature being what it is, people value what they have to pay for. They work harder to make each counseling session count. Accordingly, many counselors and organizations give the first several sessions, and charge between thirty to fifty dollars each session from then on. The money helps the counselor of course, but the purpose is mainly to spur the counselee. Some counselees will ride on the largess of a giving counselor, enjoying the attention, having no firm intention to get at problems and be done with counseling. A stiff fee usually ends that.

Occasionally an unbeliever happens to come to us for

counseling. We are as straightforward as we can be, saying, "We counsel as Christians. Our method and only power are the cross and prayer. If you can accept that, we'll be glad to help, but if not, you are free to find some other counselor." We may go on to include that while we will not demand that the counselee accept Jesus as Lord and Savior, nor even ask that he have faith (Luke 5:23-24), we will not be restrained in ministering by faith, and he needs to know and accept that. Somewhere in the counseling process, the counselee usually receives Jesus as his Lord and Savior.

We do not believe in prayer for the inner transformation of someone with whom we have not counseled, or who is not present with us. The inner regions of another are holy and private ground. We have no right there, except by verbal, present invitation. Some time ago a teacher in the Body of Christ began to instruct people to pray for others while they were asleep, asking God to change them. We regard that as reprehensible. That is unfair, a manipulation of the other, bordering on magic. Though God has all power, He never changes anyone in such a way as to violate his free will.

We make two exceptions. Parents are ordained of God to raise children, thus to form their character. Children before teen-age years can be prayed for concerning the inner man by their parents while the children are asleep. A couple came concerned for their little boy, who could not stop wetting the bed. We instructed them to go into his room after he had fallen asleep and pray affirmative prayers softly aloud giving thanks for their son, filling him with love. They did, and within a week he had stopped bed-wetting. We did not instruct them to pray about or mention the bed-wetting problem, only to pray affirmative prayers of love for the inner child.

My cousin (John's) was given up by psychiatrists as a hopeless cause. She would be confined to an asylum for the rest of her life. That is the second exception. Such a person does not have the fullness of her own mind nor willpower. Nevertheless we regarded her inner being as holy ground. We prayed for the healing of her inner man, apart from her, without telling her or my uncle about it. Within a few weeks she was rediagnosed as totally well, and released. Today she has a husband and children and a perfectly normal life. We have never told her that we prayed, especially not what nor how. Nor would we have prayed at all had not the Holy Spirit called and commanded (we can visualize Christians having read this, trying to empty asylums by prayer—wearing themselves out to little avail!).

We believe that Body ministry should be happening regularly in every church, especially in small groups. As that happens, there will be instances in which the small group feels the expertise of someone especially gifted to counsel is needed. Such persons could then be sent within the Body to counselors who are recognized by pastors and elders. In the church in Spokane that is what we had in operation. Counselors worked with those sent by the groups, and returned them to their groups for support and continued ministry. Sometimes what could be reported without breaking confidence was told to the leaders of the groups to help them continue to minister.

Pastors may counsel, but it is our experience that pastors cannot carry a full counseling load and continue to shepherd the entire flock. One of the most compelling reasons we write this book is to say to pastors and churches the counsel of Jethro to Moses:

"The thing that you are doing is not good [counseling from morning until evening]. You will surely wear out, both yourself and these people who are with you, for the task is too heavy for you; you cannot do it alone. Now listen to me: *I shall give you counsel*, and God be with you. You be the people's representative before God, and you bring the disputes to God, then *teach them* the statutes and the laws, and make known to them the way in which they are to walk, and the work they are to do. Furthermore, *you shall select* out of all the people *able men who fear God, men of truth, those who hate dishonest gain;* and you shall place these over them, as leaders of thousands, of hundreds, of fifties and of tens. And *let them judge the people at all times;* and let it be that every *major* dispute they will bring to you, but every *minor* dispute they themselves will judge. So it will be easier for you, and *they will bear the burden with you.* If you do this thing and God so commands you, then *you will be able to endure,* and all these people also *will go to their place in peace."* (Exod. 18:17-23)

It needs to be remembered that Moses was the leader of a church-state. There was no separation of church and state. Moses was actually sitting as a magistrate over a civil court, settling civil disputes in the public body. From Jethro's counsel to Moses, our entire jurisprudence system has grown.

Nevertheless, the same counsel pertains to all pastors. Pastors cannot settle all the affairs of the heart for all the members of their churches, not even of as small a church as 100 members. No pastor can have that much time and energy. Therefore today shepherding elders are being raised up. Unfortunately the theological errors and psychological abuses of dominance and control which happened in some branches of shepherding and discipling some years ago have burnt the fingers of many who should learn shared leadership.

Faith Lutheran Church of Geneva, Illinois, set twelve elders over small groups. In a few years, they found that only half of those possessed the gifts and time, etc. to counsel and shepherd. Undaunted, they simply reformed and tried again, relegating under-shepherding to the six whom time and experience had revealed to have a true gift for it, finding other tasks as elders for the others. This church, under the wise leadership of Pastor Del Rossin and Pastor David Dorpat, has avoided the pitfalls some earlier groups fell into. Jim Clapper, head shepherding elder, has prepared a manual for elders, and the pastors and Jim form deputation teams to share with other pastors and churches. Paula and I have spoken there on several occasions to teach elders and the Body. The Body of Christ *can* learn to minister. It *can* enter shepherding by elders without a controlling spirit and without meddling in the personal lives of the members, and without robbing individuals of the right to their own decision-making in the Lord.

Some Christian counselors may have to overcome unscriptural off-balance childhood teachings concerning confession. When Paula and I grew up, our arm of Protestantism was overreacting to what was regarded as abuses of the confessional in the Roman Catholic Church. We heard many false teachings, such as, "One should never confess his sins to another human being, only to God." "Confess your sins in secret to God only; He will hear in secret and reward you openly." Nowhere in the Bible is there a commandment to confess sins in secret! The one reference to praying in secret is in Matthew 6:6, "But you, when you pray, Go into your inner room, and when you have shut the door, pray to your Father who is in secret, and your Father who sees in secret will repay you." The context has to do with personal piety and alms giving (v. 4), not confession of sins. Jesus repeated His admonition to pray in secret in relation to fasting (v. 18). But none of that was a command to confess our sins privately. Rather, the command is to ". . . confess your sins to *one another* . . ." (James 5:16).

Consequently, many elders and Christian counselors have felt unnecessarily awkward or out of place pronouncing God's forgiveness. Praise God that He is rediscovering to us today that the pronouncing of forgiveness is not only ours to do, it is the *first* gift connected with reception of the Holy Spirit! "And when He had said this, He breathed on them, and said to them, 'Receive the Holy Spirit. If you forgive the sins of any, their sins have been forgiven them; if you retain the sins of any, they have been retained' " (John 20:22-23). By giving authority to forgive sins immediately upon breathing the Holy Spirit upon them, Jesus was saying that the very first consequence of having the Holy Spirit is authority to forgive sins! By placing these together, Jesus was saying that the power to forgive the sins of others is the natural birthright and position of every Holy Spirit-filled son of God! He was also thereby making a powerful statement of importance, as though the forgiving of sins is the first and most-needed work of every normal Christian. Notice also that authority to forgive sins was given before any other manifestation of the presence of the Holy Spirit! Not until ten days later did the power of the Holy Spirit descend. As though Jesus wanted the disciples to know that ability to pronounce forgiveness is in no way dependent on power (*dunamis*) but solely on authority (*exousia*). They were to forgive sins before they had any power in the Holy Spirit! Perhaps also this gift had to be given immediately, before Pentecost, because in those ten days the one hundred and twenty would need to confess their sins one to another and pronounce forgiveness for one another, in preparation for fullness to descend on Pentecost!

It is still so today. It is as though the Church has been breathed on but is not living in the fullness. We have not yet come to Pentecost, thinking the first signs were the fullness. But none yet can walk up to a man lame *from birth* and say, "I do not possess silver and gold, but what I do have I give to you: In the name of Jesus Christ the Nazarene—walk!" (Acts 3:6). Notice Peter's use of the personal pronoun "I." *I* possess. *I* give. Miracles do happen today. We have the first breathing of the Spirit. But who among us has the audacity to *command*, *knowing* the miracle *will* happen right then as we say and expect? Who among us has the humility to say, "What *I* do have *I* give?" Kathryn Kuhlman and others can call out when and where God is working a miracle, but that is by description, not by personal command, knowing beyond all doubt it will happen as Peter knew. None of us dares to say as did they, "Look at us!" (v. 4). As you see, we do not have the fullness of Pentecost. We maintain that perhaps the primary reason the fullness has not come is because we have not spent our ten days confessing to one another our sins! We heard the word "tarry"; and some have fasted and prayed long—*individually*. But "Church" has not yet happened. We are not yet corporate. We have been too falsely taught, too frightened of vulnerability, too unwilling to be open, honest, and real. Pentecost happened when "all were together in one place" (Acts 2:1). We aren't together yet, even if geographically in the same room. It is the task of Christian counselors to hear confessions in order to get the Body of Christ together in one place, that Pentecost may truly happen.

Whoever hears a confession should pronounce forgiveness in first person, "In the name of the Lord Jesus Christ, according to His Word, *I* pronounce that you are forgiven your sin of ___ . As far as the east is from the west, so far. . . . " It is not as effective merely to say, "Your sins are forgiven in Jesus' name," or "The Bible says you are forgiven." When a man sins, that sin denigrates mankind. When Achan sinned, all Israel lost power (Josh. 7). When David sinned, his son died (2 Sam. 12:13-14). "If one member suffers all suffer" (1 Cor. 12:26) can also be taken, "If one *sins*, all suffer." Whenever we hear a confession, we have been placed in a position to represent mankind. Mankind has been injured; mankind needs to forgive. Our saying *"I forgive you"* is essential to accomplish forgiveness, from man. "In Jesus' name" effects forgiveness from God and heaven. We need to pronounce the forgiveness in several ways, repetitively, until the inner being is fully comforted and assured.

Hearing of confessions one to another is vital because the foundation stone of Christian transformation is the cross of Christ! Apart from the cross, there can be no Christian healing or transformation. Every Christian counselor must know that indelibly and irrevocably. That means our primary method is always prayer, the route always repentance and forgiveness. Having heard of a violent father, for example, we fail to transform if we only comfort. By such "healing" alone, the victim is left able to "throw a pity party." Nothing is resolved. The person feels only momentarily relieved because someone has heard him and buttressed his self-excusing stances. In actuality, the counselor has thrown water on a fire God was building and thereby postponed confession of anger and bitterness. The counselee may feel falsely justified and most assuredly will continue his patterns of retaliation, whether by aggression or withdrawal.

Nothing can defile us from outside. Only what comes out of our hearts can defile (Mark 7:15-21). Therefore, we are always dealing not so much with what was done to us as with our sinful responses. Reactions of resentment and judgment, however hidden and forgotten in the heart, must find their way to the cross, or guilt remains—with all its appendages. Habitual patterns of response must be transformed by repentance, death and rebirth. Otherwise, no permanent or even valuable change of personality or behavior will result.

Every Christian counselor must know and see that sanctification is the work of the Holy Spirit, and only His. He moves upon us in His own mysterious ways, within the Father's timetable. His plan is the Father's. His actions are totally in tune with the Father's perfect will for us. Psychological counselors may use techniques, hoping to bring forth results. Christian counselors must not rely on techniques. They must speak or act only as prompted by the Holy Spirit, else we disturb His work.

Hypnotism in counseling involves not only occult error, it may release power to demonic and/or fleshly forces to discover what the Holy Spirit would not yet or perhaps ever reveal (so, by the way, may many methods in counseling, even under the check of the Holy Spirit; such is the Lord's ability to risk His work with us faulty workmen!). No Christian counselor should be involved with hypnotism. "Let no one be found among you who sacrifices his son or daughter in the fire, who practices divination or sorcery, interprets omens, engages in witchcraft, *or casts spells*, or who is a medium or spiritist or who consults the dead" (Deut. 18:10-11 NIV, italics mine). If he needs to know what is hidden, let him use the gifts of insight in the Holy Spirit, not forbidden resources of the flesh.

However psychological his training, however informed his mind, a Christian counselor remains as we have said earlier, a midwife, assisting the Holy Spirit and the other in the arena of birth. He must not draw forth by force or too soon, nor should he fail to catch the idea that plops from the deep womb of thought. The Christian counselor is therefore not the initiator of what happens, nor the controller. He catches the vision of what God is doing in the other, celebrates and assists.

He is not thereby passive. All his energies are bent to identify with both God and man, to empathize with both the Holy Spirit and the counselee, so as to sense wherein and how the Holy Spirit is moving upon the man, and what is rising in the counselee. Consequently, again he is not using psychological models to try to analyze. He is restfully active in the gift of insight, a coach upon the sidelines (Isa. 11:2).

Because the Holy Spirit leads, the counselee is the responder. Rogerian counseling teaches that the counselor should not interrupt or distract the counselee from what the individual's inner psyche brings forth. That stance grants the initiative to the flesh rather than the Spirit. The kernel of truth for the Christian counselor is that he ought not to detract from what the Holy Spirit is bringing to light. Unfortunately, many who followed the Rogerian method had insufficient awareness both of the Holy Spirit and of human deceptiveness by sinful nature. They found themselves tracking the deceits of the flesh and confirming them by silence or seeming agreement, rather than speaking the truth in love so as to hold the counselee to the Spirit's track of truth. Sometimes a Christian counselor must confront a counselee directly and rebuke sharply (Titus 1:13). Failing to do so leaves both counselor and counselee vulnerable to the warnings of Ezekiel 33:1-9 (that a prophet must warn, or the blood of the other is on him and both suffer). The Christian counselor's task is to recall the counselee continually to the whispering of the Spirit's truth in his ear. In short, a Christian counselor helps the other to understand how the Holy Spirit is working in his life, and how to respond in repentance, confession, action, or whatever the Holy Spirit prompts.

The Holy Spirit is working, in myriads of countless details, in every life, to inform, teach, prepare, please, enthuse, enjoy, convict, create, worship—whatever enhances fellowship with God and man, whatever sanctifies and matures in faith. The counselor's task is not to oversee all that work, and thus usurp God's position, but to be attentive to that move of the Holy Spirit of which God in that moment would have the counselor be aware. Perhaps the counselor cannot help but see many patterns of deceit, or talents that need to be encouraged. He is not called to act by that seeing. He opens only that can of worms the Holy Spirit prompts, or affirms when He says to.

It is not enough to see what the Holy Spirit is doing or what He would reveal to the counselee; the call for wisdom is to learn what part the Holy Spirit would have the counselor play. Should he blurt out an insight? Ask a question? Pose a parable or a riddle? Tell a story? Or set a trap, as Nathan caused David to judge his own case (2 Sam. 12:1-14)?

The problem usually is not the difficulty of seeing, nor to cause the other's *mind* to comprehend, but so to assist the process of discovery that the Holy Spirit can write understanding *in the heart*. For that difficulty, St. Paul prayed that "the *eyes of your heart* may be enlightened" (Eph. 1:18, italics mine), and for the inner man to be strengthened with might through faith that "you may have power to comprehend . . ." (Eph. 3:14-21, paraphrased).

Counselors must be restrained by the knowledge that it is the Holy Spirit who sanctifies by leading us out of old ways into the Way. As was said earlier, sometimes He cleanses and purifies without our ever knowing or needing to know what was wrong. The temptation upon the counselor is to do too much, or to hurry the process. It is the Lord who permeates us with His death as our death, and raises us to resurrection life. But since the counselor empathizes in the process and has been there many times both for himself and others, he may assume too glibly that the other comprehends, or leap too quickly to the denouement (successful conclusion). If he does, then like a hasty ferryboat captain, he may discover to his chagrin much of his cargo still on the dock! Or he may encourage the counselee too much to try, and thus throw him into the common error of psychological counseling—Pelagianism—"You can do it," or "I can lift myself by my own bootstraps," or "I can see and change my own character." Pelagianism is the trap of self-striving, doomed to failure in the end. Only Jesus will bring to the birth and not fail to bring forth (Isa. 66:9-11). Only He will not fail to present us without spot or wrinkle before the Father (Eph. 5:27). In that fact is our rest, for counselor and counselee alike. We don't have to make the other grow up (or ourselves). It is God who will sanctify us wholly—spirit, soul, and body (1 Thess. 5:23).

That is the *primary* difference between psychological counseling and Christian counseling. Often both may see the same thing. The secular psychologist waits for something to happen in the other, once seen and understood. His faith is in the power of the other's flesh to change. The Christian counselor, whether he is psychologically trained or a beginning layman, stands and watches as Christ delivers and transforms by the power of the cross. Countless times men and women have come to us saying, "I have been going for six years (or so) to psychiatrists. I know all my hang-ups, and why I have them. And I still have them!" Again, this is not meant to criticize psychologists or psychiatrists; a Christian counselor may be both. It is to say again that for all who counsel as Christians, our base is not psychology, either in hearing or acting for the counselee. Our power is the cross and the Spirit. We have the answer that works. Let's use it.

Counselors should also remember, if sanctification is the work of the Holy Spirit in us, needing only the continual response of a counselee's willingness, it is not so with transformation. Transformation requires more than willingness. Sanctification is largely *done to us.* Transformation involves *our* more active *participation* as He accomplishes the work in us. Transformation is effected by the "renewal of your mind" (Rom. 12:2). Since as we have said, renewal of the mind comprises more than conscious mentality, and the mind, surface and deep, must ponder (Luke 2:19), we have a larger part in the struggle. "But Mary treasured up all these things, *pondering* them *in her heart"* (Luke 2:19). "I buffet my body . . ." (1 Cor. 9:27). "I . . . [myself, of my own discipline in Him] count them [all things as] but rubbish . . ." (Phil. 4:8). "The carnal mind is enmity against God" [therefore requiring personal struggle to bring it to death] (Rom. 8:6-8 KJV). Such change involves our *will* momentarily, daily. *We* must consign our nature to the cross. In Gal. 2:20 the word is "We have *been* crucified"—something done to us. But in Gal. 5:24 it is, *"We* have crucified . . ."—something we do to ourselves. Herein is balance, for it is both that we are crucified and that we crucify ourselves. We help Him do it to us. The counselor must coach but never do so much that the counselee fails to put himself upon the cross.

Transformation is not complete until we treasure all our life, and praise God from a full heart for it. The end result is that we are grateful for everything in our life, for we see that whatever happened was blessing in disguise, either sent or at least allowed of God. The Father knew what degradations we would choose or fall into, what would be put upon us and how we would respond, and in His predestinate will planned in Christ Jesus to transform dust and ashes to love and joy, ugliness to beauty, and weakness to strength.

> The Spirit of the Lord God is upon me; because the Lord hath anointed me to preach good things unto the meek; he hath sent me to bind up the brokenhearted, to proclaim liberty to the captives, and the opening of the prison to them that are bound; To proclaim the acceptable year of the Lord, and the day of vengeance of our God; to comfort all that mourn; To appoint unto them that mourn in Zion, to give unto them beauty for ashes, the oil of joy for mourning, the garment of praise for the spirit of heaviness; that they might be called trees of righteousness, the planting of the Lord, that he might be glorified. (Isa. 61:1-3 KJV)

Section II

Early Life—Hidden Sins

8
Crib Time

Baby cries. Somehow mother knows in the cry the sound of hunger. She lifts him from the crib and the child responds excitedly—reaching, breathing quickly, at once laughing and crying, nestling into oneness with the warmth of her, patting, pinching, pulling, drawing from the free-flowing fountain—milk leaking out the corners of his mouth, squeaking, gulping—round tummy, fat cheeks, feet that seem to pump to make more room, soon heavy eyelids, satisfaction, falling limply to sleep again—tiny lips that nurse in sweet dreams of more and more . . . .

Any mother who has loved her child as she nursed it at her breast knows that the babe was drinking far more than milk. There was a meeting taking place in which she knew the sometimes breathtaking joy of her baby's new spirit flowing into hers, seeking, asking. And her own spirit, full to bursting with sweetness, rose to embrace and pour into that little one with power she couldn't begin to understand. She knows that there has been a sharing of life and love beyond description, a sharing that has fed and fulfilled them both.

That quality of nurture can never come in a bottle. It has always been the Lord's best design to feed each infant with his mother's own liquid-love-with-skin-on-it. Man will never improve on that plan, though certainly the Lord is capable of blessing all necessary substitutes.

Our purpose here is not to quicken feelings of guilt nor to arouse the pain of loss in any mother who out of misinformation or incapability did not nurse her baby. It is solely to make the reader aware that there may reside in an adult unidentified senses of hunger, insecurity, rejection, anger, frustration, disappointment, or emptiness traceable to very early experiences at, or away from, the breast of the mother.

Perhaps a mother attempted to nurse, and her milk was lacking nutrients. Though her child was fed, he was not satisfied. That continually repeated disappointment can register in the foundation stones of his being and create an expectancy to ask but not to receive richly and abundantly. It can dwell in him as a vague and mystifying fear and inability to rest in and trust another's love or ministry. It can contribute to an inner drive to search or strive beyond necessity. Such a person may later be blessed beyond measure in many ways, yet never seem (at the deep feeling level) to have enough.

A baby may be thriving on mother's milk, but circumstances may interrupt: Mother becomes suddenly ill. Baby's teeth appear early. He bites and will not be taught not to. An infection develops in the nipple. For whatever reason, the baby is suddenly deprived. In his spirit, he may resent the substitute. He may feel at levels below reason a sense of rejection, of losing what is rightfully his. He has no well-developed intellectual faculty with which to put his feelings into proper boxes. He simply reacts, and lives with those seeds of "I've been robbed" and "I won't get mine." Later experiences in life may reinforce and trigger those deep feelings. As an adult he may find himself responding in relationships in seemingly unexplainable, childish, self-centered behavior. Sometimes we have found the loss of breast feeding to be the reason some people cannot stop smoking; the oral sensation, the comfort and peace of smoking reach too deeply into unsatisfied areas.

The good news of our Christian faith is that when we become aware that we have such reactions, we have only to confess by faith that we do own hidden resentments, and avail ourselves of the blessedness of giving and receiving forgiveness. We may invite the Lord Jesus to meet us at that deep level of our being; in the person of His Holy Spirit, He will comfort and satisfy the little child within. He will then release us from bondage to childish structures, and we will find that we more and more easily catch outselves in what have now become recognizable habit patterns over which we have some authority. In the process the Lord will graciously give a gift of growing trust which will open the heart to receive more readily the warmth of human affection from friends, who will then be enabled to help us to come more and more to life. Quite often we counsel married couples who are unable to talk out their differences because when irritation rises or the threat of quarrel appears, one (or both) may experience instant fear which sends them fleeing either into isolation or into frantic attempts to explain, settle, or smooth over. Or they are simply overwhelmed by emotion, paralyzed in any capacity to act in relation to the other. "I feel trapped. I want to get out but I can't!" They may be convinced they want out of the marriage altogether, that the only thing holding them is the children, or responsibility to God, or lack of enough money to live separately, or the fear of what people might think, etc. The truth of the matter may be that deep within there is a seed of anxiety which was planted firmly when they were in the crib and parents were quarreling loudly in the room. They felt the tension, took into themselves the destructive energy of the anger, and reacted in panic as they felt the protective strength of mother-father love cracking and splitting. The sky was falling! The world was coming apart! A mechanism of self-defense by fleeing or turning off was born. Now when they are grown, any argument releases the explosive power of the baby's terror, magnified by years of reinforcement each time the family atmosphere became tense or a position was threatened or the clamor of voices was heard.

For such people, the Lord is close at hand to identify the seeds of fear, sort them out and bring them all to the cross. The appropriate type of prayer is, "I see that I reacted in fear when I heard my parents shouting. I made a sinful reaction to that. I fled from life (or the opposite, I charged in order to control). Forgive me, Lord. Enable me to forgive in the deepest levels of my heart. Set me free from that habit pattern. Fill me with your love which is never threatened and never threatens. Establish me in you, root and ground my spirit in love and protect my heart that I may not need to react wrongly." It is not enough to pray that the grown one be set free; there would remain a baby still cringing in fear deep inside. It is to that little child we invite the Lord.

It is seldom as effective for a person to pray for himself as it is for another to pray for him. To choose to expose the fear in our inner child and to open our heart to another person is an act of trust which denies the tyranny of our feelings. This act prepares in us the way of the Lord, which has always been to bring us to life by the loving nurture of family and friends. What was not done for us in the beginning can now be done for us in prayer by others who care. Expressions of care and prayer may need to be repeated again and again until the inner being catches on to respond in a new way.

Since the heart of a child naturally opens in trust to quiet, sensitive strength, the voice of the one who prays for the innermost being of another needs to communicate the tenderness, warmth, and enfolding love of the Father. The attitude of the person praying needs to convey the unconditional love of God through Christ Jesus. The counselor should pray with an arm around the shoulder or invite the other to rest his head against him. Prayer for the inner child is most effective when vividly pictorial. We have found this way of praying to be not at all dependent on our own insight, but rather a gift of the Lord through committed and consecrated imagination. The Holy Spirit is quite capable of turning our perceptions of the confessions of a counselee into a beautiful picture of healing for the other, projecting upon the screen of our minds as we pray aloud the new reality He wants to communicate. We may find ourselves praying something like this, "I see, Lord, that there is a little one deep inside my friend who is afraid, lonely, hurting, and hungry. He needs to be held in arms which are secure and strong. Thank you, Father, that your arms are like that, and that right now you are reaching deep down inside to enfold that baby with the warmth and strength of your own being. I know that you, Father, are delighted with the little one whom you fashioned out of your own heart of love. This one, Lord, is chosen and precious, a treasure to you. You are pouring your sweet light into your child till all hunger is satisfied, all anxiety is settled out, all fears are calmed. Hold this one, Lord, until the love that you are permeates every cell of his being, and enables him to melt into you, trusting. Thank you, Father, that you are light pushing back darkess; you are music displacing noise; you are a perfectly safe place to lie down to rest. You will never leave; nor will your love fail." The Lord may inspire the prayer with pictures of rocking, walking the floor, comforting with hugs and pats, tucking into bed, standing watch—all the things a parent is called to do for a baby.

In the depths of a woman who finds it difficult to confidently express a need or her opinions to her husband or any man, there may be a tiny child whose cries in the night were answered by an angry face looming large over the rails of the crib, and an angry voice booming its displeasure. At the root of overwhelming irrational feelings of loneliness may be many childhood experiences of being left alone for hours at a time to cry in a room behind closed doors. Beneath the apologetic attitude of an adult who cannot easily receive loving attention for fear of burdening others may still live the heart of a baby who remembers in his subconscious mind rude, rough, angry handling by a bothered parent, for instance as his messy diapers were changed.

Recognizing foundational experiences behind the structures in our nature and thus seeing the driving forces within us today is only the first step in the process of transformation. We must then assume responsibility for the choices we made, confess attitudes which sowed the original bramble seeds in our life, and lay the entire matter on the altar of God, submitting ourselves to him without explanation or defense. The Lord will then accomplish that forgiveness in the heart (1 John 1:8); He will bring to death the old structure with its practices (Col. 3:9), comfort and strengthen us from inside (Eph. 3:16, 2 Cor. 1:3-4, Isa. 51:3), give us a new heart (Ezek. 36:26; 11:19; Jer. 24:7), and grow us up into new life (Gal. 2:20). We are not capable of changing our hearts by an act of our wills. But by the continual act of our wills to invite the Holy Spirit to do that work of transformation in us, and by the consistent quiet discipline of "reckoning as dead" (Rom. 6:11) those symptoms which may continue to persist for a season, we can contribute substantially to our process of coming alive— or we can by prideful stubbornness and untrust remain in our predicament.

More difficult to deal with than the negative experiences of our infancy is the lack of those positive experiences which should have brought us to life. It is by warm, affectionate touching and holding that the spirit of a child is called forth to fullness. If a baby has not been held, cuddled, rocked, sung to, walked with, and talked to, but has been cared for only in terms of rigidly scheduled feeding and bedding, he will most likely become an adult who interprets all of life in like manner. For example, he will be uncomfortable with spontaneity and unable to open wide the heart and nestle trustfully into another's love. His security and satisfaction will be in the smooth operation of schedule and plan, his definition of love in the giving of material gifts and services. But because his spirit knows there is something more to life, he will experience hunger he cannot identify. He may find anger welling up from inside which he tends to project onto those around him as though they should be providing some comfort for needs he cannot name. Family and friends may be offering that nurturing comfort consistently and abundantly, but he may fail to perceive and receive what is given. He still thinks he is being starved in the midst of a family banquet of offered love.

A person's soul (as we understand it) is that structure of character and personality in which his spirit resides. If that structure has been imperfectly formed by a lack of affectionate nurture and discipline early in life, or if it is damaged by abuse, the spirit of the person may fail to develop or lack equipment to express healthily. He will then in adult life be crippled in his capacity to receive and contain spiritual nurture from friends and loved ones. Blessedness may be heaped upon him but he can not make it his own. The answer for him is not found in an exhortation to "count your blessings," nor to "try harder," nor to "wake up." He has no tools in hand with which to do those things. He simply is incapable to do so no matter how hard he tries. The answer lies in consistent, repeated prayers for the spirit of the little child within to be held in our loving Father's arms, for the Spirit of the living God to flow into him with lifegiving power to affirm, to quicken, to resurrect, to bring him into all the fullness of life in the Father (Eph. 3:19). The inner one is like a little child, and so he says, "Tell me again . . . Tell me again." He needs many repeated prayers. Christians who pray with him may need to associate on a regular basis as spiritual mother and father in Christ to do for him what the natural parents failed to do.

Though we do not rely on techniques of role playing, psychodrama and the like to minister to deep needs in people as much as we do the simple working of the Holy Spirit in the hearts of people following prayer, we do not at all discredit their use where the Lord directs. Many times we have seen tears streaming down the face of a person whose stance had been long-practiced, cold intellectual poise. The stimulus which unlocked the emotions was no more than a brush of hands on the shoulders and a hug here and there as he walked slowly between two rows of loving people as they sang, "Cause me to come to thy river, O Lord!" What began as a drama to illustrate our flowing through the river of life banked by supportive love of friends became an instrument by which God could penetrate into the depths of the heart. The mind, not expecting the exercise to amount to more than sentimental ritual, was off guard, and love scored a victory, penetrating behind defensive barriers.

We have witnessed strong men sobbing as they were rocked gently by groups of two or three. "Rock-a-my soul in the bosom of Abraham" was sung as a lullaby, and in the simplicity of the experience, love somehow pierced through strongholds of controlled emotion to hidden needs, and melted the stony heart. In most instances, there arose a new ability to feel and to reach out, because the baby spirit inside the grown adult had received a portion of the ingredient of love so essential to life.

Such experiences, however, must be followed by ministry which supports, encourages, and protects, or else the newborn can become like the seed in the parable of the sower which dies by being choked by tares (Matt. 13:1-23). Without continuing ministry to enable him to become rooted and established in the Lord in his new capacity to experience life (which includes at the same time vulnerability to hurt as well as openness to blessing), he may feel abandoned, exposed, and fearful. If he flees back inside himself to the seeming safety of the old familiar prison, it may be a long time (if ever) before he allows himself to be put in a position where he might be awakened again.

In counseling, it is often difficult for a counselee to accept that his present emotional responses are rooted in and fueled by experiences and reactions made in infancy. This is especially so if life has written on the conscious mind vivid recollections of some positive nurture.

A young man who was about twenty-two years old came to me (Paula) broken-hearted that his wife had left him, condemning himself that it was largely his uncontrolled temper that had driven her away. He could not understand the eruptive violence in himself that caused him to hit her occasionally when pressed by argument. He was mystified by his fierce possessiveness and by the intensity of his fear that the relationship could not be mended. He was even more mystified by his feelings that he would not be able to live without her. He had been raised by loving, attentive, affectionate grandparents who had brought him up in the church. They had disciplined and affirmed him well. There were other children in the home with whom he had enjoyed good fellowship. He had no recollection of having been abused, unduly criticized, deprived or rejected. He was not aware of any partiality that had been shown to others, nor of having developed a competitive spirit. Family had always seemed to be there when he needed them. Everything he could consciously remember of his life would seem to have equipped him well for participation in a comfortably happy marriage relationship; consequently, his behavior seemed a total contradiction.

"What happened to your natural parents?"

"I don't remember my mother at all. I think my parents were divorced soon after I was born. I don't know. My dad came around once in a while. But my grandparents were always mom and dad to me. I don't remember being an unhappy kid."

I explained that the spirit of a young child experiences far more than he can know with his mind, and suggested that he had known in his spirit the absence of his parents, and had felt hidden hatred of his mother for leaving him altogether. Further I told him that it could be that an unconscious desire to punish his mother might cause him to project onto his wife the anger and fear belonging to his mother, causing him to hit his wife when in verbal battles she seemed to desert him emotionally. I asked if the possessiveness he felt toward his wife could not actually be an intense, unidentified reaching out to claim the mother he had never really had. I asked if the jealousy he directed at anyone who claimed his wife's attention might more properly be aimed at those faceless people and events which had taken away the mother he could not find even in his memories.

"Wow! That sounds far out! But I suppose it *could* be. I haven't found any other answer."

The young man consented to offer to God, on faith, what he could imagine might have been in the heart of a baby who felt abandoned by his father and mother through whom he had received life. *By faith* he repented of anger and resentment for being rejected, of all judgments he could have made toward his parents, particularly against his mother. *By faith* he repented of possible anger and mistrust of God for having allowed such a thing to happen. In all this he was not aware of any negative feelings in himself. "I am conscious of nothing against myself, yet I am not by this acquitted; but the one who examines me is the Lord" (1 Cor. 4:4). "Who can discern his errors? Acquit me of hidden faults" (Ps. 19:12).

I (Paula) declared that by the authority of the Word of God (1 John 1:9) he was forgiven the unconscious sin of dishonoring his parents. And together we invited the Lord to wash his heart clean all the way back through his years to the beginning, and to comfort and strengthen the little one in his innermost being, to fill him with the Lord's gift of forgiveness that could flow to those parents wherever they were. We prayed that the cross of Christ might in a real way come between him and all his past, that he might be free from inside to become the new creature the Lord called him to be.

He left our office, touched by the prayer, grateful for the session, but with the attitude of: "Okay—I'll wait to see if anything comes of this. Nothing else has worked."

Several weeks later the phone rang. Greeting me was a jubilant young man anxious to share the unbelievable.

> You'll never guess what happened! My real mother looked me up! Right out of the blue she called me! We met and had a wonderful visit!

He went on to share the pieces of the puzzle he had never been able to get hold of.

> My mother loved me! But my parents were *so* young. And they couldn't support a marriage. My grandparents had the marriage annulled just after I was born. And there was some kind of big court battle for custody of me, and my grandparents won. And my mother wasn't allowed to see me! She's been hurting and afraid all these years. Now I have to work at forgiving some other people, but my mother really loved me! Isn't that terrific? I don't know if my wife and I can get together again or not. But I feel different inside about it. I'm going to *live* no matter what happens. I know I don't have to *force* her to do anything any more.

The circumstances of that young man's life had not been changed by his trying harder to demonstrate Christian love or virtue or by his striving to be a loving husband. The important thing to note is that it was the bitter roots within him from childhood on (his hidden, unconfessed sinful nature) which had continued to produce bad fruit in his life despite his conscious efforts. Not until he confessed by faith that hidden area of sin did the Lord have invitation to take up residence in that protected, unconverted depth of his heart.

In inner transformation (as we said in chapter two) we are always evangelizing, converting level after level of the heart in order to bring us wholly into line with what our conscious mind has committed to the Lord—all this to bring ultimately to an end that inner battle described by St. Paul in Romans 7:18-19 and 21-24:

> For I know that nothing good dwells in me, that is, in my flesh; for the wishing is present in me, but the doing of the good is not. For the good that I wish, I do not do; but I practice the very evil that I do not wish. . . . I find then the principle that evil is present in me, the one who wishes to do good. For I joyfully concur with the law of God in the inner man, but I see a different law in the members of my body, waging war against the law of my mind, and making me a prisoner of the law of sin which is in my members. Wretched man that I am! Who will set me free from the body of this death?

The "body of death" does not mean here the physical body, but the sinful character we have become.

It has always amazed me (Paula) that we in the Church family do what we would not think of doing in the natural family. Who of us would bring a baby home from the hospital, put him in a crib, toss him the car keys, and a list of chores to do, and leave him with an ultimatum to do everything right, or else? But that is exactly what we have done to countless newborn Christians. Because they have been "born again," we have heaped responsibilities upon them and have demanded instant performance according to standards in Christ which they are as yet in no way prepared to accomplish emotionally or experientially. And how quick we have been to judge their errors with condemnation!

Lest I fall into the trap of condemning those who condemn others, let me close this chapter by laying that judgment of mine (that the Church *should* know better) on the altar, and go drink another glass of milk (1 Cor. 14:20).

9

Toddling Terrors

From an adult perspective, toddlers are a delightful mixture of cuddly comic, lap wiggler, furniture climber, drape swinger, messer-upper, and living floor mop. They come open armed and begging for hugs in one moment, and elude us, giggling, to hide from kisses in another. Sometimes proud to please, often defying to tease, adventuring without fear to the extremities of their capabilities and our discomfort, they try their wings and our patience. Bumps and bruises, skinned knees and noses are a part of the daily fare. As John and I look back we wonder with gratitude to God that our six survived so well the multitude of normal toddling terrors—and so do most parents.

Physical hurts are easily ministered to with kisses that really do "make it well," by magic Band-Aids, piggy-back rides, and cookies while we rock and sing the wounded one to sleep. Nap time seems to accomplish a forgetting of minor accident and injury. After a good sleep the toddler will bubble up into unbelievably fresh and vigorous activity whether propelled on all fours or on legs that always seem too short to keep up with the enthusiastic thrust of curiosity running pell-mell. Such vigor, enthusiasm, and curiosity need encouragement to grow, plus a loving discipline to provide limits which become security for the toddler. He is the center of his own world emotionally and experientially and knows nothing yet of the magnitude of challenges and challengers to be encountered.

John and I have sometimes tried to put ourselves imaginatively in the toddler's position to gain his point of view—a world of knees, enormous behinds, tall and tiny heads that always seem to be jabbering strange noises toward us. We're supposed to respond to those confusing sounds. There is one sound that comes again and again—"No, no!" Often that sound comes with a shout, a scowl, and inflicted pain. And we wonder why. What we were doing *felt* so good! We do that thing again and we experience repeated displeasure from the people who stand four times our height. We soon learn to associate the act we do with the pain that comes through the huge hands of the tall people. That pain is called "no-no." Those hands are the same hands that feed us, give us loving strokes, and pick us up when we fall. So we quickly learn to measure the "feeling good," which the doing of the "no-no" brings, against the price of the momentary pain of the slap on our backside. We understand the light pain. It brings cause and effect to sharp and simple focus, though it elicits a tearful, angry response. A tirade of angry words throws us into confusion; we feel compelled to respond to directions which are to us a mystery. Equally untranslatable is "sweet reasonableness"; it sugar-coats the angry energies we feel rushing toward us. We are frightened. We rush into the big arms and hands which sometimes give loving strokes, and demand acceptance. If we are rebuked, we flee wounded into tears or temper. But soon we learn to gain the best of two worlds. We can do the "no-no" when no one is looking!

Identifying so with the toddler, it is easy to see how qualities of self-preservation and manipulation are born in normal healthy families and nurtured by responsible, caring parents who only do what they *can* do. *If* there were a way to be a perfect parent, it would be impossible to raise a perfect child. Before consciousness of right and wrong is developed, before conscience is activated, we "sin" for personal gratification or to gain advantage. By the time we grow into consciousness and conscience, we have already developed habit patterns of manipulation, control, striving, sneaking, and lying so deeply ingrained they form without our knowing it the motivational foundations in us by which we can do all the right things for all the wrong reasons. The Lord Jesus would redeem and transform to the depths of our foundations.

One of the primary things a toddler must learn to do is to

control his bladder and bowels. A mother understandably looks forward to the end of dirty-diaper laundry. But if she is so anxious to arrive at freedom, she pushes the child into a discipline he is neither physically nor emotionally prepared to handle, she may build into her child habits of striving, structures of rigidity, and attitudes of fastidiousness which limit his freedom to be and to express who he is. These structures will find expression in him in adulthood.

A mother may express great pride that her six-month-old was potty trained when in truth the mother was trained to anticipate time patterns and recognize symptoms of approaching need to eliminate. The mother imposed her training on the child, at great cost to the child. Often in such a case ego involvement is expressed strongly when her child, not trained at all, has an "accident." "Shame on you! Oh, nasty! Pew! Bad! Dirty!" At this point the child can begin to view his body and its normal functions as something shameful, to be despised. This becomes an unconscious part of his foundational attitude toward his body, and more pertinently, towards his sexuality.

More devastating to the toddler is pressure which confuses love with performance. The child has just done a successful job on the pot. Thinking to encourage, the mother says, "You did good! Mommy is proud of you! Mommy *loves* you!" The child needs recognition for having succeeded, but never should performance be associated with love, or failure be rewarded by lack of loving expression. Love must be poured out unconditionally, especially to undergird and encourage the child to venture in his learning of new skills. The toddler who stands humiliated and rejected with a malodorous lump in his britches and loudly proclaims he didn't do it, may be one and the same with the adult who cannot admit his mistakes because he cannot feel loved as one who has failed. Or he may be the man who unconsciously retreats from his wife, avoiding more than surface sharing, because he cannot at the root level of his being believe that the woman would be sensitive to him in his imperfections. He is afraid to allow himself to be vulnerable because of the specter of his mother—the screaming voice, the biting tongue, and the accusing finger. He may have made a deep inner vow never to be "found out," and so strives to maintain a facade of macho-niceness and self-sufficiency, while actually dying inside in the absence of real intimacy.

To exhort such an adult to trust, to be open and truthful, to relax, to make himself vulnerable, is to insist that he do what he has been structured and programed *not* to do! He may try. But his early fear will rise from the depths of his inner being to prevent him, triggered by no more than mildly impatient prodding by his wife.

If a man has been strongly programed to feel loved only within a confused need to perform well, any exhortation will throw him into self-defeating striving. The more he tries to relax, the more tense to succeed he will become. The more he tries to be open and truthful, the more he will control and judge his success or failure. When he fails, as he must sooner or later, the more frantic he may become to cover it in order to be accepted. "Don't tell me I'm not doing it right!" (See chapter 3, "Performance Orientation.")

If ministry to such a person is to be effective, it must speak to the heart of the little child who still lives in the innermost regions of the adult. The little one still feeds the grown one with anxiety, and imprisons him in childish emotions. Jesus came to set prisoners free. He is the only one who can reach to the child inside to enable the little one to forgive and be forgiven. He is the only one who can "Create in me a clean heart, O God, And renew a steadfast spirit within me" (Ps. 51:10). "When I was a child, I talked like a child, I thought like a child, I reasoned like a child. When I became a man, I put childish ways behind me" (1 Cor. 13:11 NIV). That maturation waits upon a gift of power from the Lord, else the counselee cannot accomplish that "putting away."

When we are praying for a person, his inner child needs to hear again and again that he is not loved more if he does it right, nor any less if he does it wrong, whatever the "it" is.

The inner child needs to apprehend as reality for him personally that he is loved by our Lord *unconditionally*, at *all* times, no matter how well or poorly he performs.

Our grandson Nathan, when he was not yet three, was extremely independent and willful, and quite fond of peanut butter. His mother, Beth, left him alone with his peanut butter sandwich one day, with strict instructions to leave his bib on. Nathan had noticed that older people do not eat with bibs. Anxious to be an older person himself, he promptly removed his bib. Beth returned to find that Nathan had completed his lunch, but peanut butter was everywhere—all over his hands, face, shirt, table and chair! Before she could say a word he blurted out, "Ise clean! Ise clean!" She took him firmly in hand, slapped him on the behind, and lovingly marched him off to the bathroom, saying gently but firmly, "You are not clean. You disobeyed and ate without your bib. Now we'll have to wash you and your clothes." She called him to account. She brought discipline to momentary painful focus with the light spanking. But she in no way withheld her love from him. Neither did she humiliate nor rail at him. Firm discipline in love builds basic abilities in toddlers by which they as adults will be able to confess to the Father God or to another human being, "I've done wrong. Forgive me. Let me make amends." But a childhood base of rejection and humiliation may cause a person to rationalize, lie, cover his tracks and always be on the defensive—until the cross of Christ brings the old way of the child in him to death and gives birth to a new way of thinking, feeling, and acting. "Truly, truly, I say to you, unless one is born again, he cannot see the kingdom of God" (John 3:3). The kingdom of God is secondarily a place; it is primarily a way of relating to God and to one another without guile and without shame.

Consistent firm discipline provides a toddler with the assurance that he will not be allowed to run amok. Having that, he can rest securely and be unafraid to venture. Loving discipline blends firmness with acceptance. Love tempers consistency of discipline to prevent rigidity so that discipline is appropriate to the occasion and to the changing needs of the toddler.

My little brother, Norman, was told to stay away from the old wringer-type washing machine. His curiosity, along with his desire to be as big as the rest of us who were helping mother, got the best of him. He caught his arm in the wringer and was pulled in up to his armpit. Disobedience by general principle would have been rewarded with scolding or spanking. But neither was in order here. He had clearly already reaped the reward of that particular disobedience. Further discipline would not have been discipline at all, but cruel punishment. The primary purpose of discipline is not to punish, but to structure. The message already built into his inner being that day was, "When you disobey the rules laid down by those who by experience know more than you do, you get into painful trouble. When you are hurting, you are not condemned for being what you are, but you are met and loved and healed by the very ones who gave you the warning in the first place." Is not that the way parents communicate the nature of God before children have the intellectual capacity to comprehend? "He will call upon Me, and I will answer him; I will be with him in trouble; I will rescue him, and honor him" (Ps. 91:15). Children cannot abstract. They experience *particular*, specific pains and joys. God comes to them in the hands of parents.

Parents who vent their emotions on a child who is already terrified and "bleeding," communicate an altogether different sort of message to the heart of a child. They bind him to his pain in condemnation for having done a "stupid thing." As adults we need to be free to risk doing things which might turn out to be stupid. We need to be free to say yes or no, from our own individual center of decision inside ourselves, and to reap the consequences of our choice without condemnation. God calls us to be sons, not robots. Emotionally or physically battered children are seldom capable of freedom as adults.

While we are yet toddlers, we are practicing to be free. Of course toddlers must be controlled and protected. They have not gained by experience the wisdom to keep from killing themselves and others. Witness a fifteen month old who sinks his teeth into his friend's arm and registers surprise at the reaction. But our controlling behavior must never completely squelch the toddler's courage to say "no," or to express his displeasure. A teen-ager who has ego strength to say "no" to his peers is one who as a toddler was allowed freedom to say "no" without being condemned, and who was also not allowed to run willfully over authority by the "no."

I (Paula) was seated on the couch one afternoon. At the end of the couch was a table which held one of my favorite house plants. Our grandson Jason, then not yet two, began to stir in the dirt with his fingers. I said, "No, Jason." He withdrew his fingers quickly, watched me intently for a few moments, and deliberately stuck his hand back in the dirt and began to squeeze whole handfuls. I took his hand out, brushed the dirt from his fingers and repeated a firm, "No! No! No!" He quickly repeated the aggressive action, and I slapped his hand. He stepped back, clenched both his fists, screwed up his face, shrieked one long, disapproving screech, and then came to sit in my lap. The matter was settled. I felt no compulsion to punish him for screeching what was on his mind. He never again ventured to play in my potted plants. At age six he is very much his own person, has a respect for authority appropriate to a six year old, and still loves to play in the dirt when and where it is allowed.

Sometimes toddlers say "no" not because they mean "no" but just to delight in the privilege of saying the word. Our children loved things like car rides, romping on the floor with daddy, and ice cream. Sometimes as toddlers when invited to one of these, they would practice saying "no" and then happily enjoy anyway. We knew they didn't mean no. With all of our six children we went through periods, when they were toddlers, of playing games of "saying"—for the sole sake of saying.

"Yes," we would begin.

"No," they would respond.

"Yes," we would insist.

"No," they would return emphatically.

We would change our response to, "No"—and they'd change with a giggle to: "Yes!"

Just as they learned by the peek-a-boo game that we could move out of sight and return again, and it was okay to trust, so they learned by the "yes-no" game that it was all right to express an opposing opinion. They would not be rejected for being different. That did not guarantee that our children would always stand against peer pressure later. They did their share of sinning, but the basic structure of freedom to choose was in them, and in those areas warped by our mistakes, the Lord's grace was there to redeem and remold. As the years progressed, we learned that the best and most effective prayer to bring our children into tune with the purposes of God was to pray as St. Paul did, that they be strengthened with power and might in the inner man (Eph. 3:16). That is another way of saying, "Lord, set them free from all bondage—even my anxiety for them—and give them root-level courage to make good choices and to become who *they are* in you, not just what I want them to be."

But suppose we are ministering to an adult whose freedom to be and to express freely was damaged or destroyed in the beginning?

Bud was one of the "nicest" people I have ever met. He would bend over backward to do anything to help someone. He would never say a bad word about anybody. Yet he continually struggled with angers. He was driven to find the "right" way to do things, and though he would never express it, he had little patience with those who didn't perform according to standard. But he could never vent his frustrations openly—except to his wife, who received the brunt of all he had suppressed inside. Then he would condemn himself for those outbursts. He struggled with sexual lusts, had some difficulty with voyeurism and found it a strain to relate to women, especially to sweet women. The more his wife related to him lovingly and forgivingly, the more upset he became. As we talked with him, and sought the Lord's wisdom about how to pray, we found that Bud had been controlled from the time he was a little child by the sweet, smothering, manipulative reasonableness of his mother.

"No, Bud, we don't want to feel that way, do we?"

"We aren't going to do that, are we?"

"Now, honey, nice boys don't stomp their feet."

He had learned to stuff down every real, rotten impulse he had, including his hatred for his mother—who had never allowed him to be himself! His sense of humor had completely died, if it had ever lived.

Prayer for the little child to forgive and be forgiven was first in order. Then prayer for love to cast out fear. We asked the Lord to lift off of the little boy the oppressive burden of performing and to set him free inside to be himself. "Lord, take away the dread seriousness of life and give the little boy the freedom to goof and to laugh at himself—to stomp his foot, say a nasty word, get dirt all over his clothes, and know that you're still there with open arms and an understanding heart." We persisted in those prayers and saw the Lord accomplish resurrection in Bud. He even learned to laugh at what he had been.

Toddlers are naturally all curiosity, full of adventure—exploring, tasting, testing, finding out what their bodies can and can't do. Each one is different. One cannot stamp a principle on all, and make it work. Each has to be met and dealt with as a unique person. We used to pursue our little ones to the edge of the dock, or haul them back out of traffic, or catch them as they jumped off the back porch, breathlessly wondering if they'd make it to voting age. At eighteen months Loren thought nothing of plunging headlong into Lake Michigan. He'd seen his father do it many times, and after all, wasn't it wet like the water we had such fun splashing in at home? With equal abandon he would rush down any street or alley in pursuit of flocks of pigeons, "Look at de birds! Look at de birds!" With Ami in a stroller and Loren so full of spontaneous enthusiasm and my hands full of groceries, I learned that it was best to put him in a body harness in busy downtown Chicago and attach him to the stroller lest he have some sudden inspiration to leave us on the first departing Elevated. From little old ladies who didn't know Loren as well as we did this brought many looks of, "What's the matter with that mother!" When Loren was ten-and-a-half months old, a neighbor in our apartment house at The University of Chicago opened the door for him (because "He looked like he knew where he was going"), and we found him across the street on the second-floor fire escape of the veterans' student housing. A few months later someone found him on the nearby Midway Plaissance and turned him into the Rockefeller Chapel office. He was unconcerned as we picked him up. He knew where he was; he'd been there before. Ami was more conservative. She stuck her foot into a basement drain and for a while we thought we'd have to get a jackhammer to extract her, but at least we knew where she was. On the other hand, on hot days she thought nothing of removing all of her clothes to make the most of the breezes; the neighbors all called her "Crinkle Buns."

With Mark we had a respite. He was content to spend hours playing in a corner, studying pictures in a magazine, chasing birds of thought, exploring inner space; but he could be active when he wanted. He would run from the cat until the cat took a flying leap to get a claw hold in Mark's drooping diapers. And they'd sprawl together, he giggling and they leaping to do it again.

Then came Johnny. He stood up in his crib at five months, took his first step at nine months, immediately tacked thirty-nine more to the first till he wound up swinging from a drape in the living room, and from there on he was undaunted. We thought about billing him as the "human fly"; he could climb anything, and usually did. Timothy, at age three, fell in the men's restroom at a campground in British Columbia (because he wanted "to do it himself") and cleanly extracted four front teeth when his mouth hit the toilet bowl. Andrea came along in our later years and the Lord had mercy and gave us another quiet one who, like her sister, was happy to explore cupboards and flush things down the toilet rather than occupy herself with more dangerous pursuits. The only time I remember being really upset with Andrea as a toddler was the day she and her little friend decided to decorate the bedroom wall with a large crayon mural. They were so proud of the job they had done, and so perplexed by our not-too-controlled rage!

We wrote all of the above to say, "Each child is different! Don't try to stamp them in the same mold; what works for one may not work for the other. Rejoice, as God does, in the variety."

Over the years we have appreciated more and more of the wisdom of the Lord in giving us our children while we were young, and for most of us, one at a time. At the same time we grieve for those modern-day young people who flee from the responsibility or the discomfort of raising children. We look at those years as being rich and exciting if oftentimes frightening, and know that with each child came for us a new dimension of the capacity to live and to give and receive blessing.

The temptation we all must check as parents is the urge to overprotect. There is a fine line between mothering and smothering, fathering and bothering. We have known adults who have never been able to enjoy the delicious freedom of walking barefoot in the cool grass, or stretching their bare toes in front of TV after a hard day's work because as children they were made to feel guilty for taking off their shoes. "You might step on something and cut your feet!" Some grownups have varieties of fears of heights for no other reason than that they were never allowed to climb trees or play in tree houses. "Be careful! You might fall!" Many people live out their lives with a fear of animals because of repeated warnings, "Don't go near that dog! He might bite!" And some never get over the fear to venture into new experiences because of the continuous refrain, "You're too little to do that." "Here, let me do that for you." "Watch out!" "What makes you think you can ride like that?" "Let somebody who knows how, do it." "You'll get lost."

Over-protective parents, thinking to save life, snuff it out, projecting their fears into their children. They actually are protecting their own comfort. What *can* we do that we might shepherd our children in their adventures? We need to get at those things in our flesh that feed our own fears, call to death in prayer those needs to control and manipulate, and ask for wisdom to "Train up a child in the way *he* should go" (Prov. 22:6). Again, for the adult whose fears of risking are rooted in experiences with over-controlling parents—the way to freedom is always to forgive the sin against you, to be forgiven your response to that sin, to be given a new heart, and a gift of trust. And finally to be loosed to live and laugh and run and risk.

In our book, *Restoring the Christian Family*, we devote an entire chapter, "A Place for Fantasy," to the subject of shepherding the imagination of a child. Suffice it here to say that the imagination of a toddler is very active. His spiritual sensitivity is keen, and he is often aware of spiritual realities adults have long ago tuned out. A toddler may cry out in the middle of the night that someone is in his room and that he is afraid. He may have dreamed, he may be imagining, or he may very really sense a presence there. It is not so important that we determine the cause of his fear as it is for us to stand *with* him in his fear with quiet confidence that Jesus is there to protect and overcome in all circumstances. By our manner we will communicate that there is nothing to fear. We can also communicate that by simple prayer. If we ridicule the child's perceptions, we undermine his confidence in his ability to see. If we express anger at his insistence, we will thereby be telling him we cannot be trusted to understand and accept and help him to overcome the enemies he finds in the dark. But if we respect his realities and invite the Lord into them as one before whom every knee in heaven and earth must bow (Phil. 2:10-11), we will instill confidence in the child that God is always at hand, understanding, ready, more than adequate to overcome all that threatens. The Lord who descended into hell and led a host captive (1 Pet. 3:18-19, Eph. 4:8) will certainly have no trouble banishing shadows from a nursery wall, be they real or imagined.

Like the disciples who tried to keep little children from bothering Jesus, many people would brush toddlers aside, not realizing that the deepest lessons of life are learned in the early years, in the tiniest, often most repetitive details.

In the church we often put children who are less than three years old with baby sitters who have no awareness or inclination to teach because we are too unaware of a child's capacity to learn at that most pliable and sensitive age. We should put our most loving, creative teachers with the little ones! I remember most clearly a class of two years olds I once taught. We climbed into a boat (the table) with Jesus one Sunday and the storm came and the boat rocked and we were all so afraid that some actually started to cry. And then we all "saw" Jesus awakening, and "heard" Him speak to calm the waves, and the sea obeyed. And we climbed down out of the "boat" and thanked Jesus for taking such good care of us. Years later, one of those now-adult children recalled to me the vividness of that experience.

When a death occurs in the family, sometimes everyone assumes too glibly that the baby is too little to understand, so he is left alone to absorb the energies of the family grief with no one to minister sensitively to his feelings of loss and confusion. He cannot yet intellectualize, but his little spirit is most certainly aware. In times of bereavement, in the busy world of adults, even the normal fare of hugs for little ones may be neglected.

There are other kinds of losses, significant to a toddler, but lost to us grownups. A favorite toy is run over in the driveway. "It's only a toy. He'll get over it." A pet is hit by a car. "Don't worry about it. Get him another puppy. He won't even remember it next week." Parents are fighting. The toddler hears, and more importantly, feels the tearing between his parents. They do not know that his base of security is being ripped from under him, that in his spirit he may be pulled apart as they separate. "He's too little to understand."

Let the reader know that in the first year of a child's life, basic trust is gained or it isn't. Basic trust is that capacity to hold the heart open, to risk in sustained heart-to-heart involvement with imperfect people. Basic trust is the inner strength and resilience necessary to human relationships, the capacity to remain vulnerable to people who cannot always be believed.

If a little child were to fall and break a leg, and if that leg failed to mend well, he would go limping through life. We can see that fracture and its cause and easily sympathize. But emotional wounds are as real as broken legs, and a child may go limping throughout life because of them. Such fractures cannot be seen except by the X-ray of insight. Not seeing, people tend to be less aware and compassionate. Repeated wounding and repeated sinful reactions to hurts result in character-structured habits, ways of responding to life in defensive or hurtfully aggressive actions. The Body of Christ, especially its counselors, need to have their eyes open to the terrible fact that very many of the practices in our old nature, with which we struggle so fiercely as Christians, were formed in our first two or three years on earth! Once we come fully to comprehend the awesomeness of that fact, our hearts and minds will be easily filled with our Lord's gentle compassion.

The assurance we have in the Word of God that "Surely our griefs He Himself bore and our sorrows He carried" (Isa. 53:4) is not only for present ills, but also for all our yesterdays, all the way back to our beginnings. Jesus Christ is able to touch, heal, and transform *all* that has gone on before, *all* that has shaped us, *all* that has driven us from within our unconscious since our first years. He does not erase the past, or cause anything to fall into forgotten memories. He transforms every experience of our lives into strength, understanding, compassion, and instruments of healing—from the very substance of our former woundings and humiliations from our sin.

10

From Walking, to School

Train up a child in the way he should go, Even when he is old he will not depart from it. (Prov. 22:6)

The most common responses from anxious parents to Prov. 22:6 are: "I want to believe that, but how old does the child have to be before he stops departing!" "If that's true, then where did we go wrong?" "We gave Susie everything! She doesn't appreciate anything!" Missing from all those comments is basic understanding of what we consider to be the key word in the Scripture, "Train up a child in the way *he* should go. . . ." The important thing is to discover what is the way *he* should go, according to the *Lord's* purposes for him, and lovingly, sensitively, invitationally train him so as to set him free to become the most God has created him to be. "For we are His workmanship, created in Christ Jesus *for* good works, which God prepared beforehand, that we should walk in them" (Eph. 2:10).

God's peculiar preparation of good works for our son or daughter may or may not coincide with our family traditions. "We hoped Jimmy would be a lawyer like his father and his father before him." God's plan may run totally counter to our dreaming, hoping, and planning, "But I always dreamed of having a doctor in the family!" "Love does not insist on its own way" (1 Cor. 13:5 RSV); to superimpose even the most noble aspirations on our children is not love. I (Paula) firmly believe that each and every person is created for good works, and uniquely equipped for those by seeds of natural interest and talent implanted by God. He is not limited by these, for God can broaden any person to do a specific task by enabling him to learn new skills to meet needs. But that which most restfully fulfills a person and enables him to most fruitfully and joyfully contribute is for him to be seen, respectfully met, nurtured, disciplined, and matured in his own natural gifts by parents and teachers. If a child is so trained in the way *he* should go, it will feel so right, rewarding, and fulfilling, he will be at home in it. The way will be a part of him, and he a part of it.

A friend of ours, Roger Youmans, M.D., Associate Professor of Surgery at Oral Roberts University Medical School, shared with us this definition of health: "Health is that relationship between an organism and its environment which enables the organism to fulfill its purpose." Love in a family, like education in a school, should be designed to produce healthy human organisms. By Roger's definition, the child who has been conformed principally to fulfill purposes not his own is not a healthy organism. He may go limping through life striving to please people but never doing what he was designed by God to do. He may be shriveling inside for fear of failure and rejection. He may be overcome with shame for not living up to expectations. He may be polluting the atmosphere by sins of rebellious anger and resentment for never being accepted for who he is, rather than only for the role he consented to play.

Prayer for the healing of the inner man always involves at root a decision to forgive, a plea to be forgiven, and a discipline of walking in the new life. The purpose of healing is not merely to enable him to do successfully what others have wanted him to do all along. It is not merely to make him feel better. It is to restore a person to the original purpose for which he was created, to gift him with the courage to be. It is to set him free from judgment, condemnation, and fear about what others think of him.

That is not a complicated process. It is a simple matter of recognizing that a part of the house of our life is weak and crumbling, or filled with unhappiness and strife because there was a serious defect in the foundation of character upon which our house was built. We are told in Luke 6 to dig deep and lay our foundation on the rock (who is Jesus) so that when the floods of life arise we will be able to stand, whatever pressure hits us.

> The good man out of the good treasure of his heart brings forth what is good; and the evil man out of the evil treasure brings forth what is evil; for his mouth speaks from that which fills his heart. And why do you call Me, "Lord, Lord," and do not do what I say? Everyone who comes to Me, and hears My words, and acts upon them, I will show you whom he is like: he is like a man building a house, who dug deep and laid a foundation upon the rock; and when a flood arose, the river burst against that house and could not shake it, because it had been well built. But the one who has heard, and has not acted accordingly, is like a man who built a house upon the ground without any foundation; and the river burst against it and immediately it collapsed, and the ruin of that house was great. (Luke 6:45-49)

Often we recognize that our lives are expressing actions and attitudes which do not manifest a good treasure in the heart. If we neglect to search out the rottenness in some of our foundation stones (the early years of our life upon which all the subsequent years of our life are built) to allow the Lord to transform those stones into the solid substance of His own nature, it will be only a matter of time before the pressures of responsibility and the difficulties of circumstance (the floods of great waters) bring us to spiritual, emotional, and physical cave-ins and washouts.

The following stories illustrate many of the kinds of flaws in foundation stones which occur in pre-school and early school years.

How to Bury Your Children with Their Talents

Eugene was the first of two children. Fearful for the safety of their little boy, his parents determined to protect him from all harm. He was not allowed to leave his yard to play with a friend. Neighborhood children were not made to feel welcome at his home. Playtime was never carefree because mother was always interfering. Messes were not tolerated. He was never allowed to ride a bicycle nor to roar down the sidewalk on roller skates. When he started school, his mother walked him to the schoolyard every day, then met him and saw that he arrived home safely. This continued into the third grade. By then he was allowed to leave his yard, but he had no friends. He continued as a loner through his school career and did poorly in his studies despite volumes of "help" lavished by a mother who had no idea she was undermining confidence by her overprotectiveness and undercurrent messages, "You couldn't get along without me." When he married, he was unable to hold a job and became dependent on his wife for every emotional and then material support. He became an alcoholic to comfort the insecurity he felt about himself as a man, and was always fearful about traveling more than a few miles off familiar paths. He accepted the Lord in a real born-again experience, but was too embarrassed to let himself be known by becoming part of a church. He never grew up in his salvation (1 Pet. 2:2).

Jealousy prevented the development of a relationship between him and his younger brother who seemed to be determined to be his own person and to succeed no matter what.

Eugene died at an early age, never having developed the outstanding gift for writing and storytelling with which the Lord had equipped him from the beginning.

> For to everyone who has shall more be given, and he shall have an abundance; but from the one who does not have, even what he does have shall be taken away. (Matt. 25:29)

In Eugene's case it was not that only a few of his foundation stones were flawed. It was that his life had been built on a mishmash of having had everything done for him, of never having been allowed to exercise his own muscles of responsibility which would have developed in him a measure of self-confidence. Whatever spirit of adventure he might have had in the beginning was so bound by parental fears and controls that he lost all courage to risk. Healing for him would have only *begun* with forgiveness. Then he would have needed continual prayer and association with others who could call him forth to life. Being born anew, he needed others to support and affirm that coming forth by spending time with him, completely rebuilding his foundations through expressed love of Jesus, in daily actions. But his carnal conditioning overcame him—he fled from life.

Sibling Sufferings

We also exult in our tribulations; knowing that tribulation brings about perseverance; and perseverance, proven character; and proven character, hope. (Rom. 5:3-4)

As adults we tend to look upon the trials and upsets of small children as being relatively unimportant immaturities which will soon pass. Or being discomfitted by their quarrels and tears, we may ignore them altogether, ridicule their silliness, or rush in to settle matters prematurely. We need to realize that the tiny tribulations of a young child are mountainous to him, and his emotions all-consuming. The events with which he struggles may soon fall into forgetfulness, but the reactions of primary people to his handling of those events become a part of the storehouse of his heart and continue to influence him from within. A young child has not yet developed faculties to think through his experiences to put them in a context of past and future. He hurts now, and vents the steam of hurt as an appeal for immediate comfort and aid. For instance, Joey has spent considerable time building a tall tower with his blocks. He leaves the room to call mother to look and admire. While he is gone, little brother knocks the entire construction down, and gleefully sits on it. Mother consoles Joey and gives him an ice cream cone, which the dog grabs out of his hand, and in his urgency to save his treat from the thief, he trips over little brother and the pile of blocks and falls to the floor, hitting his head on the corner of a chair. Hurt and rage need a place to land, so he pops baby brother with a block. To Joey that series of events is as devastating an experience as that of a grown man who after hours of hard work loses a coveted business deal because of the bungling of an inept colleague, then makes a recovery only to lose credit for it due to misrepresentation by one of the company "glory boys" who hops on the bandwagon at the last minute. In either case, the outraged cry of "It's not fair" needs to be met with sensitivity before teaching. If Joey's mother only punishes him for lashing out, she will feed in him a judgment of not being understood, of being pushed aside in favor of the younger brother, of being given a raw deal by those he is supposed to be able to trust. Many people seek counseling who as adults are having trouble with "brothers" in business or in organizational groups. Such people may have stones at the base of their foundation which bear the imprint of many such incidents with natural brothers and sisters. They have judged, hated, built an expectation, and now they are reaping.

Jealousies

Marilyn's husband is leaving her for another woman, her best friend. She feels betrayed, rejected, ugly, and worthless. Counseling reveals that from the time her younger sister was born, Marilyn felt second best—not as pretty, talented, or lovable. Mom and dad seemed always to be giving her sister advantages. She protests she loves her sister, but her sister was the one whom friends always called first, the one who later had all the boyfriends, won all the awards, etc. Others in the family remember Marilyn's history differently than she. They knew the animosity. The counselor's task is not first of all to straighten Marilyn out about the truth of what went on when she was a little girl. It is to connect the little child in her with Jesus through prayer, that He might begin to reveal to her the truth about herself and enable her to let go of the judgments she has made from childhood in relation to her sister, her parents, God, and herself. The Lord, through counselors and the church, can then help her to grow into an appreciative awareness of her own beauty and worth in Him. Not all childhood judgments we make concerning siblings become a lasting part of us. My (Paula's) brothers, Jerry and Stan, were born only twenty months apart. They enjoyed many early adventures together, including a lot of healthy rough and tumble. When Jerry, the older, started to school, Stan naturally thought he should be allowed to go also. When he was denied that privilege, he was angry at Jerry, thinking it was Jerry's fault. Apparently he nursed that blame for at least a year, for when he was allowed to enter kindergarten, he insisted on walking to school on the opposite side of the street from Jerry. But the misunderstanding took no deep root. A part of that is probably due to parents who could arbitrate lovingly with no partiality. A large part was due to choices the boys made at that early age to forgive and choose one another. They remain good friends to this day and each has succeeded well in his own field.

Choice plays a great part in determining whether tribulation ultimately produces character and hope. No amount of counsel or prayer for inner healing can change the heart of a person who has not yet made a choice deep down to forget what lies behind and press on toward what lies ahead (Phil. 3:13-15). Healing comes to the one who has determined not to "use" the events of his life to excuse himself or to prove others wrong.

Economic Downs and Hand-Me-Downs

We have counseled many who were small children during the Great Depression and post-depression years. We find two major reactions to their common experience of compulsory frugality. Some continue to nurse feelings of deprivation and try to compensate with periodic buying sprees. Or they have determined not to let their children go without as they had to do, splurging too much for them. They are offended by the offer of hand-me-downs. "I never had anything new that I could call my own! I'm going to see that my children have the very best!" Others in depression times seem to have developed a keen ability to determine the difference between want and need, a developed talent for using scrap materials creatively, and appreciation for bargains and shared resources. Sometimes prayer needs to be administered before they can buy for themselves or accept luxurious gifts without vague guilt feelings, but they are not driven to excesses to fill emotional pits of deprivation. The difference lies again in the quality of the foundation stones. (Train up a child in any way at all, and until something enters his life to change it, he will not depart from it.) If a child was given plenty of affection, if his family unit stayed together, if there was an absence of quarreling, if sharing was expressed as sacrificial love, if there was fun and game times in the family, the small child probably did not even notice he was poor materially! Or if he noticed, it did not matter significantly. In families in which financial stress was allowed to overcome love to warp harmony and break unity, their small children most likely absorbed anxiety, and the resulting insecurity became a part of their basic attitudes toward life.

In both poor and affluent families, the story is usually the same where there are many children. Hand-me-downs naturally come to the younger members. In one family the younger children are proud to wear big brother's or sister's outgrown clothes; it may symbolize to them that they too are maturing into the image of their sibling heroes. Or if the siblings are not heroes to them, they may respond jealously or angrily to being treated like second best. What goes into the storehouse of the heart to wound or bless is *not the event or circumstance itself, but always the individual's reaction to it.* Second-best mentality in the heart can rise to find expression in many ways throughout life—expectation to be bypassed for job promotions or awards, inability to believe one's own mate chooses you above all others, reticence to put oneself forward to serve or to claim one's place, awkwardness in response to compliments, difficulty even to believe that "Jesus loves *me. . . ,*" etc.

Belonging—Confusion and Exclusion

A child commences to move into the "gang" when he leaves the familiar protected surroundings of his home and begins to venture into his and the neighbor's yards to play. He soon begins to experience a confusing disparity between the way mom and dad act and the way things are done down the block. For instance, he learns a strange new vocabulary which wins him approval among his peers, and is rewarded with soap in the mouth when he uses it at home! He finds himself wrestling with questions of justice when he is spanked for violations of rules, and his friend is not. I (Paula) remember when our son Loren, then four or five, ran down the alley with his friend Ernie and the two of them plucked ripe tomatoes which they threw for the fun of the splat. Loren was spanked and required to apologize to the neighbors; Ernie was not. Loren was outraged.

Peer-group loyalties take an increasingly firm hold on every child, and a wise parent will relate sympathetically to pressures on the child while administering appropriate discipline to build in solid healthy value systems. A child may react with violent emotions to what at the moment he considers to be unfair. But if sensitivity and love are expressed concurrently with whatever the shape of discipline, that will serve as good mortar base for the laying of solid foundation stones.

If judgments are made against parents for excessive (or perceived as excessive) discipline, forgiveness can be accomplished later. But lack of discipline leaves a child without bounds for his energies and drives, and this results in more than a need for inner healing as an adult. At some point he will have to be given what was not given, someone will have to give him some form of discipline as a parent in Christ, or he will flounder and err forever without structure. He will not have self-limits built within him to know when he is trampling on others or taking unfair advantage. He will be vulnerable to the urgencies of the moment, unable to take into account easily the dynamics of cause and effect. "Like a city that is broken into and without walls Is a man who has no control over his spirit" (Prov. 25:28). Frequently we have prayed with people to enable them to forgive parents for not disciplining them. A child's mind may shout hallelujah for "getting by" with a transgression, while his heart feels unloved and afraid.

Every child has a tremendous need to be accepted among his peers. Our oldest son demonstrated this dramatically in the early 1950s when we were living in the University of Chicago community. The students in our seminary housing took great delight in Loren's ability as a two year old to mimic the current theological vocabulary without missing a syllable. As he played in the front yard of Kimbark House many students and teachers going to and from classes would stop and chat with our little towhead. They were invariably astonished to learn that he was so young because of his facility in conversation. It was not long before Loren was attracted to the far end of the block where many children played in a courtyard area behind a group of apartment houses. He had been given a little blue tricycle, and daily he would pedal down the sidewalk in search of playmates. Again and again he would return in tears because of the taunts of the children, "You're a dummy! You don't even know how old you are!" It was difficult for them to believe that one who rode and spoke in such a grown-up manner could be only two years old. We would hug him and wipe his tears, and he would return once more to try to become a part of the gang he referred to as the "roughie toughies." That effort developed in Loren an ability to persist in the face of adversity. It also created in him a deep thirst for approval which had to be ministered to in later years.

Ami, our second child, during her preschool years in Streator, Illinois, was the only little girl on the block. Sometimes she was allowed to tag along with Loren and his gang, but never as a full-fledged member. She felt this exclusion keenly, and responded to it in several ways: 1) She assumed what she felt was the upper hand by becoming more righteous than her older brother, reminding him quietly but persistently about the rewards of virtuous living. This practice did nothing to win her a place in the group. But it did give her an identity in relation to them. 2) She became a pint-sized champion of the underdog, her heart bleeding for anyone who was underprivileged, taunted or teased. She'd take them under her wing, no matter what the cost, and mother them. In one community where we lived there was a very poor family named "Pitts." The children's parents took good care of them, and they were respectable in every way, but they dressed in clothing that was ill-fitting, and they bore the marks of an inadequate diet. Neighborhood children took up the cruel taunt, "Pitts Pitts—you look like the pits," and they passed a warning to newcomers, "Be careful—you'll catch the Pitts!" Ami identified and became one with the rejected, defending them faithfully. We admired her for the love and strength she demonstrated. We worried a little for fear of feeding her self-righteous stance. We worried more for the pattern of mothering that was so much a part of her. When she married, the Lord blessed the mothering as she applied it to her children. But He had to purge and refine the mothering insofar as it was for a time inappropriately, unconsciously applied to her husband. It was not enough to make the grown one aware mentally of what she was doing. The little girl inside had to be comforted, forgiven, and released from driving urgency in her heart. Then she could choose to relate freely to Ron in a love that nurtured him according to his need.

Teasing

Even when teasing is intended not as ridicule, but as an affectionate expression, it can be damaging to preschool children. They do not understand teasing, tending to interpret what is said very literally. Most of us have experienced the tearful response of a little child who has just been told, "The cat has your tongue," or "I have your nose" followed by a tweak of said appendage (with the thumb thrust between second and third fingers to prove it). Or the loud response to, "You have epidermis all over you!"—"I do not!" Most of us have not realized the wounding we have inflicted by continual use of expressions such as "Hi, twerp!" "How'd you grow so short?" "Come on, dummy," "Hey, stupid." We adults may think we were communicating such epithets as jokes by our laughter, but the heart of the child received it as ridicule and rejection. He felt attacked unjustly for his size or his ignorance, over which he had no control. Perhaps the most common thing we pray for to enable a person to live beyond feelings of being inadequate or unacceptable in his adult peer group, is in relation to teasing by other children years ago. The adult mind can remember and identify the occasion and the confusion. The little child inside needs to forgive and be forgiven for anger and possible continual habitual lashing out or withdrawal from others, and to accept a renewed identity.

Ridicule

The child who is ridiculed in front of his classmates may carry the scars of the knife thrust for years. He may carry anxiety within his heart about embarrassing himself in front of other people. A child who wets his pants in class and is pointed out as a baby who can't control himself may from then on harbor feelings of embarrassment and rejection about his body and its natural functions. He may carry hate in his heart for the teacher who would not recognize his need to leave the room. He can then project that hatred on anyone who ignores his desires or puts him on the spot for whatever reason. But the good news is that today he can also by his choice describe that hurtful incident to the Lord and let someone pray in order that forgiveness be accomplished. He can pray that the power of that incident to push or inhibit him be broken. Jesus will answer that prayer.

As a child I (Paula) was very performance oriented, so much so that when I was fitted for new glasses, I faked the ability to read the print in a storybook (I had memorized the story by repeated listening) because I thought new glasses meant I was *supposed* to see clearly. I couldn't let anyone know I was failing to do what I was supposed to be able to do. I can laugh about that now, but it was a very serious matter to the little girl. I carried my "ought world" into the classroom, mixed with a good measure of shyness. I can't remember the names of the teachers who were sensitive and considerate; that part of my heart rests in peace. At age six I made a powerful hateful secret judgment on a teacher who called me "stupid" because I would not follow her directions about spelling my name. I quietly persisted in writing "P A U L A" on the blackboard while she accelerated to a public display of temper at my expense because I didn't know how to write my name "correctly" as "P A U L I N E." Later she sent me on an errand which I blundered because I didn't hear her clearly, and she scathed me publicly for being "stupid." I remember her name because it was written in blood in my heart and fed with resentment. For years I was hypersensitive to remarks that were made thoughtlessly perhaps but innocently, which I received as insults. Having judged her for calling me stupid, I found myself reaping that judgment by putting others down. They felt "stupid" though I never called them so. Only recently have I come into a deep dimension of freedom from that bondage. Jesus cannot free us from hatred and resentment when we think we have a right to hate and resent. God bless Miss Shackleton.

Family Position and Other
Assorted Opportunities to Foul

We may be loved, taught and nurtured marvelously and yet be imperfect and erring. For example, an only child may have striving in him because he was always running on tip toe to live up to an adult model. He may be self-centered because in the home he was always the center of attention. He may find it difficult to share his space because he never had to. He may not know the freedom of good-natured rough and tumble with others in talking things out because he never knew how to rough and tumble with brothers and sisters who came up laughing after rolling and pounding on the floor. If we were last children we may always feel tacked on, a tag along in relationships, or that we never quite measure up to others' abilities. If we were first children, we may be too dutiful and serious, or have a habit of fleeing from responsibility, having been given too much too soon. We may feel controlled and pushed because we were that first project of parents who were practicing on us. Middle children may flounder, not knowing whether belonging is with the older kids or the younger ones. If our family is talented, we may have trouble coming up with something that is only ours to do. If our family has no talent, we may feel like nothing can sparkle from a setting like that. If our home was always neat, we may have in us an inability to tolerate disorder. If we lived in disorder we may feel inside a guilt and helplessness about that, especially if as children we heard again and again apologies for "messes the children make."

All of us are filled with memories of little things we made into big deals. Everyone in my second-grade class wore short socks while I had to wear knee socks, so I rolled my knee socks down to be like everyone else. Our son Tim didn't feel handsome in glasses, so he managed to "lose" multiple pairs. Perhaps our jeans didn't have the "right" kind of pockets. It may be that the way people related to our differentness was wounding. All such things may leave hidden trigger points inside us, or not-so-hidden harmful practices. But in Jesus we are healed simply by inviting Him to minister to the inner child and to bring such practices to death on the cross. From then on, no one forces us to pick our scabs.

Abused

If we were abused physically or emotionally as children, we will indeed have foundation stones of fear, rejection, anger, and a thousand variations. We will need to have basic trust restored in us before we can reach out with confidence to Father God, or to any authority figure. If a counselor ministers in the nature of Jesus by the wisdom and power of Jesus, tuned in to His direction so as not to rape the process, always aiming sensitively to connect the person he counsels to Jesus, there is no wound beyond healing, no experience beyond redemption. We need only to remember at all times that the calling is to minister to the inner heart, and the solely effective method is the cross.

I pray that the *eyes of your heart may be enlightened*, so that you may know what is the hope of His calling, what are the riches of the glory of His inheritance in the saints, and what is the surpassing greatness of His power toward us who believe. These are in accordance with the working of the strength of *His* might. (Eph. 1:18)

We cannot enter the narrow gate into the fullness of life in the Kingdom carrying a load of garbage. Having examined that which is in our hearts to determine what is garbage, we must leave it at the altar of God and go on. If we do not do that, we cannot go on to freedom and maturity.

I (Paula) was a first child. My parents were almost as inexperienced at being parents as I was a novice at learning what it is to be a child of God. We blessed one another. We made mistakes. We sinned against one another in our ignorance and our immaturity and because of our basic sinful nature. But in Jesus we are forgiven and forgiving, transformed and renewed. I have needed to see the shape of me, to dig to the foundation stones to let Jesus happen in me. Now, as the adult child of my parents, leaving the hurtful part of the past behind, I can grow forward with the cherished remembered heritage of the wealth of my parents to strengthen, encourage, and instruct my life.

Observe the commandment of your father, And do not forsake the teaching of your mother; Bind them continually on your heart; Tie them around your neck. When you walk about, they will guide you; When you sleep, they will watch over you. And when you awake they will talk to you. (Prov. 6:20-22)

I wrote the following on the occasion of my parents' fiftieth wedding anniversary:

Out of the Chosen Treasure of My Heart
I Remember Dad

Skating hand in hand
  when I was two—
  the left skate on him.
  the right on me,
  and feeling together.

His calling me "Baby,"
  but never
  making me feel like one.
  "You can do anything
  you really want to do."

His pretending to "only look"
  in our mouths
  for loose teeth—
  and coming up grinning
  with quick and painless extractions.

His coming home after
  days of travel on the road
  to take us for a ride in the car—
    buying special treats
    we each could choose
      when wonderfully delicious things
      could be bought for a nickel,
      and nickels were hard to come by.

Sitting on the piano bench
  announcing his homecoming
  with chiri-biri-bin on the clarinet—
    A special quality of order
    settling over the household
    with the music of his presence.

Rocking the little ones to the only songs he ever sang—
"The Old Gray Mare" and "Bye O Baby Bunting"—

His grossing mother out
with ridiculous humor
when life became too serious and cares too heavy—
Teaching us to laugh at ourselves.
A legacy our boys have inherited.

I remember him
buried under piles of weekend job reports,
pecking away at his typewriter—
taking time from that important task
to let his dentures slip out of the corner of his mouth
for our amusement.

His creative cookery—that special sauce for pork and beans
His books—tomato plants—his picture taking
His "dag-nab-it" when things went wrong.
(I never heard him swear.)

He could show tender emotions
and yet
Stand sturdy in the face of our anxiety
and say
"It will be all right."
With believable authority we could touch.

He could charm the proverbial "face off a clock"
without departing from the truth,
Plug away at life without being dreary,
Lay down his life without putting any under obligation,
And win a prize for being human,
without expecting a medal.

He even cried with the rest of us when our kitty died.

Every special day—
Birthday,
Christmas
Father's Day—
It was the same.
I spent my dime,
My two week's fortune saved

For a gift for Dad:
  White wrapped,
  Ribbon curled,
  Small and flat—
Always the same, and ever a surprise
To him.
He'd smile and effervesce,
"Well, look here what it is!"
And proudly wear
My love
And me
In his pocket.

I Remember Mom

Rocking, singing
sharing her repertoire
of a hundred nursery rhymes to give her children.

Loving us through
bumps and mumps and whoops and sniffles
    with milk toast, clean white sheets,
    and sometimes purple plaster on our chests
        under soft flannel—
    such fun to peel off in the morning.

  I remember
the delightful smells from her kitchen—
    chicken pot pie
    meat loaf
    grape jam simmering
    peanut butter cookies
    green beans with bacon and onion
And we always sat together at the table
With a prayer of praise to the Provider.

She played the piano while we sang
    for hours.

If we were scattered in a thousand alluring directions,
We were reunited in a foundation of the
   great old songs of Christian faith.
   And they remained,
   And we were stayed.

I remember her presence at every school function.
We knew her interest,
And we understood authority;
   "If you're spanked at school, you'll be
   spanked again at home."
And our house was not divided against itself.
It stands.

She could iron her way through
   baskets of freshly laundered clothes
And tromp with us
   on aching legs
   to the zoo—or through an art museum.
Her answer to rambunctious
   troops of neighborhood boys
Was an afternoon trip to a packing plant or jam factory.
   In our family
We were free to be rotten
   But not to get by with it.
   The discipline was pruning—never excommunication.

   Sunday
was always the first day of the week in our home
from the beginning.
   And it was Sabbath:
      Sunday school and worship,
      Family dinner and rest,
      Funny papers and games,
      Music through a long afternoon.
      Edgar Bergen and Charlie McCarthy and "One Man's Family"
         in the evening
         with the aroma of toasted cheese, peanut butter,
         and sassafras tea.
   Life and God all flowed together.

(Sunday evening still smells like that
  whether the sandwiches are there or not.
And if the Lord's Day is given away,
  the month is one long dreary week.)

  Charlie and Edgar have passed away
  But the family goes on
    and multiplies in blessing . . .

Renewed each day by life from roots
  that never die.

Hot summer sun and
Row on row of bright clean clothes
Flapping on the lines.
  Mother:
    stooping,
    stretching,
    folding,
    carrying,
While we played in the yard and vacant lot—
    exploring trails,
    weaving clover chains,
    and capturing grasshoppers
    for our Mason-jar zoo.

Some plan and scheme and push as children grow
And bind their offspring to them as they go
In selfish striving.
But Mother launched her dreams from ironing boards,
And blessed their rising.

Section III

Six to Twelve—Most Common and Vitiating Malformations of Character

11

Inner Vows

Come now, you who say, "Today or tomorrow, we shall go to such and such a city, and spend a year there and engage in business and make a profit." Yet you do not know what your life will be like tomorrow. You are just a vapor that appears for a little while and then vanishes away. Instead, you ought to say, "If the Lord wills, we shall live and also do this or that." But as it is, you boast in your arrogance; all such boasting is evil. Therefore, to one who knows the right thing to do, and does not do it, to him it is sin. (James 4:13-17)

Again, you have heard that the ancients were told, "You shall not make false vows, but shall fulfill your vows to the Lord." But I say to you, make no oath at all, either by heaven, for it is the throne of God, or by the earth, for it is the footstool of His feet, or by Jerusalem, for it is the city of the great King. Nor shall you make an oath by your head, for you cannot make one hair white or black. But let your statement be, "Yes, yes" or "No, no"; and anything beyond these is of evil. (Matt. 5:33-37)

A woman came to us who could not bear a male child. Several times she had become pregnant, and had miscarried boys about the third or fourth month. Gynecologists could find no physical cause. She wanted fervently to give her husband a son. We asked concerning her life with her father, and could find some hurts, but her reactions did not seem great enough to create such a destructive, obviously psychosomatic condition. Her brother, however, was not like the usual sibling who teases because he loves. This brother was vicious, continually embarrassing and physically hurting her. Her father failed to protect her. She remembered then, at about nine or ten, walking beside a river, picking up stones, hurling them into the water, crying out, "I'll never carry a boy child. I'll never carry a boy child." That was an inner vow, a directive sent through the heart and mind to the body. Though the conscious mind had long forgotten, the inner being had not. Though she now wanted to give birth, the earlier programing was still intact and functioning.

We took up authority in Christ, knowing that whatever we loose is loosed (Matt. 16:19; 18:18). Having pronounced forgiveness for her hatred of her brother, and induced her to forgive, we spoke directly to her body, even as Jesus rebuked the fever (Luke 4:39). We commanded the body to forget that hateful order and to return to the original command of God, to subdue and fill the earth (Gen. 1:28). Mentioning "subdue" was a polite way of reminding the body as part of nature, to obey the voice of the Lord even as Jesus commanded the waves and the winds, and they obeyed Him (Matt. 8:23-27). We prayed comfort and healing for her heart and spirit, and for her body. In the prayer, we visualized her being able to produce a healthy, normal baby boy. She did conceive and carry to full term a normal healthy son.

An inner vow is a determination set by the mind and heart into all the being in early life. Vows we make currently also affect us, but an *inner* vow is one set into us as children, usually forgotten. Our inner being persistently retains such programing no matter what changes of mind and heart may later pertain. The distinctive mark of an inner vow is that it resists the normal maturation process. "When I was a child, I used to speak as a child, think as a child, reason as a child; when I became a man, I did away with childish things" (1 Cor. 13:11). We may have many childish peculiarities, but we mature and leave them behind, reminded only by friends, relatives, and family reminiscenses. Normal childish proclivities do not harm us other than to embarrass or prevent us as children, goading us to mature, until we "do away with them"; i.e., shyness, awkwardness, absentmindedness, insensitivity towards others' feelings, etc. But inner vows resist change. We do not grow out of them.

Inner vows may not become manifest immediately in behavior. Like the programing of a clock on an electric range, they may not kick on until the time set by the vow. They may rest totally forgotten and dormant, until triggered by the right persons or situations. Having forgotten them, we are unaware they exist or could have any effect.

We all have made many inner vows, of varying intensity and tenacity. Inner vows are as common to children as peanut butter in America. There are good and helpful vows as well as destructive ones. Even the good vows need to be released, so that we are not impelled by the flesh, but by the Spirit in freedom. Vows do need to be seen, for their nature is to prevent departure from them. They affect us like a railroad track affects a train. The conscious mind may be a very good engine, but it can run only on the track of the inner vow set for it in childhood. No matter which way the engineer may desire to go, the train will not change direction unless someone switches tracks. Inner vows, being lodged in the heart like an engram, respond not at all to the fleshly will of the inhabited. The person cannot, unaided, uproot or change that track. Such vows require authority. Only one who knows his authority in the Lord Jesus Christ can break a vow and reset the inner being to another way of acting.

Many marriages resemble a rail yard. Many tracks lead in. But the engine is not on the track leading to marital bliss. It runs on the track of hidden inner vows far from happiness. Unless someone switches the track, the train to marital bliss will never arrive. Though perhaps a person alone, with Jesus, could reset his own tracks, he should prefer not to. It is much easier, humbler, and better to let another in the Body of Christ do it for us. Pride is best humbled by the Body of Christ ministering to us.

A young wife came to us who could not conceive. She greatly wanted to bear children for her husband. Tests revealed no physical reasons for barrenness, either in her or her husband, according to her gynecologist. She should normally have conceived easily long before. Questioning revealed that she had been the eldest of nine children born to a Catholic woman who became ill early on in each pregnancy and remained so until long after delivery. It took little imagination to see what happened each time her mother conceived. Feelings of imposition increased yearly, as she had to take over and run the household. Anger mounted day by day, pregnancy after pregnancy, at her mother for continuing to become pregnant, at her father for causing it, at the church for its rules, and at all the babies who caused commotion and labor. Ultimately she cried out over and over again, "I'll never be like my mother; I'll never act like that." The inner being easily interpreted such vows as orders not ever to allow pregnancy. Who can say how much power our determinations have to influence the functions of the body? Her later healthy, natural instincts and desires, even her love for her husband, could not overcome that earlier directive. I (John) pronounced forgiveness for her disrespect of her father and mother and the church, and by authority in the name of Jesus, broke that vow and directed the inner being and her body to receive and nurture life. At this writing, she is about to deliver her second baby. Would she have conceived in due time anyway or did her inner vow in fact prevent this from happening until the vow was broken? Who can say? We have seen this and similar inner vows broken so many times in prayer, with immediate beneficial results, that to us the revelation is confirmed.

Many wives have discovered the trouble is that their husbands were raised by mothers! We don't mean that critically, however facetiously. Boys soon learn that mothers have elephantine memories. They discover that "whatever you say can and will be used against you in a court of law." Often whatever emotion that hangs out noticeably, good or bad, will be used by mama to control. So boys learn to hide from their mothers. The less she knows the better. Whatever she knows may be hauled up for criticism or scolding—weeks, months, or years later. Though all this is normal, sometimes the situation is so tense or the reaction so vehement, the lad forms a most obstinate inner vow: "Never share what you really feel with a woman. It's not safe."

Later on, when chromosomes and hormones change a boy's aversion to girls, he may want to share, and find himself unable. Most likely he may find it easy to communicate with girls, until he marries. Marriage puts the woman in position to trigger in him inner vows made relative to such primary females as mothers, grandmothers, and sisters. Frequently couples have come for counseling, perplexed by the fact that they had good communication until the honeymoon. Now her complaint is:

"He won't tell me anything any more."

Evening conversations sound something like the following:

"Hi, honey, how was your day?"

"Fine, just fine."

"Tell me about it."

"What do you want to know?"

"How did it go? What happened today?"

"Just great. Went just great."

"Like what?"

"What what?"

"You know, tell me some incidents. Tell me about your day."

"Oh, I don't know. Just like any other day I suppose."

"Well, what happened?"

"Whaddaya mean, what happened?"

"Tell me some incidents. How did your day go?"

"I just told you, just like any other day. You know how the office goes."

In no way does he know that his inner being has no intention to share what is really on his heart. Unknown to him or her, an earlier programing has kicked into action. Even if he hears his wife and is wounded and perplexed about his inability to be vulnerable to her, he may not be able to change his heart to open and share. He may repent a dozen times, only to return automatically to the pattern. The problem is that his repentances in the present concerning his wife cannot overcome the earlier programing of the vow concerning his mother. The repentance is true, but for the wrong sin. Like an arrow shot into the center of the bull's eye—at the wrong target. The repentance and prayer needed is for childhood resentments towards his mother (or other primary females) and for the breaking of that inner vow he set into his being. Present surface repentances alone cannot touch such deeply set directives.

Such inner vows are among the most common problems men and women face. Many a husband, unaware perhaps that he isn't sharing, gradually becomes more and more estranged from his wife. Lacking him, she may be emotionally wilting and dying and may eventually find other places, like the church or bridge clubs to find sharing and fulfillment. The husband meanwhile becomes lonelier and lonelier. Now he ripens for the almost inevitable affair. He has no way of knowing that if he divorces his wife and marries this woman who, "thank God, understands me," the moment he marries her, she will then be in the identical "ruled out" position his wife presently occupies. That inner vow confines him to isolation from any wife and exposes him to vulnerability (limited but more than with his wife) to anyone who does not trigger the action of the vow. He is doomed to loneliness and possible superficial affairs until the vow is seen and broken.

Unlike the two former examples, merely seeing and breaking the inner vow will not by itself set him free. In the former two, I (John) could speak to the body, which was eagerly willing to return to the original command of God to produce life. The body leaped, unimpeded, to fulfill its purpose in creation. Few structures in the soul remained to block. But in the case of vows not to share, many other character structures remain after the original inner vow is broken. Those who have seen the movie, "Star Trek," know that when Voyager VI returned, a "planet of machines" had built a vast complex sub-planet of mechanisms around the original small probe—which was still seeking to fulfill its original mission! Just so, inner vows of this type have built huge surrounding complexes in the character structure, and all are still seeking to fulfill that original purpose, to hide the person from hurt. There may be, for example, a heart of stone, or unconscious, evasive and defensive habitual flight mechanisms, automatically triggered angers, many bitter-root expectancies, key words, phrases or actions that stimulate automatic reactions, deep anxieties and fears, incapabilities to trust, etc. After all these negatives are overcome, there will still exist the need to create totally new habit structures to replace the old. Extended counsel may be required, as one by one all the auxiliary structures are dismantled or transformed. Patience by all—wife, counselor, and husband—will be necessary, plus forbearance, compassion, and continuous forgiveness. It may take a long time to overcome the many complex "machines" of one little vow.

In women, the most common malformation we encounter is likewise an inability to share who they are with the man of their life. Not, however, usually in the area of talking. On the surface, in communication, women almost invariably are more desirous of sharing than men are. So much so that sometimes that fact itself is part of the problem, "Your desire shall be for your husband" (Gen. 3:16). Eve's desire was already by creation for Adam. The Lord meant that her desire would become inordinate, made so by insecurity. "A sandy ascent for the feet of the aged, such is a garrulous wife to a quiet husband" (Ecclesiasticus 25:20, Apocrypha RSV). God created woman to desire to please her husband, but right there is the entrance to trouble, for women were likewise raised with their fathers.

Little girls want to be the apple of their daddies' eyes. They come into earth innately knowing they are God's gift to ravish their daddies' hearts, to comfort, delight, and please. Being received by an appreciative father builds confidence in what it is to be a woman. A wife fulfills her husband from her own sense of beauty and desirability. If she knows she is a precious gift of God to him, she can bless him restfully with her. If she doesn't, and therefore requires constant stated approval and reaffirmation, she becomes a wearisome burden to her man; he always has to prove to her anew that she is desirable to him. That wears him out. He becomes vulnerable to some "siren" who is confident of her desirability.

Unfortunately, all too many fathers are unaware of their value. Less are dead enough to self-centeredness to be aware for their girls' sake rather than their own. Too many times little girls have bounded joyfully into their daddy's presence, only to be ignored or pushed away. New dresses were not noticed, or dad only said, "Yeah, it's okay," or to mama, "What did it cost?" School papers may not have been rewarded with compliments. Worse, the little girl, who lived from a romantically emotional world her father had long since forgotten, may have seen mother's heart crushed again and again mostly by what daddy failed to notice. Men, to her, eventually became regarded as "dumb," "off-base," not noticing or knowing where life really is. For this reason, God in His Word almost never has to remind the woman to love the man, she would have already; but "Let the wife see to it that she *respect* her husband" (Eph. 5:33, italics mine). "Thus Sarah obeyed Abraham, calling him lord, and you have become her children if you do what is right without being frightened by any fear" (1 Pet. 3:6). The "fear" is not usually of physical abuse, but of anxiety born of distrust—"The man will not see and do what will make me feel secure."

From constantly repeated neglects and slights as a little girl originates a subtle inner vow. A man's childish vow is not as subtle. It's simply, "Don't share." But a woman retains a hunger to meet and fulfill her man. Hidden to the grown one, the most common forgotten inner vow of little girls has been, "Don't let him really have or know all of you." Sharing means from then on, first that the wife wants to share *his* life, to know *him* and talk about *him*, not the other way around. And second, her inner vow makes a clever game of what she does share with her husband. She may share enough of her, and give enough to him, to convince herself that she is the open and sharing one, unaware that she has unconsciously, carefully controlled how much she is sharing. He does not really have all of her, in the very moments of sharing in which her surface life protests otherwise.

How often have little girls clenched their fists in frustration when daddy didn't notice them? How often have daddy's words revealed he never really understood her at all? From reactions to such experiences grow distrust and disrespect, which strengthen the inner vow not to be vulnerable, not to really risk who she is with a man. "See if I ever. . . ." As in a boy, by the time natural desire reverses childhood aversion, the earlier directives are not only forgotten, most often they would be vehemently denied.

For one out of five women in America that inner vow is only the tip of the iceberg, for beneath it lies molestation by some trusted man—father, grandfather, stepfather, brother, uncle, or cousin.* When little girls broadcast their desire to be seen and held, many men receive the signals but interpret them bestially. They fail to honor the call to be fathers and honorable men who can love a girl to life as a desirable woman. They respond sexually, and thus violate not only the girl's body but her precious ability to trust herself openly to be her own lovely person with the right man. From the moment of molestation she may fear to let the beauty of what she is shine for fear the result will be nastiness. A most passionate inner vow screams through her being—"Shut down!" From then on,

---

* This was written in 1980. Rachel Johnson reports (August, 1981) that statistics now reveal that one in every four women has been molested by a family member.

though she may become either frigid or promiscuous, behind both clings the same root, an inability to give herself fully to the man of her life. She may appear sexy, and have intercourse often, righteously or unrighteously. She may enjoy sex or detest it. But behind all is a covert inability to be all she is to the man. She cannot meet her man unreservedly with all her heart and spirit through her body. Sex is confined to physical stimulation, because her spirit is not free to flow out and nestle into the man. Her man may find himself bemused, confused by something intangible he senses is lacking. He cannot understand why, with a willing wife (if that is her case), he still hungers for others. The truth is that he has never yet had her. Loneliness is most poignant when there seems no reason for it.

The first difficulty for a counselor is to see the problem. All apparent clues may indicate that she gives, but the husband doesn't, and that he can't or won't receive her. A lack of clarity may be compounded by the fact that in truth he can't open or receive, both in communication and in their sex life. We have found it a wise principle that problems in marriages are never one-sided. Whatever problem appears in one mate, in the other is something either counter-balancing or identical, usually equally disturbing or destructive. This is especially important to remember when the sight of the eyes celebrates a beautiful saintly woman with a callous, uncouth man. We suggest reading 1 John 2:16 in this context, "For all that is in the world, the lust of the flesh and *the lust of the eyes* and the *boastful pride of life*, is not from the Father, but is from the world." Again, we must not judge by what our eyes see.

The first task of the counselor is to help such a woman see. Once she sees, to help her come to a real hatred, not of any person or thing outside herself, but of that practice in her old nature which blocks her from real life. She must come to hatred of that inner vow which caused the blocking practice. Such hatred is not automatic, and should not be taken for granted, no matter what the counselee protests. Fruits, not words, reveal truth. It takes time before fruits are steadfastly manifest. Prayer should be immediate, for the parental dishonorings to be forgiven, for the vows to be broken, and the new life of freedom to emerge, but it may take awhile for proper hatred of the old nature and consequent death of self to arrive.

Again, the fullness of transformation can not be achieved without resurrection. A woman whose father never loved her to life may come to know herself outwardly as beautiful and desirable, and even flaunt it while inwardly feeling ugly and undesirable. A truly confident person does not need to flaunt, preen or brag. Flirting, or any hint of making use of sexual allurement, is usually a dead giveaway to inner arid deserts and distress. No matter how many things come to death on the cross, lasting results cannot happen without resurrection. Resurrection happens only by love. A person cannot come to life without being loved to life (1 John 4:19). The little girl needs a father.

Paula and I have acted as father and mother in Christ to many such women. But all too many times we have seen ministers and other counselors caught in transferences and being seduced. We warn every counselor stringently to keep the cross between the counselee and himself, to guard his own heart and feelings carefully, to be secure in his own mate (or in the watchful counsel of others if unmarried), to be girded surely in the moral law of God's Word, and to be regular in devotion and worship. The attempt to love others to life must be kept by the counselor, not by the counselee, in most secure, safe relationships. Counselors must know themselves to be fathers and mothers in Christ—and nothing else.

Fruits are not hard to detect. They cannot be hidden. "You are the light of the world. *A city set on a hill cannot be hidden*" (Matt. 5:14, italics mine). Whatever degree of physical glamour a woman may have naturally, when she also becomes beautiful from within, nothing can hide it. Beauty suffuses from inside and settles about her, without attracting wrong attention. Men treat her as the lady she has become. Quiet inner joy now radiates, no matter whether for the moment she is sad or happy. She is free to give to her husband without demanding tit-for-tat reciprocation. Because he is free from demand, he usually begins to respond. One lady reported with delight, "He can't keep his hands off me. He's always patting me and telling me he loves me." Because she has become free, many talents long bound (Luke 13:16), begin to be discovered and soon flower. Counselors need to stand back, and let her happen.

Inner vows are as multifarious as people are. Some are simple, like a boy who swears he will never sing (because of early embarrassments or a demanding parent) only years later to discover a rich voice released. Some are complex, like a girl who refuses to put her head under water in swimming, but counsel discovers it has nothing to do with early swimming experiences and everything to do with a vow never to be risked beyond her control. In Paula's case, that vow had started in the water in the womb and had been strengthened by performance demands before she was able to answer them. Only now, years after the infilling of the Holy Spirit, and more years of seeing and praying over root causes, is she beginning to be free in the water!

People can make vows never to speak in public, or never to develop breasts, or never to grow up. Never to give not only of self but also of simple things like clothes, or to allow personal space to be invaded, or to wear hand-me-downs. Many inner vows have to do with ambitions, or rebellions against them— "I'll never fail again," "I'll be the best ever," or conversely, "I'll never try again."

The most vitiating are those concerning personal relationships. Children can make other powerful determinations against parents than we have discussed earlier, which also destroy marital relationships. "I'll get even with her" (the mother or sister), later projecting a consequent unconscious need to take vengeance on all women, specifically on the wife and children. "I'll never let him (brother or sister) get the best of me again" (either in reaction to teasing or in sibling rivalry), which results in automatic hidden competitive and/or evasive mechanisms with a mate and close friends. Some inner vows set the being upon untenable courses that lead to breakdowns or explosions. "I'll never let my temper go again; see what resulted when I did." Such a person thereafter may store up repressed angers until a merest spark sets off a holocaust. "Never again will I be unprepared when people ask me a question." Such a person may be tense in every group until he has figured out how to respond to every possible question. When he is put into too many situations involving too many quick adjustments, his inner vow becomes a major contributing factor to a breakdown.

Good inner vows need to be released lest they block normal healthy interchanges. I (John) turned each of my parents' good teachings into a strong inner vow: "Never hit a woman," "Never raise your voice to a woman," "Keep your temper," "Treat every woman as a lady." Such vows might seem good, but they are of the flesh, and binding, not of the spirit in freedom. Those and others of their ilk made me unreal with Paula. Rejecting them did not release a boomerang to violence. Never yet have I hit Paula or tried to wound by insulting, and the fact that I am free to lose my temper and raise my voice has never resulted in my becoming a loud or angry person. Conversely, I am probably less likely to become so for the fact that the Lord, rather than my fleshly determination, has me in those areas. My vows, not released to the Lord, would have locked me into reactions which later would have had to find some form of outlet. Perhaps more importantly, our righteousness must become His, by the flow of His Holy Spirit in us, not by the strivings and consequent prides of fleshly determinations.

How do we find inner vows? By asking. Counselors should look for inner vows behind stubborn practices in the old nature. Compulsive behavior may (or may not) indicate inner vows at their root; other factors may be at work. We must discern in each case whether a vow is in fact at the root of trouble. Where inner vows do lie at the root, seldom are they the sole factor even if major. They work in tandem with bitter roots, hidden resentments and fears, etc. The crucial factor concerning inner vows is that if they are at the root, they are often the key. Their stubborn resistance to change, until seen and repented of, may be what blocks release from all other areas, seen or unseen. Especially whenever counselors find themselves puzzled by continuing lack of change in a counselee, most specifically when many factors have already been discerned and repentance should already have accomplished freedom, inner vows ought to be suspected and ferreted out.

Again, power (*dunamis*) such as would be needed to heal the physical body is not needed, but only the power (*exousia*) of authority. The least Christian who understands his authority (*exousia*) in Christ can break any inner vow. The prayer should not be merely hortatory, not "Help him, Lord, to overcome this inner vow," nor petitionary, "Please take away this inner vow, dear Lord." These will accomplish little if anything. The situation requires prayer in first-person authority: "In Jesus' name, I break this inner vow." It cannot be said as a magic ritual, by one who does not truly know the Lord nor believe his own authority in the Lord. Though demons are not usually involved directly (an inner vow being a structure in the flesh) the same impotence would result if we pray in unfaith, merely copying the ideas given here, as the seven sons of Sceva discovered when they tried to apply the name of Jesus in an unbelieving manner (Acts 19:13-16). No one likes to run naked and defeated. A counselee is set free only if his counselor has his own personal faith in the power and will of the Lord to act.

The prayer should be voiced fully, expressed several ways for the sake of the inner child of the other. "I break this inner vow of withdrawal. I speak directly to the inner child and I say in Jesus' name I release you from this habit of withdrawal. I restore you to the original delight of your soul to share you with your brothers and sisters in Christ. I release you to open your heart and be *with* others. Thank you, Jesus, I see (name of counselee) talking and laughing, no longer afraid to make a mistake, giggling in freedom rather than embarrassment. I praise you, Lord, that you will continue until (the person's name) realizes one day with an exclamation of joy, 'Hey, it's true, I'm free, even as we prayed that day.' Thank you, Jesus, Amen."

12

Hearts of Stone

Moreover, I will give you a new heart and put a new spirit within you; and I will remove the heart of stone from your flesh, and give you a heart of flesh. (Ezek. 36:26)

Do not harden your hearts, as in Meribah, As in the day of Massah in the wilderness; When your fathers tested Me, They tried Me, though they had seen My work. For forty years I loathed that generation, And said, they are a people who err in their heart. And they do not know My ways. Therefore I swore in My anger, Truly they shall not enter into my rest. (Ps. 95:8-11, italics mine).

God wants to raise a people with whom He can have fellowship, "That you also may have fellowship with us; and indeed our fellowship is with the Father, and with His Son Jesus Christ" (1 John 1:3). He has saved us for himself. It is not so much that He wants servants, as friends (John 15:15). "And the Scripture was fulfilled which says, 'And Abraham believed God, and it was reckoned to him as righteousness,' *and he was called the friend of God*" (James 2:23, italics mine). "Jesus answered and said to him, 'If anyone loves Me, he will keep My word; and My Father will love him, and We will come to him, and *make Our abode with him*'" (John 14:23, italics mine).

To have fellowship with God requires capacity within our spirit to commune with Him. "God is spirit; and those who worship Him must worship in spirit and truth" (John 4:24). In human conversations almost everyone has experienced those rare moments when communion of spirit enabled us to so read each other's hearts we seemed to comprehend before words were spoken. Other times, our words appeared to bounce off invisible walls. We know then we have spoken *at* each other but not *with* each other. Real fellowship is dependent upon the ability of our spirits to reach out and blend with one another.

We can understand and be refreshed in one another's company solely because our spirits reach beyond our bodies to meet and nourish one another. Anyone who has touched the clamminess of a corpse has recognized the absence of spirit. A "dead fish" handshake is defined by that fact, lack of meeting and embracing. How often have we spent hours with someone, only to realize "I never really met him," or in a moment's embrace felt that we had always known as a friend, someone we just met?

To be able to meet God, we must have God's Spirit within us. "For who among men knows the thoughts of a man except the spirit of the man, which is in him? Even so the thoughts of God no one knows except the Spirit of God" (1 Cor. 2:11). Men can understand men because each possesses a man's spirit. Similarly, all creation seeks its own, cats with cats, dogs with dogs, and so on. No cow ever mistakes a horse for a cow, because a cow's spirit knows its own. *By design*, each species communes with its own. But God has created us human, and yet desires to have fellowship with us! In the beginning, He made us able, endowed with His own Spirit (Gen. 2:7). Adam and Eve walked and talked with Him in the Garden (Gen. 3:8-24). But in the Fall mankind lost that capacity. We died in sin. Our attempts to commune with God became like a machine wired for 100 volts trying to plug into a billion. No wonder the Israelites cried out, "Speak to us yourself and we will listen; but let not God speak to us, lest we die" (Exod. 20:19).

So God came in human flesh, in Jesus, that through Him we might be restored to fellowship. Our Lord Jesus Christ poured out the Holy Spirit upon us so that we might have within us again the power to comprehend Him and His love

(1 Cor. 2 and Eph. 3:18), to commune and walk with Him in spirit (Rom. 8).

The difficulty is that the Holy Spirit comes to reside inside the barbed wire of our still-too-inhuman nature. The Spirit, like water, must flow out through the shape of what we are. And God's approaches to us have to be interpreted by our still-imperfect, corrupted mentality. The union of the Holy Spirit in our *spirit* may be full and true, but meanings can become twisted altogether by the *heart* and *mind*. For example, if He comes to embrace us because of His love and compassion in the midst of our suffering, we can and often do take that moment of glory in His presence as confirmation that our wrong way is not only right but His will for us.

It follows then that the more our hearts are open to Him and the more our minds comprehend, the better our fellowship. Conversely, the more hard and stubborn our hearts are and the less our mind is akin to His, the less our ability to abide in fellowship. If our spirit meets His, understanding must match or we can not sustain. That is why Jesus said, ". . . in spirit *and truth*" (John 4:24). Spirit to spirit without truth causes a relationship to flow like a bankless river in the desert—soon gone! Truth alone is only mind to mind—and barren! Neither without the other can produce or sustain fellowship. Both spirit and truth together spark and enhance in crescendo to blessedness.

In the beginning, our marriage to the Lord overflows all our barriers, like a flood spilling over a dam. But we are still too carnal, too immature in faith to maintain that fullness of relationship. Soon the flow is behind the dam again, and we wonder where the Lord went. He is right there of course, but we can't sustain full fellowship due to our hardness of heart and lack of faith. Truth didn't match spirit; we couldn't abide.

The same happens in human relationships. At times our spirits overleap all barriers and we enjoy enriching fellowship. Other times we live in pockets of loneliness.

In order to enable true fellowship between humans and with himself, God has to pierce or melt our hearts of stone so that His Spirit and ours can flow *through* to one another rather than only occasionally *over*. In our fallen condition, we are like medieval knights in armor, peering out slits to slash and poke at one another, wishing that other fellow would open up so we could really meet him.

The problem is a malformation of character, formed long before age six, but between six and twelve it is either overcome or cemented. The spirit which God breathed into us at creation (Gen. 2:7) found itself confined within the body, required to find expression through the corrupted soul of mankind's inherited nature. Whether we began at creation as some believe, or at conception, as others assert, once in the flesh we are all equally subject to the sinful condition of mankind, but each spirit may also experience uniquely harmful factors. Parents may not want the pregnancy. Quarreling, tension and too much violence may rend the atmosphere. By the time a person emerges from the womb, or shortly thereafter, his spirit's ability to trust and open to life may be greatly hindered or blocked altogether. "The wicked are estranged from the womb; Those who speak lies go astray from birth"(Ps. 58:3). All of us are "the wicked," "no one does right" (Ps. 14 and Rom. 3).

All conscientious, well-intentioned mothers are normally frequently unable to interpret their baby's signals correctly. Baby is hungry, but mama changes its diaper. Or the child is not hungry; a pin sticks or diaper rash bothers, or voices have startled him or maybe he just wants to have a good cry, but mother puts her breast in his mouth! Perhaps papa burps the infant with a rough hand when all he wanted was a gentle rocking to sleep. Or brothers and sister keep on pestering, making noises and funny faces, when all he wants is peace and quiet. Or, most likely at 2:00 AM when baby wants to giggle and play, everybody else wants to sleep! In the best of homes constant irritants are a normal part of a baby's life. What can he do with his emotions? With angers? Resentments? Loneliness? Fears? Longings? Or with needs for solitude? He doesn't yet know the Lord, so as to be able to forgive. The mind has not developed so as to rationalize. Self-control has not yet been built. There are no stopping places; he has to *be* stopped, by touch and comforting, strength of daddy and warmth of mama; but often parents aren't there or they fail to understand. He just plain hurts when he hurts and revels when he revels.

Include along with such normal irritants, in some cases, rejection, prolonged absences and consequent unabated loneliness. Every baby knows and seeks his own daddy and mommy. As John the Baptist at six months *en utero* could recognize the presence of Jesus in Mary (Luke 1:44), so every baby spiritually knows his own. But many are given up for adoption. However adults may rationalize and believe what they do is best, to the baby that is nothing else than horrendous rejection. Or the father may little realize his own value and fail to rock and play, hold and comfort, walk and talk in the long night hours. Mama may have been trained, in that most horribly wrong school, never to hold lest she spoil—four hours in the crib, feed, and four more in the crib. Or mother may decide not to nurse or be unable to do so. How can a baby handle such hurts? With what emotional tools?

In far too many instances, add violence and terror. Some parents are bestial. Red, shouting faces loom over the crib. Again and again, raving drunken noises shatter sleep. Hitting and screeching may break out at any moment. There are no dependabilities to rest in.

What can a baby do to protect himself? He hastens to build walls around his heart! He learns to check the impulse to let his spirit flow out unguarded to another. Gradually, but most surely, he forms a heart of stone. Babies in deplorable homes can hardly keep from forming strong turtle shells. Every person on earth has fashioned such a heart, some softer, some harder and thicker, depending usually upon the degree of pain suffered.

One family we knew made it their ministry to receive foster babies from violent or broken homes. When the tiny babies arrived, they were rigid and tense, unable to let down into an embrace. Their eyes stared, seeing nothing. After a few weeks of love and prayer, the babies became warm, cuddly, soft, and laughing. Their little spirits leaped joyfully into whoever held them.

But what of the many tragically wounded not so healed by love?

All of us, having formed hearts of stone, have to that degree failed to become fully human. To that same degree, we have closed down the very faculties needed for real interchange of heart and mind. We will not let the spirit be vulnerable, open to touch and embrace. It hurts too much. We hide behind stone walls. We are like the boy in Wordsworth's "Ode on Intimations of Immortality"

> Our birth is but a sleep and a forgetting:
> The Soul that rises with us, our life's Star,
> Hath had elsewhere its setting,
> And cometh from afar:
> Not in entire forgetfulness,
> And not in utter nakedness,
> But trailing clouds of glory do we come
> From God, who is our home:
> Heaven lies about us in our infancy!
> *Shades of the prison house begin to close*
> *Upon the growing Boy,*
> But he beholds the light, and whence it flows,
> He sees it in his joy;
> The Youth, who daily farther from the east
> Must travel, still is Nature's Priest,
> And by the vision splendid
> Is on his way attended;
> *At length the man perceives it die away,*
> *And fade into the light of common day.*

Our spirit's faculties, shut up and imprisoned, wither and atrophe like unused muscles. We become like Sleeping Beauty or Snow White, asleep within while all our dwarfed talents weep without. It takes a prince charming (Jesus) to awaken our numbed spirit to life again. Or we become like the tin man, rusted to a stop, needing the oil of the Holy Spirit before we can walk the long yellow brick road to find a heart. That, by the way, is why such stories as Snow White and the Wizard of Oz continue to live—they tell the truth about us, and something inside is still alive enough to know it! Some people have talked all their lives, and have never known a moment's communication. Some have never enjoyed true human fellowship, much less divine. Worse, such individuals may have little or no consciousness of their lack. They get along by surface, monkey-see-monkey-do sharing, insensitive not only that their heart and spirit has not met the other but ignorant that something else is available. They have become zombies walking through a luscious garden, wearing glasses which prevent them from seeing anything but dandelions.

Real conscience arrives solely by the ability of our spirit to love, to meet, to enter in and share another's life for the other's sake. That is why Jeremiah wrote, "Were they ashamed because of the abomination they have done? They were not even ashamed at all; They did not even know how to blush. Therefore they shall fall among those who fall" (Jer. 6:15). Their spirits were too nonfunctional to have enabled true conscience. That is one reason St. Paul also wrote, "Do you not know that God's kindness is meant to lead you to repentance?" (Rom. 2:4 RSV). It is God's kindness which so touches the heart with the kiss of life that the spirit revives, enabling the conscience to function; only then can repentance happen.

In "I-Thou" encounters, each "I" meets and treats any other person as a revered "Thou," spirit to spirit, heart to heart, mind to mind, openly and without impediment. I-Thou can be pictured by imagining two sparks radiating light into and through each other until, if one is blue and the other yellow, a green field suffuses both equally without eradicating either, at once brightening both the original yellow and blue. Whoever learns to live in I-Thou relationships learns to cherish the other. He hurts in anticipation of the other's hurt and therefore stops *before* a personal action might damage the other. This is the true function of conscience.

To the degree of adamancy (hardness, imprisonment, stubborness) in their hearts, people are unable to enter into I-Thou relationships. Their encounters are thereby delimited to "I-it" (Martin Buber, *I-Thou*). Attempts originate not purely from their "I" but also from their shell, reaching only meagerly the "Thou" of the other, mainly only his shell. So the picture is of two much-diminished lights beneath nutshells, bouncing blue and yellow rays off one another mostly unchanged. No green of mutuality appears, except in flicks of chance in the passing rays. Such people do not have functioning consciences, because to them no other has ever become a cherished "Thou." Any other remains only an "it" to bounce off of, attack, or climb over.

The tragedy of our culture is that men and women are becoming progressively less human. God wants to raise human beings. Jesus, who is patient and kind, gentle and compassionate, loving and forgiving, is the only truly human person. We are to become more and more human, more warm and loving, vulnerable and compassionate.*

The task of fathers and mothers is to evoke humanity in their children. In the beginning, to call forth the spirit to embrace. Then to build "truth," the ability of heart and mind to interpret meanings and cherish others' intents. Thus, though each child must bear responsibility for the choices of his spirit, God holds parents accountable (Heb. 13:17) for they either enable or prevent "I-Thou" encounters. Insofar as others can *condition us to life, it is parents who either make us human, or inhuman!*

In the command, ". . . bring them up in the nurture and admonition of the Lord" (Eph. 6:4 KJV), it is those last words which tell. Only nurture *in the Lord* brings forth children who have learned how to contribute their "I" in love to another "Thou" without overriding or being themselves dominated. Above all, parents are to produce children who have dis-

---

* We are not advocating "humanism," which is Satan's copy, in which man exalts himself, but our Lord's resurrection of mankind to His fullness in humanity.

covered the secret of joy, that abundant life is found in laying down one's life in sacrificial service for every other "Thou." We are to produce children who then as adults persistently choose never to treat another "Thou" as a usable, discardable, destructible "it"!

"But realize this, that in the last days difficult times will come. For men will be lovers of self, lovers of money, boastful, arrogant, revilers, disobedient to parents, ungrateful, unholy, unloving, irreconcilable, malicious gossips, without self-control, brutal, haters of good, treacherous, reckless, conceited, lovers of pleasure rather than lovers of God; *holding to a form of godliness, although they* have *denied its power;* and avoid such men as these" (2 Tim. 3:1-5).

That prophecy receives increasing fulfillment today primarily because fathers and mothers have failed to cherish. Hardened, inhuman hearts are the result. Consequently such persons have no true conscience. They cannot relate to the power of God, which is love, because they have never received it. Their spirits are dormant and incapable (dead in transgressions, Eph. 2:5). For that reason the curse of street gangs ravages city streets. Vandalism forces architects to build schools which look like prisons, without breakable windows. Parks must find indestructible toilet and sink fixtures. And crime rates soar. Repressed anger at parents must find outlets. The curse *is* beginning to come upon our land— "Behold, I am going to send you Elijah the prophet before the coming of the great and terrible day of the Lord. And he will restore the hearts of the fathers to their children, and the hearts of the children to their fathers, lest I come and smite the land with a curse" (Mal. 4:5-6).

Each sin listed in 2 Timothy 3:1-5 can happen only because the perpetrators cannot see and cherish any other "Thou." I (John) being a normal person, would have to mentally subhumanize my brother to steal from him, or else the pain would be too great. The same goes for adultery, gossip, treachery, whatever. In order to defraud Indians, Americans dulled their consciences by calling Indians "savages," something less than human, objects to be gotten rid of—"the only good Injun is a dead 'un." Blacks had to be regarded as less than human by slave owners, or else they could not have reduced them to chattel in slavery. In those who have never known themselves as loved and cherished, no other can possibly be a "Thou." Lady Macbeth, desiring to do evil, cried out, "Come, you spirits that tend on mortal thoughts! Unsex me here, and fill me from the crown to the toe top-full of direst cruelty; make thick my blood, stop up the access and passage to remorse, that no compunctious visitings of nature shake my fell purpose . . ." (Macbeth, Act 1, Scene 5), lest her too human feeling prevent. But those listed in 2 Timothy 3 have no need to dehumanize themselves; they already have become dehumanized! Increasing crime rates are therefore nothing more nor less than the mark of our defection from true parenthood in the Lord.

It is humanity that Satan desires to destroy.

It is the heart of stone which is Satan's tool to block humanity.

It is parents whom God intended to call forth to enable hearts of flesh to develop in their children.

It is parents who are to call forth a "Thou" to life.

It is parents who often force a child to build walls of stone.

It is Jesus who became human to meet and melt hearts of stone, to give us hearts of flesh.

It is a heart of flesh in Jesus which is God's gift to restore humanity.

It is Jesus who makes us human.

That is the work of a counselor in Christ, to see how and when a child reacted in pain to flee and hide. The task is to see the heart of stone and melt it in the fire of love. Though parents create the problem, the counselor must deal with the child's guilt for reacting. Therefore confession and forgiveness again are the access to the efficacy of the cross. But whereas authority can break an inner vow, and the blood can wash away guilt, and daily death of self on the cross brings a practice of the old nature to death on the cross, more is involved here than all these. For that reason Jesus came to "baptize you with the Holy Spirit *and with fire*" (Matt. 3:11, italics mine). Only the fire of love can melt a heart of stone. Hansel and Gretel were brother and sister playing happily in the fields. Along came the wicked snow queen, who cast a dart of ice into Hansel's heart, froze him, and carried him away. Gretel went through great perils a long time searching for him. But when she finally found him, Hansel was not happy to see her. He reviled and shouted at her and spat upon her. At last her love warmed him, the ice thorn slipped out, and Hansel came to himself. Gretel and Hansel played happily together in the fields again.

Just so, companions and counselors must search patiently to find the frozen hearts of their friends. But the most common sign of returning life is that the warmer the love given the meaner the response. Fear of vulnerability creates hate. Each stony heart has a life of its own. It sings lies into the mind. "You know what happened before when you risked yourself." "You don't want to get hurt again." "It may be lonely this way, but at least it's safe." Some of those songs may be true. The lie is that it's better to be alone and dying. So the person we are trying to love to life strikes back.

Jesus said, "Blessed are you when men revile you, and persecute you, and say all kinds of evil against you falsely, on account of Me. *Rejoice,* and be glad, *for your reward is great . . .*" (Matt. 5:11-12, italics mine). Why rejoice? Our reward is that the other is coming to life! The life of the person is our joy, our reward. The sign of coming to life is pain, like when our leg has fallen asleep, and the first we are aware of it is when we feel a million pricking needles of pain—the reason is that the leg is coming to life again! But our loved one built that hiding place precisely to escape pain. Therefore the attack is automatic, to remove the menace before the walls crumble altogether. Rejoicing is part of praise and worship, which keeps the flow of Jesus' life pummeling the walls with torches of fire.

Who has not seen dating couples break apart, strangely

enough because they drew so close that their hearts were becoming vulnerable? Husbands, more frequently than wives, often become meaner and meaner the more their wives express love. Just so, the transformation of hearts of stone is not accomplished by distant, safe prayers and well wishings. Hearts of stone can only be melted by persistent, pain-bearing hearts willing to lay themselves down daily, understanding and forgiving every time the quarry turns to attack, until the ice thorn melts. Precisely this kind of love is fire. "God is love" (1 John 4:8) and "Our God is a consuming fire" (Heb. 12:29). The love of God is made manifest in Jesus, whose walk of love on earth culminates in crucifixion in love for mankind. "I have a baptism to be baptized with and how I am constrained until it be accomplished" (Luke 12:5 RSV). What He accomplished was the cross. The baptism of redemptive suffering for another is fire. It is when a heart suffers unjustly while loving the attacker that love turns to fire. That kind of fire melts stone to lava—isn't it striking that it takes mountains of pressure to produce fire and molten rock!

Sam cannot understand what his wife is talking about. He brings home the bacon. He never goes out with the fellows, never drinks, never swears, never hits her, and goes to church with her regularly. But she is miserable. He does not know that he does all these things only by duty, like a robot. When he kisses her, which is seldom, it is because duty and unmistakable signals demand it. But for Lucy, living with him is like continually knocking on the door of an empty house. Each time she steps in and calls out, "anybody home," she hears only echoes. There's never anybody home in Sam's inner house! Neither of them can understand. On the surface even to her he is such a nice guy. Sam's parents were good people. They provided well. He never lacked for things. And they were never unkind or brutal. But they never touched or held. Sam came into marriage with a hidden heart of stone. He is still a tin man. He can not feel, meet, cherish, and be cherished. Lucy lives in a desert—nice, always nice—nevertheless still a desert.

Ann came to me (John) discouraged because depression and thoughts of suicide continually beset her. She had a good husband, healthy children, plenty of money, friends and good things all around her. In short, Ann had arrived. She had everything. Performing had won her a nice life. But all that blessedness was empty. There seemed no reason for sadness, and for that, guilt increased the depression. Ann couldn't feel. She never had been able to feel. Her parents were cold, principled people. She had done well in school, and even yet remained artistically superior. Recently, she had tasted enough real life in a Holy Spirit-filled prayer group in her church to discover hints of life. She wanted more, but she couldn't get going, like being stuck in neutral, unable to get in gear. She had a heart of stone.

Frequently, people who have hearts of stone are like Sam and Ann. They perform well. They do for others. But they can't feel. Most often, the telling mark is that they can't let others do for them. In those who cannot do for others, the heart of stone is no longer hidden. Everyone recognizes it, and we speak of it in the vernacular, "Who, that hard-hearted so and so?" But in people like Sam and Ann the heart of stone is most difficult to see because everyone sees their actions and thinks of them as loving people. The last thing most people would suspect of them is hardness of heart.

Ministers, doctors, and lawyers most commonly are afflicted with hidden, ossified hearts. Those who were born with loving natures, but prevented from learning true give and take, built strong walls to protect those naturally tender hearts. Now, for example, that loving nature expresses itself in the family doctor in a most compassionate bedside manner. He becomes a greatly loved father-confessor to most everybody in the town. Everybody praises him. All the town and church tell the doctor's wife what a fortunate woman she must be, to have such a saintly, gentle, loving husband. Suppressing a desire to scream, she agrees politely and rushes home to surreptitiously gulp another jigger of whiskey, hoping she can survive another day. "If only they could see him like I do!" He can't let anyone love him, especially close family members. He must minister to everyone else. All who know about her "problem" pity that saintly man stuck with that drunken wife. But they don't know; "He will not judge by what His eyes see, nor make a decision by what His ears hear" (Isa. 11:3). Hopefully, something will happen to break through. "God is not so unjust as to overlook your labor of faith and love" (1 Thess. 1:3). God wants to reward His servant by setting him free.

God himself may send such a person a breakdown. Perhaps, when weakened he will learn to receive. We have noted that strong, serving people (who have never learned to receive) often have long, debilitating illnesses before they die. If everyone in heaven has only learned to serve, who will receive? Or the Lord may send a true persistent friend, who will risk enough to tell him hurtful truth. "Faithful are the wounds of a friend; profuse are the kisses of an enemy" (Prov. 27:6 RSV). Perhaps his own inmost spirit will begin to raise questions—"The spirit of man is the lamp of the Lord, searching all his innermost parts" (Prov. 20:27 RSV). "Stripes that wound scour away evil, And strokes reach the innermost parts" (Prov. 20:30). Some way, God will reach the heart. Our point is to friends and counselors that most often such blessings will come in disguise. We need to celebrate the stern hand of God, and stand by ready to pick up the pieces.

Better of course when hearts can be reached in easier ways. A Christian counselor must penetrate—by logic, touch, the Word of God—whatever accomplishes insight in the other's *heart* (not mind). Talk and prayers must be to that end, to reach to the causes in early family life. But from there on the struggle is not ended, it has only begun. The heart alternately receives and rejects, comes forward and retreats, embraces and attacks, storms and lapses into silences. Counselors need to remember this teaching, and not be dismayed or become discouraged when the patient flips out and reverts just when everything seemed to be going well. We cannot beat such people forward into life. They have to be moved there by the "kisses" of the Prince Charming (Jesus) through us. (This does not mean physical kisses or hands inappropriately touching, but only warm touches in the Lord.)

Counselors must not abdicate their responsibility. The person's budding life is for that time dependent on our steadfastness in loving. We must not hand the person back solely to Jesus. Agnes Sanford, greatest of faith healers at the time, came to us (John and Paula) needing love to come out of her walls of depression and live again (after the death of her husband). We couldn't believe this great saint needed us. We handed her back to the Lord in prayer. She went away crushed. She could move mountains by faith to give healing to countless others, and had no faith at all to receive from God for herself! She needed God's love through human vessels. Counselors must know their worth as God's messengers of love.

Sometimes Jesus will sovereignly and quickly melt a heart of stone. Testimonies of such abound. But far more frequently He chooses to do it slowly—oh, so slowly—through human vessels. Perhaps so as to create the bonds of love in His Church. To heal hearts of stone, He calls us to be true friends. Counseling is then not gimmickry and not mainly prayer, but friendship. "There are friends who pretend to be friends, but there is a friend who sticks closer than a brother" (Prov. 18:24 RSV). "Two are better than one, because they have a good return for their work: If one falls down, his friend can help him up. But pity the man who falls and has no one to help him up! Also, if two lie down together, they will keep warm. But how can one keep warm alone? Though one may be overpowered, two can defend themselves. A cord of three strands is not quickly broken" (Eccles. 4:9-12 NIV).

The best oven for melting hearts is not a single counselor only but a group in the church. One frozen intellectual in our church stormed in and out of fellowship regularly. But the prayer groups persistently prayed for him and met him at the door with hugs. They lightheartedly sidestepped his brilliant mind and met him with embracing spirits and bodies. Before long, he found excuses to let people know he was leaving, in order not to succeed in passing the door without being hugged half a dozen times. No way was he ready to admit what he was doing, or what was happening. Eventually he received the Lord and became the warmest greeter at the door, hugging everyone.

To sum up, hearts of stone, like inner vows, lie hidden, often behind warmest exteriors. The telling mark is not an expressively loving nature but inability to receive love. Like inner vows, hearts of stone resist change. Unlike inner vows, authority will not beneficially affect a heart of stone. Only prayer and persistent touch will set fire and bring to life. Love becomes fire when refused or attacked and given anyway. Rejoice and persist.*

---

* For further information, see chapter two, "A Heart of Flesh and a Heart of Stone" in *Restoring the Christian Family.*

13

Flight, Control, Burial and Possessiveness

Brethren, my heart's desire and my prayer to God for them is for their salvation. For I bear them witness that they have a zeal for God, but not in accordance with knowledge. For not knowing about God's righteousness, and seeking to establish their own, they did not subject themselves to the righteousness of God. For Christ is the end of the law for righteousness to everyone who believes.
(Rom. 10:1-4)

Since therefore the children share in flesh and blood, he himself likewise partook of the same nature, that through death he might destroy him who has the power of death, that is, the devil.
(Heb. 2:14-15 RSV)

Imagine the position of a child, two to twelve years old. Father and mother, and perhaps others such as grandparents (who live in the home), are all adults. Older brothers and sisters may be there too. In the beginning, everything these older people know is foreign to him. He must accomplish everything they have long taken for granted. Walking, talking, controlling body functions, eating (properly, no less), embracing, refraining from touch, not interrupting, dressing, being mannerly, teasing, laughing and joking, remembering, picking things up, placing things in order, and countless other skills—all have to be mastered, quickly it seems. Adults are on the last legs of the marathon, but an infant is just beginning. Punishment, scorn and laughter often accompany failure.

Fear is therefore indigenous to childhood. It comes with the package.

Several kinds of fear beset infants, and continue to plague them well into maturity. The greatest of these is anxiety. Anxiety is normally a healthy precursor to fear itself. Anxiety is a state of apprehension (see *Anxiety* by Rollo May) in which our spirit senses something wrong. Like the DEW line, it is an early warning system. Anxiety is meant to marshal energies for action. We sense something wrong (that's anxiety); instant cascades of messages pour through the body, producing adrenaline, preparing the body. We locate the energy (a growling dog, an angry face, something hurtling at us), and that energy is instantly channeled into appropriate action— flight, fighting or whatever.

There is nothing wrong with anxiety, pain, fear, or anger, or most any other emotion. All are normal, healthy functions. Part of the task of maturation is to learn how to handle them. Without anxiety, energies could not be at hand on time. Without fear we would not know to leap out of the way of a speeding car. Without pain we would not have sense enough to remove our hands from a hot stove. Anxiety, fear, and pain are most blessed parts of our equipment. They act like sentinels, preserving us from harm, or alerting us for blessing.

But all are meant to be temporary. Like minutemen, at constant beck and call, they are meant to flash into action long enough to move the body to safety or to whatever end is desired, and then to return to rest, ready but dormant. We cannot stand to live too long in any heightened emotion, even joy, without becoming hyper or exhausted.

When an animal cannot locate its enemy, or having done so, cannot come to a decision concerning how to act, anxiety paralyzes it. Deer and rabbits can move as quick as a flash, but often they are smashed by cars because though anxiety summoned great instant energy, blinding headlights squashed their ability to decide which way to flee, until that life-saving energy itself became the cause of death by "overloading the circuits," paralyzing the victim.

Infants and children, like adults, soon learn to sense when some word or action of theirs causes a reaction in others. How often have we all sensed resistance or shock, or some negative reaction as we were speaking, and quickly changed emphasis or attitude? In a split second energies were summoned, decisions arrived at and battle was averted or started, or blessedness resulted.

We make those flash decisions on the basis of built-in patterns. Some practiced patterns in our nature serve us well, enhancing communication, and some defeat our relationships. Patterns of flight, manipulation and control break blessedness. Patterns of empathy, compassion, courage, openness, understanding, and love enable. We build those practiced patterns of response in infancy and early childhood; they have become "foundation stones" in the house of our character.

The crucial building factor is gentle love or its absence. Where the river of love flowed from spirit to spirit among adults, couched in firm but gentle, sensitive actions, our infant spirit sensed moments of error without dread. Anxiety then hooked into no stored wells of fear. Happy adults, at ease and easily forgiving, encourage the building of habits which facilitate rather than hamper relationships. We see an example of this in what happens when a baby cries. Babies need to cry. Physically, it strengthens the lungs. Emotionally, it releases tension. As a baby cries, his spirit senses reactions in adults around him. If whoever holds him is angry, anxiety alerts, increasing the wailing. Gentle love soothes the spirit, calming anxiety, turning energies into delightful embrace. Repeated negative experiences build automatic responses either of tightening up in fear or rebelling in punitive anger. Continual gentle touches say to an infant, "It's okay to cry. It's okay to be you. I can receive you no matter what you do." Love thus creates freedom to be, freedom to venture, freedom from dread of error, and consequent ability to be spontaneous and happy. There, in our first experiences, are built the structures by which we respond to others throughout life.

Through many early encounters, we learn either to laugh and love, risking easily, or to recoil in fear behind defensive walls and bitter expectations. We build habit structures much like learning to walk. Just as we never again have to think about how to walk, so we develop practiced ways of relating to others which require no further thought. Soon the framework by which we interpret the approach of others is either factually appropriate, or delusory, and our responses from then on either enable or distort and disable true communication and friendship.

The most common malformations are flight mechanisms. We build them in the first six years, but from six to twelve we either outgrow, overcome, or cement them. By the time we are into our teen-age years our character is set in its mold. Doctors can discover the age of a child by the development of bones and cartilage. An experienced counselor can pinpoint mental age by the development and degree of firmness or rigidity in mental and subconscious patterns. More importantly, the degree of rigidity normally reveals the amount of trauma endured.

Flight patterns bury our talents!

Then the man who had received the one talent came. 'Master,' he said, 'I knew that you are a hard man, harvesting where you have not sown and gathering where you have not scattered seed. So I was afraid and went out and hid your talent in the ground. See, here is what belongs to you.' His master replied, 'You wicked, lazy servant! So you knew that I harvest where I have not sown and gather where I have not scattered seed? Well then you should have put my money on deposit with the bankers, so that when I returned I would have received it back with interest. Take the talent from him and give it to the one who has the ten talents. For everyone who has will be given more, and he will have an abundance. Whoever does not have, even what he has will be taken from him. And throw that worthless servant outside, into the darkness, where there will be weeping and gnashing of teeth.' (Matt. 25:24-30 NIV)

That parable is not merely a story to illustrate a point. It is an exact description of the way reality works! It describes the inevitable operation of the impersonal law of retribution—whoever buries his talent *will* lose what he thinks he has! What does the one have to whom more is given? Trust. Courage to be. Willingness to risk. What is missing from the one who has not? The same.

The first and deepest malformed condition is called by psychologists amniosis. It means an inability to come out of the amniotic fluid and be born, or flight by regression to return to the safe hiding place of the womb; thus either never having come out or having fled back to. Amniotic people want to be taken care of. They want to find strong people—ones in whom they can nestle, upon whom they can become dependent, and by whom they can be mollycoddled. They avoid decisions, confrontations, public speaking or performing, physical risks, competitions, new situations, meeting new people, and creative challenges. They want security, petting but not intimacy, caressing but not fullness of sex, walls rather than open spaces, soft lights rather than glare or darkness, sure things rather than gambles, comfort and not hardship.

Ideal life, to amniotic people, is a comfortable cave (reminiscent of the walls of the womb). Their constant refrain is, "Oh, don't ask me to. . . ." Or, "Why, I wouldn't dare to. . ." (accompanied by fluttering eyelids and a hand over the chest). Or, "Who would ever think of such a thing?" Prophets, or anyone else who would rock the boat, are threats to such people, to be avoided like the plague—or run out of the church by one's husband or aggressive wife.

Paula and I knew one lovely lady who met a fine young man in college and having married him, promptly fell into the nest-making syndrome. Nothing could lure her out. She had her nest and her fine young provider and nobody was going to get her away from it. She wouldn't go skiing with him, or sailing, or water-skiing. She didn't like to socialize with him. She soon had her three boys, and life centered around feeding and bedding. She would have overprotected her sons if her flambuoyant husband had not refused, and had not energetically taken them out to do things. He tried again and again to draw her out into the good earth with him. If she agreed and tried, like going water-skiing, her spirit was so not with it, and coordination so consequentially poor, it dampened the whole party, and she fled with great relief to her secure home. Her husband's adventurous, fun-loving spirit was soon lonely and finally despondent and angry. He had trust, zest, hunger, and questing for life. She had none. She refused not to bury her talent. He had his own many faults, and she had others than flight and burial. Marital counseling took care of some in both, but the bottom line remained her unwillingness to choose to venture—in social life, fun with him, or in marital sex. The result was no surprise; he finally divorced her. What was hers was taken from her and given to another, to a wife who already "had." Had what? Trust, adventure, and zest for life, a wife who had decided to live, to pay the task master's hard price— the pain of being open and vulnerable.

Paula and I see the parable of buried talents being reenacted countless times, in marriages especially, and throughout life. We know men who go just so far in education or business, who so fail to risk or grow further that another who is willing to risk reaps the promotion or the business deal only a little more venturing would have landed for them. We meet countless people who want to sit down on a plateau with God and build tabernacles to what they have already experienced rather than challenge the next mountaintop, who will not receive the fullness of the Holy Spirit nor operate a gift already received. (See Paul's letters to Timothy—1 Tim. 4:14, 2 Tim. 1:6). We have all experienced knowing people who grab a few friends and settle into comfortable routines rather than venture into something new, to whom a dare is a scare and no fun at all, with whom life is "Peace at any price."

But life is not a stagnant pond. It is a dynamic river. Sooner or later the flow has gone on by, and the boat has gone on without them. Then even what they think they have crumbles and is gone.

People who bury their talents also usually have learned subtle and/or aggressive ways to trap loved ones into their style of life. Amniotic or fearful mothers become smotherers, who cannot let their children be free within the nest, or get out of it later. Turtle-neck fathers hide fear behind responsibility to discipline and protect, and so curb and kill their children's zest to risk and discover. Paula and I have grieved to see some children and adults, from well-behaved families who do everything properly, walking about dead-eyed, with no bounding energies for anything. Their stance says, "If I can just get through life without making any ripples. . . ." We want to throw them off a high bank and say, "Sink or swim, buddy!" We wouldn't; we know that's not the way. But we want to.

When positive confrontations are ruled out by fear, and the controls of discipline are required in a family, such parents resort to manipulation. Amniotics become wheedlers, "Please, mommy doesn't like you to do that. Come on, now be mommy's good girl (or boy)." "That's daddy's good girl; you don't want me to feel bad, now do you?" A sharp, clean "Cut that out!" would have done very well. Manipulative parents tie controls onto natural affections until so many checks invade every impulse that a child or later adult is afraid to venture anything lest someone be offended or left out. Such mothers quite often suddenly become deathly ill just as the son is about to be married, and of course he must "take care of mother; how selfish it would be of me to think of marriage just now."

We believe that the most common, basic reason so many churches split whenever the Lord does something new is simple flight and burial; for example, the fearful reactions and persecution which may result if God impresses a people to build a new sanctuary or to start a new program, or if He suddenly pours in a fresh infilling of the Holy Spirit, or wants His people to discover new dimensions and gifts of power in Him. "What's wrong with the old building?" "We've gone as far as we can go." "Don't bother us with the new." "We've got all we can handle." "We want to settle down with what we've learned to manage." "Mission begins at home you know." "We've got to learn to take care of our own first." These things actually say, "We're comfortable." "Our real god is the nice life." "We're in control." "Don't rock the boat." Prophets and pastors are persecuted sometimes simply because they hear the beat of a new drummer. They say, "Get up and move."

The nine plagues in Egypt may have been more to break the hold of slavery and comfortable ruts on Israel than to bother Pharaoh. Note, *God hardened* Pharaoh's heart not to let Israel go (Exod. 4:21 and 7:3). Why? Because He knew if He didn't frighten and disgust Israel thoroughly enough about Egypt, through the nine plagues, they would soon flee back to slavery for the comfort of abdication from the responsibilities of freedom. Even so, they wanted to flee back (Exod. 17:2-3). So many people are so conditioned in fear and comfort in childhood that mankind never yet has consistently chosen the rigors of freedom! Our nation today flees back to such overdependence upon such otherwise good things as Social Security, Aid to Dependent Children, Workmen's Compensation, pensions, insurances, and assurances, that no man can get elected who seems willing to cut back on these things. The nation that fought a revolution for the right to be independent of the provision of a king, now says to its government, "Take care of us." Flight and burial proliferate in a society which turns away from God. The freedom we think we have is soon surrendered and then easily taken from us.

For years scientists wanted to study wild, razorback hogs in Arkansas, but they couldn't catch and hold enough to observe their habits. One wise, old black man volunteered, and in six weeks brought in an entire herd. "How did you do it!" "Easy, ah jest put out some food. Pretty soon dey done get so used to it, dey couldn't do without it. Ah done brung 'em in easy." The point is manipulation and control, by comfort and feeding.

"Where the spirit of the Lord is, there is freedom" (2 Cor. 3:17 RSV). The inverse is a law, "Where the Spirit of the Lord is not, there is lack of freedom." Where there is no freedom, manipulation and control are the prison house. We manipulate and control one another in families until it seems natural and right to do so, and to live under such in society and government. Amniotics are not always milk toasts. Aggression is a common tool for control. Once a loved one begins to knuckle under to an amniotic's controlling devices, the amniotic's heart gains courage in that arena to try other things. Anger is soon added to the arsenal of controlling weapons.

Honest anger helps. Dishonest anger manipulates. Anger is not sin. Jesus never sinned, but He "looked around at them with anger, grieved at their hardness of heart" (Mark 3:5 RSV). "Be angry. [That's a command.] But do not sin; do not let the sun go down on your anger" (Eph. 4:26 RSV). What we *do* with anger is either sin or blessing.

Paula used to become angry at me when I would retreat into my cave. Her anger was not manipulation. It was born of love for me. It hauled me back to the vows I made to be with her. It left me free to choose my cave if I wanted to but it also let me know she didn't like it. That was honest anger, and it helped.

Dishonest anger is not born of love for the other. It is born of a desire to get one's way, a tool to that end. It is not *for* the other, for *his* sake, but *at* him, *for the manipulator's sake only.* Its desired end is not blessing and fulfillment for the other, that he might come into all he should be. It is precisely to keep the other from becoming what he would be so that the manipulator can return to rest, having prevented and controlled the other for selfish, self-centered purposes. Honest anger is born of death of self in love for the other and is willing to risk loss of acceptance and position if it will only set the other free to become. Dishonest anger is the exact opposite. It is born of self-will as a technique and would not dare to be ventured if the perpetrator thought it would risk loss. Its aim is to keep, not for the other, but for the manipulator. Its purpose is to prevent the other from becoming, so that the other will become only an extension of one's self, a satellite in one's orbit.

Many couples have never been set free from cycles of angers and manipulations in their parental homes. They know no other style of life. Their marital life therefore becomes a teeter-totter game—"It's my turn to be *it*, I'm the one with the power. Now you let me run you for a while (better yet, forever)" or, "Now you're *it*. You get to shout and rave and I play knuckle under." Whoever has the truth, whichever one manages to get hold of the recognized righteousness of the moment is entitled to be "it," and so the participants battle until it is clear one or the other gets to dominate because he got closer to the truth (kind of like the school-ground game of "stink base," whoever came last off the base of truth had the power and everybody else had to run). Almost all families' "battles" have behind them this delusion, that whoever has the best grab on truth holds the power to make everyone else knuckle under (all of which is totally irrelevant to life in Christ—though religious denominational battles through the centuries have had this same base of delusion behind them!).

Healing for manipulators is not like the way we heal other conditions. Authority breaks inner vows. Friendship overcomes hearts of stone. Forgiveness expressed by a counselor washes away guilt. Joshing and teasing help a performer quit. All these are done by a counselor for the counselee. Nothing a counselor can do can help a manipulator if he does not want to quit! Of course the same is true for all other conditions, but most especially so for flight and manipulation. Nothing but *personal*, individual, inner *decision* can help a manipulator.

All other helps need to be offered by the counselor. He must help the brother (or sister) see what he is doing, and help him to see the roots in his life as a child. He becomes a midwife for the amniotic person more than for any other. He assists God in the birth of the other. He helps God draw the other forth to life. He enables and pronounces forgiveness for hatred of parents in the inner child. He prays love into a starved inner foundling. He encourages, exhorts, scolds and perhaps becomes a father or mother in Christ.

For you know that we dealt with each of you as a father deals with his own children, encouraging, comforting and urging you to live lives worthy of God, who calls you into his kindgom and glory. (1 Thess. 2:11-12 NIV)

But all these will be to no avail in the end if the person himself does not make a determined, resolute stand to choose life, to refuse to bury talents or flee back from the risks of life, nor to manipulate others.

Talent-burying manipulators more than all others have developed huge reward systems behind their sin. They have learned how to make others jump to their tune. To one who feels empty of power because he has forfeited his own life in fear, such power feels *good!* He wants to feel powerful. How often we have seen physically small people rule others with a rod of iron. It feels *good* to that weak, little, old grandmother to make those great, big, powerful sons reel and jump. Sin, by the way, almost always feels good (to the flesh). We wouldn't keep at it if it weren't fun (however painful).

The only way out for turtle-neck, hard-shell controllers is to learn to hate. "Hate . . . evil" (Rom. 12:9 RSV). Only their own virulent hatred of that putrid habit of manipulation and control can hold that thing to the cross long enough to die. We must forgive ourselves for becoming manipulators, but hate it like a death-dealing cancer, or else we won't choose to give up the rewards of power long enough to get rid of it.

Counselors should invite their counselees to do the praying. Other things may be healed as the counselor prays for the counselee, but not the habit of manipulation. The counselor may pray away all the resentments and causes for flight and manipulation, but in the end the counselee must pray, preferably aloud in the counselor's presence—two prayers. One, "I choose life, Lord Jesus. I choose to be here, naked, without devices to cloak me. I choose to trust you and be open to life." And most importantly, "I renounce and reject all these ways of controlling people, Lord. I'm sorry for it, I cast it away from me. Haul me up short, Lord, every time I fall back into it. I hate it. Get me out of it, Lord. Wherein I don't hate it enough, create in me a perfect hatred of this thing which makes me a destroyer of my friends and loved ones."

A person may not be amniotic and yet be one who flees or buries talents. We easily regress in situations of strife to earlier more comfortable or successful patterns. Many times God does not want to answer our cry for help, not because He doesn't want to help but because our cry is that of a regressed little child. If He were to answer, the result would be childishness. He would have confirmed us in immature ways of pleading with parents. He wants mature sons.

Sometimes children have learned that parents don't know how to handle temper tantrums. They may eventually mature beyond loss of control, but may not know that they have learned a more deadly thing. From then on their anger may often be dishonest; they have learned that people will jump to behave or back off if they make a mad bluff rush. We sometimes say of such people, "He is such a strong personality." In fact, the truth is the opposite. Behind that seeming courage and aggressiveness is a learned technique of flight. Below conscious thought the self says, "Attack will cause others to back off. I won't have to reveal myself, or let anyone come close to me, or be real, or stand and talk rationally (which I fear because I'm afraid after all I don't really have it)."

Rape and murder often have fear and flight at root. A person who could not admit his very real angers at his mother, who suppressed his feelings from fear, may later project anger into rape and violence. The real root is fright, fueling anger, and hatred. A frightened little boy lives inside every vile and attacking murderer. Even war is flight from real encounter.

It takes courage to sustain relationships, to stand in and continue to take unintended slights, much more to receive intentional hurts and continue to hold the heart open, knowing it will be lacerated. It takes endurance to continue to return to embrace and to continue to be vulnerable, considering the peccability of mankind in general, much more to keep forbearing the murderous things we know are in those we love (Col. 3:13). Truly it seems life is a hard taskmaster, reaping where it seems most unfair—again and again. So we slip back easily to hiding places.

Silence is a man's most common weapon. He learned as a boy that nothing could get his mother's goat so much as not responding. Now it has become an automatic, forgotten pattern. He has an inner built-in laughing place when fear comes around in the person of his wife. Powerful men, six inches taller than their wives, able in a moment to break them in pieces physically, are often terrified of the primary women in their lives, and consequently they flee from real meeting and embrace. Courageous to a fault in the world, the same man may be a coward at home. Again, only conscious decision, voiced again and again in prayer, will hold a man presently in the arena with his wife. Even the glory of her may frighten him ("I can't live up to this"). He has learned to manage objects and his job well. He feels confident there. But here is this wholly other "Thou" who claims him, and can get to his inmost emotions, who can't be managed or boxed in—help! The very advent of closeness may spark forest fires of flight in his heart. Flight may hide behind office duties, social obligations, church functions, visits to friends, or duties to parents, anything to excuse and purchase time away from the wife and children.

I (John) have often prayed many times the same prayer, "Lord, hold me open to life." "Jesus, make me vulnerable." "Lord, keep me from fleeing from Paula." "Father, let me be all you designed me to be in relation to her." As our sexual relationship has caused me wondrously (as Prov. 5:18-19 says) to be "ravished always with her love," I have perceived another part of me in the moment of rapturous embrace designing how to flee, for fear of further vulnerability! At such times I have learned to pray, "Open me to Paula, Lord, and keep me there. Don't let me flee." Whoever takes it for granted or congratulates himself that he has courage to abide heart to heart in a relationship is like a lawyer who is his own counsel—he has a fool for a client.

Consider the possibility that Adam and Eve may have succumbed to the temptation to eat of the fruit of the knowledge of good and evil simply out of fear—fear of growing into maturity without something going for them—some knowledge, some understanding, some way of controlling life. Perhaps what most caused them to choose to eat of the tree of knowledge was simply fear of standing open ("naked") to life, trusting God blindly; fear of becoming daily something new, with no handles, only trust. Perhaps it was even fear of failure, not knowing the rules of the game. Such knowledge seemed "desirable to make one wise" (Gen. 3:6). How? By appealing to that in man which fears vulnerability to life without the seeming controls of cunning and clever manipulation.

The immediate result of turning from trust and openness before God to fleshly knowledge was hiding by cleverness, "The woman whom *Thou* gavest to be with me, *she gave me* from the tree, and I ate" (Gen. 3:12, italics mine). All this is to say that flight and burial are not the propensity of a few weak ones; they are basic to *all* mankind. Flight is the sinful inclination of the best of us at all times. We choose, and must choose, again and again, every day, to be open to life, to choose God, to choose to risk, to be vulnerable, to pay the daily price of life.

14

Bitter-Root Judgment and Expectancy

*See to it that no one comes short of the grace of
God; that no root of bitterness springing up
causes trouble, and by it many be defiled.
(Heb. 12:15)*

*Do not judge lest you be judged yourselves. For
in the way you judge, you will be judged; and by
your standard of measure, it shall be measured
to you. (Matt. 7:1-2)*

*Do not be deceived, God is not mocked; for
whatever a man sows, this he will also reap.
(Gal. 6:7)*

Burt and Martha came to me (John) for counsel. Burt
thought the problem was pure and simple—Martha was too
fat, and he couldn't stand it! Martha felt awful about herself
but claimed it wouldn't be so hard to get the fat off if Burt
would just quit criticizing her all the time. A few minutes of
questioning revealed some root causes. Burt had grown up
with a mother who not only became obese, she was slovenly.
She failed to care for her appearance. The house was poorly
kept. And she would use the toilet with the door open and the
children running in and out. Burt judged his mother for her
appearance and habits. His bitter-root judgment and consequent expectancy was that his wife would become obese and
slovenly.

Martha had grown up with a father whom she could never
please, no matter how much she tried. He always found
something to criticize; at least that was her perception.
Whether her father was actually that critical was not what
was important to me as a counselor. What was crucial was that

she had judged her father. Since she could not honor her father in that area, life would not go well for her in all similar aspects of life (Deut. 5:16). Her bitter-root judgment and expectancy was that the man of her life would always be critical of her; she would never be acceptable or be able to be pleasing to her man.

When Burt and Martha met, Martha was a slim and beautiful girl. They fell in love and married. In a little while Martha became pregnant. As she grew in size, so did Burt's difficulty to appreciate and compliment her. After delivery it took a while to lose the weight. Burt became increasingly upset and critical.

Burt now was sure he had married someone like his mother (though he couldn't have consciously admitted that inner realization). He found himself increasingly critical and scolding. But that was of course what Martha already expected would happen! Under attack, she became agitated and insecure, so she ate more, for comfort—and grew heavier. As Burt became angrier and more critical, she became more upset, more nervous, more hungry and fatter. All of this affected her ability to keep herself and the house neat. Their judgments and reactions spun to more and more painful levels, until at last she was living with an angry demon and he was living with a blimp!

What created such a destructive spiral? It was not merely psychological expectancy. It is true that he expected his wife to become fat and she expected to be criticized. But psychological expectancy by itself lacks sufficient power to have overcome their determinations to lose weight and to stop criticizing. They had already seen what they were doing to each other before they came. Being Holy Spirit-filled Christians, they had set their wills to quit. They came because they found themselves powerless to stop. They knew they needed help.

The law of judgment *does* have that kind of power. When Burt judged his mother, the law which declares that the measure he metes out he must receive, went into effect. When his judgment dishonored his mother (regardless of whether she merited his judgment, even if his judgment was true) that meant that Deuteronomy 5:16 ensured that life would not go well for him in that regard. Most cogently, his judgment was a seed sown which by law had someday to be reaped. Just as a tiny mustard seed grows to produce a large tree, so a seed of judgment sown increases the longer it remains unrecognized and unrepented of. So we sow a tiny judgment and reap again and again, larger and larger in life.

Every time we do a deed or hold a judgment in the heart, that can be compared to throwing a ball against a wall. If a physicist knows the weight and size of the ball, the distance to the wall, and my hurling power, he can predict when and with what momentum the ball will return. That is natural law. We comprehend that easily enough. But God has not made one law for the natural and another for the spiritual. All things are governed by the same basic laws. The law expressed in physics is, "For every action there must be an equal and opposite reaction." In chemistry it is expressed, "Every equation (or formula) must balance." In moral and spiritual life it is, "Whatsoever a man soweth, that shall he also reap" (Gal. 6:7 KJV) and "Judge not, that you be not judged. For with the judgment you pronounce you will be judged, and the measure you give will be the measure you get" (Matt. 7:1-2 RSV). All things will come to resolution and balance (justice). It is one basic law, described differently in each field.

The law of sowing and reaping, however, adds another dimension. We do not sow one seed and get back one seed. All things increase in God's kingdom. God desires increase in all beneficial things. The first command given to Adam and Eve was to be fruitful and multiply and fill the earth (Gen. 1:28). The man who buried his talent was excoriated by our usually gentle Lord Jesus for not at least putting his talent where it could increase—"Then you ought to have put my money in the bank, and on my arrival I would have received my money back with interest" (Matt. 25:27). The longer a judgment continues unrepented of and unconfessed, the greater increment it gains. We sow a spark and reap a forest fire, or sow to the wind and reap whirlwind. When the Word says, "The measure you give will be the measure you get," I think perhaps it means "in the same regard or area of our life," rather than the same amount (otherwise the Word would contradict itself).

The lovingkindness of God our Father is that He moves on us again and again to prompt us to do some good thing. When we finally act, He lets us reap an hundredfold as though it were all our own idea. He sends servants on earth and in heaven to persuade us not to do some bad thing; but when we do it, He moves heaven and earth to cause us to repent and confess so He can reap all our evil for us in His Son Jesus on the cross!

The law of sowing and reaping was eternally in operation for all the universe before Adam and Eve were created. Before the entrance of sin, the law was designed to bring multiplication of blessings—and it still does so today. But the advent of sin meant that the same law from then on rebounds to destruction. Therefore, the Father, knowing from the ground plan of creation what men would do, planned to send Jesus to reap the evil we deserve. In the following diagram, we can see how our judgments return upon us. Proverbs 13:21 says, "Adversity *pursues* sinners, But the righteous will be *rewarded* with prosperity" (italics mine). The Law of God actively *causes* reward and punishment to come upon us, as surely as any other natural law exacts its due (see diagram 1 on next page).

The seed we sow may be tiny—an anger, a resentment held against some family member as a child—and forgotten. The longer it remains undetected or neglected, the larger it grows. So we may sow a ping-pong ball and reap a nine-story bowling ball!

The grace of Christ on the cross delivers us, as diagram two shows. Colossians 2:13-14 says, ". . . having forgiven us all our transgressions, having cancelled out the certificate of debt consisting of decrees against us and which was hostile to us; and He has taken it out of the way, having nailed it to the cross." There is no cheap grace. Every sin demands resolution.

Forgiveness does not mean God looked the other way or changed His laws. Jesus said, "Do not think that I came to abolish the Law or the Prophets; I did not come to abolish, but to fulfill" (Matt. 5:17). The full legal demand of the law of sowing and reaping was fulfilled in pain upon the body of Jesus in anguish in the heart and soul and spirit of our Lord upon the cross! (See diagram 2 on next page.)

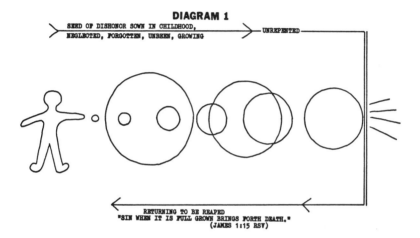

DIAGRAM 1

SEED OF DISHONOR SOWN IN CHILDHOOD, NEGLECTED, FORGOTTEN, UNSEEN, GROWING

UNREPENTED

RETURNING TO BE REAPED
"SIN WHEN IT IS FULL GROWN BRINGS FORTH DEATH."
(JAMES 1:15 RSV)

Nevertheless, the cross is not automatic. If we do not repent and confess, we reap in full despite the fullness of mercy available at a moment's utterance.

Since Burt had judged his mother for obesity, he was due to reap obesity—who would be a more likely person through whom to reap than his wife? His judgment helped first to draw to him a woman who was likely to have a weight problem; then it pushed Martha to gain weight. His necessity to reap what he had sown was therefore returning to him like a mighty wind. For Martha, that was like standing in a hundred-mile-an-hour gale, pushing her to fulfill his legal requirement by gaining weight.

But Martha had her own set of judgments, which first drew her to marry a man who was likely to criticize, and then pushed him to do so. Her seed sown ripened and was reaped through Burt.

Burt and Martha, like most couples, found that they were designed to grind against one another's problems. His judgments exactly matched what she was most likely to become, and her judgments matched his carnal tendencies.

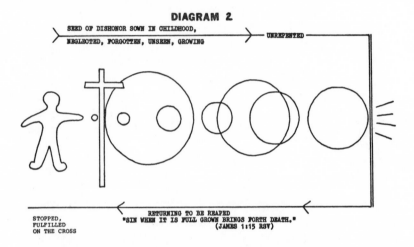

DIAGRAM 2

SEED OF DISHONOR SOWN IN CHILDHOOD,
NEGLECTED, FORGOTTEN, UNSEEN, GROWING
UNREPENTED

STOPPED,
FULFILLED
ON THE CROSS

RETURNING TO BE REAPED
"SIN WHEN IT IS FULL GROWN BRINGS FORTH DEATH."
(JAMES 1:15 RSV)

Burt and Martha are not unique. We have found bitter-root judgments and expectancies in every couple we counsel! Bitter-root judgments are the most common, most basic sins in all marital relationships—perhaps in all of life. These three simple laws affect all life: 1) Life will go well for us in every area in which we could in fact honor our parents and life will not go well in every area in which we could not honor them; 2) We will receive harm in the same areas of life in which we have meted out judgment against others; 3) We will most surely reap what we have sown. We regard these laws as the most powerful keys God has revealed to His people for the healing of relationships. These three laws are the basis of almost all our counseling.

Most couples enter into a relationship with little or no awareness of what they are bringing with them in the heart, or what power those unconscious forces have to influence, drive, and control perceptions, attitudes and behavior. Let diagram *A* represent me (Paula) at the beginning of my marriage with John.

A.

I have pictured myself as an incomplete part of a whole circle; I had some awareness that I was imperfect, unfulfilled, needing completion. But like most young brides I felt I was beginning my new life rather clear, clean and fresh. I had no idea what a large and complex bundle I was bringing into that new life. Like multitudes of Christians, I did not understand that though my sins had been forgiven, I was still the shape of person my experiences in life and my reactions to them had made me to be. I did not know I would be inclined to "see" my husband and relate to him according to the attitudes and expectations of my old nature until in Christ I could experience an interior cutting free from the past and a growing into the new life. The weighty contents of that bundle dragged me down to prevent uninhibited sharing of myself.

B.

They were also at times the trigger points for ammunition to be hurled John's way.

Another factor had to be dealt with. I held an ideal image of who John was and had to be in order to complement me.

C.

IDEAL IMAGE

Notice that the diagram pictures me as being incomplete but rather symmetrically balanced (I *tried* hard to be the person I thought I was, and liked to think I had succeeded in some measure). It was my hope that John's shape of person would fit mine comfortably. Where I had weaknesses and undeveloped areas I earnestly hoped he would be strong and capable so as to fill and strengthen me. Where I had areas of natural skill and strength I hoped he would have the decency to stand back and give me room to express myself. I thought our coming together should be as effortless and painless as possible.

We had not been married long before I discovered that we were not at all shaped for a struggle-less coming together as one. It seemed to me that the picture looked like this (John saw it the other way around):

D.

LIGHT DAWNING

It was obvious that the closer we moved to one another the more we were going to have to make adjustments. It took awhile for the two of us to realize that we were both a mess and that it was part of God's plan in calling us together that we should grind blessedly against each other's natures and so become polished and perfected.

244

God gives us a beloved enemy to force us spiritually lazy people to face what is undealt with in our flesh, else we would go through life ever congratulating ourselves that we are okay without Him.

E.

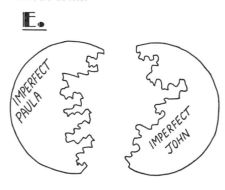

REALITY

Unfortunately what happens in many marriages is that when couples begin to grow close enough to one another that the grinding and polishing process is going on in earnest, they withdraw from the pain, erect defensive walls to hide their vulnerability, and find themselves in a marriage that looks like this:

F.

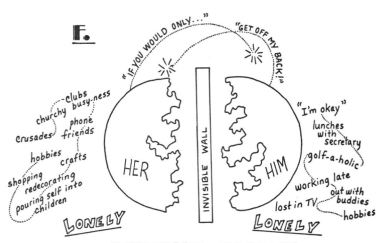

DEFENSE, FLIGHT

He lives on his side of the wall spending more and more time at the office, immersed in hobbies, playing golf, anything to avoid prolonged exposure at home where it hurts. And he looks for places to express himself where there is no threat to his ego. She pours herself into her children, spends her time at crafts, clubs and church, and talks to her women friends about the things she no longer feels it is safe to confide in her husband. Being together becomes excruciating as it seems only to accentuate the loneliness they both feel in isolation from one another. Occasionally they may throw rocks at one another from behind the wall, "If *you* would only change, I'd be all right!"

The world's culture feeds them continually with lies. "If it *feels* good, it is right." "Love is warm and fuzzy and makes you *feel* tingly all over." "If you were really in love you'd be living happily ever after." "If you aren't happy in a relationship, get out of it." Their marriage certainly doesn't feel good, and they begin to think, "We must have made a mistake. I have the wrong partner. God never intended for us to be together."

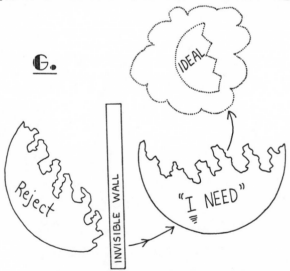

RATIONALIZED COP-OUT

And so one or the other (or both) wanders from the marriage in search of that "ideal partner," that "soul mate," who must be out there somewhere. The wandering partner may indeed find someone who initially makes him "feel good." But because he has not let the Lord deal yet with the things in his heart, he will choose that new relationship with the same eyes, the same sensitivities, the same criteria which equipped him for choosing in the first place. And should he marry a second time, the moment the new mate begins to penetrate his heart, he will find himself repeating the same patterns all over again. More cogently, the same necessity to reap seeds of judgment not yet stopped on the cross will most likely still draw a mate through whom to reap, usually more detrimentally. In this way some people go from marriage to marriage to marriage—right on to dead-ended frustration, "I guess I'm just not marriage material." (By the same token people go from church to church and from group to group and from friend to friend, searching endlessly for someone to make them feel good with no challenge to grow and change.)

There is only one answer for any marriage or any vital relationship. That is to exchange that dividing wall of hostility for the cross of Christ. *It is to stop all demands that the other change.* It is to die daily to self, to continually ask the Lord, "What in *me* is contributing to the breakdown of this marriage?" "Lord, why doesn't my mate get better by just living with me? What is there in *me* that needs to die?" "Bring me to death." It is to confess, "Lord, I can't be loving to John. But you can. Give me the love you have that I may give it to him." "I can't forgive. But you can. Express your forgiveness through me." It is to ask the Lord to enable

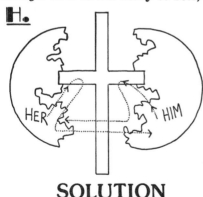

SOLUTION

compassionate identification with the other's hurts and fears, and wisdom to minister to those. It is to "forget what lies behind" (Phil. 3:13-14), by identifying it and dealing with it on the cross of Christ so that it no longer has any power and "press on toward what lies ahead" by embracing each step of God's sometimes painful plan to transform your life as you live *with* your mate and work *through* problems together. It means choosing to be vulnerable and trusting the Lord to defend and protect.

If one partner in a marriage refuses to enter into that process of transformation in the Lord, all is not lost. The unbelieving partner is sanctified through the believing partner (1 Cor. 7:14). What happens in the heart of one affects the other, if not consciously, at least beneath the level of consciousness. Eventually it will bear fruit. The more immediate effect of one partner's finding a stopping place on the cross is just that; the vicious cycle is stopped. The remaining partner may continue to behave in the same old habit patterns, but those ways find no place to land in the Christian. They can no longer hook into sensitive trigger points.

I, (John) was raised with a mother who was hypercritical. I judged her for that. My bitter-root judgment was that the woman of my life would always criticize and seldom affirm me. My mother also made me work long hours, and then gave little comfort or appreciation for it, and so my bitter-root judgment was that any woman close to me would expect me to work long hours, and then be unhappy with me anyway, and insensitive to my needs.

I (Paula) was raised with a father who was a traveling salesman, gone two weeks at a time. Though my mind said, "I'm proud of my daddy, he is working for us," my heart sang a bitter tune, "Oh yeah, why isn't he ever here for me when I need him?" I was covertly angry at men. My bitter-root judgment was that the man would always be gone from me. What better place to reap that than to marry a workaholic pastor!

It takes little imagination to see how we were designed to

grind on each other. I (John) would work long hours for the church (whose symbol is mother or woman) and find myself constantly criticized both by the church and Paula. Paula would be angrier and angrier the harder and longer I worked to please. The power of law is such that had I not possessed a built-in workaholic structure, Paula's seed sown would have pushed me to become a workaholic, or in one way or another to be away from her. Her anger made me ask myself, "Who wants to come home to a buzz-saw anyway?" My necessity to reap bitter judgment guaranteed that Paula would criticize had she not already been so disposed.

Not only was John a workaholic, he was always late. In the first years of our marriage John came home from calling on parishioners habitually late to dinner. I would get after him, and he would promise to watch the time and try to arrive home promptly. But neither my scoldings nor his determinations helped. He seemed to have some kind of block about time. It was just something not to be noticed. We ruefully laughed about "Indian time," while I hurt and hurt and grew angrier. Then we learned about bitter-root judgment and expectancy patterns. I repented (by faith alone) of angers I had never yet (nor ever have) felt against my father, but supposed must be there, and asked the Lord to haul to the cross my bitter-root expectancy that my man would always be late. Then I could begin to remember a little, red-haired girl sitting disconsolately waiting for her daddy to come home on the weekend, being more and more disappointed as the seemingly endless hours dragged by. This was the more difficult to see because my father was in fact always punctual. But a little girl's grasp of time is not that factual. I repented and asked for a new heart. John soon found himself easily coming home on time— no sweat, no struggle.

My (John's) bitter-root expectancy from my judgment of my mother was that I would be criticized even when doing my best. And since no one can perform well under a critical eye, I had often as a child blundered absent-mindedly or stupidly and had been criticized roundly for it. So both by judgment necessitating reaping and by psychological expectancy, I looked for the woman of my life to criticize me, and expected to blunder into it continually. That trait was nicely matched by the fact that Paula was raised with three younger brothers. The first two especially were normal, rambunctious boys who were always into something which embarrassed their righteous older sister. They loved to tease her unmercifully—like running in to throw earthworms in her bath water! Being adventurous, they got into a plethora of "dumb" scrapes. And who was it who did the dumb things which caused the teacher to make the entire class stay after school? Boys, of course. Who stuck her long, red braids in the inkwell? Who threw paper wads and splattered ink? Boys! Paula's bitter-root judgment was that boys (men) would always do dumb things and get everybody into trouble. How better to reap that than to marry an immature, head-in-the-clouds, mystic, dreaming, absentminded preacher?

During the first years of our marriage, I suffered "hoofin-mouth" disease. I was always saying some dumb thing. I preached on Sunday morning. Paula preached on Sunday afternoon! "Do you *know* what you said to those people?" It was so bad that each Sunday morning Paula would say, "You aren't going to say something startling today, are you?" and then of course I had to, just to declare independence. I even found myself continually inverting words much to my consternation and embarrassment, like instead of saying, "Look up 1 Peter 3," it would come out, "Look up 1 Threter Pee."

Then I was called to teach out of town, away from Paula. Much to my surprise out rolled uninterrupted wisdom, with no dumb-dumbs. I thought, "Hallelujah! I'm healed. Wait till I get back home!" Only to fall right back to spoonerisms and all kinds of blunders. Finally the Lord revealed that Paula's bitter root was defiling me ". . . and by it the many become defiled" (Heb. 12:15). She repented of her judgments on her brothers and other men and boys, and asked that the Lord give her a new heart, crucifying the expectancy that men would do dumb things. Since then I have never suffered more than the normal goofs anybody makes, and they are my own, not her reaping.

My (Paula's) bitter-root judgment and expectancy that the man would leave me matched John's workaholic nature in another way. John would always be finding someone to help, too much sacrificing family time for others. Though that was actually out of order (God was calling him to first priorities, his wife and children), John had that one neatly masked under noble serving for God. God wasn't calling him away from home. As a boy he had had to be out milking cows, feeding chickens, and doing chores while the rest of the family played and visited, and had formed a bitter expectancy that life would always go like that. That perfectly matched my judgment of men. It was so bad that even on vacation, five minutes after setting up our own camp, John would be out walking through the campground finding someone else to help—and I was furious!

Law is so powerful that the requirement to reap what was sown can overcome our strongest good natural capacities. My mother (John's) was part Osage Indian, part English. Both cultures have produced very reserved people, and it was not easy for her to express emotion or affection. I judged my mother for not giving enough affection. So the expectancy was that I would be a suffering-servant martyr who would work long hours, only to be criticized and then not receive enough expressions of love. But I married a butterball of affection! In seminary I had determined to be a secluded scholar, but Paula would come and sit *on* my books *on* my lap and express affection to me. I protested—while lapping it up! In five years that didn't happen any more. Paula was no longer that affectionate. Why? My bitter-root judgment had to be reaped. Law overcame her good intentions. My necessity to reap (plus psychological expectancy) *kept her from giving affection.*

My (Paula's) father was seldom home to protect me. Those three rambunctious brothers gave me a hard time (no tougher than normal, actually quite healthy teasing, as brothers will do). But my heart was bitter. No man would be there to defend me. I would have to do it all myself. John grew up with stern English training to lay down his life to protect a woman. He had seen his father live that in many ways for his mother emotionally. And there is scarcely a stronger or more fierce trait in Indian nature than for a brave to defend his squaw! By both inheritance and training it was one of his strongest characteristics to defend a woman, especially his wife, against all attack. He found himself totally bemused that something almost always blocked so that he seldom was able to defend me. I had sown seeds, and the reaping was so powerful it overcame his strongest good intentions.

Women who are raised with alcoholic fathers, and judge them for it, often either marry a man who is already an alcoholic (they are used to that, and it confirms their judgment), or their man sooner or later becomes one. And so it goes—weak father, weak husband, poor providing parent, poor providing husband, cold and distant father, so is the mate, etc. If the husband does not fit the pattern, either the little girl did not judge and so is not forced to reap, or having judged, has been delivered from reaping by the grace of God.

Men whose mothers were domineering attract the same, unless grace intervenes. Men whose mothers often left them with baby sitters, or by sickness, marital separations or death, find wives who do the same to them. And so it goes— cold, insensitive mother; cold, insensitive wife; etc. If the condition is not exactly the same, the parallel is unmistakable. Again, not the actual history is important but whether the child judged the parent. Reaping is then inevitable. Either Jesus is allowed to pay the full legal demand and so set us free, or we reap, usually through the mate.

When one receives Jesus Christ as Lord and Savior, all that bitter-root system is dealt a death blow. But observe that St. Paul was writing to *Christians* when he *commanded*, "See to it that . . . no root of bitterness springing up . . ." (Heb. 12:15, italics mine). Note the words "springing up," like a plant suddenly appearing from a hidden root. He did not say, "Lop off visible branches," nor "Deal with the obvious." But rather to see to it that no (hidden, beneath the surface, problematic) root become manifest and cause trouble.

Sometimes, repentance prior to accepting Jesus as Lord and Savior has reached to a bitter root, so that the moment of conversion is also the moment of deliverance. Most often, however, vast subterranean tap roots and spreading, hidden tributary shoots remain untouched until we obey St. Paul's command to get at them.

We wish we could train every Christian counselor, on principle, to look for bitter roots in each counselee in every interview. Physicians are trained to examine meticulously for certain possible conditions routinely, especially in first interviews. So also do dentists, chiropractors, and other professionals. Paula and I routinely ask questions concerning early childhood, checking to see whether bitter roots lie behind conditions.

"You say your husband never listens to you? Tell me about your father. What was he like?" After a few basic general questions such as, "Did he give you affection? Was he 'home' when he was home? Did he stay with your mother? How did they relate to each other?", we will ask, "Could you talk with your father? Could he hear and understand you?"

In nearly every instance in which a husband will not listen, we find the same began with her father. "Oh, he was always too busy. He never listened to me."

"Your wife is always sicker than she really is, and it grates on you, and you can't make yourself help her like you should? What was your mother like?" "How was your mother's health?" It is amazing how often the response is, "Oh, she was always complaining about this or that ailment, and taking to her bed," sometimes accompanied by, "She made dad wait on her hand and foot," or "I hated that."

If his statements are: "My wife can't keep the house neat," or "The laundry's never done," or "She's always shopping and spending too much money," or "She gossips too much. Always talking." Our questions will be: "How did your mother take care of the house?" "Did your mother keep your clothes clean and ready when you were a little boy?" and so on. Usually we ask several other general questions first and then slip in the relevant ones so as to camouflage our intent, lest the counselee answer dishonestly.

If her statements are: "He won't ever take me out anywhere; just sits in his darn ol' easy chair and falls asleep," or, "He never notices whether I look nice," or "He never disciplines the children; he just abdicates and leaves it all up to me." Our questions will be: "Did your father do things with the family? How about picnics, or fishing trips—things like that?" "Did your father like to do things around the house, or did he get lost watching TV or sleep a lot?" "Who wore the pants in your family?" "Did your father do the disciplining, or your mother?"

Sometimes it was not the father who failed a daughter and was judged, but the mother; but the grown wife is reaping through her husband. Or sometimes we reap through the children, or another who lives in the home or nearby, or a boss, or pastor, or colleague at work. Sometimes likewise a son may have judged his father but reaps through his wife.

Sometimes patterns of judging and reaping are not so obvious or so neat and clean. For instance, a little girl may have felt greatly rejected by her father. Questioning reveals, however, that her father seldom was gone from the home, had no great obvious vices (such as alcohol, violence, or a critical tongue), attended church regularly, was a good moral man, etc. But perhaps he was inattentive, or one who fled into books, or seldom spoke. A girl may just as easily take those simple flaws as rejection, but finds it difficult to fault her father since love and loyalty cover feelings of hurt (James 5:20). All of what she can remember is rosy. She may marry a man who insists on remaining in a teen-age gang mentality, frequently leaving her in order to go out with the guys. Or he may be alcoholic or a workaholic. Whatever the surface manifestations, it is the same root—one way or another he fails to take note of her, and she feels rejected.

As much as we wish we could train every counselor to look

for bitter roots, *we would hope to induce each to look for cross-over patterns.* We could almost make it a hard and fast rule: Whenever one partner has a bitter root, the other will have something exactly matching! A counselor ought to suspect that possibility simply by the law of attraction and repulsion. We manage to attract to us and are ourselves attracted to those whose characteristics closely match or oppose ours. After watching this phenomenon through twenty years of counseling hundreds yearly, Paula and I are still amazed at the consistency of law and of human nature.

Sometimes it is not through others we reap but through mother nature, circumstances, or our own selves. For instance, I (John) have seen cases in which several generations suffered business failures, sometimes by ineptitude but often by accidents, economic depressions, weather, etc. Generational sin (Deut. 5:9) may not fully explain the strength of such a pattern; whereas bitter-root judgments by sons upon fathers may turn out to be the main way that particular generational pattern continues to descend.

In cases in which a person is reaping upon himself, another law usually is foundational. "Therefore you are without excuse, every man of you who passes judgment, for in that you judge another, you condemn yourself; for you who judge practice the same things" (Rom. 2:1). It is also an irrevocable law that when we judge another, we doom ourselves to do the same thing (or something so similar the root cannot be missed)! For example, a wife who exclaims, "My mother was always shouting at us kids. I swore I would never act like that. And now I'm doing it just like she did, only worse!"

A young man came whose father had been an alcoholic who was unfaithful to his mother. The counselee had hated those things in his father, and swore that he would be different. He loved his wife dearly. He had become a Holy Spirit-filled Christian, attended church regularly, read his Bible, and loved Jesus. Now seemingly inexplicably, he found himself compulsively going out to drink, and had already committed adultery. Guilty, worried and confused, he came to us. A few minutes of questioning revealed the bitter-root pattern of judgment. Though Christian, he had never distinctly repented of his judgments against his father. That doomed him by the power of law to do exactly as his father had done. Jesus of course longed to protect him from himself, and after he fell, Jesus longed to set him free; but free will prevented our gracious Lord until the young man could see his roots and repent specifically. Under our counsel, he did so repent, and was set free.

Sometimes bitter roots lie hidden far beneath levels of what we have commonly thought of as "rememberable" incidents. One lady came whose behavior totally baffled her. She loved the Lord and her husband. She believed the Bible, belonged to a solid evangelical church, and was Spirit-filled. Now she too found herself compulsively leaving her husband to go out drinking. She had become involved in a fully adulterous affair with an alcoholic married man whom she did not even like or want to be near! Her husband was a gentle, loving, born-anew, Spirit-filled man. "Whatever in the world am I doing?" she cried out, "And why?"

So I asked more questions and discovered that she had been adopted at birth. Her natural mother had never been married, and at forty had dated an alcoholic married man! Her natural father had never told her natural mother that he was a married man. When she became pregnant and informed him, he vanished from her life by returning to his wife and refusing to acknowledge any connection with her. Her mother had carried her nine months in shame, in days when condemnation was much more severe than today, and medical proofs of parentage were unknown. Sometime during the nine months, she determined she would have to give up her child for adoption. She did so, and Ann had never known, outside the womb, any other than her gracious, loving, God-fearing adoptive mother and father.

By now the reader must understand that in our spirits we know and comprehend whatever is happening around us in the womb, as John the Baptist knew Mary was pregnant with our Lord and leaped for joy (Luke 1:41-44). In her spirit in the womb she had judged her father and her mother for fornication, her father for drinking and adultery and for rejecting her mother and her. That doomed her to: a) reject someone (her husband) as she was rejected; b) drink; c) commit adultery. Not all tiny judgments we make have such power. Some may be cleansed away by the blood of Jesus immediately (1 John 1:7). But deep-set, virulent judgments do have such power. As she had hated being in that womb of shame during the nine months and had hated becoming a person, so her girl child forming within her triggered into her hatred of herself, and she subconsciously projected her self-hatred onto her baby.

When we explained to her the laws of bitter-root judgment, she could see how her compulsion had taken hold of her. The Holy Spirit revealed the reality of her life to her heart and we prayed for forgiveness and death on the cross to all bitter-root structures. From *one* session of counsel and prayer results were immediate and full (perhaps because she had such good faith)! She brought her adoptive mother to rejoice and confirm, and to pray for her older sister, who was also adopted, who could not understand why she too hated her daughters. Her husband also came. By now can the reader fail to know what questions I asked him and what were the answers? Of course, though he had been a devout Christian for many years, he had a matching bitter-root judgment and expectancy that his woman would leave him and be unfaithful!

The most pathetic thing Paula and I see daily in Christian counseling is that day by day, year after year, good Christian people are driven by forces of which they have no awareness! We are not speaking merely of libidinal psychological forces. Those are bad enough that most any psychiatrist or psychologist could agree with that statement. All kinds of counselors have discovered the truth of Ecclesiastes 1:18, "Because in much wisdom there is much grief, and increasing knowledge results in increasing pain." Beyond such grief is a depth of pathos for Christian counselors, for we see not merely psychologically but the invincible operation of inevitable laws of judgment, especially of sowing and reaping, acting with impersonal, unrelenting force in human life (short of the cross of Christ). The pathos is because Christians ought to believe, should know and see and let Jesus Christ do what He came to do—to set them free.

But Christians have failed to see. If this book has no greater purpose than this chapter, it is enough if Christians will only come to see how the law of sowing and reaping affects them drastically day in and day out, in multifarious details in common daily living.

Paula and I wrote of bitter-root expectancy in *Restoring the Christian Family* (chapter 11) and have spoken of it everywhere for years. (It may also be found in the two four-tape series, "Restoring the Christian Family," "The Refreshment of Forgiveness," and the single tape: "Bitter Roots Revisited"). We have learned to our chagrin that most who read or heard failed to grasp the point! They thought we were speaking only of psychological expectancy. In small part we were. Bitter-root expectancy is a psychological construct in our carnal natures by which we expect a self-fulfilling prophecy to happen, like always being criticized or rejected or left out of things. By it we do indeed coerce people or manipulate unconsciously until they do that bad thing to us which proves our judgment, "I knew it!" "I knew it would happen that way. It always does."

Such psychological expectancies do have some power in our lives. But compared to the laws of which we actually were speaking, psychological bitter-root expectancy is like a flickering candle flame beside an atomic blast! It is the Law of God which alone possesses limitless power!

The inability of most to hear told us something else more wounding. We wrote about it in chapter 4, "The Base of Law" —that most people cannot and do not think in terms of the operation of God's law in their daily lives. They do not see or understand how what they did as little children (or as adults) can still be like a boomerang swishing to return with ever greater momentum in their present or future. Not comprehending that *every* action in life must reap a result, they find themselves continually being hit on the blind side and smashed by events, and wondering why. Life seems unfair. It is to help the Body of Christ see in order to repent and stop the reaping of destruction that we write this chapter. Oh, that men will hear!

Let us repeat what we said in chapter four, that no law of God is an inert, dead thing. The laws of God will operate whether we know of them or are ignorant, approve of them or disapprove, love or hate them, believe or disbelieve. Therefore, God's impartial laws will affect us whether we unintentionally activate them by judgments as children, or intentionally sin as mature people. It makes no difference. Law is law. If we disbelieve, what we think or feel about the reality and effectiveness of the laws of God will have about as much effect as a gnat trying to knock down the Empire State Building! The laws of God will roll right on controlling the universe no matter what our puny minds think or don't think.

The law of sowing and reaping is so simple it is deceptive. We just don't think anything that simple can be that real, that pervasively powerful and effective. Perhaps for that reason St. Paul warns, *"Do not be deceived, God is not mocked; for whatever a man sows, this he will also reap"* (Gal. 6:7, italics mine). It is impossible to hold a judgment or do a deed without setting in motion forces which absolutely must return to us. If a man were silly enough to believe with great certainty that he could fly, the law of gravity would not be affected one whit! He would plummet as surely as the foolishness of his technique allows. Only the operation of devices within other laws enables a man to fly. Just so, a thief will eventually reap, no matter how brilliantly he escapes human detection. A secret adultery will result in destruction of the soul and in later reapings no matter what modern "feelosophies" say. *The law of sowing and reaping guarantees unconditionally that no one ever gets away with anything at any time in any place!*

If a Christian counselor sees that the law of sowing and reaping is so effective, he is prepared to use it as a key for understanding human life and dilemmas. But in counseling we must remember to include the dimension of time in our reckoning, and to explain it to the counselee. Reaping is not immediate. As a farmer must wait first for seeds to die and rise, then to grow, then to bloom, then to form in the head, only at last to mature, so reaping in all of life must wait. For counseling one difference is crucial. A farmer not only can see his plants growing, some tending may be required. But since in the case of bitter-root judgments sown in childhood, most commonly seeds sown are forgotten, and seldom can the shape of bitter-root judgments be seen in earliest childhood, perhaps never having been fully consciously admitted, it seems inexplicable when reaping arrives as a whirlwind when the sowing to the wind was so long ago, so small, and so hidden or forgotten. People condemn one another and themselves for failure. It seems unfair that sins of judgment sown in infancy destroy adult relationships. But that is because we attach blame to a process in which there is none, only impartial law.

When man was created and set in the garden to take care of it, law already had long regulated growth. In that innocent order, all things did indeed work together for good (Rom. 8:28, now only by the cross, then without need of it). The good deeds of Adam and Eve rebounded to increase the blessedness of Eden, and there were no sinful things setting in motion terrible later reapings. The entire universe was designed to upbuild itself in love (Eph. 4:16).

But since law is impersonal, when Adam and Eve opened the door to sin, every succeeding generation has reaped the result. That means that infants come into a fractured and sinful world with hearts already corrupted by Adamic sin, and so make judgments and hateful reactions which must later be reaped in vast increase—*by the same law which would have brought ever-increasing blessing had Adam and Eve never sinned!* God does not blame. He knew before anything was ever created that men would fall, and that the very laws which He had built to govern all things in blessedness would then be turned to bring destruction. So from the ground plan of creation he predestined Jesus to reap all harm, to pay on the cross all the price demanded by His own impartial law.

We must understand, especially as counselors, one vitally important fact. Human free will is so precious to our Lord that He will not let the efficacy of the cross be applied to us without our consent. It is as though He has brought us a present on Good Friday, but wrapped it up until our own invitation allows our own Easter morning to open it to personal application. In each detail of our life it is the same. Our gentle Lord is always standing outside some new sequential inner door, softly knocking, but the only latch is on our side. Bitter roots are normally not taken care of until we invite Jesus to accomplish that specific task. Our compassionate Lord hurts more, not less, in the waiting till we do. He pays the price even for our tardiness in confessing.

Is it fair that a tiny child should live with an angry, violent father and reap thereby a life with similar bosses, or with a husband who acts out the same, only worse? Of course it isn't. Whoever said, since the Fall, that life was fair? On the other hand, should our infants reap, all undeserved, all the benefits of our fathers' fathers—house and health, technology and medicine, appliances, clothing, rich foods, knowledge and spiritual blessings, and then be exempted from reaping the harms that come in the same package? God is just and fair. Life on earth since the Fall of Adam and Eve is not.

So it is that the tiniest children, who hardly can be blamed for making angry, bitter judgments at parents who may richly deserve such evaluations, nevertheless set in motion forces which must move to resolution. It is not that God is mean, and picks on children. It is the opposite, that God in His kindness and compassion sees the gathering storms from all our sowings (though we may see neither the sowings nor the impending reapings), and He moves, unseen by us, to intercede on our behalf. When the prayers of others on earth and the intercession of heaven fail of access to our stubborn natures, then despite the perfect will of God, we reap what we have sown.

Jesus always lives to intercede on our behalf (Heb. 7:25). "For I, the Lord, do not change; therefore you, O sons of Jacob, are not consumed" (Mal. 3:6). Let all Christendom understand, were the Lord to change, that is, to stop interceding for one short while, the weight of our sowings of sin is so great—"This tape (earth) will self-destruct in five seconds!"

Destruction is reaped not merely in our marriages and in our families, but in all aspects of life. Earlier we told the story of a businessman whose father had continually gambled away the family money. When our friend went to work at eleven or so for the family, if his father could find the money he earned, he would steal it and gamble it away. He judged him for that. His bitter-root judgment was that his father (therefore, subsequently all businessmen) would cheat, lie, and steal. Needing partners for his real estate projects, he continually drew to him men who failed him one way or another—lying, cheating, being lazy, and leaving our friend to hold the bag, unaided. In his business office he managed to find partners who invariably failed him. One split his family in two. Being determined, he searched and found a man of faith, a most highly recommended man, born anew, church attending, a responsible deacon. This man so failed to be responsible in business, our friend was almost driven to bankruptcy. While he was in the hospital with back trouble, this partner went to his doctor, lawyer, and counselor (me) to try to have him declared incompetent so he could steal his business!

Subsequently, we talked of his judgments against his father and how his bitter root was being reaped through all these men. He repented and was forgiven. In prayer we called that bitter root to death on the cross, and prayed for a new heart, a new expectancy by which to draw to himself dependable, honest men. One by one the Lord has weeded the leeches out of his company and brought to him men of honor and dependability. Recently his banker, extending a sizable loan which saved his business, said to him, "Now that you have gotten rid of those men, and you are running your company again (he meant out of the hospital and back on the job) and now that you have around you these men we can trust, we will back you again." Our friend's bitter root nearly destroyed his business, and the cross of Christ saved it.

Note the words, ". . . and by it the many be defiled" (Heb. 12:15). Our bitter root, by the force of reaping, actually defiles others. We *make* them act around us in ways they might successfully resist, apart from us. Every married person or other kind of partner ought to ask, "How come he didn't become a better and stronger person by associating with me?" And, "Can it be that my bitter root is defiling him?" "Am I reaping something through this person?"

We need to understand, however, that guilt is always fifty-fifty. Our bitter root could not overcome the other's free will unless something in him is still flesh (no matter how good and strong), or weak and sinful. The other is always responsible too. Guilt in a family is always shared.

When questions reveal a bitter root, there are several factors needing our attention. First there is the original event. The grown person may have no awareness, as Paula has never been able to *feel* any kind of resentment against her father. But we are not dealing first with feelings of the flesh or spirit. We are dealing with facts and law, by faith. Forgiveness for the sin of judgments should be pronounced if present circumstances indicate reaping. Where reaping is, judgments and/or sinful actions were the sowing, no matter what the other's reasoning mind or feelings may protest. The counselee need not presently feel anything during counseling or prayer. The counselor is now a confessor, pronouncing absolution for the inner child, ministering beyond the adult to the little one within. Forgiveness needs to be said several ways so that the inner one can take hold and receive.

The counselee should be asked both to forgive and to be forgiven, purely by faith if necessary. Forgiveness is essential. Without it, no subsequential healing can happen (Matt. 6:15, Mark 11:26, Matt. 5:23-24).

The original event(s) created structures in the character. These are practices of judgment and psychological bitter-root expectancy which only the cross can transform. The counselee or counselor or both should pray aloud together asking that Jesus' work on the cross be applied to that practice in the old nature. It will help and may be necessary for the counselee to say in prayer, "I hate it. I reject it. I don't want it."

A science-fiction, space movie several years ago told the story of a spaceship lost upon a planet devoid of its former population. A second spaceship, sent to find the first, found only a professor (the scientist aboard the flight) and his daughter still alive. Soon members of the second crew began to be torn apart one by one by an only partially visible monster. The captain discovered a machine invented by the former population. By placing a cap on the head and turning the machine on, great mental powers were released. Unfortunately so were all the inner powers. The hidden demonic urges of the former population had thus materialized, causing them all to destroy one another by their covert hatreds! Meanwhile all the new ship's crew were being destroyed until only a few remained, locked behind a supposedly impenetrable door with the scientist and his daughter. Now the demonic thing was smashing through even that! At the last moment the captain, perceiving the truth, called on the scientist, who he discovered had tried the machine, to realize it was his own despotic thing, jealously overprotecting his daughter. At last the scientist stepped in front of the door and cried out, "I hate you. I reject you. I don't want you." Dramatically the sounds of rending and tearing descended into silence.

I know of no better way to depict the power of such subconscious practices in our nature, or how they can only be destroyed by holding them to the cross by hate. ". . . hate what is evil (loathe all ungodliness, turn in horror from wickedness) but hold fast to that which is good" (Rom. 12:9b TAB). Sometimes we have prayed with counselees about such practices, in full faith, only to have them continue, seemingly unabated. The missing factor which denied success was hate. We spoke earlier of reward systems. All bitter-root systems contain rewards. I grew up determined to serve well no matter whether my folks appreciated or criticized. Actually that built a noble martyr who loved that stance. That fed my ego. No matter how much I protested that I disliked being criticized and was tired of serving for little reward, the inmost truth was that in reality I preferred it so. That proved me the magnanimous suffering-servant Christian, and all those others less than me, even hypocritical. So long as I enjoyed that reward, I was not about to let go and face as sin my defiling others by causing them to act in an un-Christian manner toward me.

So long as John kept working too late, spending too much time away from me (Paula) and the children, my noble martyr self could "bear that cross" all alone and unappreciated while serving anyway. That fed my ego. So long as I enjoyed proving the man wrong, so long as I enjoyed being "one-up" (on my brothers in sibling rivalry projected onto John), so long as it was precious to me that my bitter root view of life was being confirmed again and again, I had no real intention of letting go of my bitter root. The rewards were too sweet.

Perhaps now we are prepared to comprehend the necessity for the command, *"See to it. . . ."* Sometimes overturning a bitter root requires upsetting the entire stance of life by which one has defined his life and found his (fleshly) worth. It may mean coming to hate that fleshly righteousness by which we have congratulated ourselves that we are the good guys standing for Jesus and being persecuted by all the dirty guys.

Further, real repentance may require that we repent of our pushing those very people whom we have been blaming for hurting us to do so by being in proximity to us. Oddly, we may have to repent that we hurt them by causing them to hurt us! We may not become whole until we bless them for loving us enough to be the ones through whom we could reap! Truly forgiveness is not fully fulfilled until we bless those who despitefully use us (Matt. 5:12-13, Rom. 12:14, and 1 Pet. 3:4).

Finally, the counselee may have to catch himself at the game in many little ways for days thereafter. The big battle may be won but there may be hundreds of pockets of "guerrilla resistance" here and there in our nature. Habit structures are like morning glories, weeds which keep sending up sprouts from a long, persistent root system until every part of the old root is uprooted or finally too weak to send up a shoot.

The blessed end of transformation of bitter roots is first that we find ourselves continually surprised. Things just don't happen like they used to. New things happen. People compliment who didn't, or give affection, or whatever is the reverse of what used to happen. Good rather than bad "accidents" happen. Things begin to work together for good, visibly. One can't miss seeing it.

Perhaps the most blessed shock is that often the very people we have been hating become the ones we love or appreciate the most. We even become grateful for their former persecuting ways (or whatever they did) because by that we saw and were set free. Life takes on a new lease. It is as though new vistas open before us—and we come (slowly perhaps) to realize they were there all along; we just couldn't see them. What used to bother us now falls like water off a duck's back. We giggle instead of tense up. We laugh *with* those we used to get mad at for laughing *at* us. And we see others and our own self with real compassion.

Truly in that area we are born anew.

Section IV

Sexual Sins and Difficulties

15

Fornication, Adultery, Inordinate Desire, and Aberrations

Let your fountain be blessed,
And rejoice in the wife of your youth.
As a loving hind and a graceful doe,
Let her breasts satisfy you at all times;
Be exhilarated always with her love.
(Prov. 5:18-19)

So husbands ought also to love their own wives
as their own bodies. He who loves his own wife
loves himself; for no one ever hated his own
flesh, but nourishes and cherishes it, just as
Christ also does the church.
(Eph. 5:28-29)

For this is the will of God, your sanctification;
that is, that you abstain from sexual immorality;
that each of you know how to possess his own
vessel in sanctification and honor, not in lustful
passion, like the Gentiles who do not know God;
and that no man transgress and defraud his
brother in the matter because the Lord is the
avenger in all these things, just as we also told
you before and solemnly warned you. For God
has not called us for the purpose of impurity, but
in sanctification.
(1 Thess. 4:3-7)

God designed us to enjoy sex. He united our sensitive spirits to delicately intricate, wondrously strong, feeling bodies to give us great heights of blessing and joy in sexual union. There is nothing we can do with one another through our bodies that is so holy and perfectly fulfilling as marital sexual union. God meant it for refreshment, fulfillment, recreation, realignment, release, sharing, procreation, healing, lessons in loving, practice in sensitivities, development in the art of laying down our lives for another, completion, entrance into the kingdom of being corporate, gratitude, longing, hope, endurance, fun, laughter, mysticism, embrace, and so on through endless catalogues of blessing. It is perhaps God's best physical gift to mankind.

Precisely because it possesses so much power to bless, mankind to that degree can warp and twist sex to unleash destructive power.

Sexual blessedness, more than any other form of human encounter, depends upon our having become *human* beings. A human being is a person who has a loving, living personal spirit by which he empathizes with others and cherishes others more than himself. We do not become human simply by existing. We have to be made human by being given copious affection in infancy and thus drawn forth to love. Sexual blessedness depends upon the capacity of our spirits to reach through our bodies to nurture, bless, enfold, enrich, and enrapture the heart and spirit of another. That capacity is activated, nurtured, and disciplined by our relation to our fathers and mothers. Before we are six, the ability later to enjoy sex fully has either been enabled or destroyed. Failing to receive from our father especially, we cannot enter into the fullness of what ought to be. Aberrational forms subsequently await us like reefs under the shallow waters of our living.

To become human means (at most) to become like Jesus.* Jesus was the one fully human person. We use the word wrongly when we say, "I did that (bad thing) because I am only human." No, we did that wrong thing purely because we are

---

* Again, we do not speak here of humanism, which is Satan's copy, by which man is prompted to elevate himself and his supposed rights, but of our Lord's work in bringing forth the sons of God on earth.

inhuman. If we were human we would do as Jesus did! We would be compassionate, warm, open, giving, embracing, and nurturing. Our spirit, perfectly wedded to our body, would rejoice to embrace another, for His sake rather than ours alone. That life of living to bless others would be so natural and fulfilling to us, we would be willing, like Jesus, to suffer loss for the happiness of another. That sacrificial willingness is the quintessence of success in marital sexual union, for only as both husband and wife are willing to give all they are through their bodies to fulfill the other can either or both reach the fullness of blessedness in sex.

To become human means (at least) to become capable of empathizing with another. It means to have a functioning spirit which through our bodily senses can commiserate or rejoice with another. It means ability to hurt empathetically *for* another; concerning conscience it means to allow ourselves to be hurt in advance lest our brother be hurt. Thus the least indicator of the ability to be human is to have a working conscience. The essence of humanity is told by conscience. When we do not have a functioning spirit, filled with love, we cannot care how our brother feels, nor do we feel bad if we happen to be the ones who have brought him harm. To be inhuman is to be dead to concern for the welfare of our fellowman. Witness the bestial acts of street gangs, and the lack of conscience among increasing numbers of fatherless children today (2 Tim. 3:1-5). We are born possessing a spirit. But our spirit does not yet know *how* to love another. That capacity must be awakened, brought forth, instructed and disciplined. The task of nurture and discipline is spoken specifically to fathers, "Fathers . . . bring them up in the discipline and instruction of the Lord" (Eph. 6:4). Mothers give life and nurture. Fathers are primarily responsible to call forth that life and shape it.

The capacity to be sexual as an adult is formed in a girl as her spirit learns to nestle safely in the strength of her father's arms. As she romps and plays, rocks with him in his chair on his lap, curls up on his chest, and delights him with her, she learns what it is to bless and be blessed, to trust herself restfully into the hands of a man, to let her spirit flow into another's and back again. She learns how to let her spirit come alive in the embrace of another of the opposite sex. A woman who has never been allowed such life with her father may not be able to reach a climax in sex, because the high moments of climax require letting go control of herself into the man, and she can't do that. She may enjoy the physical titillations of sexual union, but the glory is far from her because that capacity has never been aroused to function. She may never even know she has missed what God intended. Only one who has tasted mountain air can truly be aware that the muggy heaviness of a river bottom atmosphere is not all there is to breathing.

The capacity for a man to be sexual is formed in the same way. Though he may drink proportionately more from his mother than a daughter does, the capacity and shape of his spirit to meet and embrace is *formed* by his life with his father. Hugs, romps, rides on the shoulders, walks in the fields, banter and laughter, mock fights and games teach his spirit the shape of responses to others. The way his father embraces or keeps distant from his mother soaks into a growing boy as his definition of how to be a man with a woman. The way a father gives sympathy or jumps to false conclusions, the way he empathizes with hurt or shouts obscenities for weakness, the way he touches with gentle hand or slaps with violence—countless such daily experiences write upon a growing boy how his spirit should express itself through his body and character.

God intended for fathers to teach their sons and daughters the blessedness of sex, and the warnings we need to keep us away from immorality. See Proverbs, chapters 1-7, especially 5:1-5,

My son, give attention to my wisdom,
Incline your ear to my understanding;
That you may observe discretion,
And your lips may reserve knowledge,

For the lips of an adulteress drip honey,
And smoother than oil is her speech;
But in the end she is bitter as wormwood,
Sharp as a two-edged sword.
Her feet go down to death,
Her steps lay hold of Sheol.

A tree cannot grow roots into the air and leaves under the ground. We have sense enough to know that God has firmly fixed certain things to grow only in particular ways. Nor would we try to run a car on its top and hope the wheels could spin on air fast enough to move us somewhere. We have sense enough to know that even the things man makes must abide by law, or they won't operate. Strangely, however, Bible-believing Christians can get it into their heads (as we said in chapter 14) that God didn't mean it when He said, "Thou shalt not commit adultery!" Scientifically we know that all machines must be operated in obedience to law, or they plug up or explode. Nutritionally we know that some things are poison to the body, no matter what we may feel or think about them. How then did we become so blind as not to see that venereal disease runs rampant wherever people practice sex without God-given right, and not where husband and wife share sex in the beauty of a God-sanctioned relationship? Ought not that fact alone be enough to convince our foolish minds of the reality of God's laws? "And receiving *in their own persons the due penalty of their error*" (Rom. 1:27, italics mine).

Every Christian counselor must know without a shadow of doubt the irrevocable, unbendable absoluteness of God's law. He meant what He said, exactly as He said it, to ensure for us the blessedness of His gift. It is not that He gave the "thou shalt nots" to keep us from having fun, but that we might truly enjoy the fullness He created us to have.

Sex outside of marriage absolutely can have no blessedness! It is God's Holy Spirit which sings through our spirit the love song of the universe in sex; the Holy Spirit will not flow in forbidden places! Sex outside of marriage, any form of sex between any other than husband with wife, is not only sin and loss, it is degradation of God's creation, insult to Him, rebellion and foolishness. Never should a Christian counselor upon hearing confession of sexual sin say, "Oh, that's all right," or "Don't feel so guilty." Nor should one ever counsel another, "Try it. It will help you get over your inhibitions." That is abomination before God. Though God looks on the heart and circumstances with compassion and forgiveness, there are no exceptions whatsoever to the moral laws of God.

Behind each sexual sin or aberration is some form of ruination or blockage in early childhood. A counselor's heart must be ruled by compassion, and he should dig for root causes. But his mind must be keen-edged with the sword of God's Word. Said the other way around, perhaps no one would ever fall into an aberration or sexual sin if he were truly human and capable. His spirit's conscience would sing out so loudly and strongly, he would turn in revulsion *before* committing the act. But we are not that human or capable. Perhaps for compassion's sake we who counsel should remember that we are more sinned against than sinning—we being but one and there being many to corrupt us.

In this chapter we want to deal primarily, however, not with the present fact of sexual sin, but with incidents and structures formed in early life which create the fertile ground for transgression. Behind any sexual aberration or sin is a flawed nature. Let us settle it as a rule: *no whole person falls into sexual sin* (1 John 3:9)! Sexual sin, however enticing to our carnal nature, is abhorrent to our spirit. We do not naturally gravitate to sexual sin as whole people *in Christ*, but away from it. If the flow of our desires continually pulls us to sexual sin, that comes from a bad root in us. Good trees do not produce bad fruit; bad ones do (Matt. 7:17).

We posit all this in the beginning to end once for all the lying notion counselors hear so often, "Well, I couldn't help it. I just fell in love," or "I guess I love her too much to stay away from her." Or, "If you love someone, why, of course it couldn't be sin, could it?" Nonsense! Rot and deception! Love does no wrong thing! Good trees do not produce bad fruit. Lust, a flawed nature, death of conscience apart from Christ, and deception produce that sin. Whoever commits fornication or adultery did not fall in love; he fell into hate. If love was the starting point, what followed became use and manipulation. Human love alone would have respected the sanctity of the other. God's love in the couple would have respected God and His laws and the sanctity of the other's soul and body. Whoever commits sexual sin flaunts all that is holy for egocentric, selfish reasons. Let us once and for all strip off the romantic, excusing, glossing-over veneer. Immorality is ugly, not beautiful. Destructive, not freeing. Disgusting, not ennobling. Hateful, not loving. Indescribable loss of the holy, given of God privately to only two, not fulfilling.

Pornography, and R-rated and X-rated movies, do not glorify sex, they denigrate it. Quantity of sexual involvement does not fulfill an individual outside the marriage bed; it empties him and leaves him feeling hollow. No one who has never married has ever had true sex, no matter how many affairs he has had, no matter what reputation he possesses as a "lover." He is not a lover; he is a self-centered little boy playing falsely at being a man.

Legend has it that Don Juan, famous for 1,003 sexual affairs, was offered only a jester's jacket by Satan in hell. "What?" he protested, "I'm no fool. I was a great lover." Satan offered him a bargain. If he could recognize and remember just one of his many "loves," he would not have to assume the fool's cloak. One by one, his romantic partners came before him. He failed to remember even one. At last, he had to admit it. He had not been a lover; only a fool. The jacket was appropriately his to wear for all eternity.

No man who is truly a lover ever *uses* another. No man who truly loves embraces the bosom of one who is not his wife (Prov. 5:18-20). No man who truly loves demolishes the glory God designed for blessing only one other person. "For this is the will of God, your sanctification; that is, that you abstain from sexual immorality; that each of you know how to possess his own vessel [make love to his own wife] in sanctification and honor, not in lustful passion, like the Gentiles who do not know God; and *that no man transgress and defraud his brother* in the matter . . ." (1 Thess. 4:3-6). To enter another man's wife is to defraud him of the glory God has given only him, "An excellent wife is the crown of her husband, But she who shames him is as rottenness in his bones" (Prov. 12:4).

Today's young people are being barraged with a Niagara of lies through countless media—movies, novels, magazines, newspapers, comic strips, periodicals, false counselors and teachers, radio, TV, popular music, gossip columns, etc. all proclaiming that sex is okay anywhere, anytime. Or worse, perhaps quasi-morally, "It's all right if you're in love." The worst part of the flood is often parental example— separations, subsequent dating, divorces, the infidelities children see or sense, even false sexual partners sometimes brought into the home behind not-too-closed doors. I (John) often think the flood Satan pours out of his mouth (note, from his mouth) after the woman (in Rev. 12:15) may be nothing other than the floods of sexual, immoral, and theological "verbal garbage" men continually spew out, especially in this generation.

Fornication is sexual intercourse before marriage. The cause is not the above-mentioned flood; that may indeed bid to sweep away an otherwise moral young person. But the primary fact is that if a person is strong and whole in Jesus, he can and will stand, "In a flood of great waters they shall not reach him" (Ps. 32:6). Our purpose here is not to deal with surface pressures, but to minister to the root reasons for falling. Piaget, a French sociologist, states the root reason: "If a person keeps himself virginal sexually, he (or she) loves and respects his (or her) father and mother. . . . If a person commits fornication, he (or she) hates and/or disrespects father and/or mother."

Many times people have come to us who have commtted fornication a number of years earlier. They have confessed privately and to others, and have heard the words of forgiveness, but still feel guilty and unclean. Questions soon uncover the fact that their sexual sin was not isolated, but was connected to other things. There may have been anger and rebellion toward parents, or a need to throw oneself away to prevent one's parents from rejoicing in their child's glory. Or a hunger for a father's love, so that the touch of a man became so tonic, a "no" could not be spoken. Or a need to punish the parents. Or simply the lack of a functioning conscience because the father had never been "there." Or a need to prove again and again that men, or women, are "like that" (like their judgment against one or both parents). In each occasion of confession, it was our task to discover the real reasons behind each fornication. Most often in a woman who cannot be moral, there is lack of a father's expressed love, and a consequent lack of love and respectful care for her own being. She believes she is worthless anyway, so why not be the tool of any man who comes along? Especially since to be touched seems to reach such vacant and needy places deep inside.

Merely pronouncing again an absolution for the sin of fornication most likely will not set such a person free. A counselor should talk about and pray through all the hidden (and not-so-hidden) childhood wounds and resentments. He may also have to resurrect in the other a love and respect for her (or his) own person. The seeing of causes must not be allowed to be taken as an excuse for sin, but as root rottenness producing sin in the present. When a person recognizes root causes, and understands that the real reasons for promiscuity were not first sexual but psychological, that can help him (or her) to cease viewing all sexual impulses as nasty, and enable the person to allow true and proper human impulses to flow in sexual areas. A new sexual identity which can be cherished rather than feared can be developed. Counselors should work to that end.

Any complete sexual act, whether fornication, adultery, homosexuality or some other aberration, unites a person's spirit with the other. "Or do you not know that the one who joins himself to a harlot [or any other illicit partner] is one body with her? For He says, 'The two will become one flesh' "

(1 Cor. 6:16). God has so built us in our spirits that whatever woman a man enters, their spirits are united to each other from that moment on. Each person's spirit seeks, from the moment of union, to find, fulfill, nurture, and cherish the one who entered into that union with him/her.

If a flower is planted in good soil, it sends out roots and blooms where it is planted. It cannot bloom and produce properly or fully in alien, arid soil. In exactly the same way, God has designed us to be planted by marriage ceremony and subsequent sexual union in the fertile soil of our own mate's body, heart, mind, soul, and spirit. We cannot come to fullness of life in any other soil. For this reason, the Scripture says of those who commit adultery (specifically of a man with his daughter-in-law, but the principle holds true of any adultery), "Their bloodguiltiness is upon them" (Lev. 20:12b*). Only Paula is good soil for me. Only Paula can tell me who I am as a man. Any other woman, however comely of face, figure or character, must tell me a lie which confuses. For that reason the Bible says, "But whoso committeth adultery with a woman lacketh understanding: he that doeth it *destroyeth his own soul*" (Prov. 6:32 KJV, italics mine).

Unfortunately, however, once a wrong union has been entered, our spirit still remembers that union and seeks to fulfill the other. If there have been many immoral unions with many partners, our spirit becomes like an overloaded transformer, trying to send its current in too many directions. Having been delivered by confession, absolution and prayer for separation, counselees have often cried out, "I have never felt so free. I didn't realize how scattered I felt. I feel together again." Of course! Their spirits were no longer having to search heaven and earth to find and fulfill dozens of forgotten partners!

Every Christian counselor should comprehend the fullness of his task. If he hears a confession of sexual immorality, he should not only pronounce absolution (forgiveness by

---

* Marginal note in NAS: "Literally, *confusion*, i.e., a violation of divine order."

authority in Jesus), not only seek out and forgive roots, not only transform malformed structures, he should also by authority in Christ pronounce that in Jesus' name the spirits of persons involved in immorality are separated. I (John) usually say, "In the name of Jesus, I direct your spirit to forget that union (or unions). You are loosed from that one (or those people). I set your spirit free to cleave only to your own husband (or wife), I loose you in Jesus' name, grateful that what I loose on earth *is* loosed in heaven."

Adultery is sexual union with a person other than one's own mate. If a married person has intercourse with an unmarried person, the first commits adultery, the other fornication.

The same causes pertain to adultery as to fornication. Childhood roots may not appear to have significantly influenced the behavior of an adulterer, since present troubles in the marriage are obviously creating vulnerability and driving such a person to seek illicit relationships. He or she may protest sincerely that were it not for the present untenable circumstances in the marriage, there would be no difficulty in remaining faithful. *Present* causes need to be given full consideration, but causes need to be searched for mainly in childhood roots. Memories in our deep unconscious determine largely how we receive and react to *present* stimuli to our conscious awareness. Because such memories are unseen, they have more power to drive us beyond our control when *present* circumstances pressure us. For example, the most common *present* cause we see is failure of one partner to communicate. Loneliness and vulnerability result. Any person in such circumstances is dying emotionally inside, whether aware of it or not. Sooner or later someone comes along who is able to penetrate behind barriers to communicate heart to heart and soul to soul. It feels so wonderful to come alive again, and he cannot feel guilty as sexual desires begin to awaken. He finds that bewildering. He expected great warning signals or feelings of heavy guilt. A man, for instance, may be unaware that his spirit is so dead it sends no signals of conscience. His coming alive again emotionally in his soul's faculties feels so good, he can't believe the relationship is wrong or sinful. If he continues, and enters into adultery, he may find his mind weakly reminding him of God's laws, but his heart is singing. He thinks he is "in love." Now he is thoroughly confused. Can God's laws be wrong? Can they be only men's imaginations? Surely he wouldn't feel so alive if this were sin? He does not know that if he divorced his wife and married this "soul-mate," she would soon be identified as a "mother," and thereby also become one not to be shared with, and he would soon have to find another "soul-mate." (See chapter 11, "Inner Vows".) Nevertheless, no matter how compelling the *present* loneliness or how confusing the seeming happiness in the sinful relationship and its accompanying lack of guilt, behind all may lie a poor relation with his mother or some other bitter root. That bad root is the real cause, activated by present problems. The pattern appears with many variations—the secretary, a partner at work, a best friend's husband or wife, someone who counsels another or who receives counsel, the next-door neighbor, someone in the family such as a brother or sister-in-law, someone who worked on the same committee in some good work, and so on. Some people go out specifically seeking adulterous relationships. Such people are to be pitied. But most often normally "good" people are blinded by some hidden need or broken area until proximity to just the "right" wrong person develops. A counselor needs to discover what was actually operating in adulterous relationships and deal with causes, not merely results.

The Scriptures are clear and adamant concerning all aberrational forms of sex. By aberrational forms we mean incest, mating with animals, *ménage à trois* (three in one bed), homosexuality, etc.

> If there is a man who commits adultery with another man's wife, one who commits adultery with his friend's wife, the adulterer and the adulteress shall surely be put to death.

If there is a man who lies with his father's wife, he has uncovered his father's nakedness; both of them shall surely be put to death, their bloodguiltiness is upon them.

If there is a man who lies with his daughter-in-law, both of them shall surely be put to death; they have committed incest, their bloodguiltiness is upon them.

If there is a man who lies with a male as those who lie with a woman, both of them have committed a detestable act; they shall surely be put to death. Their bloodguiltiness is upon them.

If there is a man who marries a woman and her mother, it is immorality; both he and they shall be burned with fire, that there may be no immorality in your midst.

If there is a man who lies with an animal, he shall surely be put to death; you shall also kill the animal.

If there is a woman who approaches any animal to mate with it, you shall kill the woman and the animal; they shall surely be put to death. Their bloodguiltiness is upon them.

If there is a man who takes his sister, his father's daughter or his mother's daughter, so that he sees her nakedness and she sees his nakedness, it is a disgrace; and they shall be cut off in the sight of the sons of their people. He has uncovered his sister's nakedness; he bears his guilt.

If there is a man who lies with a menstruous woman and uncovers her nakedness, he has laid bare her flow, and she has exposed the flow of her blood; thus both of them shall be cut off from among their people.

You shall also not uncover the nakedness of your mother's sister or of your father's sister, for such a one has made naked his blood relative; they shall bear their guilt.

If there is a man who lies with his uncle's wife he has uncovered his uncle's nakedness; they shall bear their sin. They shall die childless.

If there is a man who takes his brother's wife, it is abhorrent; he has uncovered his brother's nakedness. They shall be childless. (Lev. 20:10-21)

Homosexuality will be spoken of more fully in chapter 17, "Archetypes and Homosexuality." Here we discuss other forms. In *Restoring the Christian Family*, and in chapter 11 of this book, "Inner Vows," we reported that one in five women has been molested by someone in her own family. Since that writing, we have learned that the rate is now one in every four, and increasing. As the nation turns from God and His Word, we are given over "to degrading passions . . ." (Rom. 1:26).

When a father or stepfather molests or lies with his daughter, the greatest possible harm is done not only to her but to himself. He is confused, shamed and destroyed, whether or not he is aware of loss. His very manhood has been degraded. He has shattered the essence of what it is to be a father, as one who protects the women in his care and who nurtures his daughter's sexuality in holiness. She has been destroyed. The essential capacity of her spirit to become a wife sexually, to entrust the holiness of her spirit through her body to a husband, has been shattered and defiled at its source. Her spirit's loyalty to honor her father has become confused with the union of her spirit to his as a mate, and desecrated. Her ability to relax and let her spirit refresh her husband in holy union is now dead. Only the grace of the Lord, not only to forgive, to heal and separate, but to recreate in her through His power to resurrect, can restore her as a wife and mother. After nearly twenty years in counseling, we have discovered nothing more destructive and defiling than incest!

Girls becoming women should feel free and secure to practice their allurements on their fathers. The young girl and both parents should know it is only a game, and allow it honorably. A father should be delighted with his daughter, and should tell her so. But many men read "come on" signals and fail to comprehend, or their conscience is so weak they override its signals and respond bestially.

For this reason many molested or raped girls feel guilty. They often *feel* they have done *something* to bring it on. What a shame it is that her God-given power to allure a man properly has now become something nasty to her! She may be afraid ever to let her physical beauty shine again. If in anger or rebellion she goes the other way and flaunts her physical beauty to trap men sexually, such a woman is not truly confident, even if she wields great sexual power to seduce. She is afraid to let her real beauty live, for dread of pain at deepest levels in which her spirit still recoils in shame and hurt from her father. Her heart and spirit will need forgiveness as though for real guilt for seducing him, but her mind should be released by comprehension of what really went on.

Further, a girl taken by her own father or stepfather finds her relationship to her mother fractured as well. Should she tell her mother? What would that do to her mother's marital life? What will it do if she doesn't tell? That she has taken her mother's bed-place causes ambivalent feelings of the flesh to run rampant: unwanted glee and guilt that she has beaten her mother in the game of allurement; shame that she has defiled her mother's bed, but unpreventable nasty delight if for any reason she needed to wound or punish her mother; strong feelings of matehood toward her father, perhaps as strongly self-rejected; great desire to share with mama countered by fear which blocks; possible fear of pregnancy; perhaps virulent hatred or aversion to the father—for which she can make no reply when the mother says, "Why can't you be nice to your daddy?" or "What's the matter between you two lately?"

The entire history of confusion needs to be talked out with a counselor. Satan works on her to tell her that she is different than any other girls she knows. "After all, how many of *them* have managed to seduce their own fathers? You're just a slut. No one would like you, or even be around you, if they really knew. . . ." She needs to learn by experiences of sharing that she is not alone. Perhaps isolation could be listed as one of the most damaging results of incest. A counselor should try to win the confidence of a girl or woman so that eventually she can speak of it as freely with him as she would share last night's trip to the ballpark, but *only* with him. A too-glib tongue with others could undo all the good accomplished by sharing.

One-time occurrences, or even several, are not so damaging as being forced to become a regular incestual partner. In each of the many cases we have counseled, we have seen the same effect, a deadness of heart and eye concerning what it is to be a woman. It is as though such women have given up, and know themselves to be nothing but tools to be used and discarded. In such cases, much healing may have to be administered, in which a counselor has touchy ground on which to walk. It will be difficult to avoid transference, confused emotions, etc. He must bring her to life, knowing that she is apt to latch on to him rather than to the Lord. Yet it must be done; only let the counselor by his own prayers keep the cross between himself and her. Better yet, let him counsel with a partner, preferably his own wife. Resurrecting another is not always as clean and clear as calling out "Lazarus, come forth!" We are not the Lord, though He acts through us; resurrection of another affects us—and we must guard our own hearts as we serve. More counselors fall in this attempt than in any other.

Ménage à trois refers to two women in bed with one man, or two men with one woman. Behind *ménage à trois* is often a hunger to fill longings in the heart which could only be satisfied by true sexual blessedness. Some forms of lust occur when true hungers are prevented right satisfaction, causing that energy to seek false release (augmented by carnal desire and Satanic influence). When deadness of spirit prohibits true fulfillment, and hunger couples with other flaws in human nature, the answer for resultant lust can be identified by the mind in terms of some aberrational form such as *ménage à trois*. No aberrational experience truly satisfies, but thrills enough to hold promise, and so captivates and becomes compulsive. Once started down that path, the person must either tire or find more and more degradations to explore.

Sometimes *ménage à trois* happens as a throwback to excessive performance orientation. There is great hunger to experiment, and greater lust to do something to defile, to destroy the performer. One eastern pastor we knew could not receive my warnings concerning performance orientation and his need to destroy his good-guy role. He wound up in *ménage à trois*, and so frightened himself that he plunged back into performing with a vengeance. We wonder what will come next—unless grace intervenes.

Sometimes it is strict obedience to law which fuels fires which erupt into *ménage à trois*, "The strength of sin is the law." Here the motive power differs from performance orientation only in that the specific way of performing is legal rigidity. That coerces repression, for the Pharisee must not let even his feelings or thoughts enter such fields. One wise old pastor said to me, "John, no man can keep the birds from flying over his head, but you don't have to let them nest in your hair." No one can keep lustful thoughts out of his mind or heart. But a man has not "committed adultery with her already in his heart" (Matt. 5:28) until he purposefully entertains such things in his imagination, and dwells upon them. One has only to pray silently, "That's me, Lord, a normal sinner. Forgive me," and go on, forgetting what lies behind. But the rigid ones fight the slightest thought, trying desperately to maintain fleshly righteousness, and thereby doom themselves to endless struggle, until some explode into *ménage à trois* or some other form of degradation. Their obedience was for the wrong reason, not from a live spirit which rests in Jesus, but from the vainglory of a self-righteous heart and mind.

Pornography has this same appeal—a no-no offered to a child needing to rebel. To those who have long ago cut free from parental taboos and found their own foundations in love, pornography is something rank and detestable, not something alluring. A counselor can break the hold of pornography by getting at roots of rebellion and resentment in childhood. Whatever the aberration, a counselor needs to find out what is the unique causal factor in each case and so deal with roots.

There is no sin so great that God the Father cannot forgive through the Lord Jesus (save that against the Holy Spirit), however abhorrent the sin to the counselor. I (John), even after all these years, sometimes have such anger and revulsion at a man who regularly sexually abuses his daughter that I am sure I must be a most unfit vessel to pronounce that man's forgiveness. But the work of mercy is the Lord's, not mine, and so the prayer for forgiveness always works wonders, no matter what I feel. Just as communion and baptism are valid, no matter what the spiritual condition of the celebrating priest, so counselors need not worry. Their yet-undealt-with angers cannot block the efficacy of confession, repentance, and forgiveness, though they may indeed block the counselor's ability to be the counselee's friend. A counselor in Christ is called to honor the office of a confessor, not whatever wayward feelings assail his or her own heart.

Counselors need to be aware that sometimes in counseling, if the counselor is a burden bearer (one who empathizes with others and experiences their feelings in his heart), sexual counseling may become needlessly confusing. Sometimes the way I (John) know a counselee struggles with lust is that by empathy with him or her I feel lust in my own heart, sometimes seemingly toward the counselee. By faith and experience I am able to identify what that actually is. Having placed myself as a counselor daily in my Lord's hands, and the cross between the counselee and myself, I know Jesus keeps my heart. I know also my security in Paula's love, so that even if my sinful, lusty heart were itself really stirred, I would not entertain or act on such feelings. I know then that those strange feelings of lust are not my own, but the other's lust which the Holy Spirit enables me to feel as one way discernment can operate in me. A question or two usually discovers that to be true, and the feelings in me, having existed only to alert me to the inner need of the other, quickly depart.

Beginning counselors may find this extremely confusing. But the lesson needs to be learned. Too many have fallen into honoring those feelings as real, and have succumbed to temptation.

Each counselor must know his own heart. Paula and I have labored long to search our hearts for any untoward or unwelcome feelings and lusts. After many years I have come to view myself much like a gynecologist. Exposure to the emotional, sexual nakedness of a woman or man, even if it involves letting me feel the lust which bothers them, is something as detached for me as talking about a quarrel, or about a parental problem. I have prayed and studied to show myself "a workman that *needeth not to be ashamed*, rightly dividing the word of truth" (2 Tim. 2:15, italics mine), and I trust my Father to protect me in the counseling office—and perhaps most importantly practically, I share with Paula whatever happens (as much as possible without breaking confidences).

Some teachers have insisted, some adamantly, that no man should ever counsel a woman, and that no woman should counsel a man. Such counsel seems wise but it stems mainly from fear, not godly wisdom. Many women need the ministry of a man to become whole. Jesus, of course, did not have the benefit of such teachers' wisdom or He would never have been caught counseling so long alone with the woman at the well (John 4)! Nor would St. Paul have dared attend the women's prayer meeting with Lydia (Acts 16).

Some insist that a man should counsel a woman only if his wife or other witness is present. That is wise and preferable, but not always possible; it is helpful more because two are better than one (Eccles. 4:9) than for fear of sexual wrong-doing.

Let us not celebrate the strength of the flesh or of Satan and his hosts. If a Christian is not strong enough to be trusted in the arena with either a man or a woman, he ought not to be counseling, period. A man who lives alone, or who is presently in trouble with his wife, ought to protect himself whenever possible by having others with him. At the first signs of untoward involvement he should resign that counseling situation, or refuse to continue unless others are present, so as never to give the flesh opportunity. The fact that some counselors have fallen must not be allowed to stampede us into wrong solutions. There are many risks in counseling, but we do not answer them by worldly wisdom devoid of scriptural backing. The example of Jesus is disciplined freedom, not fear and retreat—or shall we insist that no male medical doctor examine a woman or deliver her baby, for fear of sex?

On the other hand, I have shared many warnings throughout this book because I know of many counselors who have become involved sexually with their counselees, especially when ministering in the area of sex. The two greatest pitfalls we have seen counselors fall into are: (1) depression and (2) sexual affairs with counselees. Most often such affairs started because the counselor naively thought the feelings of attraction he felt were really his, instead of simple empathetic identification. Let every counselor be sure to be at one with his wife or her husband, as we have said. I have no hesitation to advise that counseling stop until the heart is settled again. To unmarried counselors I say, "Beware," and add, "Share somewhere in the refreshing family life of some friends."

We cannot leave the field without discussing two other areas of great sexual concern in some counselees. Many come to us confessing an obsession with masturbation. We treat that condition quite oppositely from all the others we have described. Usually what has occurred is that a child, growing up in a tension-filled home, coming into puberty, learned that the experience of ejaculation (for a man) or climax (for a woman) brings a great feeling of release and peace. When the need for relief from tension is coupled with the power of a repressed no-no, masturbation often sets in as a habit. It becomes compulsive over the years by a process of fleshly struggle and continued identification with relief. Though masturbation may or may not be an offense against the law of the Lord (to this date I have not found a Scripture which directly says so, though some Scriptures speak of wet dreams and uncleanness—Lev. 15:16, Deut. 23:10), we do treat it as a cause of guilt because the counselee feels guilty. But though in other circumstances I (John) often speak to make others feel guilty, knowing that is the route to the cross, here I act in the opposite way. This is the one time I will tell a person not to feel guilty (about the masturbation itself).

The true guilt concerns not sexuality first, but idolatry. The counselee is using his body to find the release he should find in prayer to God. This is the same kind of guilt one experiences as a result of inordinate smoking, drinking, golfing, fishing, or whatever we overuse to find the release we should have found in God directly through prayer. I explain to the counselee about identification of masturbation with relief and the power of repression and the guilt of idolatry, and say, "Let's find forgiveness for that idolatry, and see if we can take some of the steam out of this habit by not struggling with it so hard." I may add, "If you slip, okay, forgive yourself. But let's not make such a big deal out of it. Struggling with it as a no-no only increases tension and gives it added power." (Note, I never counsel the same way for any other sin, such as adultery. That simply must be stopped, whatever the cost.) This particular habit has built-in channels inside the body—reflexes which are best defeated by ignoring them rather than frontally attacking them.

The same principle was involved when I as a youth had developed a habit of cursing. When I decided to stop, the battle was on. I discovered then that the more energy I poured into the struggle, the more fuel somehow went to the habit. But when I turned to Jesus and put my eyes on Him, and ignored the battle, trusting His forgiveness for each slip, the battle was soon over. Fleshly struggle adds power to the problem. Rest in Jesus defuses it.

So I teach the person that the moment the temptation to stimulate oneself arises, to recognize it but not to be fearfully concerned, just to turn the eyes of the mind to Jesus, and find someone to pray for, to distract the train of the impulse from its track. In prayer I say, "In the name of Jesus I forgive each instance of masturbation, and now I speak directly to the body, loosing it from this habit. I break this identification of peace and emotional release with masturbation and say to the inner being that it is to find release now in prayer at the foot of the cross, not in physical stimulation." Many have returned to say, "What do you know, John, it worked! I don't have to struggle with it any more." Some add, "Once in a while I still slip, but it isn't a compulsion any more. I forgive myself, and don't get caught up in self-condemnation."

I plead with counselors not to treat masturbation as a demon to be exorcised and not to come down harshly on the counselee. Masturbation is simply a bomb in the flesh we want quietly to defuse.

The second great concern many have is about oral sex. Again, I have found no direct discussion in the Scriptures. It may be there, but to date I have not found it. The Word does say, "That each of you know how to possess his own vessel in sanctification *and honor*" (1 Thess. 4:5). That is the key I follow. Whatever honors the other seems right to me. A second principle is, "Whatever seems natural, the way God designed things to be, is okay." Oral sex does not seem natural to me. The tongue is made for food and speech. Genitals are built for genitals.

A number have come to me saying, "But my wife wants it, and oral sex seems to be the only way she can become aroused enough to enjoy intercourse." Often a wife complains that her husband demands oral sex, or that his sexual needs are excessive. Frequently the cause here is simply that he feels her withholding a part of her inner self from him (though she may be quite willing to go through all the physical expressions of love). Because he never feels "met," and cannot identify what is missing, he is compelled to ask for more and more, and the "more" never satisfies, for the sharing is experienced through walls.

A long time ago the Lord said to me, "John, fight the warfare with whatever level of faith and whatever weapons you have. And what you can do in innocence today may not be appropriate to tomorrow's need or level of faith." Therefore my counsel to such people has been, "The real reasons she cannot be aroused are probably psychological. Let's go after roots. Meanwhile it may or may not be sin, but do what you have to do to keep the relationship from failing." I may change that counsel as the Lord reveals His Word more clearly and gives me more wisdom. To be more clear, I do believe that a regular practice of oral sex would be much less than God intends, perhaps sinful, though perhaps some may need to practice it occasionally. We do not ourselves, because we meet spirit to spirit and heart to heart, and such means of arousal are not needful for us. Again I would counsel against putting a heavy guilt trip on married couples who have found it pleasurable to them. (We speak only of some oral stimulation for arousal, not the use of it *rather than* normal sex; we would simply say stop to that practice.)

Many have written to us, having heard us speak on this subject, wanting us to speak out more forcibly condemning oral sex. We need to make clear that even if our predilection were to do so, and though our own tendency is to avoid oral sex, as prophets and teachers of the Lord, we can only speak out forcibly (as we have about adultery) where the Word of God is unequivocal, either by direct statement or by inference. Prophets and teachers must be careful as St. Paul was in 1 Cor. 7, to distinguish when the Lord was speaking (verse 10), or when Paul spoke, but thought himself trustworthy (verse 25), or when what he said was his own opinion (verses 12 and 40). We plead with well-meaning Christians not to let their zeal cause men to twist God's Word to say what it doesn't say, nor to push or condemn God's servants for not taking stands in areas of controversy in which the Word of God is not unmistakably decisive. We cannot make a definitive statement when God's Word (to our knowledge) does not, no matter how much we might want to.

Finally, concerning dating and "making out" (which in our day meant only what petting, sparking, or spooning, meant to other generations). The question asked so often is, "How far can I go before it is sin?" This question (and all the dating difficulties young people find themselves involved in today) arises because our culture is distinctly unbiblical. There was no dating in Bible lands. We cannot return to that culture, nor perhaps should we. The point is that therefore the Bible does not lay down direct guidelines. There was no need then. The Song of Solomon does say, "I adjure you, O daughters of Jerusalem, By the gazelles or by the hinds of the field, That you will not arouse or awaken my love, Until she pleases" (Song of Sol. 2:7).

Today's children have been freed from the Docetic mind of previous centuries which taught some people to think sex was nasty (see chapters 9, 10, 11 of *The Elijah Task*), and which caused them to fear all bodily emotions and passions. That freedom is good. They also have been delivered from inhibitions of touch and sight which were born of prudery rather than respect for the holiness of a person. That also we view as good. However, today's culture is much too devoid of the sense of the holy, and of proper respect for modesty. Moral laws have been scoffed at and scrapped by most of the culture. Therefore young people have few of the safeguards in dating which we older ones felt compelled to observe. Add to that today's relaxed views of chaperoning, and the mobility available to young people, and parents are reduced to nothing but bare trust in God and prayer. The culture also teaches the opposite of Christian love—to get what you want, with no respect for others. Christian girls are now often disrespected and rejected if they "won't give out." It is a frightening time for parents of teen-aged young people, and young unmarried people.

As we will make more clear in chapter 18, the teen-age years are too late for basic teachings. By then we reap what was sown or not sown in childhood. A child well coached during the pre-teen years, whose parents' lives exemplify what they say, is well-armed for entrance into teen-age dating dilemmas. We have known girls who walked home many miles in the night, or chose the path of loneliness during high school years, to keep themselves for the Lord and for their husband-to-be. Praise God for their testimony and for their parents' solid teachings and example.

Some kissing may be advantageous for young people, because it can teach them many things. But I (John) could not bring myself to kiss a girl unless I had known her a long time.

To me a kiss meant more than physical touch; it involved meeting and cherishing. I could not kiss a girl apart from meaning, just for the "thrill" of it. That was a travesty to me; it meant to my heart the same kind of dishonesty as to come into the House of God and go through the motions of worship without meaning it. I only went with two others before Paula, and was quite serious about each. I watched Paula several weeks before asking her for a date, and then did not ask to kiss her until we had dated several weeks. Loren had the same kind of approach to dating. Mark is the same. Johnny never seriously dated anyone other than Marty. And Tim thinks in like manner. Morality is engrained; it is "caught" from one's parents.

We warn young couples that what they do today, still managing to stop without going too far, they may not be able to continue to do and to be able to stop, as their relationship grows. So there is no hard-and-fast rule for what one can do without it being too much. During certain times of the month desire is greater and resistance lower. Couples ought not to "stir up nor awaken too much desire until it please." Certainly all genital areas should be off limits before marriage. The breasts should be reserved for the husband only (see Prov. 5:18-19, and especially verse 20, "For why should you, my son, be exhilarated with an adulteress, And embrace the bosom of a foreigner?"). How can a young man know whether this one whose bosom he desires to embrace will be his or another's wife? Our counsel to couples as they become more serious is that they not give themselves opportunity by being together alone too much, and to double date and go to parties together. Flesh cannot be trusted once increasing trust opens doors. Not love, but carnality, will push us to go too far.

Again, a counselor's work may not be so much to bring forgiveness for overstepping bounds as to uncover the childhood flaws which create vulnerability. Most often, unfortunately, we do not have opportunity for preventative medicine; we are only invited to restore ships already on the rocks. Let us hope that these few words may help to prevent some from ruining the gift God gives us for one only. Every year (we have now been married thirty-one years) Paula and I rejoice in the Lord more and more, that by His grace He has kept us all of our lives only for each other.

16

Archetypes and Homosexuality

For though we walk in the flesh, we do not war according to the flesh, for the weapons of our warfare are not of the flesh, but divinely powerful for the destruction of fortresses. We are destroying speculations and every lofty thing raised up against the knowledge of God, and we are taking every thought captive to the obedience of Christ, and we are ready to punish all disobedience, whenever your obedience is complete. (2 Cor. 10:3-6)

The Toughness and Mercy of God's Word

Homosexuality is not a thing by itself. It possessed culture and history long before Sodom and Gomorrah. Other aberrations seem to be occasional, or if they are obsessional, they do not claim to be a valid style of life. But homosexuality wraps about itself rationalizations, defenses, veneers, postures and a way of living which sometimes even claims to be Christian.

"Dear friends, although I was very eager to write to you about the salvation we share, I felt I had to write and urge you to contend for the faith that was once for all entrusted to the saints. For certain men* whose condemnation was written about long ago have secretly slipped in among you. They are godless men, *who change the grace of our God into a license for immorality* and deny Jesus Christ our only Sovereign and Lord" (Jude 3-4 NIV, italics mine).

Today some civil rights groups appeal for acceptance of homosexuality as normal, God-given and healthy. They pull

---

* Many biblical scholars believe "certain men" refers distinctly to homosexuals; the point is clear, whether this is the case or not.

upon the desire of men to appear to have an open, liberal, live-and-let-live mentality. No one can survive as a counselor without a generous, loving, and accepting nature. But every Christian counselor must also stand firmly on the foundation of our Lord Jesus Christ, according to His Word, and nowhere else. Gentle desire to accept must not be allowed to blind eyes to reality. The Word of God is absolutely clear concerning homosexuality.

Nevertheless, men practice cunning and try to twist His Word:

> Rather, we have renounced secret and shameful ways; we do not use deception, *nor do we distort the word of God.*
> (2 Cor. 4:2 NIV, italics mine)

> Bear in mind that our Lord's patience means salvation, just as our dear brother Paul also wrote you with the wisdom that God gave him. He writes the same way in all his letters, speaking in them of these matters. His letters contain some things that are hard to understand, which *ignorant and unstable people distort,* as they do the other Scriptures, *to their own destruction.*
> (2 Pet. 3:15-16 NIV, italics mine)

> In a similar way, *Sodom and Gomorrah* * and the surrounding towns gave themselves up to *sexual immorality and perversion.* They serve as an example to those who suffer the punishment of eternal fire. In the very same way, *these dreamers pollute their own bodies,* reject authority and slander celestial beings.
> (Jude 7-8 NIV, italics mine)

Kindness to homosexuals is not achieved by lessening the severity of God's Word. The strictest law of God is nothing but kindness. His laws were given purely for our benefit. We think to change or improve upon them only to invoke the silliness of man's carnal reasonings.

Homosexuality is sin. The Word of God allows no other statement.

---

* It is these references which lead scholars to conclude that verse 4 also referred to homosexuals.

If there is a man who lies with a male as those who lie with a woman, both of them have committed a detestable act; they shall surely be put to death. Their bloodguiltiness is upon them. (Lev. 20:13)

You shall not lie with a male as one who lies with a female; it is an abomination. (Lev. 18:22)

For even though they knew God, they did not honor Him as God, or give thanks; but they became futile in their speculations, and their foolish heart was darkened. Professing to be wise, they became fools, and exchanged the glory of the incorruptible God for an image in the form of corruptible man and of birds and four-footed animals and crawling creatures. Therefore God gave them over in the lusts of their hearts to impurity, that their bodies might be dishonored among them. For they exchanged the truth of God for a lie, and worshiped and served the creature rather than the Creator, who is blessed forever. Amen. For this reason God gave them over to degrading passions; for their women exchanged the natural function for that which is unnatural, and in the same way also the men abandoned the natural function of the woman and burned in their desire towards one another, men with men committing indecent acts and receiving in their own persons the due penalty of their error. (Rom. 1:21-27)

Or do you not know that the unrighteous shall not inherit the kingdom of God? Do not be deceived; neither fornicators, nor idolators, nor adulterers, *nor effeminate [i.e. "effeminate, by perversion"—marginal note], nor homosexuals,* nor thieves, nor covetous, nor drunkards, nor revilers, nor swindlers, shall inherit the kingdom of God. (1 Cor. 6:9-10, italics mine)

Realizing the fact that law is not made for a righteous man, but for those who are lawless and rebellious, for the ungodly and sinners, for the unholy and profane, for those who kill their fathers or mothers, for murderers and immoral men *and homosexuals* and kidnappers and liars and perjurers, and whatever else is contrary to sound teaching. (1 Tim. 1:9-10, italics mine)

But for the cowardly and unbelieving and *abominable* and

murderers and immoral persons and sorcerers and idolaters and all liars, their part will be in the lake that burns
with fire and brimstone, which is the second death (Rev.
21:8. Remember that Lev. 18:22 calls homosexual activity
"abomination").

The only change from the Old Testament to the New
Testament concerning homosexuality has to do with treatment. In the Old Testament the sole answer was death,
whether from stoning by Israel or fire from heaven upon
Sodom and Gomorrah. Today the answer is still the same—
death. But Jesus has become that death for us; so the answer is,
"Brethren, even if a man is caught in any trespass, you who are
spiritual, restore such a one in a spirit of gentleness" (Gal. 6:1).
The Christian answer is forgiveness and death on the cross,
thus redemption from sin, whenever a homosexual will allow
that to take place. It is to that end we write. Our hope is to place
in every Christian counselor's mind and heart tools for the
deliverance of repentant homosexuals. Homosexuality is not
an irreversible trap. We have seen a great many homosexuals
delivered once for all. All Christendom needs to join in prayer
for the deliverance of every homosexual and lesbian.

The role of a Christian counselor for all people is to love
the person, to hate that which destroys the life of Christ in him,
and to assist as the Lord sets him free to become who he is
meant to be in Christ. That task for homosexual individuals is
made most difficult by the stance of the "gay community." Gay
society acts to pull back ". . . by fleshly desires, by sensuality,
those who barely escape from the ones who live in error" (2
Pet. 2:18). The gay community parades upon the ground of
Christianity as though anyone ought to see that their sickness
is normal. (This is based on the Hitlerian maxim that a big
enough lie will be accepted as truth.) Whoever doesn't agree to
that lie is of course judgmental and filled with hate. Never
mind that a homosexual can understand and agree that a man
can view liars, cheaters, thieves, and murderers as wrong
without hating them—in their eyes one cannot view a homosexual as wrong without being hateful and judgmental! They

try to discredit any counselor who disagrees with them and to dislodge the counselee from his care.

A gay person may agree with a Christian counselor in grieving for parents and children in child abuse cases, or in the deliverance of an alcoholic, or in setting free someone who is psychotically paranoid. "Square" and gay can find common ground in recognizing, even biblically, the undesirability of such conditions. Normally, neither gay nor "square" would have difficulty in concurring that the command, "Thou shalt not steal," is to be obeyed, and that mercy is to be applied to a thief according to Galatians 6:1. Gays may celebrate the compassion of a Christian counselor relative to everyone and everything else, but let that same counselor move to set a brother free from homosexuality as sin according to the Word of God, let him move to heal a brother of that condition, and suddenly the counselor is apt to be named a bigot who is judgmental, hateful—someone to be discredited and avoided.

We write, therefore, only to and for Christian counselors, to teach them how to set free those who desire deliverance, not to please, convince, or even give any credibility or acknowledgment to the gay community. We owe it none. We regard it as an enemy of Christ no matter what it thinks of itself in its delusion. We make no apology to them. We have no help for anyone (other than rebuke) who wants to maintain, contrary to the Word of God, that homosexuality has any right to exist.

Let the gay community detest or protest whatever we say; they are simply, clearly, and utterly wrong, sick and deluded, and a defilement in the eyes of God! We insist to every Christian counselor; take no other stance. There is no middle ground. Kindness and liberality happen by the grace of Christ for all sinners, not by relaxing one of the least of His commandments. We do not help the sick by refusing to call them sick for fear of being called judgmental. Be unashamed of the moral rectitude of the Gospel of Christ. Be willing to take whatever abuse the gay community may hand out. There are no halfway, "safe" stances concerning homosexuality.

If, like Alcoholics Anonymous, who exist to fight alcohol,

the gay community would band together to destroy their disease, we would applaud them and support them. But as they exist to oppose the truth of God's Word, no Christian counselor or church should grant them the same kind of respect that is given to Alcoholics Anonymous, for instance. This does not mean that we should hunt them down as we would a criminal gang, however. They are not to be persecuted. We write to insist that Christian counselors and the Church have the spiritual backbone not to defer one iota.

Archetypes and Principalities

We have not spoken of demons or deliverance anywhere else in this book (or in our previous two), because we do not want to give Satan any glory. We know that if a counselor transforms a person's inner house of character in Jesus, whatever demon inhabits, if any, must flee, having no longer a house to dwell in. Seldom do Paula and I have to do an exorcism directly. We know that the devil and all his hosts were once for all defeated and disarmed, "When he had disarmed the rulers and authorities, he made a public display of them, having triumphed over them through Him" (Col. 2:15). Therefore, we seldom have to speak directly to demons to defeat them. We have only to wash the other in the blood of forgiveness and bring unregenerate practices to death on the cross. Thereby the blood has removed Satan's ground to accuse, and the cross has dismantled his theater of operation. So though we occasionally do exorcisms (one Christian psychiatrist used to send patients regularly to us whenever he diagnosed them as inhabited, and the Lord would set them free), we very infrequently say anything about Satan, and concentrate on teaching how to bring people to Jesus on the cross. That is the only lasting form of exorcism, for the devil's forces will return after exorcism to a house not dealt with (Matt. 12:43-45, Luke 11:14-16). The cross gives glory to Jesus, whereas too much direct attack upon Satan gives him the attention he craves. We accomplish the same end—deliverance— but we celebrate only the power of Jesus.

Nevertheless, we cannot teach concerning homosexuality without first presenting a basic teaching concerning not merely local demons, but principalities. For it is principalities and "world rulers of this present darkness" (Eph. 6:12 RSV) who use devices to entrap, blind and hold captive all homosexuals. We are not saying that all homosexuals are demon possessed, or even inhabited. Some may be. We are speaking of world rulers of darkness who use empty philosophies and deceits (Col. 2:8) to overcome the minds and control the wills of homosexuals. The point is that such powers can control homosexuals without ever having to come near them, though they may do that as well in some instances.

In many cases, homosexuals cannot be set free until "the strong man" (the principality who blinds his mind and controls his will) is bound. Only then can we plunder his goods and set homosexuals and lesbians free (Matt. 12:29).

The following teaching is therefore not only for counselors but for all intercessors in the Body of Christ, applicable not only to homosexuals and lesbians but to many dark forces in many areas of life which threaten to undo the free will of our friends and neighbors.

Archetypes

"See to it that no one takes you captive through philosophy and empty deception, according to the tradition of men, according to the elementary principles of the world, rather than according to Christ" (Col. 2:8). One might ask, "How can philosophy or empty deception take anyone captive? Do not men have free wills? Is not philosophy an inert, inactive thing? How could it grab hold of anybody who didn't want it to?" We used to think one could dabble in philosophies and nothing more than mental exercise would come of it. But in our generation, we have all seen increasing numbers of young people totally thought-controlled by various cults, pinning flowers on people and badgering for contributions, accosting people in airports, parroting the jargon their controllers have pumped into them. Free wills *can* be overcome. Minds can be "brain-dirtied" (we refuse to say brainwashed). People can be thoroughly thought-controlled. How? "In whose case the god of this world has blinded the minds of the unbelieving, that they might not see . . . the image of God" (2 Cor. 4:4). How does Satan block and blind? One way is by ancient archetypes in the mind of man, wielded by powers of darkness. We now purposefully reach outside biblical terms to borrow a term from Plato and Carl Jung. Too many differing meanings have been attached to such words as "traditions," "philosophies," and "empty deceptions." It seems easier to borrow a secular word and coin a new meaning for it than to try to launder these biblical words from present associations. Most likely neither Plato nor Jung would be happy with our use of the word, "archetypes." By an archetype we mean a ruling way of thinking, feeling, and acting, built by mankind into the common mentality we share; an archetype, therefore, being a device built into the flesh of mankind generally which acts upon us to control us individually.

Inside an individual, a habit or "practice" (Col. 3:9) can be developed until it has an automatic, autonomous life. If, for example, the habit is jealousy, we may decide not to be jealous, only to find ourselves taken over and expressing jealousy anyway the next time we are caught off guard. That habit has obtained a life of its own in our flesh and does not want to die. It looms up and controls us whenever it is triggered, until and unless we break its hold. Some habits are so strong that fleshly will power cannot break them; and so we discover anew our continuing need for the intervention of Jesus as our Lord and Savior.

An archetype is simply a habit or practice not inside an individual but in the flesh of mankind. An archetype (as we define it) is any developed way of thinking—a tradition, a cultural norm, an "empty philosophy," an habitual way of emoting and rationalizing—which can clamp upon individuals. Under the influence of an archetype, our minds become like preprogrammed computers, we develop tunnel vision, our wills are circumscribed, and our emotions are no longer those of our spirit or the Holy Spirit in us but they become outer-controlled, predictable and usable. The specific function of an archetype is to rob us of our free will, to prevent true conscience from enabling good decisions, to turn us into robots programed to perform, manipulated by forces outside ourselves.

Just as a practice in our individual nature may be only flesh, but serves also as a house for a demon, so an archetype (a "practice" in the flesh of mankind) may only be flesh, or may also be wielded by a principality (ruling demon). In the case of homosexuals the archetype always has a principality of delusion behind it.

Before World War II, Hitler began to preach Aryan superiority to the German people. The archetype of racial prejudice had been built centuries before, active in culture after culture, history after history, teaching one nation after another to think itself better than others. That way of thinking was not an inert thing, like a silent rock, but more like an octopus writhing in the sea of thought, ready to wrap living tentacles about whatever foolish minds ventured near enough. The moment the German people began to open themselves to that teaching, the powers of darkness could maneuver that archetype over their minds until whoever was not securely grounded in God's Word lost ability to think in any other terms. Hitler could then begin to preach the "divine right" of the Germans to conquer the world, to establish the great Third Reich. That moved the German people under another great, long-established archetype of aggression and war. Soon, men were proudly goose-stepping into battle to destroy other men and take their lands. Christians who protested, such as Dietrich Bonhoeffer, were put in prison. The German mind was controlled by "world rulers of this present darkness" (Eph. 6:12 RSV), through the ancient archetypes of racial prejudice, hatred and war. Recently, having shared this teaching in a meeting, I found it sadly confirmed when several who had lived in Germany prior to and during the Second World War came to me with tears in their eyes to exclaim,

"Oh, you don't know how true your teaching was. We saw friends and neighbors taken over and controlled one by one. It was horrible!"

Have we not all grieved to see friends and neighbors, married ten or twenty or even forty years, who began to think of separation and divorce—and suddenly our friends' thoughtful, balanced minds were deluded? Overnight it seemed, they were confined to tunnel vision. They could not remember the good things of the past nor look to better days ahead. They could gain no perspective to look upon their problems in helpful ways. They began to spew the same half-baked sophistries and deceits of mind and heart our other friends did who went the same way. No longer could we have free and open discussion with them as we had in the past. They could not reason; they only emoted and reacted to "red herring" words and signals. Their free wills were gone. The hidden factor is an archetype. Men have long thought and built deceptions and lying ways to rationalize separation and divorce. That web of thought lies not merely like a spider web across the path but like a writhing, power-filled mesh of patterns of thought, a net (Ps. 25:15, 31:4, 35:7-8, 57:6, 140:5) cast by ". . . spiritual hosts of wickedness in the heavenly places" (Eph. 6:12 RSV). The purpose is to destroy what God would build—the family!

Have we not often been stunned by the change in a teen-ager, overnight it seems, when drugs begin to catch hold of him? Teen-agers naturally change like weathervanes, flipping in one direction and then another. The key in discerning the presence of an archetype is loss of freedom to reason or to turn about—as though the weathervane gets stuck pointing only in one direction no matter which way the wind of reason blows! The influence of drugs alone is bad enough. More causal, however, is the power of the archetype. Long before mankind could write, men had begun to discover hallucinogens, and drugs for healing. The archetype of drugs is almost as old as the mind of man. Powers of darkness wield it to captivate and destroy the human mind. When one of our sons became involved with drugs, there was suddenly no reasoning with him. No matter how many scientific articles we showed him *proving* the danger and damage of drugs, he could not hear. When the grace of God brought change, he dropped the drugs. A few weeks later he could not imagine how he could have thought that way. Later he testified brilliantly to his cousins, warning them what happens when people dabble in drugs, and was astonished and stymied that now they refused to hear him—already, only a few months older than they, he had become part of the "older generation"! Archetypes not only blind and rob, the powers that wield them also invent and use catch phrases that have no real, logically defendable meanings. Archetypes thus hook into deep unexaminable feelings by such catch words to block meaningful thought and sensible conclusions.

Dispensationalism (an approach to theology that holds that miracles, tongues, signs and wonders ceased about the time the biblical canon was established) has behind it another debasing archetype. Throughout history, whenever men have hardened their hearts and refused to hear God, rationalizations, false loyalties, idolatries, "feelosophies," "foolosophies," and fleshly theologies have been built to justify and secrete the deceptions of the heart. Not having the fullness of the Holy Spirit, men found reasons to justify rather than receive. That constant sinful proclivity to falsely justify in many areas has formed archetypes of clever unbelief which act upon stage after stage—heresies, deceptions, circumcision, partyisms, Phariseeisms, etc.—all to block and blind. "To this day whenever Moses is read, *a veil lies over their heart*" (2 Cor. 3:15, italics mine).

Perhaps the most obvious archetype among Americans is what men have been attempting to break out of through the efforts of such leaders as Martin Luther King and such organizations as the NAACP. Having grown up in Missouri and Kansas, I can testify to puzzling greatly as a child over the confused mentality of people. My spirit leaped to embrace black people as brothers (and still does today) and found itself darkened and bewildered by adult hatreds and silly prejudices. I am not unique. No one is born with racial prejudice. Every child is confused and made heartsick by the snide remarks, jokes, stories, and actions of brain-dirtied adults concerning black people in America. Racial prejudice is a sickness kept alive by the powers of darkness through archetypes. I hate it virulently (perhaps partly because of my American Indian heritage). I passionately hate such statements as, "I don't hate niggers, I just don't . . ." (followed by such statements as) ". . . have to like them," ". . . want to ride beside them in buses," or ". . . want them to marry my daughter." Another often-heard remark, "I want them to keep their place, that's all," is the essence of the function of an archetype, to lock people into places that are not their place in the Lord at all. I want to cry out, "Wake up, America!" Thank God that seems to be happening, if not so quickly as some of us want.

Some have asked me, "Could not sound doctrine and theology and even biblical teaching and the Word itself be archetypal too?" Men can fall into the flesh and use any holy thing corruptly. But whatever flows from God by His Holy Spirit sets free. "The law of the Lord is perfect, restoring the soul. . . . The commandment of the Lord is pure, enlightening the eyes. . . . The judgments of the Lord are true; they are righteous altogether" (Ps. 19:7a, 8b, 9b). Sound doctrine and the Bible are not of the flesh; they are of God. Flesh corrupts and ensnares. The Holy Spirit sets free (Gal. 5:1). So long as the Spirit flows in us according to God's Word, what we preach and teach is no archetypal thing. The telling mark is fruits. If we take "every thought captive to the obedience of Christ" (2 Cor. 10:5), paradoxically by that the mind and will are set free. Whereas if archetypes act upon us, free will is trammeled and independent thought is shut down. Nevertheless, our fleshly theologies, doctrines of men, and religious traditions can be used by the flesh to become the most unyielding, captivating archetypes of all, destructive to the unity of the Body of Christ, hateful and more wounding to our Lord than all others.

"For our struggle is not against flesh and blood, but against the rulers, against the powers, against the world-forces of this darkness, against the spiritual forces of wickedness in the heavenly places" (Eph. 6:12). How do the powers rule men? Perhaps more by archetypes than by any other way. Principalities so wield huge archetypal forms of thought over the minds of men that wars, rebellions, racial strife, divorce, pornography, demagoguery, cultism, etc. move men like lemmings leaping off cliffs to drown in the sea. Through archetypes, powers of darkness polarize men and hurl opposites at each other, such as male chauvinism and women's liberation—both more driven and controlled than either could suspect or admit. The real battle is not between capitalism and communism (though the battle exists and ought not to be minimized). We do not war against flesh and blood. Behind both capitalism and communism are ancient archetypes of greed, aggression, and control. Rugged individualism is an archetypal form by which principalities strive to prevent the corporate life of the Body of Christ. Truly, it is only "When a man turns to the Lord the veil is removed. Now the Lord is the Spirit, and where the Spirit of the Lord is, there is freedom" (2 Cor. 3:16-17 RSV).

Every Christian possesses power to defeat world rulers of this present darkness. We are given power and authority to bind and loose (Matt. 16:19, 18:18). Whether or not we are called as counselors, we are called to be intercessors (1 Tim. 2:1). We are all called to stand, "Finally, be strong in the Lord and in his mighty power. Put on the full armor of God so that you can take your stand *against the devil's schemes*" (Eph. 6:10-11 NIV, italics mine). We are more than conquerors (Rom. 8:37). We are to overcome evil with good (Rom. 12:21).

When we see the operation of an archetype on the minds of our friends, we are called to warfare. We need only bind the archetype by name, and command it to be still. One day I (John) was visiting with a brother pastor. The conversation turned in a way that was appalling to me. I found myself listening with increasing revulsion to judgmental tirades about other denominations and pastors. After a while (having covertly asked the Lord whether I ought to) I silently bound that archetype of judgmentalism, divisiveness and hatred. Perhaps to teach me, the Lord opened my spiritual eyes, and I physically saw a sheet of fire and love rain down over that pastor. The pastor flushed deep red, stammered a moment, and said, "I don't know what I got into that for. Forgive me. Let's talk about something else." I never told him, merely praised God and gave thanks inside, and went on visiting.

Paula attended a ladies' circle which devolved into gossip and critical attack. She silently prayed against that "thing" which had invaded the women, and prayed awhile, silently in the Spirit. Soon, one of the women shook herself and said, "What are we doing? This is not right," and changed the subject.

In *Restoring the Christian Family* I told the story of a young couple who fell under false teaching of male dominance and women's suppression. I wrote about how the wife called in tears to say, "My husband has just gone to spend a week with another woman and tells me that being a submissive wife means that I should let him do this so he can find out if he really wants to choose me or her!" (*Restoring the Christian Family*, pp. 157-158). I told about praying for him. And how that night he called his wife and came home. What I did not include then was that that was an archetype of male dominance, cultism, and control. I did not know then all this about archetypes. I merely rose in righteous anger against that "thing" which was destroying my brother's marriage, and commanded it to let go of him. I "saw" him raise his head, look about and say to himself, "What am I doing here?"

One cannot cast away a demon if the demonized person wants it. Similarly one cannot in the opening warfare, without counseling the other, cast away an entire archetype and all the demons and principalities behind it. But we can "buy time" for the other. We can break the hold and prevent the influence of the archetype and principalities long enough for the other to come to his senses. One could wonder, was it perhaps that ancient archetypal form of teen-age rebellion, of greed and lust, that had laid hold of the prodigal son in Luke 15? Certainly he had become lost from himself, for the Scriptures carefully report, "But when *he came to his senses* . . ." (Luke 15:17). Was the father doing more than waiting? Was he praying for his son? Whether or not, the message is clear for us: we are called to do more than wait. We have power in intercession to break the hold of cults, or drugs, or divorce, or greed, or gambling, or homosexuality, whatever may be gripping our brother or sister (that is, if God so calls—we are not to rush out like Don Quixote to charge at every windmill).

We cannot minister the fullness of deliverance to a homosexual until he asks for it. The point of this prelude concerning archetypes is that perhaps our loved one will never have power to cry for release unless someone pays the price of intercessory warfare. The strong man, the world ruler who wields the archetype which holds his mind, must be bound. His power must be broken. We can purchase that space of time our loved one needs, that moment of clarity. We can strengthen his inner spirit (Eph. 3:16) and give him power to see (Eph. 1:17-18). If anyone has been desperately ill, and has felt a few minutes reprieve by the presence of a few praying friends, he can begin to grasp how precious that bit of time can be.

During my wild flights into mystical adventures in earlier years, I lost track of reality for a few hours several times. I know minimally, but enough to appreciate deeply, the gnawing anxiety, restlessness of spirit, tumbling of thoughts, confusions and sickness of heart and mind which can become so pervasive one can even lose track of what it felt like to have been whole. The sick condition can become familiar to the point of seeming normal. I know the blessedness of feeling myself being returned to normal. I know what it is to come back to one's senses. The only way I have found to begin to describe it was to say, "It feels so good to quit hitting one's head against the wall, one knows for the first time by that peace that he *was* hitting his head against the wall!" We can be so sick that we no longer have any awareness of any other kind of life. We cannot remember what wholeness felt like. Preaching to homosexuals about how good it is to feel normal is like pouring nickels into a defective vending machine; the coins fall on through to "reject" with no place to catch or take hold. Their minds are simply so captive that they cannot register what is being said. Binding the principalities can set the mind and heart free for a while to hear. Call friends. Gang up on that "thing." We *can* set our loved ones free. It works.

Healing Homosexuals

When a homosexual or lesbian asks, there are certain things necessary for freedom. First, we counsel as we would any other, discovering the counselee's early life with his or her parents. Several conditions are the most likely contributing factors. *In all our years of counseling, we have never found a homosexual or lesbian who had or related well to a strong, gentle, loving father.* Commonly, the father was crude, violent, unstable, critical and abusive, or absent altogether. The growing boy rejected masculinity as a model, and fled to the female side of his nature, usually with over attenuated attachment to his mother. The young girl rejected letting emotional responses live in relation to men, and found gratification with women. Mothers likewise can drive boys to reject becoming close to a woman, and girls to despise becoming female. Overprotective, maudlin mothers can contribute to homosexuality in either sex.

Sometimes the spirit of the fetus is aware of great parental desire for a baby of the opposite sex. Boys born, for example, fifth or sixth in a line of boys, can try desperately to become the girl the parents wanted. Or girls may want to be their daddy's boy.

There are hermaphrodites. These individuals are born with physical manifestations that are both male and female. That is an organic condition which may or may not result in homosexual activity. We suggest that lay counselors refer such to medical specialists and psychiatrists.

Sometimes tendency toward homosexuality is an inherited condition. We have counseled some who could trace homosexuality through several successive generations. To stop that, one simply places the cross through prayer between the person and all previous generations, claiming according to Ezekiel 18 and Jeremiah 31:16ff that all the sins of the ancestors are now stopped on the cross of Jesus, and shall not descend by reaping, by inherited physical tendencies, or by example to the children or children's children.

Homosexuality is often "caught" by exposure of young boys or girls to practicing sodomites who so involve their victims that stimulation, practice, and false sexual identification overlay sodomy on an otherwise normal child. The innate sense of a child can sometimes either throw off homosexual advances before anything happens, or overcome such practices before they can take root, unless some inner fractures from earlier childhood, or other latent conditions act as fertile ground. So many normal children carry so many vulnerabilities, it is for this reason that school boards should be allowed to refuse to hire known homosexuals regardless of gay protests and their confused cries about civil rights. As counselors, having heard numerous stories of involvement at crucial times in puberty, in swimming pools, restrooms at school, situations with camp counselors, choirboys and girls at church, etc., we know it is nothing but head-in-the-sand foolishness to maintain that practicing homosexuals will not molest young people! Of course not all will. But the likelihood is as frequent as sparks on tinder to flame. Not all sparks catch, but why be foolish?

Before I knew any such thing as homosexuality existed, it was a swimming instructor in a YMCA program who offered to teach me how to float on my back, who tried to make approaches. The moment he touched where he should not, my spirit darkened, I was angry, and I fled out of there. I did not know from what I was fleeing, but I knew in my spirit whatever it was, was bad. But what of the many we and others have counseled who were not so parentally fortunate as I, who were vulnerable? Countless times Paula and I have pronounced forgiveness for homosexual and lesbian experiences which did not lead to sodomy as a way of life, but left a dark blot of guilt and sexual confusion in the heart. I do not care what legal sophistries and moral confusions may possess the minds of lawyers and judges (archetypes again), up to and including the Supreme Court of our land, if and whenever we cannot protect our children from exposure to sodomites, we interpret law in defiance of God's law and incur the wrath of God! Our culture has become lax about many such matters as adultery, rape, molestation, incest, etc. but our jurisprudence system is based upon biblical commandments. On that basis we incarcerate a thief, rapist, extortioner, etc. Somehow the gay community has gained acceptance to the lie that the Law of God's Word does not rightly apply to them!

Unfortunately our prisons have become major breeding grounds for homosexuality. I do not say that we should put homosexuals in prison. But neither should we be forced to have to allow their contagion near our children.

In each case, whether in experiences in life or in prenatal traumas, fractures happened which led to homosexuality, we ask the Lord to enable the person to forgive, and we pronounce forgiveness, healing the condition by transformation through the cross and the resurrection life of the Lord Jesus Christ. Often, after several prayer sessions, in which roots have been discovered and "prayed through," I have realized that the counselee cannot come into fullness of manhood or womanhood through lack of an acceptable primary model. At such times I have for a while become a parent in Christ, imparting by my life what manhood is for the other (or Paula has done so for women). That is not so much a matter of amounts of time spent with the counselee as it is of acceptance in the heart and "carrying." The closest model I can think of is osmosis; it is almost as though the counselee needs to drink or absorb what it is to be a man or a woman by relating at deep, heartfelt levels to me and/or Paula (or any other counselor or friend).

One can bind the demonic, transform the root causes, and

become as a surrogate parent to the other, and still fail to deliver. The Lord revealed to me a further step. I had seen that what we then knew to do was not enough. Something more and deeper was needed. What the Holy Spirit revealed I do not pretend to understand. I tried what He showed me, and it worked, whatever the reality behind it may be.

The Lord reminded me of the Scripture, "Male and female He created them" (Gen. 1:27), and said that His Word did not say, "Male *or* female created He each one" as we so often mentally misread it. God pointed out to me that He meant by the Word that all, whether male or female, are created both male and female. He explained that He has created us to possess both poles within us, whether male or female. He went on to say that men develop mainly within the male sphere but also have within themselves a female nature, which their wives later fulfill for them, thus in that sense literally becoming one flesh. He explained also that women likewise have a male nature which husbands fulfill. (In all our reporting, readers should remember that a prophet's hearing and prophecy is imperfect—1 Cor. 13:11-12. Perhaps this exegesis of Genesis 1:17 is suspect. But let the reader take home the meaning.) Then the Lord said to me, "In the case of one who has indeed become homosexual, what has happened is

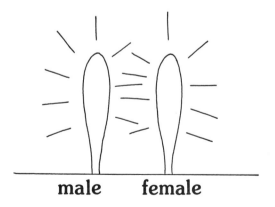

male female

that either prenatally or by sinful experience the poles have become reversed." Then he represented it to me by a vision, first of the normal, like anode and cathode poles, radiating in balance with each other.

Then he portrayed an abnormal or homosexual condition:

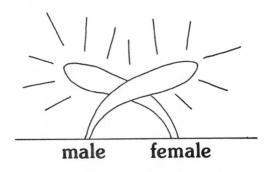

He continued by teaching that when the poles have become reversed, natural desires are affected accordingly. So that a man whose poles were reversed in early childhood may struggle subsequently all his life against strong impulses to try sex with a man, wondering why such occasional desires plague him. Finally, when he tries it, it seems so natural and right for him, he may conclude he must have been created that way. He may proclaim then that God created him to be a homosexual and that he has at last been liberated and has come home to what he ought to have been all along. The Lord explained to me that what has actually transpired is that he has surrendered to the hidden, sick condition which had lain dormant since childhood, and thus he falsely concluded that homosexuality must be natural and God-given for him! It seems liberating and "right" only because he has resisted it for so many years that ending the battle brings a relief he then confuses with rightness. Then the Lord said, *"John, when you have done all else for a homosexual, by vision see the poles*

reversed as I have shown you, and then stand and see as I reach in to disentangle those poles and set them in order."

The first occasion following that revelation was a young man who came confessing to more than fifty homosexual encounters in the previous month alone! We tracked down the early history—father a failure, a smothering mother, etc.— and prayed for resultant structures to be transformed. Then I prayed as the Lord had directed (with my heart in my chest, feeling like I had walked out of the boat onto the sea). I did "see" the Lord reach in and set the poles in order. It not only worked, that was over ten years ago, and very recently we received a letter from that young man reporting and giving thanks that he has remained whole!

What happens after such prayer is that normal desire of a man for a woman revives and desire for men ceases. Women cease to lust for women, and natural desire for a man lives in the heart as it should.

Dr. William Johnson, head of the psychology department at Whitworth College, Spokane, Washington, heard us teach this way of ministering to homosexuals. Later he talked about it with me, both of us confessing that we couldn't fully understand what the Lord was revealing. We did not and still do not know whether the Lord was speaking of some as yet undiscovered physical reality, perhaps in our nervous system, or something psychological, or spiritual only, or all of the above. But we agreed that if it brought good fruits, whatever the Lord actually described, it was worth trying. Subsequently, young men came to Bill wanting deliverance from homosexuality. He bound the archetype, traced down psychological causes, and prayed accordingly, and then prayed by vision and authority concerning the male and female poles as the Lord had instructed. He reported with joy that the first young man had returned to testify to a great change; he didn't know what had happened but now he no longer felt temptations or even attractions to men, and had begun to feel real longings for women. In short, he felt normal! Bill said, "I don't know what it is, John, but I know it works. Hallelujah!"

Great mysteries await us inside mankind. The Lord has only begun to reveal the wonders of our makeup. Suffice it to say that we have shared this revelation by testimony rather than as confirmed scriptural teaching, to indicate that what we have shared concerning male and female poles is not as other teachings in this book, but a step of faith on our part to hear what may or may not be scripturally, psychologically, or physically defensible. We want to make it abundantly clear that this teaching is based on our own faulty listening and experience (in 1 Cor. 7, St. Paul also distinguished between what was his own and what was clearly of the Lord). Let the reader try what is offered on the basis of his own faith, his own willingness and wisdom.

All I know is it works! Praise the Lord, so far as I know, we have never yet suffered one failure praying for homosexuals since the Lord revealed this bit of knowledge.

Homosexuals *can* be delivered. *Lay people* can do it. Let's battle for the freedom of this distressed people. Perhaps no more lying misnomer can have been applied than the word "gay"! I know of no people who are more miserable. It ought to be called the "miserable community"!

Finally, concerning homosexuals in the Church. The Word proclaims that "Neither fornicators, nor idolaters, nor adulterers, nor effeminate [by perversion, footnote in NAS], nor homosexuals, nor thieves, nor the covetous, nor drunkards, nor revilers, nor swindlers, shall inherit the kingdom of God" (1 Cor. 6:9-10). That list seems, at first glance, to eliminate us all! Who among us is not occasionally covetous, or does not sometimes revile someone, or lie, or cheat someone one way or another? And who can keep his heart totally from thoughts or feelings of fornication or adultery? I suggest that the Word means not those of us who infrequently slip into one or another of such sins, even homosexuality. Else our salvation experience means nothing; we would all be doomed anyway. I maintain we are not liars or drunkards because we fall once in a great while. I believe these Scriptures refer to those who are *habitually* fornicators, adulterers, liars, etc. Further, that even the addicted in any such area are not meant to be included here if they are struggling to find freedom in Jesus. Rather, I believe this Scripture, and others like it (1 Tim. 1:10, Rev. 21:8), refer to those who have not received the Lord as Savior, or having attempted to, still persist unrepentantly that that particular sinful way does not need to change. I believe this Scripture refers to those who have become identified with those particular sins. That is, they are not merely Christians who occasionally fall into reviling or alcohol or some sexual sin. They are people who have accepted that sin as an excusable form of life. Or whether or not their consciences excuse them, they make no further attempt to change. They have become that sin. It has become a way of life for them.

Thus, if a person is revealed as a homosexual, I do not believe he should immediately be put out of the Church. If he declares he wants to be free of it, the congregation should retain him in the fold. I believe he should not be allowed to act in office until he is declared whole. Whether pastors, teachers, evangelists, prophets, apostles, or any other lesser offices such as administrators, choir directors, etc., I hold that all should be subject to this ruling. An ordained pastor or deacon who wants deliverance ought not to be defrocked, only forbidden exercise of his office until healed. This is the identical policy we should hold for any other sinful condition—stealing, adultery, psychopathic lying, etc. The church should unite in prayer and ministry to restore (Gal. 6:1), even as the deacons labored to restore the adulterous pastor spoken of earlier. The body of believers should persist compassionately as long as it takes to heal.

But if a person declares his sin acceptable or persists in it with no evident attempt to change, I believe the church *must* act, even as St. Paul did among the Corinthians in 1 Corinthians 5. After all healing efforts have been tried and either failed or were refused, the leadership must ". . . remove the wicked man from among yourselves" (v. 13). Later (in 2 Cor. 2:5-11), St. Paul wrote to assure that he did not mean to stop loving the man, only not to associate with such a one, and to "reaffirm your love for him" (v. 8). Anyone who persists intentionally in homosexuality, who in the face of Scripture proclaims it acceptable, should be put out of the Church!

Certainly and absolutely no church should ever ordain a confessed, intentional homosexual! Never should a "homosexual marriage" be performed! Those are abominations— detestable defilements and desecrations in the sight of God. No one knows what is the abomination set up in the holy place in the end time (Dan. 11:31), but sometimes I wonder if it is not at least in part the knowing ordination of homosexuals to perform the holy sacraments of God! Surely that Scripture refers to more than sodomy, but homosexuality clearly is an abomination, and as a counselor I can testify that it does create desolation. It can be nothing but defilement when admitted to the priesthood.

We *can* set homosexuals free. Let's get at it.

17

Parental Inversion and Substitute Mates

Parental inversion is our term to describe what happens whenever one or both parents are so immature or ineffective that a child takes responsibility to parent his parent(s). That inverts the God-given order. Part of each parent's task is to provide a secure home in which a child can be free to be a child. Parents are to care for children, not the other way around. Chores and responsibilities are good training for children, but the *weight* of care and responsibility for the family should rest on the parents' shoulders, never on the children.

Children today have too often been made to feel useless. The more our labor-saving devices have done away with previously necessary household chores, the less our children have been given the opportunity to learn life's greatest secret, that happiness belongs to those who have learned to lay down their lives in service to others. Consequently, it has not been easy for some to see that parental inversion is harmful. Counselees often report with pride and joy how in their childhood they took hold when their family needed them. Well and good; far better that trouble should arrive by the route of a child's overserving than that he should fail by selfish unwillingness. Nevertheless, sin is involved, and we need to help counselees see it in order to set them free.

The heart is never pure no matter how noble the service. No matter how pleased all concerned may be that a member of the family has been helpful, and no matter how much our Lord wants to reward his servant for trying to honor his parents by serving, the sin side of our actions still demands reaping until transformation by the cross sets free. God sends the Son that He may reward the servant and prevent destruction. "For God is not unjust so as to forget your work and the love which you have shown toward His name, in having ministered and in still ministering to the saints" (Heb. 6:10).

Insofar as parental inversion is sin, it has as its base, disrespect for failing parents. It is good if a child tries to honor and respect his parents, but none can keep the heart completely free from disappointment, hurt, judgment, resentment, and disrespect. Whether a parent fails in place or by being absent, it is almost impossible for the child to avoid the sin of usurpation. He is taking over functions which belong to another, thus is in the position of usurpation, whether intended or not. Nor is it altogether possible to avoid the sin of not trusting God. Parents color God to children so that whether consciously or hiddenly the child's picture of God begins to resemble the failing parent(s). From then on the child may not be able to trust in reality in the heart that God is on His throne. "The world will fall apart," if the child doesn't hold it together.

Parental inversion robs a child of his childhood. It builds into children an inability to rest. It rapes rest from then on. Parents provide security, but when parents fight or the home is filled with unspoken tensions between them, one or more children may take responsibility to try to hold them together. Once that stance is established in the heart, a child may manifest that fear-filled attempt to hold life together inappropriately everywhere. Such an adult cannot let people fight things out healthily—"Oh, I just can't stand it when people fight, let's get this settled." They shush quarrels too soon, unable to trust in healthy dissensions until things can be fully worked through. They may so smooth things over, or hold such tight controls, nothing can be fully resolved. They may be compulsive peacemakers, their sin masked behind the beatitude (Matt. 5:9). Others may honor them and so perpetuate their error, not realizing what is really behind their peacemaking.

P.I. (parental inversion) people overwork and overachieve much like P.O. (performance orientation) people, only from a different wrong motive. Their service is not to gain them acceptance or earn love, it is to keep the world of fear and chaos from the door. P.I. people become far too busy and may often be heard to say, "Well, I'd rather do it myself," unable to trust that others will hold up their end, or do things rightly. Thus they may fall into being noble martyrs, their stance actually an unconscious insult to everyone else around them. The insult and put-down come from unconscious angers at parents for not doing what they should have. Have we not all witnessed how some people can be helpful in such a way a person feels honored, while others help in such a bustling, self-martyring way the recipient feels dishonored and insulted? Such are usually P.I. people.

P.I. people cannot rest on vacation or anywhere else. Being a P.I. person myself, on vacation in a campground, five minutes after arrival, I would be wandering around looking for somebody to help—this after a full year of helping people! At home, P.I.'s learned not to let down their guard for a moment, lest some spontaneous, thoughtless act add one final straw to an already overburdened marriage. Little children need to be nasty. They discover many things about themselves by foolishness in the "school of hard knocks." Self control needs to arrive by the slow process of trial and error and inner decision, not from outer compulsion for fear of results in a shaky family.

P.I. people usually cannot relax and be refreshed in the home. In childhood, home was identified as the place of tension and consequent demands for emotional responsibility, and of attempts to control self and others. It may require years before a P.I. person can learn at heart to mature into the reality of "the *heart* of her husband doth *safely trust* in her" (Prov. 31:11). Rest has become identified with solitude, or fun and games away from the home. It is a strain and an added discipline of self to learn to find rest among primary people in the P.I.'s life. A P.I. cannot initially rest *in* another. He did not learn that in the home (see chapter 3). Instead, he will always care *for* the other—thus effectively holding the other at a safe distance from the heart.

Paula was a P.O. person, but my besetting sin was P.I. My father was gone much of the time, and though gentle and kindly, he nevertheless failed greatly to be strong and present, more and more as the years wore on. Gradually I assumed more and more responsibility. I became strength for my mother and younger sister and brother. I kept the garden and yard, cows, chickens, orchard, and pets. It was a shock to learn recently that Frank, my brother who is ten years younger than I, had been angry at me because I, as his surrogate father, had left him to go to college. But it was a greater shock to learn very recently that my sister, Martha Jane, only four years younger than I, had been angry at me for identically the same reason. I cried out, "How on earth did I get in that position, dear Lord?" I repented again of usurping my father's position and resigned anew as savior of my family.

God has honored and blessed me in reward for my poor attempts to serve. But there are two sides to every coin. Every symptom listed above, and more, fitted me. Now, He is setting me free from compulsive service and from an inability to rest in my home.

God wants to use our Elijah House ministry to help prepare His family for His return; until I could come to death of my lack of trust in His ability to be head of His family (by projection from untrust of my natural father), no way could my service be untainted by disrespect of His Lordship, or His Fatherhood.

A businessman I counsel has only lately begun to discern the source of his striving. His father was a drinker and a gambler. As a lad of eleven, he went to work to earn money for the family. In every way he tried to support his family. From then on he has had compulsively to take care of everyone—employees, friends, wife, children, church, God, anyone, and everything. He was the compulsive Good Samaritan for every flat tire and trouble in the way. He could not purchase and enjoy something for himself without inordinate guilt. As a boy he had built into himself that he must give everything to save his family. Now he could not stop trying—long after the family

322

and everyone else could and should take care of themselves.

Worse, his mother had long since learned to control him and pump him for unnecessary services by simply putting him under guilt. He would jump whatever hoop in order not to fail to serve like his dad did. Business employees not only milked him for higher than normal wages, they were ungrateful, and attacked him if he couldn't deliver on too-extravagant promises. Only lately is he learning he doesn't have to carry the world on his shoulders. P.I. people need to be taught to resign over and over again the general managership of the universe—and to discover with gleeful chagrin that somehow God manages to get along without their help!

P.I. people get into wrong positions with other siblings, as I did. That usurps, and prevents right relationships. Never mind that someone *has* to do the job; the lateral side of whatever is not done by the right person is damage.

Again the antidote is repentance and forgiveness. The blood of Jesus will wash away resentments from the heart of the inner child. His perfect love will cast away the hidden fears which have propelled overstriving. The cross will effect death of resultant structures—busy-ness, self-suffering stances of martyrdom, controlling, putting others down, etc. Those all may need to be seen and dealt with one by one, or may simply die and wither away as deeper taproots are dealt with. The presence of the Father will heal and restore the tired and untrusting heart.

But a second more confusing and damaging condition may follow upon parental inversion. Sometimes, when one parent fails or is gone from the home, one of the children (usually the eldest of the opposite sex) steps in to fill the vacant spot. A son may become the breadwinner. He may become the mother's confidant, or her strength to lean upon. He may discipline the younger children. In short, in one degree or another, he may set about to run the household in his father's place. That puts him in position of a husband—without the bed. Nevertheless, nuances of meaning and practiced mate feelings flow as an undercurrent between mother and son.

Even if the mother never lets herself think a sexual thought towards her son, he is in position, and stimuli flow, purely from being in that position. If he never thinks a sexual thought towards his mother, he still must unconsciously turn off untoward feelings and stimuli. The deep mind's unvoiced thought is, "This is mother; I must not think or feel that way." Or he may have conscious feelings and consciously have to refuse them. The result is that a pattern of withdrawal and shutting down is built into the subterranean passages of the heart.

Later, that man may become a model husband, trained to be responsible, knowing how to be strength for his wife, but what may happen is that suddenly, unaccountably to him, he may be unable to make love to his wife. He is not impotent, merely turned off. Something is blocking him, and he can't imagine what. The block is a built-in turn-off mechanism, activated usually the moment his wife becomes a mother. Projection-identification processes then activate the turn-off mechanism.

One young man came to me completely frustrated and bewildered. He loved his beautiful wife, and had greatly enjoyed and found fulfillment in sexual intercourse. Now he couldn't bring himself to touch her. He kept thinking something about "respecting her too much" but that didn't square at all either with his ideas about sex or his previous freedom to enjoy her body. It turned out that his lovely mother had been divorced just as he entered puberty, and he had tried to be strong and protective for her. Her beauty had affected him. He could remember, as we talked, having to turn off his feelings. We simply forgave the boy his confused feelings and commanded that old, no-longer-needed structure to loose its hold on him, and set him free from identifying his wife and mother as one. His wife wrote (with him) in great happiness, thanking me for returning her husband to her. The blockage has never returned. Praise the Lord.

The same may happen the other way around. The wife may die or become an invalid or simply fail. A daughter may step in to clean the house, shop, cook, do the laundry, and whatever else may be necessary, including watching over younger children. Now she is in position as a mate, with the same confused unconscious feelings and results. Or there may be no such crossover between the sexes, simply that a daughter takes over in the father's place to help her mother, or a son in the mother's place to help the father. Confusions still abound, for each is acting in a position not natural for them as children or teen-agers. The girl may become too manly, or at least so learn to try to run the home that she has difficulty later letting her husband be head of the home. Or a boy may learn wifely roles and unconsciously seek them until that becomes confusing and seductive to his wife, inducing her to play the vacant authority role. These things once seen are easily prayed about so long as we remember to minister beyond the grown mind to the little child within.

Each person must then be helped to break out of the old mold and find and build into himself a new identity in Christ. He does not so much try to build a new self as to discover and celebrate the new identity resurrecting out of the old, thus appreciating and praising God for what He is doing in making him new, so healing the first and deepest hurt, lack of ability to trust the father.

The concepts of parental inversion and substitute mate are simple; we can see easily how such patterns are formed in the heart. It is not so easy to overcome them, once fully installed. Here again a counselee must take firm hold in his own healing.

P.I. is not an easy thing to hate as sin. The difficulty is that it has become a most noble definition of life. The whole purpose of life may be invested in it, justified a thousand times scripturally. How about "Greater love has no one than this, that one lay down his life for his friends" (John 15:13)? Another Scripture that may be used is:

Then the righteous will answer Him, saying, "Lord, when did we see You hungry, and feed You, or thirsty, and give You drink? And when did we see You a stranger, and invite

You in, or naked, and clothe You? And when did we see you sick, or in prison, and come to You?" And the King will answer and say to them, "Truly I say to you, to the extent that you did it to one of these brothers of Mine, even the least of them, you did it to Me." (Matt. 25:37-40)

Who were more deserving little ones than our own parents? Our entire life has been a commitment to serve. How hard it may be to see that as sin. Let us be as clear then as possible. Our serving was not wrong. It never has been. God wants to reward us for it. But our motive for serving was not pure. That impurity made some of our serving as much or more damaging than helpful. It is for that wrong motivation that the Lord calls us to death. It is a good death; we will most likely never stop serving. God loves us for it, "You are My friends, if you do what I command you" (John 15:14). "Jesus answered and said to him, 'If anyone loves Me, he will keep My word; and My Father will love him, and We will come to him, and make Our abode with him' " (John 14:23). Our death will mean that corruptions of the flesh will die and fade away from our serving (1 Pet. 1:24). Striving will die, and it will be the Holy Spirit who prompts and checks what we do, not the compulsions of flesh.

P.I. and substitute mate are not simply attitudes; they are habitual structures. Prayer may initiate struggle, not end it. We will be called upon to check habitual thoughtless responses again and again. Here we plead with every counselor and counselee to develop humility. Facets of P.I. practices may be revealed by others than the primary counselor. The counselor must adhere to, "I planted, Apollos watered, but God was causing the growth. So then neither the one who plants nor the one who waters is anything, but God who causes the growth. Now he who plants and he who waters are one; but each will receive his own reward according to his own labor" (1 Cor. 3:6-8).

No counselor should arrogate the entire process of discovery to his own counseling, even if he in wisdom wants to be the primary guide. It is the Holy Spirit who would teach, rebuke, correct, and counsel us all through the Body. This advice applies to all counseling, not merely for P.I. people; we apply it here for the fact that some counselors are themselves afflicted with P.I. Arrogation of the whole counseling process to one counselor is the very thing a P.I. person as a counselor is most apt to do.

Counselees must be willing to hear the frequent admonitions and rebukes of friends, "Speaking the truth in love, we are to grow up in all aspects into Him, who is the head, even Christ" (Eph. 4:15). No one likes to hear rebuke, but Scripture is clear about it. "Stern discipline is for him who forsakes the way; He who hates reproof will die" (Prov. 15:10). "He is on the path of life who heeds instruction, But he who forsakes reproof goes astray" (Prov. 10:17). "Whoever loves discipline loves knowledge, But he who hates reproof is stupid" (Prov. 12:1). "Poverty and shame will come to him who neglects discipline, but he who regards reproof will be honored" (Prov. 13:18).

When I (John) was a child, swollen adenoids and tonsils created a habit of breathing through my mouth. At seven a tonsillectomy enabled me to breathe through my nose—but the habit of breathing through my mouth had long been established. My father instructed all the family to keep saying to me constantly, "Shut your mouth, Jackie." And he ordered me never to be mad at them, to appreciate it as love, and take it. They did, day after day, and finally the habit was broken. More importantly their continual corrections built into me an appreciation for brothers' reproofs as love, well meant for me, and an ability to take it. For that reason the Lord has blessed me with brothers who do chastise me, regularly. They may not always feel like it does much good, but I have never been angry or hated them for it. That childhood experience taught me to love correction, and those who do it. "Do not reprove a scoffer, lest he hate you, Reprove a wise man, and he will love you" (Prov. 9:8). That capacity is vital for those who are afflicted with P.I. If brothers and sisters can't feel free to let us know when we are trampling all over them, doing too much, they are not likely to speak the truth often enough to us; so we are not likely to break the habit. It is difficult enough to rebuke someone who is obviously doing wrong, much more difficult to correct someone who is trying to be helpful. Truly "Faithful are the wounds of a friend; profuse are the kisses of an enemy" (Prov. 27:6 RSV).

In short, P.I. and substitute mate are practices in the flesh (Col. 3:9), but about which the Lord has far more compassion than most. To be corrected is to be rewarded. God has chosen to set us free. He wants to bless us. Freedom means then that the Holy Spirit will serve through us restfully, though perhaps more actively than before, but He will observe the checkpoints, and give us wisdom to serve in ways that bless.

18

Individuation and Destiny Malaise

My son, if you come forward to serve the Lord, prepare yourself for temptation. Set your heart right and be steadfast, and do not be hasty in time of calamity. Cleave to him and do not depart, that you may be honored at the end of your life. Accept whatever is brought upon you, and in changes that humble you be patient. For gold is tested in the fire, and acceptable men in the furnace of humiliation. Trust in him, and he will help you; make your ways straight, and hope in him.
(Sirach 2:1-6 Apocrypha)

There is an appointed time for everything. And there is a time for every event under heaven—
A time to give birth, and a time to die;
A time to plant, and a time to uproot what is planted.
A time to kill, and a time to heal;
A time to tear down, and a time to build up.
A time to weep, and a time to laugh;
A time to mourn, and a time to dance.
A time to throw stones, and a time to gather stones;
A time to embrace, and a time to shun embracing.
A time to search, and a time to give up as lost;
A time to keep, and a time to throw away.
A time to tear apart, and a time to sew together;
A time to be silent, and a time to speak.
A time to love, and a time to hate;
A time for war, and a time for peace.
(Eccles. 3:1-8)

There are two great and conflicting lessons to be learned in maturation. One is called individuation, which means to separate oneself from all formative influences and become one's own person. The other is incorporation, to become a corporate person, part of a group, sensitive to the desires and wishes of others. One definition of maturity is to learn to think in "we" terms rather than only "me, myself, and I." These two tasks cross over in conflict drastically—and both are presently tasks to be dealt with during one's teens.

How shall a teen-ager cut free to be his own person, and yet be part of a family? At thirteen to fifteen, mom and pop may sometimes treat him as though he is still ten, and expect him to step to old family loyalties and activities when other drummers beat wildly in his ears. At eighteen college cliques clamor for corporateness just when his bones cry out for individuality. About nineteen to twenty-one, no sooner does he become his own person than genes and juices start working to unite him to his spouse—and corporateness.

Without individuation, we cannot become healthily corporate. We either cop out from who we are to mimic accepted gang roles, or we try to beat the drum everyone else must step to. Only a fully free individual has what is needed to give himself to a group, to accept the give and take of healthy relationships.

A teen-ager has two primary tasks before becoming corporate. First, *individuation*, to cut free from everything and everyone who has formed him—who have birthed, fed, housed, clothed, instructed, disciplined and given him love. Second, he must *internalize*. Everything in his life has come to him from *outside* him, from others. None of it has yet become fully his own, from *within*. Since he may "own" many possessions, and the family is his, his parents may say, "Everything we have is yours," not comprehending how he feels, since it was all theirs given to him, not something of his own creation and choosing as a mature person, from within himself. He must now ponder all the teaching and example of his parents (and teachers), burn his fingers, and find out for himself why law is law and life is what it is. Wisdom, understanding, morality and faith, purpose and ambition, habits and practices, fellowship and joys, all must become his own by the painful process of inner wrestlings with his own thoughts and emotions. There is no shortcut, no easy way to do it. Individuation and internalization are the Scylla and Charybdis* through which he must pass or fail in becoming an adult.

Individuation does not begin with teen-age years; it climaxes there. It begins at the moment of formation in the womb, as fetus cells become their own entity, not the mother. Were the cells of a fetus to be absorbed again, no new life could begin. Individuation is the price of life. Birth means further individuation. Cutting the umbilical cord forces becoming organically one's own entity. Weaning, managing to walk rather than be carried, learning to talk, mastering the toilet—all are steps effecting individuation. Failure to accomplish any of these reduces the person to dependence and so reconnects the umbilical cord emotionally.

Individuation is accomplished first externally, and then internally; first physically, then mentally; and finally, emotionally, morally, and then spiritually. Birth and weaning begin to break organic dependence. Each lesson cuts more physical dependencies—walking, handling one's own table utensils, dressing oneself, etc. However, long beyond infancy we remain not only physically but emotionally and mentally dependent. Going to school initiates the process of mental weaning, and the beginnings of emotional individuation. But these are only begun. Morality and spirituality are still nascent, formative, and dependent. Each step—Sunday school, public school, exams and discipleship, church attendance, gang life, etc.—calls for further and more interior individuation.

---

* An idiom expressing great opposing difficulties, from early navigational problems; Scylla—a promontory difficult to pass (off southern Italy); Charybdis—a whirlpool opposite the entrance to Messina, also in southern Italy.

During the teen-age years it climaxes, like a volcano long bubbling to eruption. What makes the trouble usually is a two-sided squeeze. On the one hand, father and mother may be unprepared to handle a teen-ager, or even to admit their son or daughter is that old. They may not realize what is happening inside him, seeing all his changes in behavior as something horrible, needing to be corrected by tightening down the screws. On the other hand, most teen-agers cannot be consistent. One moment a young person may be responsible and sensitive and the next he becomes totally self-centered and irresponsible. One moment he wants to brave the world, and in the next, he has fled halfway back to the womb. Normally, without training, neither parents nor teen-agers are conscious of what is going on. Subliminal forces push, and old patterns no longer can contain the new urges. Impulses may be tried and rebuffed, or not tried and repressed. Attempts at communication batter down doors to empty rooms—neither the parent nor the teen-ager occupy those places any more, and neither realizes it.

Teen-age individuation becomes more difficult by the fact that the very loved ones who have given everything a teen-ager is have now become the problem! Even if parents are wise enough to understand, and let their teen-ager try some things, they—their love, their presence, their thinking—is now in the way of finding one's own—the second task, internalization. We must stand against the very people we want to love and admire, and more cogently whose approval we need, at the very moment when if they give it we seem sometimes to be put down to childhood again, or the enterprise of discovery has been stolen from us.

Surely the prodigal son of Luke 15 was the sinner we have all heard sermons about, but one thing needs to be said in his favor. Though asking for his share of his family's good was tantamount to wishing his father were already dead, he was at least doing what every teen-ager must do—taking hold of what is his own in order to individuate and internalize. The cost was all his substance (perhaps he could have learned an easier way); but it was not merely an expression of largesse that his father placed the ring of authority on his finger and the robe of ruling on his shoulders (Luke 15:22). His father saw that he had become his own man. He was now qualified to rule. The remark of the elder brother is easily seen by any experienced counselor as that of an unindividuated child:

> But he answered and said to his father, "Look! For so many years I have been been serving you, and I have never neglected a command of yours; and yet you have never given me a kid, that I might be merry with my friends; but when this son of yours came, who has devoured your wealth with harlots, you killed the fattened calf for him." (Luke 15:29-30)

Internalization means that as much as a teen-ager may admire his parents and desire to keep their moral ways, he must not simply do so or he fails to become his own person. He must examine morality for himself, test and see. He must now work through what his parents may long have forgotten they also had to examine and think their way through. But it is not merely a mental process. It is as though each ethical and moral law has to be *felt* through with deep, inner unseen fingers of his spirit, testing to see whether he really wants to own these things as his own. If he could see clearly and get at it, the task would be easy. But he cannot. It is necessarily a "fumble through" process. Incidents have to happen which reveal to him, often by pain of loss, where his heart really stands.

Being a late bloomer, I was still working through some things as late as twenty-three, in seminary. I remember wrestling with the fact that I had thought through everything so mentally, and therefore had remained so much in control that I was not certain whether my philosophy of life actually fit where my heart was, or not. I felt as though all my thinking were somewhat like a flying carpet, maybe not settled down on reality at all, maybe askew of where life really is. At the time, I was working at Delta C and S Airlines, Midway Airport, Chicago, as night shift foreman in charge of unloading and loading all aircraft on my shift. I managed to organize the crews to maximum efficiency but kept thinking that I needed something to happen totally out of my control so I could see by my reactions where my heart really was.

Then a lazy, inefficient, loud-mouthed Archie Bunker-type was placed in my command. No matter what orders were given, or how kindly, he spat back obscenities and failed to do his job. The boss would not fire him. His hateful, slothful ways disrupted both crews. One night he bungled so badly that I spoke sharply. He swung at me, missed, but knocked off my glasses. Still under control, I told him calmly that if they were broken (a crew member was chasing after them in the wind of the prop wash), I would make him pay. I meant I would report it and the cost would have to be deducted from his wages (the common practice in those days). He took it as a challenge to fight, and swung a fist at me on the ramp, in public, while passengers were deplaning, where I never would have chosen to fight.

That blew my control. I went out of my head with pent-up fury, and though he weighed 250 pounds, I was then a weight lifter, so I ducked under his blows, grabbed him around the waist, picked him up, and smashed him to the pavement. Sitting astraddle him, I grabbed both his wrists with my left hand, holding him immobile, and screamed that I would smash his face with my clenched fist. But then, rising from a deep well, there came into my mind a torrent of Scripture passages and a feeling of compassion. So I did what was actually worse—I chucked him gently under the chin and called him a baby!

That experience locked my thinking into my heart. It began to tell me a part of my reality. I could hate. I could want to kill. I could be worse than cruel. I could lose control. But another part of me, deeper it seemed, chose kindness and tried to hold me to it, while another part turned it again to cruelty. From all that, I could see that my choosing of the Lord's Word was not something exterior. In a moment of crisis the Word had flooded my mind as something *I* had chosen, from deep within.

Young people have many such experiences—a fender bender (of dad's brand new car), too much sexual exploration, an escapade with some street gang on the shady side of the law, etc. Left, alone, or met with compassion and trust, young people can use such experiences as the grist mill for grinding all their thoughts and emotions into the powder of repentance and change. They can discover their own reality and commence to stand up to life as adults.

But when dad and mom hear of some teen-ager's misdoing and come down like avenging angels, determined to straighten him out, they rob from him the enterprise of discovery. He may be forced to defend the very thing he would have used to discover reality and return to sensibility. Unfortunately then he must reach further into degradation to find some area not already preempted by his parents in order to find himself. Repeated altercations may cause him, by rebellion, to become stuck in the mire of ways he would not have owned at all were his parents (or others) not riding him so hard.

It requires courage to individuate and internalize. Those who have strength of spirit (Eph. 3:16) can do it, and those who do not cannot. We must individuate at the time our inner being calls for it, each person within his own timetable, or we do so later at great peril, or not at all. Too many times young women have come to us having moved too quickly from their father's house to submission to a husband, not having internalized and individuated. Now, urges are upon them which are blocked by wifely and parental duties. Such women cannot conveniently find the space and time to accomplish what should have been done earlier.

Incorporation and individuation are interwoven tasks which alternate in predominance and importance throughout life. Each step must be accomplished in its proper time, and the next individuation or incorporation cannot be entered unless the previous is successfully completed. Immediately after birth, the first necessity is to learn to be corporate. A child's first mental year is absorbed in learning basic trust, the basic building block which enables corporate life in adulthood. A baby must learn to open his spirit, to flow into others and receive others to himself. He must learn capacity to hold open to others despite woundings.

Basic trust as the first building block of corporateness is also the absolute prerequisite for the next step of individuation, to say "no." If a child at two has not accomplished the corporate task of basic trust, he cannot master the next task of individuation (see chapter 1, "The Demon that Rises With Us," in *Restoring the Christian Family*). It takes courage for a two year old to say no to those adults who supply everything he must have to survive. His saying of no is a practice in the art of individuating, of saying, "I am not you" and "You are not me," and "I am my own person."

Since he has failed to incorporate (to build basic trust), and therefore cannot successfully individuate (by saying no), he cannot graduate to the next lesson of incorporation, to enter the gang age, to play *with* instead of alongside of others. He must then either dominate and control or go along meekly with whatever the gang decides to do. He cannot say a proper yes or no to the gang; he either controls or is controlled.

When Ecclesiastes 3 (quoted above) says there is a time for all things, that is not merely a philosophical exercise affecting nothing other than the fun of thinking about things. That is also a description of a principle in the maturation process of human beings—indeed, of all living things. The principle is that there is a time ordained by the Lord's wisdom for all things to develop, in sequential order. Whatever does not accomplish its task in its season is out of order—and in trouble! Perhaps for this reason Jesus cursed the fig tree (Matt. 21, Luke 11, and Mark 13). It had made all the appearances of producing fruit early, out of season, but had no fruit. It was a sick plant, off kilter, out of time and harmony, producing nothing.

A child who fails to learn basic trust in his first mental year must struggle later out of time and place, to achieve what should have been learned earlier. What school teacher has not pitied and struggled to help immature children who at seven or eight have not attained the social skills appropriate for children who are two, three, four, and five? The principle is stern and unrelenting, "Whatever is not learned easily in the right time and sequence, will have to be fullfilled, with difficulty, in the wrong order and sequence." A man who has not individuated from mama cannot incorporate with his wife—until he does cut free later, usually with much struggle. A woman who has not been wholesomely corporate with her father in earliest life cannot fully individuate from him in teen-age years, and cannot later become wholly corporate with her husband—but must learn to do so, out of time and sequence, the hard way.

A Christian counselor is eventually trained like a detective to notice what is out of time and place. He comes to see what doesn't fit. If he comprehends the planned sequence of God for maturation he can sense the jarring presence of what is out of place—and start looking for it. Astronomers discovered some of our planets by puzzling over the irregularities—the jarring aspect—in the orbits of some planets, until they saw by inference that something had to be creating the disorder and hunted until the unseen planet was discovered (Pluto, in one instance). Just so, counselors who understand the true orbits of maturation can sense by what is out of place, out of order in time and sequence, that some sinful condition must have been blocking maturation somewhere in the past, needing only to be discovered to become light (Eph. 5:13).

A man came whose wife was leaving him. His was a nationally known media ministry, and she was a minister's daughter who had moved early from her father's strict home to her husband's exposed righteous style of life. Now at plus thirty, she wanted to do all the things she had been denied during her teen-age years. She thought she wanted to smoke and drink, date and dance. Her husband, his work, and her children had become identified as the prison of her life. Friends saw her as plagued by demons of lust, and prayed accordingly. But lust was only minimally a factor. Internalization and individualization were now clamoring at a more than thirty-year-old woman to do what should have been done at fifteen to twenty.

The prayers of the faithful totally missed her. Her church friends wanted to clamp her into the same behavior she needed to react against and test. Advisors scolded and called upon her "good nature" or her "love of the Lord," whatever handle they could think to get hold of, not realizing they were isolating themselves from her by lining up with the father and the "establishment" against which she needed to test herself. Being thoroughly performance oriented, she could find no way acceptable for acting out her inquiries. For her it was all or nothing—either all the way with Jesus and morality, or all the way into the dregs of sin. Those were not the real options at all! Not understanding her own inner dynamics, she could not comprehend what actually was pushing her, and could only see that those people who smoked and drank and danced were not the ogres she thought she had been taught they were. If that were wrong, perhaps the whole of Christianity was only a performance game? Certainly she could now begin to see the masks and roles people all around her were playing. She finally concluded she wanted out altogether.

Unfortunately, none in the Body around her comprehended what she was actually proceeding through. They only wanted to chase demons or scold her to return to acceptable roles. Her need to throw it all over was actually only a need to cut free, thrown into oversized rebellion by the trap of performance orientation. Had she been helped to understand, she could have been allowed to test and try things, suffered to do so by a wise and supportive Body and husband. Finally she wound up divorcing her husband and throwing herself with abandon into rank sin.

I, (John) was called in—too late, of course. She could only view my attempt as another clever ploy to pull her back into the fold, no matter what I said or didn't say or do. In fact, since she had children, what else at the outset could I be to her? I could not set her free to abandon her responsibilities to her children, much as I knew she needed that freedom. Praise God that she had gained the courage to try to become her own person, but what a tragedy that it came so late!

Presently there is an epidemic across the country of dutiful mothers suddenly throwing off the traces and opting for the wild life. Some fathers also are abandoning their families. Among the many causes, often foremost, is the lack of teen-age individuation, and thus also failure to incorporate. A wedding had happened; real marriage had not followed.

At this writing I (John) presently am thinking of three ministers' daughters, all three having received some counsel, too late, from me. All three left their husbands, sampled the wild life, and are now divorced. We were not given opportunity soon enough to save them, or their marriages. All three were regarded by relatives, friends, and their churches as having been seduced by lust. None were understood by the Church, nor perceived themselves accurately. All three could have been saved had the Church understood soon enough and ministered wisely.

Late individuation cannot and ought not be prevented or healed. Counselors must stand by ready to pick up the pieces, comprehending with compassion and mercy. Our Lord came, above all, to set people free to become mature. Perhaps this is one meaning of the cryptic words of Jesus in Matthew 10:34-36,

> Do not think that I came to bring peace on the earth; I did not come to bring peace, but a sword. For I came to set a man against his father, and a daughter against her mother, and a daughter-in-law against her mother-in-law.

"But as many as received Him, to them He gave the right to become children of God, even to those who believe in His name" (John 1:12). Observe the clarity of the Word of God. It does not say that those who received Him automatically, instantly became children of God. Of course in one sense we do. But St. John means something more than that. He says, ". . . right to *become*." That speaks of a process. The process of maturing into Christ as sons.

How carefully can we say and our readers receive what follows? Can Jesus' comparison of the prodigal son with the elder son say, among other things, that He views maturation in Christ as more valuable than always being good? Suppose we have two children, the first being one who has stumbled a number of times and returned eventually through it all to become wise and free, and the second one who has always been a model of good behavior, but with whom we cannot have the fullness of heartfelt laughter and banter because he is not real, always performing to please us. Which son are we more relaxed about? Which one has indeed become a son? The performing one remains a servant, trying to please us. The first has become a son, with whom we can have a depth of fellowship the performer knows nothing about.

Are we advocating sin? Far be it from us. Many young people can individuate and internalize without falling into rebellion and immorality.

But we *are* saying that if a child cannot individuate any other way, I am sure the Lord would rather he rebel and so become his own rather than remain as a performing Pharisee! I believe our Lord pays the price on the cross for sons to become sons, not servants only. We write this hopefully as a death knell to the scolders and a word of hope and faith to those whose sons are still rebelling. What such sons are doing is not all bad, and parents did something right or the child would not have had the courage to try something.

Our word both to parents and counselors is—let them go. The sooner released the less each must rebel. We do not mean permissiveness. Rules must remain. We speak of *inner* letting go expressed outwardly as compassion and understanding.

What those who individuate need is trust. Not naivete that really expects us to conform to good behavior, and says, "I trust you to be good." But that kind of trust which says, "I know you are going to make mistakes. I know you have to find things out. I trust what is in God and in you to come through it. I let you go, but I stand beside you in love."

If parents have not trained moral values into their

children before their teen-age years, it is too late. The time for training was from birth to twelve. Some training can continue, of course, but these become only embellishments. Foundation stones must be laid at the right time, in childhood, not later.

In *Restoring the Christian Family*, chapter 5, "Fathers, Sons, and Daughters," we wrote to parents about how to handle teen-agers. Here our attempt is to teach the unique and special ways teen-agers and those who attempt to individuate later should be counseled.

Teen-agers seldom come on their own. Most often they arrive sullenly, feeling coerced and trapped, expecting to be worked on and manipulated to return to harness. They are prepared to resist anything but open honesty and trust. Ordinarily they are also frightened about themselves and wish they could talk about it, but steel themselves not to for fear of being cajoled by sympathy into returning to mental chains.

Our word: Get *with*, not over against. Get out of the trap of being the parents' representative to work *on* them. I (John) usually begin by asking, "Tom, are you here today because you want to be, or do you feel trapped?" We talk awhile about that. I don't try to convince him I am not an extension of his parents' controlling arm. That position of trust has to be won, not sold. He would feel "soaped" otherwise.

There is a principle in the Scriptures which is a guideline for ministry to teen-agers (or anyone else), "Weep with those who weep" (Rom. 12:15b). Teen-agers in rebellion and in need of counsel are weeping inwardly, though most would not want to admit it. They weep and ache within their hearts because their parents fail to understand them. They hurt about themselves and may need to be angry at someone else, anyone else, because they find themselves acting in ways they actually despise while outwardly claiming how much fun they are having. So I weep with them. I say, "I'd like to share something with you if you don't mind." I share briefly about individuation and internalization and then say, "The trouble is, most parents don't understand that. They don't know how to let go. They treat a young man like he's eight or ten and then can't understand why he gets mad. They don't trust you to use your own good common sense. And they order you to do something as though you wouldn't have thought of it yourself, and it makes you mad as though you were a little kid or something." After a little such sharing, a teen-ager will usually blurt out something like, "Yeah, well how come she won't ever get off my case! Cripes, what's wrong with coming in a little late (or having long hair, or running around with so and so, etc.)?" He (or she) is beginning to trust and to open up. I don't try to defend the parents' position, or explain his parents to a teen-ager. It's still time to commiserate, so it's, "Yeah, they can't stand that, can they?" Or, "You wonder why it's such a big deal." That may open the floodgates to a long session of griping and sharing. Counselors must bite their tongues not to step in to correct or advise, explain or defend, only to listen. Counselors may feel like traitors to the parents and wonder whether they are helping a teen-ager to excuse himself when he ought to be hauled to account. But when trust is fully established and "catharting" (getting it all out) has been allowed, real back-and-forth talk can begin, not before.

We do not usually enter immediately into deep inner healing with teen-agers. We will if some particularly bothersome character trait needs attention, quite apart from the problem of teen-age development itself. A wise maxim is this: If everything is being torn up on the inside, keep everything in place on the outside. That is, if inner trauma is going on, keep the job, friends, church, and all other associations unchanged if possible. If job, home, church and other relationships are all being changed, don't tackle inner problems till things settle down. If the outer world is in flux, don't stir the inner. Don't fight both worlds at once—if you can help it. A teen-ager's associations are all in flux, and his inner world is already being torn up by individuation and internalization, so it is not a wise time to try to do much inner healing.

First sessions with teen-agers are to establish a base away

from home; someone he can side with, who isn't going to treat him like a child, who will hear whatever he has to say, who won't preach at him or immediately try to set him straight, above all who won't take out of his hands the initiative of his life, who won't give him answers he needs to come to himself.

Such counselees often will try to use what the counselor says against their parents, sometimes stretching things and putting words in the counselor's mouth. Therefore the counselor needs to have sessions with the parents, explaining carefully what their teen-ager is going through and how the counselor must first become a listening post. The counselor should tell the parents not to expect great changes overnight and not to worry if it seems as if he is supporting their son or daughter in wrong ways of thinking. Having grown up in ranch country, I sometimes say, "You know, down on the ranch we discovered the best way to turn a stampede of wild horses was to run with them awhile. Then we could begin to turn the leaders. I'll have to do that with _____ until he can hear what I have to say without being turned off. You know my stand for the Lord and for good morals. Bear with us awhile."

Sometimes such a dynamic is engaged between a young person and one or both parents that they can't stop. Mama (usually rather than papa in most western cultures) may not be able to stop her tongue. She persists in scolding and correcting, and the teen-ager keeps on reacting. In such cases we have no hesitation to talk with the parents about letting their teen-ager live for a while with some relative or close friend. A change of environment helps. Usually after enough experimentation and pain, a teen-ager wants to change, but the demanding tongue of mama (or papa) prevents his freedom to choose what is right. He finds himself defending what he actually wants to turn away from. In a new environment he doesn't have to swim upstream against a backlog of remembrances and accusations. In a new situation, choosing to make right decisions is no longer equated with copping out from being his own person. Out from under the shadow of parents he can choose and act out the very thing they want, only now it's his own, and not compliance.

My older brother went to live with my Aunt Tresia for a while. Paula's sister spent her last two years of high school with us. Their parents loved them enough to allow that solution to conflict. Now they are sturdy Christian people holding extremely responsible jobs, and they are free enough to be closely related to their parents.

Christian parents sometimes fail with teen-agers more miserably than unbelievers precisely because they try too hard. Teen-agers of non-believers, who may not keep such strict watch, may be freer to try things, and sooner find out which things are unprofitable (if they had some basic training and affection—otherwise they just become even more thoroughly lost). Unfortunately, whereas in former years a teen-ager might only run the legs off his dad's best stallion, today he can fry his brains with drugs, smash his body beyond repair in an instant in a speeding car, and find ways to explore sex far beyond the opportunities of earlier generations. Fear thus prompts dutiful parents to tighten the screws of control and so all too frequently teen-agers are propelled into becoming trapped in things they would only have tasted if left to their own wisdom.

The key factor in the present is the cross. Can parents pay the price of self-death and pain and fear, and pray faithfully until the teen-ager finds himself?

If love, affection, discipline, and understanding were present in a teen-ager's childhood, if quality and quantity of experiences were shared, a teen-ager has what it takes to burn his fingers lightly and return to society wiser and freer. But if there has been little physical touch, little talk and under-standing, and few compliments and affirmations, residual hidden angers are almost sure to turn normal cutting free into rebellion and immorality.

Once a counselor has fully established trust, and the teen-ager has settled down somewhat, especially if he has moved into a different home for a while, the counselor can begin to minister to deep roots. By then the counselor can explain how the Lord can reach to our innermost feelings and how what happened in earliest childhood affects us today. Prayer and counsel then proceed as with any other counselee. It is amazing how often we have seen young people turn around in their tracks. Young people have grown up in a self-conscious, psychologically oriented society. They can grasp more quickly than most adults what are hidden motives and how they originated. And their natures, like their bones, are not so rigidly set as those of older people. Young people are a delight to minister to, if we can only bite our tongues long enough to earn the position!

But when a person has been a "goodie-two-shoes" during teen-age years, and has not internalized and individ- uated, and is now in his twenties, thirties or forties, and begins at last to try to internalize and individuate, he experiences tough times. Mate and children now become a trap and a source of heaviness instead of blessing and fulfillment. Such a person can't divest himself of the workload of life which presently defines him, to discover what he would have been and would have wanted if he had not jumped so quickly into harness. Confusion sets in as he finds it increasingly difficult to discipline himself (or herself) to do the menial tasks which seemed fun and even fulfilling before. Depression may set it. Bewildering desires to go out and date may arise. We have counseled a number of women whose husbands have actually asked them if they could go out and date occasionally! Usually these men are in the habit of addressing their wives as "mama," unaware that they have transferred their relation- ship to their mothers onto their wives. Not having individuated, not having left home (Gen. 2:24), they could not cleave to their wives, and so related to them as mothers, until hunger for a mate and regression to an adolescent approach to life made them want to date someone other than their wives (see chapter 19, "Finding, Leaving, and Cleaving").

It is worse for women because both maternal instinct and cultural norms more stringently hold her to her roles as wife and mother. To go against these is to be thought the worst of sinners, by one's own self as well. And yet inner urges cry for freedom, not actually for liberty; they really cry for individuation, but the conscious mind now sees "freedom" as escape from the confinement of roles to find her own person.

The difficulty for a counselor is that though he may understand the process, and even though he may successfully help the counselee to comprehend what is happening, that will not stop it and may not help matters much at all. Once entered, the process of individuation is like a runaway freight train—awesomely difficult to brake down to control, perhaps impossible.

Our counsel to couples is first to help them understand, then to suggest some alternative actions. One, let the wife or husband have some time and expense money for hobbies, continuing education classes, trips, or whatever relatively safe arena allows for discovery of suppressed talents, skills and enjoyments. Two, let the husband or wife be careful to avoid being cast in papa or mama roles, and to say occasionally, "Hey, I'm not your mother (or father)." Three, whatever hobby or program is chosen, let the husband or wife grant some space, some area of adventure or discovery which is allowed to be all the counselee's own, not too closely tied to the mate. Let the spouse ask enough questions to show interest but not to appear as an inquisitor of a child. Four, possibly let the wife find a part-time job, or some other enterprise which propels one outside the home enough to feel as though wings can spread out. Five, let the mate of the counselee bid to become the teen-age date! Don't surrender the field to anyone else. We say, "Get out and kick up your heels *together*—even if your moral nature means you can only paint the town pink. Have some spontaneous, uninhibited fun somewhere, regularly."

"It's okay to make believe you are teen-agers together again. It may not take too many occasions before your spouse feels it's enough—but by then you may enjoy it yourself enough to want to keep at it, and you should. God is better than any earthly parents, and what parents are not happy when their children enjoy life?" Six, teach the mate of the counselee to be sensitive to when the wife (or husband) wants to be flippant and when one prefers to be serious. Above all, attempt not to scold or try to haul back to attitudes and emotions the mate has grown accustomed to. Seven, the mate should try to pick up some responsibilities the counselee is dropping, without being too obtrusive and especially without complaining, while being sensitive not to allow too much of a cop-out from duty. All these, but six especially, call for self-denial, so prayer and the cross are central to success. It's a tough role to play, in which there are no experts, so the mate and counselee should be taught to expect to fumble through. Most importantly to have faith for the other, to trust. Teach the mate of the counselee to believe that God is able to keep the wife (or husband) until the individuating one finds his adult shoes again and wears them more comfortably than before.

When the counselee is again settled in place in maturity may be the time to deal with whatever bitter roots may have surfaced in the process, but not before. Let's not tear up everything at once.

Since it requires strength in our spirits to venture out of familiar roles to find out if we really choose them, people may enter into late individuation immediately after wonderfully blessed times! Maybe the couple have been getting along better than ever, or the Holy Spirit took deeper hold in the heart. Some wonderful happening gave courage to the inner one. Right then, when everything seemed to be the best, is when one or the other may flip out. Counselors can help people to understand that the whole process, whether in teen-age years or later in life, is entered not because somebody failed, but because something good has given strength, and something good is happening through it all. The call is to patience, "And as for that in the good soil, they are those who, hearing the word, hold it fast in an honest and good heart, and *bring forth fruit with patience*" (Luke 8:15 RSV, italics mine).

The final end of incorporation is destiny. Individuals may seek and fulfill an ambition. That is not the same as to accomplish one's destiny. Destiny we see as something more corporate than individual, a contribution to society. Destiny can only come within incorporation because God designed us that way. All references to God's predestinate will in the New Testament speak of *our* place in the Body:

> Blessed be the God and Father of *our* Lord Jesus Christ, who has blessed *us* with every spiritual blessing in the heavenly places in Christ, just as He chose *us* in Him before the foundation of the world, that *we* should be holy and blameless before Him. In love He predestined *us* to adoption as *sons* through Jesus Christ to Himself, according to the kind intention of His will, to the praise of the glory of His grace, which He freely bestowed on *us* in the Beloved. (Eph. 1:3-6, italics mine)

> He made known to *us* the mystery of His will, according to His kind intention which He purposed in Him with a view to an administration suitable to the fulness of the times, that is, the summing up of all things in Christ, things in the heavens and things upon the earth. In Him also *we* have obtained an inheritance, having been predestined according to His purpose who works all things after the counsel of His will, to the end that *we* who were the first to hope in Christ should be to the praise of His glory. (Eph. 1:9-12, italics mine)

> So then *you* (plural) are no longer strangers and aliens, but *you* are fellow-citizens with the saints, and are of God's household, having been built upon the foundation of the apostles and prophets, Christ Jesus Himself being the cornerstone, in whom the *whole building, being fitted together* is growing into a holy temple in the Lord; in whom *you also are being built together* into a dwelling of God in the Spirit. (Eph. 2:19-22, italics mine)

See also Ephesians 3:4-10, 4:11-16, Romans 12:1-2 (the "you" is plural), 1 Peter 1:3-13 (again the "you" is plural), and so on.

Destiny malaise is sickness of heart when a person feels he is missing or has already missed the purpose of his life. It is not the same as male or female menopause. It is not the same as the passage a person goes through when it dawns on him he is not going to set the world on fire or be president of this or that company or society or invent the great invention or write a best-selling novel. It is not the same as settling down to become just another Joe Blow having a family or doing a job. It is not the same as despondency or depression following upon losing a job or having a business failure or bankruptcy. It is not the same as the blues upon retiring from work, or when all the children leave home. It is that deep misery which accompanies the sense of having failed to find one's place to contribute "live works" for God in society.

"For we are his workmanship, created in Christ Jesus for good works, which God prepared beforehand, that we should walk in them" (Eph. 2:10). We all know, in the depth of our spirits, that we have come into life to fulfill a mission. We know there is something laid out for us to do. We sense that our birth in life was timed and planned for that purpose. We speak of it in common daily parlance when death fails to claim us, "Well, I guess He isn't ready for me yet, I've still got something else to do for Him."

"Therefore leaving the elementary teaching about the Christ, let us press on to maturity, not laying again a foundation of repentance from *dead works* and of faith toward God" (Heb. 6:1). ". . . How much more will the blood of Christ, who through the eternal Spirit offered Himself without blemish to God, cleanse your conscience from *dead works* to serve the living God?" (Heb. 9:14, italics mine). Dead works are those which originate in our own fleshly striving and whose end, no matter what we profess, is to fulfill our own ego needs or give us personal glory. Any service, however high and holy, may be dead works—evangelizing, teaching, healing, working miracles, making mighty prophecies—even as Jesus said to those who prophesied and cast out demons and did many mighty works, "I never knew you; depart from Me, you who practice lawlessness" (Matt. 7:23). Any service, however low and secular, may be live works—carpentry (how could it not be alive while Jesus was in His father's shop?), plumbing, farming, garbage collecting, etc.—even as Jesus said to those in the Kingdom, ". . . to the extent that you did it to one of these brothers of Mine, even to the least of them, you did it to Me" (Matt. 25:40).

Live works are those which the Holy Spirit prompts, moves in and finishes. Live works give glory to God, without consciously trying to or our saying so. They do because they *are* His glory. Live works are those done in the flow of the Holy Spirit in our life, done within His plan and purpose from the groundplan of creation for us (Ps. 139:16, Eph. 2:10). Live works happen on the resurrection side, that is, when death of self on the cross is the prelude, and He is free to move and do in us as us for us.

Live works, no matter how individually done, are accomplished in concert. They are in tune with others, as a brilliantly executed violin cadenza is still only a part of a concerto. Live works can only happen *in fullness* in corporate life because God has designed maturation as corporate life (Eph. 4:9-16).

When I was eighteen my mother informed me that the Lord had appeared to her in a dream eight months before my birth to announce that she would have a son who would be His servant. That set me (or I set myself) to striving to find out what I was created to do. The hurrier I went the behinder I got. I found nothing out, in a hurry. After many years of searching, I gave up and renounced all my striving. I returned the entire mission and purpose to the altar, and simply gave myself to Him for whatever purposes He had, willing to walk blindly (Isa. 42:19), only to see in retrospect what may have been accomplished if that were to be His will. I still don't know what He wants, but it surely is fun doing what He brings to hand!

That is our counsel to those we perceive to be suffering from destiny malaise—"Give it up." We say, "Put it all on the altar. Stop searching and striving. Do what comes to hand." Moses was more than eighty when he was called to deliver Israel. Abraham was seventy-four when he was called to leave his country and his father (Gen. 12), and he was over one hundred years of age when Isaac was born. Hurry won't help. We need to die to our self-striving.

We call this teaching the "Abraham-Isaac principle," which is restated by St. Paul in Philippians 3. Whatever gain we have is to be counted as loss (v. 7). We are to cast whatever are our talents and skills, our goals and purposes on the altar, as Abraham obeyed God and would have sacrificed Isaac (Gen. 11:1-18). That sets us free from the grip of it. Now it no longer has us; the Lord has us and it.

Many great, internationally known ministries are in trouble today because (as we perceive it) their leaders have not yet let go and have not placed their ministries on the altar as their Isaac to be sacrificed. *So the ministry, rather than the Lord, has them.* Their works are mixed with flesh because they are trying to do something for the Lord instead of letting Him do the work through them. They are, therefore, caught in dying works amidst the very signs of thriving life. Not having fullness of death to their own works, they are thus not fully able to allow the Lord full charge of themselves and their ministry. Destiny malaise may become one result, if they do not die to their own striving to serve Him.

Destiny malaise is recognized by unwarranted fatigue, slumping shoulders, or by the opposite, "hype" and over-enthusiasm, too much striving and trumped-up emotionalism. Destiny malaise is recognizable through dreams of loss, or futile searching, or failing to catch a desired plane or train or some other frustration dream (though not all such dreams indicate destiny malaise). Destiny malaise is most clearly seen by encroaching defensiveness concerning the ministry and one's own part in it. It becomes evident in increasing controlling and manipulative tactics, especially in advertising and newsletters. It results in multiplying isolation, and in consequent attacks upon others. Its final end is the Jonestown suicide.

Destiny malaise begins to be overcome when we are willing from the heart to serve in the Body in whatever capacity He places us. It is beginning to be conquered when we become willing to listen to all through whom the Lord would counsel us, especially when that counsel arrives through those persons we would ordinarily reject out of hand. It is being overcome when we can see that whatever brother, however errant he seems to us, is part of the Body, and that in that seeming confusion he may be hurling at us, God may have a truth He wants us to hear. "Be devoted to one another in brotherly love; give preference to one another in honor" (Rom. 12:10).

"Truly, truly I say to you, when you were younger, you used to gird yourself, and walk wherever you wished; but when you grow old, you will stretch out your hands, and someone else will gird you, and bring you where you do not wish to go" (John 21:18). When we are newly born in Christ, we gird ourselves *individually* and run about going where we will, doing our own thing. We are like children, centered in our own experiences, however much good we do. But when we mature in Christ, we put forth our hands to minister, and others take hold of us and carry us where we would not. The mark of immaturity is a man who insists, as in the great-sounding, but faulty poem "Invictus," that, "I am the master of my fate; I am the captain of my soul" ("Invictus," William Ernest Henley, 1849-1903).

The mark of maturity is willingness, like Jesus, to forego use of personal power to escape our destiny among brothers. It is to give oneself unreservedly but not unwisely into the hands of others, trusting God though what they do may not be what we would choose at all—like crucifixion! Since Jesus has already accomplished that, often what we receive is only inner death and outward honor, the latter perhaps harder to take.

A man who is suffering destiny malaise is surely one who has insisted on "I did it all my way" as the popular ballad proclaims. A brother pastor whom I loved as a coach and shepherd sat down in a chair among brother pastors for ministry. They prayed with glorious accuracy. But he arose to say, "I cannot accept your ministry, my brothers. I know what is best for me, and I must choose my own course." The course he chose led to losing his place of service and to his own brief mental illness.

Francis of Assisi was riding a donkey. A brother on foot screamed at him in anger for riding while the poor walk. Francis fell on his knees before the man and thanked him for rebuking him. Francis fulfilled his destiny among men before God.

A Song of Ascents, Of David
How good and pleasant it is
when brothers live together in
unity!
It is like precious oil poured on the
head,
running down on the beard,
running down on Aaron's beard,
down upon the collar of his robes.

It is as if the dew of Hermon
were falling on Mount Zion.
For there the Lord bestows his
blessing,
even life forevermore. (Ps. 133 NIV)

19

Finding, Leaving and Cleaving

For this cause a man shall leave his father and his mother, and shall cleave to his wife; and they shall become one flesh. (Gen. 2:24, Eph. 5:31)

Listen, O daughter, give attention and incline your ear; Forget your people and your father's house. (Ps. 45:10)

Finding

Perhaps the greatest inequity in our western culture is that young people must decide all three major decisions which will affect all their years—their faith, their mates, and their vocations—before they have time to obtain sufficient wisdom. Decisions concerning faith and vocation are not so momentarily crucial. Important as it is for an individual to come to faith while still young (Eccles. 12:1), the Lord can redeem and change us later, even from the worst of cults. Some men have found great benefit that their call to vocation came after years of experience in various jobs or other vocations. But marriage is meant to be irreversible. That choice ought not be changed later. Genes and habits of our culture now promote us to choose a mate sometime near the age of twenty-one. That choice will bless or afflict us (unless the grace of Christ alters) all our life!

Further, our educational system teaches us the basic mechanics—"readin', writin' and 'rithmatic"—and next to nothing of the skills of interpersonal relationships needed for marriage! We are carefully prepared for vocation in on-the-job apprenticeships, vocational, undergraduate and graduate schools. Churches and Sunday schools endeavor throughout our lives to prepare us for life with God. But for the greatest blessing in this life, our marriage, and for the most important task of life, to raise children, there are no designated schools. Our families, appointed of God to teach (Prov. 1-7, Eph. 6:4), often fail miserably. We launch our children like babes, "while visions of sugarplums dance in their heads" into what turns out by ignorance and undealt-with carnal nature to be a hostile sea filled with hidden mines and submarine shots.

Our purpose in this book is to raise up the Body of Christ to counsel, but can we not also plead for preventive medicine? Could not Americans lobby for laws requiring premarital training before marriage licenses are granted? Could we not pass laws forbidding divorce without many months of marital counseling? Could not our high schools have required courses in parental duties and marital relationships? We know how much we all fear the possibility of installing bad teaching. But there are vast areas of noncontroversial general agreement and sound basic wisdom that could and should be taught. The field is full of traps, and who is to say who is to teach or counsel whom, but surely the field needs a legal champion to begin the work.

Often young people have come to Paula and myself (and to other Christian counselors) asking how to know whether the one in whom they are becoming interested is the one for them. We sometimes wish mankind could return to the pattern of biblical days, when parents chose for their children— although if truth were known that probably wasn't much better! (At least this way we cannot blame the parents; we've made our own bed.)

Counselors need to know how to advise. Many Christians try to push God (and/or their counselor) to tell them whether their intended is His choice or not. That may seem like a good idea, but we counsel Christians not to try to induce God to make up their minds. We explain that other personal choices and consequent steps in relation to God need to be made before the specific question as to which mate. We say, "Settle first the question of your life with God. Receive Him not merely as Savior, but as Lord. Give your whole life into His care. That gives our courteous Lord the freedom to move the chess pieces of your life, within your free will, so that He can stumble you across the one He planned from the beginning for you."

We explain that normally God won't let us cop out from the decision-making process by telling us who is the one. Like the wise Father He is, He wants us to make our own decisions. We often try to turn listening into divination, to find out the future so as to keep out of trouble. But God won't let us do that.

"The mind of a man plans his way, But the Lord directs his steps" (Prov. 16:9). We explain that though a tiny rudder directs a mighty ship, it can have no effect so long as the ship is not moving. So we say, "Having given your life to the Lord, decide where you are going to work or to school and where to church. Commit your life to action in serving Him. Along the way, He will bring to you your mate" (see Gen. 2:18-22).

We firmly believe in God's providence. We trust His wisdom to know how to let us remain perfectly free and yet manage to cause us to discover the right one. He can move heaven and earth to cause our prospective mate to cross our path.

Both sexes need to deal with as many interior sin factors as they can while still unattached so that the Lord's first choice can be theirs rather than someone through whom only to reap the worst. Our best preparation to find a mate is first to cleanse and heal our own hearts and minds. Some, perhaps most change in us can only happen as life with our mate uncovers our sin nature, but at least we want to uncover enough beforehand so as to attract one who can be a help rather than a destruction in the ensuing process. No wonder the Word warns to "Remember also your Creator in the days of your youth, *before the evil days come* and the years draw near when you will say, *'I have no delight in them'* " (Eccles. 12:1, italics mine).

If the Lord brings the woman to the man (Gen. 2:22) and engineers life so we will meet, how shall we be prepared to recognize? How will we know the right one when he or she appears? There are no guarantees, no sure-fire rules. It is always a heart-in-the-throat business. But counselors can offer some clues.

The first is that such discernment does not usually come by romantic fervor. It also does not normally come by "he turns me on" or "she really excites me." We do believe that sometimes there is "love at first sight," but passion is seldom the mark of it. Often it is like a deep recognition in our spirit. Something clicks. A woman often feels an alertness in her spirit, and may be surprised at sudden fervor arising for his welfare. Seldom do we recognize what it is for quite a while. Paula and I had gone together for almost six months when family financial reverses caused me one spring day to announce that most likely I would not be able to return to college the next fall. Paula knew by the sudden desolation in her heart that I must be the one.

So our second clue is not by good feelings but by hurt. We discover we ache at deeper levels than unfulfilled romantic desire when we are not able to be with the other. Pain strikes when we think, as the pop ballad states, "I am not gonna be the one"—to raise your children, or protect, or bless, or fulfill your days. We may recognize the depth of commitment by fights and flights. The closer we come to realizing what the other means to us, the more we may pick a fight, get wounded, find faults, or do anything to justify fleeing.

One of the most certain signs is that we cease to think about what we want *to get* from the other, like a "hot time in the old town tonight." We find ourselves thinking of not going to bed yet with this one. We want to respect this person. We want to nurture and bless. Such desires become more than normal courtesy or morality. About this person, we find ourselves fantasizing in noble terms. Some men have treated most dates as objects of sexual desire, and though sexually drawn even more deeply, find unaccustomed checks rising. Passion is being corralled by something new. We no longer want only to get; *we want to give.* Something in us wants to be in a position to give to this woman continually. We want to protect, from then on.

We may discover our mate by a holy kind of jealousy. Not all jealousy is bad. Our God is a jealous God (Deut. 5:9). His jealousy is love for us that no other so-called god should have His place. We may discover hurt or jealousy if some other person bids to be the mate of the one we are considering. By that hurt, not the kind born of our own wounded pride or ego, but stemming from concern for the other's welfare, we may recognize love in us for our mate.

We often counsel couples to step back and cool off awhile. If it is indeed marital love that God intends, the old saw is quite true that "absence makes the heart grow fonder." We ache when absent from that one. Emotions cool down. Thoughts settle out, but true inner "gnawing" doesn't fade. It grows. We are restless. We feel incomplete, and hollow. Finally, we know we can't get along any more without that one by our side. We may have felt free and "complete" before, but now we sense that since we have found that person, we will never again be full and complete outside of an abiding relationship with that one.

If after the wedding, we fail to move into the fullness of marital life, these same feelings of completeness and inner fulfillment may be engendered by some chance wrong fellowship, but what such feelings really are is that which we actually have for our own mate, blocked there, now transferred where they do not belong. In such a case, the feelings are not wrong, but where we have located their fulfillment is delusory and a trap. They are still the longings of our spirit for fulfillment with our own lifetime mate.

Often counselees tell me, whether or not another prospective partner has yet appeared, that they are sure they married the wrong one. Perhaps this is so, though we greatly doubt it. After twenty-four years of counseling, I (John) believe I could count on my hands the number of times my discernment has shown that a person truly did marry a wrong choice. The miracle of God's providence continually astonishes me. In the most vehemently quarrelling couples, I still can often feel and see that "rightness."

Whether or not the choice was the best, I know God can make it the most, the highest, the richest marriage. And that is where our faith should be, that by whatever helter-skelter, fearful-of-failure-process He connects us to our mate, right or wrong, God intends that right there in that union He should prove again that Romans 8:28 is true for every situation in every time (that *all* things do work together for good). So our most important counsel is not upon the effort to find just the right one, but that whatever one we do choose, we should set our sails to let God make our marriage the best.

In that way the question is settled. So many get into marriage and then look back, thinking, "I must have made a mistake." Let us settle it beforehand that whatever questions may plague the mind, the heart will be set in God to pay the price to make the most of it. Even should the mind be convinced of error, as my mother said so wisely, "Son, whoever you choose to be your wife, understand that though I love you and will always be your mother, there's no coming home. Once you've made your bed, you lie in it!"

We plead for the Church to hear us in our next suggestion. While we agree with Paul's advice not to be mismated with unbelievers (2 Cor. 6:14), we want to call into question what may have come to be too literal or too glib or facile a matter of deciding who is an unbeliever. Remember that a part of our thesis in this book is that it is not necessarily those who believe *in mind*, or public declaration, who are believers but those who truly believe *in the heart*. There may be many who have gone through the ritual of accepting Jesus as Savior who are not yet very much believers in the heart at all. Likewise, there may be vastly more who actually belong to God, in heart, but who have not yet publicly acknowledged that fact. We have grieved with many who sadly turned away from what we could readily discern would have been a great marriage intended by God, because someone insisted on the letter of the law which kills (2 Cor. 3:6). We have often run against current literalist fashions and given our blessing to young people to enter on into further dating and even into marriage when one prospective partner was not yet a professing Christian and the other was.

Are we daring to remove a seemingly safe guideline of God's Word? Rather we are saying, "Let's put God's Word in context." Jesus gave us the clue to know who is truly a believer and who is not. He said, "You will know them by their fruits" (Matt. 7:16). St. Paul said:

> For indeed circumcision is of value, if you practice the Law: but if you are a transgressor of the Law, your circumcision has become uncircumcision. If therefore the uncircumcised man keeps the Law, will he not judge you who though having the letter of the Law and circumcision are a transgressor of the Law? *For he is not a Jew who is one outwardly;* neither is circumcision that which is outward in the flesh. *But he is a Jew who is one inwardly; and circumcision is that which is of the heart, by the Spirit, not by the letter;* and his praise is not from men, but from God. (Rom. 2:25-29)

Unfortunately there are many who profess faith whose hearts are further from the Lord than many who never darken His door. "This people honors Me with their lips, but their heart is far away from Me" (Matt. 15:8).

Our counsel then is to examine the other's heart. Is the other a kind and gentle person (whether or not he knows the Lord)? How does he relate to and speak of his parents? Girls, take a long look at his father; your prospective husband will most likely turn out to be very much like him. Young men, whatever her mother is, your bride most likely will become. Christ may later change your mate for the better but *don't count on it* in your choosing. Ask yourself—can I live a lifetime with such a person? Will this person wear well over the years? Every boy marries his fanciful picture of his own mother—his wife must either be what his mother was, or desperately not be like her—whereas in fact he inherits whatever his intended learned from her own mother. Every girl does the same in relation to her father and his. Can you be content with the reality of what is?

God may later convert the mind of a supposed unbeliever. It may be wise to hope and wait for one who professes. It may be wise to try to wait until one's intended professes faith. But it is more surely unwisdom and (we believe) it is also unscriptural to walk away from one who may actually believe in the heart, but who has not yet professed. When Paula met me, I was spouting all manner of philosophies. I knew God had called me to be a minister, but I did not yet know who Jesus is. I was lost and confused though searching. I was not yet saved. I was not a believer in that sense. Paula was already born anew. But she read my heart, and wisely chose. Not for *seven more years* did God call me to salvation and fullness in the Spirit. How great the tragedy that would have been had she not chosen, or had she tried to wait all those years!

However, lest some use this counsel to excuse choice more by lustful desire than by wisdom, let us hasten to add that time is the ally of the Holy Spirit, and haste helps error. Paula and I waited a year and a half. Let believers wait and pray, hoping for the other to be converted before marriage. Rush into nothing. The Lord may give sure warnings or signs of blessing. Sometimes we become idolatrous. The lover becomes more important to us than the Lover of our soul. We are actually at heart level not content to hear a "no." We want to act, and push God to bless or convert the other. It is a most tricky business to still the soul (Ps. 131), and wait for the still small voice of God, or be sure we are not rushing ahead hoping God will bless. Time gives opportunity for the Spirit to still our selfish desires and to make God's will known. Unrest is a most sure sign (not that unrest born of inner gnawing spoken of earlier, but that born of anxiety and tension).

Peace is an indicator. When our intended comes, our heart and mind may flip every which way, while underneath is a peace totally unfamiliar to us. Outside we may be turned every which way but to peace, while inside there is no storm at all. Something has settled. When we are trying to discover, especially concerning one who doesn't yet know the Lord, our logical mind may do convolutions about itself. We may run in endless circles, opposing every thought with its opposite, getting nowhere in a hurry. And yet at the same time there may be a gentle inner knowing. Again, time is the friend of God and man, and haste is the enemy. Such inner knowing and resultant calm will stand the test of time; passion and lust will not.

Sometimes lasting friendship is difficult to divide from mate love. Especially since love sometimes enters first by the door of friendship. We often confuse burden-bearing love with romance; or transference with love. All too often counselors think they have "fallen in love" with a counselee. Such relationships might, but seldom do, develop into mate love. Relationships based on need are always unstable, and can seldom stand transition into two free equals freely choosing each other. Possessiveness frequently masks itself as love. All the above confusions are best sifted by time. The Holy Spirit is the giver of discernment, but as in healing of the inner man, ripeness is the key to capacity to hear Him. We must be careful not to pluck fruit before it ripens. Perhaps this is another meaning of the warning "I adjure you, . . . that you will not arouse or awaken my love until she pleases." (Song of Sol. 2:7, 3:5, and 8:4—three times the Word uses identical words!)

In summary, it is needful to know wise counsel, not only to prevent harm in selecting a mate, but in order to know what to forgive or confirm in what was the actual process of discovery a couple underwent. When couples come because the ship of their marriage is already on the rocks, frequently their minds are fishing for reasons to conclude that the mistake was not in present failures but, "I must have gotten the wrong one." If we know the process of the heart in selecting, a few minutes of questioning can reveal to the counselor how to assure the couple, "You have the right one; now let's settle down to find out what went wrong." Counselors need to comprehend the art of "finding," for legalities will seldom convince a couple. A counselor who understands the pathways of romantic hearts will have entrances to persuade willful hearts to cease fruitless questions, to let go of alibis and cop-outs, to settle down to the task of making a go of what is.

Leaving

Once the prospective partner has been found, a process long underway enters a new phase. From the moment of birth, a baby enters a pilgrimage from dependence to independence. In the womb every organic, emotional and spiritual system is totally encased and dependent upon the mother and father. At birth a baby becomes his own organic entity; if his own organs do not function without the mother's, death is the result. Independence or leaving is the first and continuing price of ongoing life. A baby remains organically dependent—for food, warmth, cleansing, for every life-sustaining function. He can do nothing for himself, except to eat, breathe, sleep and eliminate, dependent on others for all those things as well. Each lesson learned is a step towards independence—cessation of breast feeding, toilet training, walking, talking, dressing, accomplishing courtesy, manners, customs, morals, etc.

Teen-age individuation and internalization cut some invisible umbilical cords, but not all. Some unseen loyalties and belongings which grip our hearts and tie our behavioral responses to parental cues cannot fully be tested and cut until new, more primal loyalties call, and then not merely by presence but by many thousands of incidents and decisions. Each common daily occurrence in marital life calls for further leaving of parents and cleaving to one another.

The greatest and most common difficulty we encounter in marital counseling is this matter of leaving and cleaving. Marriage is a three-stage process, "For this cause a man shall *leave* his father and his mother, and shall *cleave* to his wife; and they *shall become one flesh*" (Gen. 2:24, Eph. 5:31, italics mine). If a man or a woman fails to leave father or mother, the second stage cannot happen; they cannot cleave to one another. If leaving and cleaving fail to happen, the third stage cannot even be entered, much less accomplished. They cannot become one flesh.

Leaving is only initially geographical. As we said earlier, it is one thing to take the boy off the farm, another to take the farm out of the boy. All the ways mother does things have set up wishes and demands, a mold in the mind of a man. His wife must become or not be what the mother was—in countless details. More importantly, loyalties, words and ways of command and control, signals and reactions, belongings and self-identifications have been built in relation to the mother which will all need to die if the new relationship is to survive.

Mama calls for assistance in a project, but this evening's plans were already laid with the wife and children. Which is the first priority? Mama of the new bride demands or scolds and advises, but the bride's husband had determined something else. Which ought she to follow? Papa insists on correcting his son in front of the son's wife and children. How much loyalty does the son owe? When ought a daughter-in-law speak out? Papa demands that his daughter-in-law or the whole family spend so much time a week at their house; what is true responsibility to honor and what is too much? Holidays and vacations demand visits home, and battles ensue over which parents are being neglected more often. Papa and mama keep butting in, saying they have a right, this is their son or daughter. When does a son or daughter have a right to say, "Bug off, this is my life?" Papa and mama want to give so many things—money, cars, appliances, etc. When ought a couple to say enough is enough?

When a husband or a wife keeps moving home to mama, how should a wise parent put a stop to that? Every day daughter calls home and spends hours (seemingly) talking to mama (or papa). When is too much too much, and when and how ought a wise parent to limit or cut that off? The children keep coming back, asking for financial help. When does wisdom say, "No more," and when and how does compassion bend such rules and help anyway? How much does a secure base aid a marriage—or undermine it?

Each instance must be examined on its own merits, but some guidelines can be firmly set. The first is that each new couple must become their own entity, apart from the parents. They must find life for themselves. They must stand on their own as though colonists on a far planet. New couples and parents must all acknowledge and grant that fact. Once that fact is granted and accomplished both ways, children can come home to visit and parents can offer help which does not entrap or hinder.

The second guideline involves a realization that the parents' job is done. Parents must relinquish the task of shaping, counseling, disciplining and advising. Parents no longer have a right to the shaping of decisions. Married couples no longer *owe* parents any obedience! No parent has any position whatsoever to *command* a married son or daughter! It does not honor to obey a parent rather than a mate. An adult may decide, in love, to do what a parent asks, but purely by free choice, not by legal, emotional, or any other compulsions. The biblical command to honor one's father and mother no longer involves obedience when married. For the married couple, honoring parents refers to attitudes and services given in proper priority *after* duties rendered to mate and children—not before.

Paula and I would never give a command to Loren or Ami or John, who are married. Mark, who is twenty-six and lives with us between seminary sessions, is not married; we do occasionally ask him to help around the house, but not as a command. That relationship ended upon their arrival at legal age. Unfortunately, many parents think they still have the same position they held when their children were only ten. A drill sergeant may shout at and belittle any recruit in his charge, but the same behavior addressed to his captain may cost him his stripes! Parents must learn that when their children become adults they are no longer recruits; they have been transferred out of their company, and must now be addressed with deference and respect.

The third guideline refers to loyalties and attachments. A wife should say to her husband the same words Ruth said to Naomi, "Where you go, I will go, and where you lodge, I will lodge. Your people shall be my people, and your God, my God" (Ruth 1:16b). Attempts to influence her husband to make their residence in her town to be near papa and mama are out of place. She must be emotionally free to go wherever he wants her to go, not using her willingness as an emotional clout over his head nor as a self-martyring stance. Nor should a husband be drawn by his parents or attempt to coerce his wife to live near his parents. Parents' love for their children must always be freely given, and never should it become chains of debt to bind their children to them. If married children freely choose to be near or to bring the grandchildren often to visit, that is as it should be—a blessing to all. But married children "owe" their parents nothing! Parents must not trade on past services for present favors, nor should they be allowed to. That day is done. Debts are canceled, as though the day of the wedding is also the day of jubilee.

Jesus gave His all upon the cross. That gift did not bind anyone to Him. He freely gave. Though His was the highest and best gift ever given, it would be an insult to our Lord to think that we therefore *owe* Him anything! His gift did not entrap us. It set us free. Just so, parental love, in everything parents do, from conception to maturity, must be seen as freely given, not an entrapment of children from then on.

Couples may want to do things for their parents, especially in their old age, and should feel responsibility to do so, from gratitude and a biblical sense of calling. It is God—not parents or laws—who calls couples to care for their parents. It was a delight to give my father (John's) a home in his old age, and to have my mother living close to us now. But parents ought never to "use" the past for the present. Having perceived an inability in either a couple or their parents to let go and cut umbilical ties, we have sometimes advised couples that 500 miles may be too close to home, and 1000 miles is better. Whereas couples and parents who have achieved freedom can live next-door to each other.

The fourth guideline refers to security—both emotional and financial. Parents need to give a two-edged word: "You've made your bed, now lie in it. You can't run home to papa and mama," and the opposite, "We'll always be here. You can always come to us." The first means, "You've got to give it your all. You cannot use us to undermine your marriage. Make it out there. And you can't come here unless you've tried it there to your utmost." The second means, "Security is here if everything else fails." Gifts and helps can only be offered to the degree that they do not weaken or undermine, especially the position and confidence of the breadwinner. Most especially, gifts and helps must not be used to entrap the children and make them dependent.

The fifth word concerns preaching and prayers. Perhaps the worst, most destructive, continuing pattern between parents and married couples is preaching. Parents must learn not to preach at couples. Couples must learn when and how to say, "Cut it out! Papa (or mama), this is *my* life." Couples must learn not to knuckle under to their parents' preachings. Parents no longer have that forum. Wise is a young person who will listen to the counsel of the aged, but there must be freedom and space between them, not control and manipulation. "Old country" parents are often the worst. Descendents of strong cultures, usually European, have far more difficulty staying clear of untoward parental interference. Some cultures consider it a virtue and traditional parental privilege to harangue and control adult children by the tongue.

Even prayers, soulishly given, can be used to try to control married children. Such prayers as, "Lord, make Sonny be good to his wife," are out of place. We would manage God to manage our children, in ways God wouldn't answer anyway. But the energy of our prayers bothers our children. To pray for them is fine. That is our one continuing duty as parents. Our blessing through prayers is the greatest, most powerful gift we have yet to bestow. But all such come under the guidelines of respect and non-interference. We can only pray successfully in ways that do not interfere, and we can only pray for what does not interfere.

When children are young, they step on our toes. When they are older, they step on our hearts! When they are young, we control. When married, they control their own lives. When older, their hearts control our hearts, and we have no shields, no controlling them so we won't hurt so much for them. We must not try to protect our hearts from hurting for them by controlling them to keep them out of trouble. We must not "use" anything to influence their lives. We stand by, willing and ready to help, but always with reticence, lest that help, even in prayer, would clip their wings.

Finally, concerning grandchildren, all the same guidelines apply. We can give them our love, but the parents must do the shaping and discipline. In our home, grandchildren can come somewhat under our discipline, as we would ask any neighbor's child to abide by our rules when on our property. But in *their* home, it's hands off. That position belongs only to their parents. If any position is consciously delegated to us by the couple, we must take it with careful deference to their authority. If a couple hosts an overbearing, still-disciplining grandparent, that calls for firmness which if not heeded must terminate the visit. Parents must not allow grandparents to usurp parental position or authority.

All too often, a father visits who has in years past molested his own daughter(s). Now the young mother worries, lest he find opportunity to molest his granddaughters. Loyalty to parents and overcompassion for past sins have no priority of any kind over the safety of children! Those children have the fullness of life before them. They are not to be risked for the later years of erstwhile, wayward parents. *Under no circumstances should known earlier molesters be allowed opportunity to be alone with granddaughters!* If that cannot easily be safely guaranteed, then visits must be very brief, and always with the mother present. We owe no parental debt, to risk our children.

It *must* be assumed, as with alcoholics, that once an alcoholic always an alcoholic, and that once a molester, always that weakness can overcome again. Our friend, Rachel Johnson, most recognized authority on child abuse in eastern Washington, adamantly states that apart from Christ child molesters *will* do it again, and even if much healing has happened, it is not wise to risk a child alone with such a grandparent. It is also our experience that men who molest will continue to do so, short of major miracles, and even then they must not be put in places of temptation. If this seems harsh, it is one of the prices for sin that a molesting father must be expected to pay and continue to pay throughout his life as a grandfather. He *deserved* nothing else than to be cut off (Lev. 18:10 and 29)! There is nothing so sacred as the trust God gives a father to protect the sexuality of his daughter, or stepdaughter, or granddaughter. One who has violated that trust must serve the consequences without complaint. Mercy and forgiveness must not be allowed to weaken vigilance. If I seem repetitious, rigid or harsh, it is because countless times I have counseled broken-hearted mothers who were sure their fathers had learned their lesson only to sob out the story of their discovery of what such men had done to their daughters. Take *NO* chances. You *owe* nothing!

Mothers, normally, have more trouble letting go and not interfering with maturing offspring than fathers. In old-country homes, sometimes the reverse. But in most American homes, mother finds it more difficult to let alone and keep still. Again, let us say, couples need to learn how to be gently and firmly incisive with such mothers. It *is* kindness to say firmly and compassionately, "Mom, you have nothing more to say in this household. I am a grown person. Your job ended the day I married. You are interfering. Cut it out." If a word to the wise is sufficient, well and good. It is still kindness to say to the persisting, "Mom, if you can't stop, there's the door." It is not kindness to a mother to let her become a disturbance in your family. False guilt says, "After all the trouble you gave her, can't you put up with a little from her?" Perhaps you alone could and should, but you are not alone, and your wife (or husband) and children are your first priority. They gave her no trouble in your childhood and should not now be required to pay whatever penalty you think you still owe! If they can put up with her, it will be good for them to make that sacrifice, but if she is too great a disturbance, the present family is first priority, and she must go.

As a counselor, I repeat this matter also so firmly because I would have no hesitancy to say that the greatest proportion of marriages which fail do so because one or both partners refused to or could not leave home! *Leaving is an absolute prerequisite to cleaving.* There can be no cleaving to the mate whatsoever so long as one or both parents occupy the place of the mate in the heart. It takes years in the best of circumstances for hearts to transfer willingly from parents to mates. I still automatically wrote "home" as my parents' address on job applications several years after Paula and I were married!

Cleaving

Cleaving is a matter of decision, not once but again and again, to commit one's life to the mate—"I am not single; I am corporate." Marital love is not romantic feelings but commitment in daily responsible acts. Cleaving is a matter of choice, in little daily incidents requiring sacrifice, again and again, year in and year out.

Whereas leaving was a matter of closing (closing the heart and mind to continuing inappropriate parental influence), cleaving is a matter first of opening to one's mate, then closing to all others. It is by God's wisdom that most marriage ceremonies include: "And keep thee *only* unto him (or her)." To keep the heart open to the mate and closed to all others is the great art of marriage, not only sexually but in countless areas of sharing. Cleaving is the primary calling and task of honorable marriage. Only Paula has the full right of unquestioned access to my holy of holies. Only Paula has the right to a full, "no secret" relationship. She alone has full security clearance. Cleaving is a matter of holding open to her no matter what the pain, and holding shut to all others in all areas of sharing that belong only to her, no matter what seeming blessedness allures me to give to another what belongs only to Paula.

Marriage is an ongoing process to a fullness of blessedness. All couples stop off now and then to rest on this or that plateau. All too few keep going on to fullness of blessedness.

Fullness is a union of mind and heart in which neither has been obliterated or stunted and both have become all that each can become, enhanced and fulfilled by the other. Neither could have come to fullness apart from the other but neither was kept from it by the other. Fullness is a rhythm, a dance, a musical duet, spontaneous and free, yet ordered and regular. Each could stand alone but chooses not to, and in the choosing, something greater than addition of one plus one has happened.

Forgiveness and the cross are central to two becoming one because no one can stand the fires of conflict in union without grace. Hurt engenders hurt, response demands response, both by psychology and the law of sowing and reaping. On the cross Jesus reaps what our evil sowings demand and sets us free to reap the fullness of blessings. We cannot be truly subject to one another unless we are first subject to Him (Eph. 5:21).

In the Garden God created man and woman for one another. The marriage state was the state of creation! Adam and Eve knew no childhood apart from one another! Eve knew no life at all apart from Adam! We are only told of creation and then union.

Together they had work to do. Labor to dress the garden and to keep it was not an added condition, or a fallen one, but the blessed condition of creation. The Fall did not create labor, it only gave it tension and sweat. So the fullness of re-creation in Jesus is not idleness but harness together in labor, without tension and sweat. It is our contention that no couple comes to fullness of union apart from labor. "For we are His workmanship, created in Christ Jesus for good works, which God prepared beforehand, that we should walk in them" (Eph. 2:10). Our vocation is *our* vocation, not something one or both *happened* to find to do, but something planned by God as *ours* from the ground plan of *our* creation for one another.

A job is not a vocation. A vocation is a calling, from the Latin *"vocare,"* to call. Tent making was a *job* which allowed St. Paul to respond to his *calling* as an apostle. A vocation may also be a person's job, in which case the couple is doubly blessed. But a married person's vocation is by definition not singular. Though they may be performing separate physical tasks, the attitude of heart is not to be singular. Each separate task is to contribute to unity and harmony in a corporate goal larger than any job. It was in the context of Adam's vocation that God saw that it was not good for man to be alone and so He said, "I will make an help meet for him." A vocation is a calling from God, for which that man was created—and his wife with him! A married man who tries to do his task alone is in jeopardy. Such loneliness culminates so that as we have seen, hundreds of men have fallen into adultery, because some woman (secretary, working mate) seemed to fulfill that part of him that needed his vocational helpmeet.

Both may not recognize the calling to vocation at once, or even for many years. They are blessed if they do, but perseverance and circumspect walking must pertain until both do. It is in the context of vocation that a couple shall come to fullness of oneness, and not apart from it, for that is their purpose and destiny in creation.

Every couple has a vocation whether they realize it or not. Many may be doing it and never have given it the name. It need not ring with recognized holiness. What seemed spiritual or holy about tilling a garden? God calls men and women to be farmers, educators, homemakers, publishers, merchants, etc. For some, garbage collecting is a job; for some the same is also their vocation. Anything can be done with the backing and artistry of heaven. For some, even to be a governor of a state may be only a job, while fulfillment of vocation is in their children or in tending their bed of roses in the garden. Who knows what any other man's vocation is? Best if a man and wife know it consciously and respond so together, but blessedness and fullness of union arrive anyway if they simply get in harness together.

The reward of heaven is never said to be clouds of fleece, suggesting laziness and rest, but greater labors:

> And the one who had received the five talents came up and brought five more talents, saying, "Master, you entrusted five talents to me; see, I have gained five more talents." His

master said to him, "Well done, good and faithful slave; you were faithful with a few things, I will put you *in charge* of *many things, enter into the joy* of your master." The one also who had received the two talents came up and said, "Master, you entrusted to me two talents; see, I have gained two more talents." His master said to him, "Well done, good and faithful slave; you were faithful with a few things, I will put you *in charge of many things; enter into the joy* of your master." (Matt. 25:20-23)

Not only is it that a man and woman come into fullness of life by joining hands in this life in vocation, it is by that vocation that God has designed to prepare them for service in the next life in heaven. The plan of marriage is to make a deposit in the soul beyond the portals of death. Marriage itself ends at death. But we do "take it with us." That which we take is what we have become. Whatever we have become has happened in relationship to our spouse in our service to God and man. That shape of character, that mind of memories we are, goes with us to our next labors in heaven. That is the end of marriage and the fullness of becoming one, to become that peculiar, distinct kind of flower God has planned to pluck for whatever bouquets He forms in heaven.

20

The Problem of Becoming One

Be subject to one another out of reverence for Christ. Wives, be subject to your husbands, as to the Lord. For the husband is the head of the wife as Christ is the head of the church, his body, and is himself its Savior. As the church is subject to Christ, so let wives also be subject in everything to their husbands. Husbands, love your wives, as Christ loved the church and gave himself up for her, that he might sanctify her, having cleansed her by the washing of water with the word, that he might present the church to himself in splendor, without spot or wrinkle or any such thing, that she might be holy and without blemish. Even so husbands should love their wives as their own bodies. He who loves his wife loves himself. For no man ever hates his own flesh, but nourishes and cherishes it, as Christ does the church, because we are members of his body. "For this reason a man shall leave his father and mother and be joined to his wife, and the two shall become one." (Eph. 5:21-31 RSV)

Then Jesus said to His disciples, "If any one wishes to come after Me, let him deny himself, and take up his cross, and follow Me. For whoever wishes to save his life shall lose it; but whoever loses his life for My sake shall find it." (Matt. 16:24-25)

The problem of becoming one is self-centered selfishness. Behind all the troubles every counselor, teacher and pastor has spoken and written about is one malady common to all mankind—simple, self-centered selfishness. The common sin of all mankind is to look out continually for number one! Its opposite is not a self-sacrificing, kind and giving person. Generous, kind and compassionate people may still be motivated by self. We do not overcome self simply by developing a practiced life style of generosity. Selfishness is not coterminous with stinginess. It does not mean merely someone who will not give of himself, or share what he has, or do for others. It means one who is "self-ish," who lives in and for his own self-definition, whether doing good for others or being what we usually recognize as selfish.

Generous people are usually well liked in society. Everyone naturally expects them to do well in marriage. Sometimes that is so but not always, because it is precisely in married life that selfish self-centeredness is most impossible to continue to mask. Our mate lives as no one else behind the front society sees, and encounters as no other the raw core of what we really are.

Self-centered selfishness is the final taproot of disease crucially destructive to the full flowering of oneness. We cannot become fully corporate so long as self still governs.

The problem of becoming one is fear. Fear to die, ". . . who through fear of death were all their lifetime subject to bondage" (Heb. 2:15b KJV). The death we fear is death to fleshly self-control. We are afraid to let go of those structures of self, those practices of character and personality, by which we think we have met and controlled our life and situations and people around us.

"Truly, truly, I say to you, unless a grain of wheat falls into the earth and dies, it remains by itself alone; but if it dies, it bears much fruit" (John 12:24). Until we die to that self by which we have attempted to control life, all primary people around us are subconsciously viewed as satellites in our orbit. So long as others around us remain in place, fulfilling our picture of the way life should go, we can be at rest and let them be at peace. But when they threaten our practiced way of life, life becomes uncomfortable and we do whatever we think we must in order to move them back into orbit—command, wheedle, threaten, scold, manipulate, comfort, hit, "love up on," give the silent treatment, harangue, etc. We do anything which hopefully will return loved ones to the status quo, in a continuum from soft and gentle ways to raging tantrums, most often unaware that what compels us is not the loving concern for others we think it is (which we often trumpet loudly) but is actually the kingdom of self. We remain alone even if surrounded by people because no one wants to be controlled. No one is willing to become a mere satellite in our orbit. We have to die to self to become safe to be corporate.

Some husbands or wives surrender themselves to the other's picture of life. A wife may submissively act out her husband's every wish. She may think that is what Ephesians 5:22 commands her to do. Many off-balance teachings about submission may buttress that stance. It seems then that she is the one who has totally denied herself and given herself in true, self-sacrificial love to her husband. Not necessarily so, however. In fact, it may be that she has first found a way of copping out from becoming, and secondly only a more subtle way of controlling.

Her submissive role may actually be a way of controlling her environment. It makes for peace (the lifeless peace and quiet of a rock) while preventing her from presenting to her husband the more risky enterprise of a lively and vivacious helpmeet who could fulfill him. She becomes an extension of him rather than an adequate counterpart. By learning what pleases him and by always doing it, she controls him. Outwardly he may be pleased, while inwardly he is dying.

Husbands may serve their wives faithfully, but that is just it, they may be *serving* rather than *meeting* them as people. As boys they may have learned to quiet their mothers by compliance; consequently they placate and control by performing whatever will keep the peace. Such men have unconsciously learned to pander to whichever emotion causes a wife to curl up and purr. They may seem to be ideal husbands. It may be difficult for a wife of such an "ideal" husband to identify the problem; she just knows she is unhappy. Something isn't fulfilled. *Wives of milk-toast husbands usually become angrier and more demanding the more slavishly their husbands perform.* Unconsciously, they are trying to provoke their husbands to angrily break out of the mold, to make them take charge of life and be heads of their homes.

Sometimes control is established not by subtle ways of kindness but by force, angriness or loudness. That type of control is easily recognized for what it is. But it is not that much more easily broken. We tend to think of such people as strong personalities, "I'm afraid to buck him; he's so strong." In reality, behind the mad bluff is a fearful little child who has learned to control his world by making others jump.

Whatever the method of control, the cause is the same—self. The result is the same—failure of full corporate life and wholeness.

St. Paul gave us the one successful route to married life, "Be subject *to one another* out of *reverence for Christ*" (Eph. 5:21 RSV). That is a simple maxim, an absolute law of marital relationship, which could be stated, "Unless you are subject to Jesus Christ, you cannot be subject to one another." Or, "If you are not dead to self in Christ, you cannot die to self in relation to others," or its opposite, "Only if you are alive in the Holy Spirit to give life to others as Jesus gives, can you give life to one another." Only as our Lord's identification with us brings our world of self to death on the cross, only as His Holy Spirit empowers us to live outside of and beyond the walls of self in and for Him, does true life emerge in any capacity, most especially in marriage.

True oneness happens not by obliteration of one for the other nor by expansion of one's self over the other, but by death to self in Christ until motives and urges arise out of His nature in us. "He must increase, but I must decrease" (John 3:30). It is not, as many have often mistakenly quoted, "I must decrease but He must increase." That inverts God-given order for death and rebirth. If I attempt to decrease, that remains only another ploy of self. Only as He increases, by His choice, by His initiative upon me, does that successfully call my self to death. Only as His life arises within me does something else and more than self become the motivating force which enables. Nor is it that His life obliterates me. His self-death is so complete that the more I die to me and rise in Him the more I become the fullness of me. I do not become a cookie-cutter copy of Jesus Christ. I become the fullness God created me to be, only I can take no credit, no pride, no boasting for what I am (1 Cor. 1:31). Nor do I have to defend it, live for it, or keep it going. That's His job. I simply live in Him for Him, and He lives in me for me.

Fullness of death and new life causes a mate to sense by the Spirit what the other wants and needs. That sensing does not pander to the flesh; it does not satisfy lusts or baser motives. One learns to read by the Spirit what in wisdom is good for the other, and to act accordingly. Oneness then is not obliteration or control of each other but the freshness of two children of God delighting in a world of discovery and adventure in blessing as they seek to bless and fulfill one another and all others. Hearts sing together. Minds are in tune so that tiniest clues catch to a symphony of thought and concerted action. One aim, one purpose, to live to bless others, ties all things in a concert of unity. Spirits so embrace and interflow that physical coordination enhances and ease of rhythm and action refreshes rather than tires, whatever the workload in harness together. Oneness becomes a symphonic harmony of two individuals freely being themselves, spontaneous and open, yet interwoven as one melody of service and worship. Oneness is not a loss of individualism, as though the corporate mass had swallowed up and ingested each one. It is more like two glowing embers in one common fire, or a tenor and an alto singing to individual fullness in a choir.

The problem of oneness frequently involves fleshly striving to create it. Oneness is not something we should directly strive for, watch over and measure, and thereby become tense about. It is a result, a byproduct of life in Christ. The antidote to fractures is therefore not to strive to return to oneness—which would result mainly in judging and measuring and so falling further apart—but turning back to worship, to serve the Lord, unmindful of self. Oneness returns as He returns.

A group of us formed into a cell. We wanted to enter into oneness, sharing problems and joys, praying for one another daily. We entered into covenants, only to be filled, like any couple after the honeymoon, with dissensions and battles. Then the Lord revealed that our lack of oneness was due to fleshly striving. Along the way, He pointed out that every attempt of men to get together He himself had frustrated. He reminded us that the tower of Babel was an attempt in unity which He himself prevented and after which He confused the tongues of men and scattered them (Gen. 11:1-9). He revealed to us that it was He himself, not satanic power which had so moved men as to cripple the League of Nations, the United Nations, etc. Whenever in history men have *attempted unity by the flesh*, He himself has broken them apart and scattered them. We cried out, "How then are we to become a corporate body?"—having become so acutely aware by then of our divisive flesh. He answered by a vision given to one member during prayer. This person saw a green pasture in which all the sheep were crowding to be near the shepherd. The Lord then said, *"As you seek me first, as each one strives to be near me, you are naturally drawn closer to one another. Anything else perverts the God-given order and results in division."*

Corporation in marriage (in church or anywhere else) comes by seeking Him first. Where he is not the head, selfishness resurrects (if it ever died), and division soon follows.

> For where jealousy and selfish ambition exist, there is disorder and every evil thing. But the wisdom from above is first pure, then peaceable, gentle, reasonable, full of mercy and good fruits, unwavering, without hypocrisy. And the seed whose fruit is righteousness is sown in peace by those who make peace. (James 3:16-18)

One partner may not actively be seeking Him. But the unbelieving partner is consecrated through the believing partner (1 Cor. 7:14), so a lack in one partner need not prevent unity and oneness in heart.

The problem of becoming one is the constant difficulty of forgiveness. Someone has said that marriage is a twenty-four-hour-a-day practice in the art of forgiveness. Unintended sleights happen as frequently as flies gather to crumbs, to say nothing of intended hurts. But so often we are not enough aware that we are being hurt so as to do something about it, until our head of steam erupts disruptingly somewhere. Or knowing, we can't quite catch hold of the frazzled ends of emotions and events to tie them successfully to the cross and so get it all done with. Eruption of fights is commonly a barometer of our distance from Jesus, for had we walked closely enough, then 1 John 1:7 would have been fulfilled in us, ". . . but if we walk in the light as He Himself is in the light, we have fellowship with one another, and *the blood of Jesus His Son cleanses us from all sin*" (italics mine). We are then relegated to 1 John 1:9, *"If we confess* our sins . . . ," because only outward confession aloud to one another can then restore unity. The prevention of hassles is devotion, but the only antidote is confession, and forgiveness.

The problem of oneness is a loss of vision and purpose. When goals no longer call us beyond self, our primal, carnal purpose (to get rather than to give) is resurrected, and we reecho the song of demand and refusal. Purpose is restored only as we return to harness. Thinking and talking about it leads only to affixing blame and erecting defenses. Serving Jesus, without a word (1 Pet. 3:1-2), is the simple sole answer.

Oneness is not the end. It is the condition by which we get there. The cause is Jesus. The end is fulfillment of life, purpose and destiny. Oneness is walking hand in hand; destiny is where we are going.

Oneness is marked by laughter and ease of heart. Trust flourishes within it. Trust is not that the other will not fail. Trust is that God will bring good and that all participants will recover from whatever error(s) may threaten. Trust is patience, that I am not called quickly to straighten out myself or the other lest all be lost. Trust is forbearance, that the other's or my own fumbles or purposeful sins are but momentary, and require only my love, compassion and forgiveness.

Only in oneness are we truly capable of rejoicing in the other's accomplishments. Prior to fullness of death of self, we only think we rejoice, while we inwardly grind our teeth in jealousy and feelings of inferiority. The arrival of oneness is the purchase of highest fulfillment for us when the other does better than we, for on the one hand we know we are part of the support system which enables, and on the other his success has become ours because we are one. "The works that I do shall he do also; and greater works than these shall he do" (John 14:12)—this becomes our aim and our joy rather than our dread of replacement. Then it is that joy in the happiness of others arises from innermost wells; it does not have to be trumped up, and its end is not a sour taste in the mouth and despondency, but contentment and a sense of well-being.

Oneness is also marked by grief. More than our emotions grieve when someone who is one with us is hurt. Sorrow weeps deep within our spirit and breaks to the surface. Hurtful as it is, such sorrow has a sweetness about it, having been born of love for the other (Eccles. 7:2-8). Such sorrow sometimes arrives long before conscious knowledge of the event because in the faculties of our spirits we sense more than our minds know. It becomes relief then to know what it is we have been sorrowing about. Knowledge directs sorrow to effective action, such as prayer or comforting the loved one, but it adds no dread. There is a joy which undergirds godly sorrow for another (Eccles. 7:2-8 and 2 Cor. 7:10).

We pop in and out of oneness, like a hat continually blowing off in a high wind. It is the resurgent demands of resurrecting flesh, the strident stentorian calls of self, which are the wind of loss. But it is Jesus who restores us, again and again, always one more time than we have fallen. The problem of oneness is to let Him. Pride is thus the essential quality of ineptitude, the obstinate and adamant factor of walls in our flesh. In the end, when everything else is said and done, it is pride which rules the empire of selfish self-centeredness, and continually locates its grave to dig up some means to puff it to life again.

"Humble yourselves, therefore, under the mighty hand of God, that He may exalt you at the proper time, casting all your anxiety upon Him, because He cares for you" (1 Pet. 5:6-7). The Greek word for casting actually means to hurl with great force, as when casting a javelin. Oneness is therefore a condition kept by vehemently hurling our fears to God. For it is fear which induces pride. When we feel empty or threatened, insecure or put down, pride is the false comforter who puffs up our deflated balloon. When we are full of His worth as our worth, we have no need to puff up, to brag or defend. Thus we can, "Be of the same mind toward one another; do not be haughty in mind, but associate with the lowly. Do not be wise in your own estimation" (Rom. 12:16). The antidote for pride is not to try to be humble. That way we only replay the game of self. To humble oneself under the hand of God is to praise Him in the midst of difficulty, to give glory and honor and majesty unto Him. That effectually humbles us. To confess our sin, instead of the other's, especially when it is the other who has hurt us and who is so obviously wrong, humiliates our pride. To seek out our own root of bitterness deprives pride of its self-justifying stances. In short, humbling the self is best accomplished by seeking death to self on the cross.

Transformation is never complete. We are always much like the man who was given a medal for humility only to have it taken away because he wore it! To consider others as being better than ourselves (Phil. 2:3) is a sign of humility, but we only do that as something other than a game of self when we are truly crushed by the realization of our own sin (Ps. 34:18).

Paradoxically, it is primarily when the blessedness of oneness takes place that our spirit gains the strength to try something to break out of successive hidden walls of self. So, strangely, it is oneness that often precedes, one might even say precipitates rash attempts, failures, and fractures. That is one reason why we pop in and out of oneness. Each touch of blessedness gives grace to attempt the next level of maturation, with all its attendant risks, threats, failures, and pride.

Oneness is therefore neither static nor boring. It is a prelude to leaps off cliffs! We cannot usually take leaps of faith without gaining courage to try. Courage comes first by God's grace, but that grace is most commonly supplied to us through human unity.

Oneness is therefore a flickering candlelight in the wind, deceptively strong, for as often as trouble puffs it out, it relights, kindled by the fire of God's love.

Oneness is the ground in which transformation produces maturity.

And He gave some as apostles, and some as prophets, and some as evangelists, and some as pastors and teachers, for the equipping of the saints for the work of service, *to the building up of the body of Christ; until we all attain to the unity of the faith,* and of the knowledge of the Son of God, *to a mature man,* to the measure of the stature which belongs *to the fulness of Christ.* (Eph. 4:11-13)

21

Fathers and Mothers in Christ

Before she travailed, she brought forth; Before her pain came, she gave birth to a boy. Who has heard such a thing? Who has seen such things? Can a land be born in one day? Can a nation be brought forth all at once? As soon as Zion travailed, she also brought forth her sons. "Shall I bring to the point of birth, and not give delivery?" says the Lord. "Or shall I who gives delivery shut the womb?" says your God. "Be joyful with Jerusalem and rejoice for her, all you who love her; Be exceedingly glad with her, all you who mourn over her; That you may nurse and be satisfied with her comforting breasts; That you may suck and be delighted with her bountiful bosom." For thus says the Lord, "Behold I extend peace to her like a river, And the glory of the nations like an overflowing stream; and you shall be nursed, you shall be carried on the hip and fondled on the knees. As one whom his mother comforts, so I will comfort you; And you shall be comforted in Jerusalem." (Isa. 66:7-13)

"How come I can only progress so far with you, John? I can't become any more whole with you. What's missing?" That drove me to see that so long as I lived for my image of myself as a counselor, no one could really become free (of me or self or anything else) because I *needed* that person to be sick so I could help him. But when the Holy Spirit had revealed the many ego trips—that I needed to help someone, to be "one up" on someone by being "more whole" than the other, to center on problems, or to martyr the self for the other, etc.—then He revealed that none or all of those sinful propensities put together answered the question. Something else was missing.

He made me aware that it was not enough merely to bring the sinful side of man to the cross. A counselee could discover every sinful deed and carry every practice to the cross and still remain a functionally incapable person! I knew then, that more important than death to the negative, is resurrection of the other to new life. The first must happen before the second, but without resurrection a person is little helped. People who have not received human love, having forgiven those who failed, and having been forgiven of all judgments, may still be unable to love and live. Someone must love such people to life! Sometimes God sovereignly does so, by himself. Most often human hands and hearts are needed to touch and draw people forward into life.

After being born anew, we are in fact babies again. As God did not design us like fish, to be hatched physically without natural father or mother, so He never intended that we should be reborn spiritually without the nurture of a family. That fact alone is sufficient *raison d'être* (reason for being) for the Church, but it is also perhaps the least understood fact of our Christian existence. Somehow we have failed to understand our importance to one another.

People could not become whole in my counseling because it never entered my head that they needed my personal love in any more special way than generally as a Christian, or more uniquely than as a friend and counselor. The Lord revealed to me that some people in my care needed Paula and me, given to them as a father and mother. Lacking this kind of relationship, they could not come to fullness of life.

I had puzzled, "Why are people latching onto Paula and me in this manner? Is there something in our carnal selves which wrongly attracts?" The more we tried to avoid it, the more people drained our energies. Then the Lord spoke, *"John, the reason they continue to latch on to you and Paula (after you have died to all the wrong reasons) is that your presence promises something you are withholding. Paradox-*

ically, if you will open up and give all of yourselves, they will be satisfied, and they will not drain you any more." He went on to explain that what they wanted was not something they should not want, that even in the cases in which some would try to seduce sexually if they thought they could, that was not actually what they wanted. What some counselees actually were seeking was what they had never received; the wholesome love of parents by which to come to life. If we would offer ourselves (Rom. 12:1) to Him as a vehicle for the Father's love, He would so satisfy their hearts that they would not only not drain us, they would become whole.

When I finally realized this was something the Father God wanted to do, and needed willing human hearts to accomplish it, Paula and I could move past the fear of doing something scripturally wrong and see that the work is indeed scriptural (1 Thess. 2:11-12; 1 Tim. 1:2). The Holy Spirit could then overcome our fears of risking ourselves too much, to show us that the work is really that of the Father, so that we could let Him do it in and through us. So we opened up and began to say in prayer aloud with certain designated counselees, "Insofar as [this person] needs a father and mother to come to life, and will accept us for a while as parents in Christ, we will be that, dear Lord. We will carry [name of counselee] in our hearts, and let you love him (or her) to life." Results were immediate and astonishing. People began to be able to take hold of their lives, and grow up more quickly. The burden was easier for us to bear, not heavier as we had feared. Perhaps making it conscious helped. Or maybe the ending of our resistance made us more transparent (not less as we had feared) and people could obtain what they needed from God more easily and quickly through us.

I began to see then that here was another key to the kingdom which had been lost to God's people. We had been afraid, too individualistic, too little aware of our need for one another, too lost from what "Church" is and too confined to what is only the temple—the location where individuals come to worship as individuals and go home the same way, minus the corporate life of the Church. We had been afraid of the verse, "And do not call anyone on earth your father; for One is your Father, He who is in heaven" (Matt. 23:19). We had not realized that such words were mainly to keep the Jews from worshiping ancestors, specifically, "Abraham is our father" (John 8:39). (Christians do need to remember this verse as a check—a counterbalance against idolizing those who love us to life.) Consequently we missed, or were blinded to those Scriptures in which St. Paul said ". . . for in Christ Jesus I became your father through the gospel" (1 Cor. 4:15) and "For although you may have ten thousand others to teach about Christ, remember that you have only me as your father" (1 Cor. 4:15 TLB). "But you know of his proven worth that he served with me in the furtherance of the gospel like a child serving his father" (Phil. 2:22). ". . . just as you know how we were exhorting and encouraging and imploring each one of you as a father would his own children, so that you may walk in a manner worthy of the God who calls you into His own kingdom and glory" (1 Thess. 2:11-12).

The Church remains weak, and incapable of rising to its glory (Isa. 60:1-2), not only because we have failed to take the negative to the cross but more because we have not done the positive. We have not resurrected one another to life. We have not yet heard Isa. 60:4 "Lift up your eyes round about, and see; They all gather together, they come to you. *Your sons* will come from afar, And *your daughters* will be carried in the arms" (italics mine). That text does not speak merely of the children of our physical wombs but of the womb of Christ. "My children, with whom I am again in labor until Christ is formed in you" (Gal. 4:19). St. Paul is speaking of labor pains; he is pregnant with their spiritual life, ". . . because I hold you in my heart" (Phil. 1:7 RSV).

We have not known how, having given birth, to raise one another as sons and daughters in Christ. Some, not knowing, have unconsciously reached out hearts of love and accomplished for one another anyway. People say, "My, what a loving church. You can feel it when you walk in." But how much better if we could recognize the call and respond knowingly, aware of the pitfalls, trained in the artistry of it? Truly, "My people go into exile for their lack of knowledge; And their honorable men are famished, And their multitude is parched with thirst" (Isa. 5:13). So many countless Christians have led faltering lives simply because no one knew how to re-parent them in Christ!

Not everyone needs re-parenting. Some, usually those whose parents were affectionate, attentive and wise, received so much naturally that when they were born anew, that blessed relation with their parents served to allow God, the Father, immediately and easily to parent them to fullness in their new lives. Such people easily drink from their pastor and from more mature friends in the body, and grow from them, without having to enter more specifically and consciously into re-parenting.

We cannot re-parent everyone we meet. How shall we know when God calls us specifically to this or that person, either to parent or to be parented? First, one learns to recognize it in the heart. Somehow a person "knows" this one is "in my bag." One comes to recognize that the feeling of the spirit and the position granted in the counseling are not merely as a friend or counselor nor as a brother or sister, but that of a father or mother. We need then to talk about it, openly, directly. We never insist where the relationship is unwanted—even if we know that is what the other actually needs. The other must welcome, whether to be as a parent or as a child. "Whosoever shall not [become willing to] receive the kingdom of God as a little child, he shall not enter therein" (Mark 10:15 KJV). One learns by experience to recognize the signs of need, and by more experience to question whether someone else is a more likely candidate to fulfill this role for a counselee, and to wait upon the Lord for confirmation.

No one can tell at the beginning of a re-parenting relationship how much will be required. Some people, though badly starved by their natural parents, nevertheless drink easily and quickly from the Lord and the Body of Christ and rise to maturity in a short while. Some take years. Some, raised by wonderful parents, take years of conscious re-parenting to mature. Each person is unique, and has within him his own agenda and timetable. Hard and fast rules will not fit every person. No one ought to be praised or blamed for either quickness or slowness in maturing. People are simply different. We need to be prepared to be continually sensitive to the Holy Spirit and the person to see when and where we are in the process of their maturation.

When we offer ourselves to re-parent another, a range of varying experiences may occur. We carry the other in our hearts. Therefore, we may feel in our own body and heart what the other person endures. We may know his (her) loneliness, fear, insecurity, anger, doubt, oppression, etc. because we identify and experience it in ourselves. Sometimes we may think that what we experience is our own trouble before we realize it is the other's. Our spiritual child's joy may well up in our own breast. The Lord so unites me with the other, and so lays his welfare into my heart, that if I do not see that person for a while, I know experientially what St. Paul meant when he wrote, "When we could endure it no longer, . . . we sent Timothy, our brother and God's fellow-worker in the gospel of Christ, to strengthen and encourage you as to your faith" (1 Thess. 3:1-2). When I come into that person's city again and see him (or her), my spirit leaps up in joy. I am refreshed.

Strangely, when that person hugs me, or drinks greedily from me, I am not wearied, I am refreshed. It is as though I am being allowed to be who I am. Consciously knowing, talking things out, eases my heart. I know then what my spirit has been grappling with in the darkness. But when a child in Christ thinks to protect me from his problems (not because of growing maturity but from the flesh) and fails to share, I am stuck with his nameless mess. I wrestle in the dark, and the burden of that child becomes unnecessarily heavy. Like a natural parent, I become anxious to know what is going on. I may press, and wrestle not to invade or coerce the other to share too much too soon.

In initial stages, Paula and I want to see that person often, as parents must spend more time forming an infant's character. Once a week at least, we need to talk together, and the relationship is colored mostly by counseling and teaching. Later, when major problems are worked through and a fullness of bond with us is established, that maturing child may not need so much proximity. The union of our spirits can conquer time and space, needing only occasional renewal. As time progresses so does weaning, until the result is much the same as with a mature natural child—friendship flavored by the residue that a parent remains always a parent, though also a companion. My natural children correct me and advise me but always with the deference and respect due their father, and so it is with God's children.

Some I misjudged and tried to release too soon, with resultant cries of pain. Later Paula and I learned to let maturation and release happen as naturally as it does with our own progeny. Each one matures and cuts free in his own timetable and in his own way, some easily and some with difficulty. Counselors need to learn to ride the waves as they come, not becoming too upset if one thinks he must become angry or another thinks he must compete and win in order to cut spiritual umbilical cords. Once one understands what the other is actually accomplishing, the way he does it can be taken impersonally and with equanimity.

Unfortunately, some are called, or think they are, to be spiritual parents, who have been possessive, domineering, cold, controlling, etc., with their own children. And the Lord may not yet have transformed them in many of those areas. From such comes blaspheming of the entire work, until some fear to venture at all.

Our counsel would be to those who need re-parenting—look to how your prospective parents in Christ have related with their natural children. If their own children are still rebellious and angry, or controlled and immature, find someone else! Steer clear! Unless mighty works of grace have progressed, they will most likely make the same mistakes with you! On the other hand if the grown children or children who remain in the home relate easily, with humor, fondness and respect, you will most likely be able to do so also. Look well to the home life before you commit yourself. Most likely you will not live in the home and will visit only occasionally, but the practices built in the home by which to relate to offspring will be those you will be blessed by or will have to wrestle with. Unfortunately so far the Lord has raised up all too few "safe" fathers and mothers in Christ, filled with wisdom, grace and stature.

Failure with our own is what mellows, humbles and prepares us to be good fathers and mothers in Christ. How then shall we know whether prospective parents whose children may still be rebellious though the parents may have changed and matured, have in fact been crucified and changed? By their fruits. Look to the other present relationships. How do they relate to friends? If he is a boss, how do subordinates react to him? If she is a leader, how do followers relate to her? Even so, entering a more primal relationship may dig into areas which secondary relationships do not touch, so be prepared to risk, and gain whatever God will teach. Once we have let God write on our heart what He intends, He can lead us to graduate to another class, and another teacher (parent) if need be, or perhaps to none, maturation having arrived. Those who were my two first fathers in Christ both stumbled and fell, but the Lord blessed me through those imperfect vessels anyway.

How shall we know when maturity calls for closure? How shall we know when it is time to fly from that nest, perhaps to another, or perhaps never to need another? One feels it deep inside. What the "parent" says no longer touches the heart as needed revelation; it bounces off our own sturdy realizations as unnecessary, perhaps as being even redundant. We no longer need proximity. We feel complete and secure alone, in whatever circumstance. "Well, what do you know? I handled that rather easily. I would have blown up before." "Hey, that situation didn't frighten me like it used to." "I didn't feel like I needed advice; I could trust my own wisdom there—how about that!" "I don't feel unloved any more." "People don't bother me like they used to." "I didn't get addled like I would have before—I'm stronger." In short, we just don't feel like we need the other one in the same way any more. Running back for counsel now seems more like a cop-out than a help. We want now to sit down and visit and maybe share our new discoveries but feel "put down" and "missed" if the parent in Christ returns to the old way of counseling. That becomes insulting. We are beyond that, and if we still retain a need, it is for that "parent" to see our freedom, and relate to us as mature equals.

There may still be times when we will want to return to "check in" or to counsel about another specific problem. One mark of maturity is freedom to do that without fear of having to regress to childishness even if the counselor tries (perhaps inadvertently) to handle us that way. We know then that we are so free even the one who raised us cannot clip our wings. (All of the above realizations are identical to what we experience when cutting free from our natural parents.)

The most important fact of re-parenting is simple love and acceptance. Once a "child" realizes at deepest heart levels that this is no game, that he really is loved by the Lord, through this parent, for himself just because he exists; once he feels truly chosen and cherished and settles it that that love is once for all "given," never to be taken back, security settles in, and healing and maturity flow as the natural outcome. A parent in Christ may fail in countless ways—incapable of understanding at crucial times, inattentive at others, bossy or too demanding, whatever—so long as the love of Jesus Christ flows into the heart of the "child" and is received, the primary work is done. From there on the counselee will gain strength to see for himself or to overcome wherein he can't see. Counseling from that moment on is the outworking of an accomplished fact of basic wholeness! One could say that this impartation of parental love is the basic, simple reason for re-parenting. We have known parents in Christ who totally lacked counseling skills and insights. They were not their "children's" counselors, advisors or teachers. They hardly ever said a word. They were merely present and available, as hug blankets. And the "children" matured beautifully.

Natural nuclear families suffer when isolated. We need grandparents, uncles, aunts, and cousins. Part of America's mounting problems, not only in the nuclear family, from divorce rates and adulteries and such, but also in increasing criminal activity, drugs and unproductiveness at work and so on, can be traced in part to increased mobility that destroys inter-family relationships. Nuclear families need the support, refreshment and counsel of blood relatives and close friends. So also do extended family relationships and parental relationships in Christ.

Parents in Christ need the fullness of the church family about them. Worship refreshes and strenghthens the heart to hold itself open. The Word of God revives the soul and instructs. Pastor and friends share and counsel. Fellow-parents in Christ can compare notes.

Sometimes children in Christ can be part of the same body, which is preferable, but sometimes not. Time and space or other conditions may prevent. We never have asked that a Roman Catholic child in Christ attend any church but a Catholic church—or for that matter that any child in Christ attend our own church. In such cases, each child in Christ should be regular in attendance in whatever church he has membership. Both "parents" and "children" need the blessing of the Body of Christ.

Brothers and sisters in Christ are part of the parcel. Sometimes the local church fills the need. Sometimes friends fill this need, quite apart from the parents. But usually our children in Christ recognize a kinship in one another and delight to visit. That sense of belonging also helps to build security, even if sibling rivalries become part of the scenario. Who better to wrestle with and learn from than a brother or sister in a family? As battling siblings usually mature into close friends, so do children in Christ. Sibling rivalries are nothing to fear, even as wise natural parents chuckle, mediate, and wait for maturity.

Parent-child relationships in Christ are far more temporary than the natural. Sometimes acceptance is the single touch needed, and in a matter of weeks the patient is whole and free. Often, our experience is that re-parenting requires about two to three years. Depending on the degree of need and the person's own developmental timetable, the "child" has matured through childish ways to adolescence to maturity within that time.

One counselee, more perceptive than most, could quite accurately assess her own inner child's age. One day she came in and said, "I'm about six emotionally now, aren't I?" In most ways to outsiders she might have appeared quite mature and free. In her primary relationships with her own immediate family she was accurate. Later she announced, "I'm a teenager now, aren't I?" And she was right. In a few months she was mature and free.

"When I was a child, I used to speak as a child, think as a child, reason as a child; when I became a man, I did away with childish things" (1 Cor. 13:11). A parent in Christ has one fundamental task, to impart such love and strength to the other that he is empowered to "do away" with childish things. Note the "I" in the verse—*I* grow up, *I* put away childish ways. Herein lies perhaps the most crucial guideline for parents in Christ—we must not try to grow the other up; that's the counselee's task and God's job in the heart of the counselee. Though a counselee may regress and relate sometimes childishly to us, we always treat the other as the adult he is. When we give affection, we know we are reaching to the inner child. And when we pray aloud with the counselee, we consciously, intentionally reach to the child. But in all other aspects of the relationship we are careful to treat the other with full respect as an adult. Many who have entered re-parenting have erred drastically in this regard. They reduce grown people to children. Some forms of shepherding and discipling become so notorious in this regard as to prevent many from entering this field who should.

Pitfalls abound in re-parenting. Some friends of ours had

to give up on a girl who came to live with them because she would not stop projecting her parental expectations upon them and consequently would not stop rebelling against what she only thought they felt and meant. Parents in Christ may (sometimes unwittingly) unplug inner volcanoes which have nowhere to come out but on them. Children in Christ may need to express love and receive touches of love so much that outsiders may think wrongly of the relationship—"Did you see the way that young girl looks at him? You'd think he'd know better!" or "Is Mary aware of the way that young man hangs around her? His intentions can't be right or he wouldn't be hanging around her like he does!" Parents must be so secure as to be able to withstand gossips and maligners without being ruffled.

A wise proverb says, "If you find a man of wisdom, let your foot wear out his threshhold." Children sometimes want to latch on and spend inordinate amounts of time just soaking up the family atmosphere. Sometimes that ought to be allowed and sometimes it gets out of hand; parents need to exercise discernment carefully about this, so as to open the home fully at some times with some such children in Christ and tactfully draw lines and limits at other times.

Sometimes having surrogate children either in the home or frequently visiting becomes a blessing to natural children. Our six children have all been blessed and matured by being part of our ministry to others. But we are careful to watch that our own children's time and attention is not given too much to others. One man and wife we know have had too many foster children in the home for too many years. Now their children feel neglected and left out, and their own space and time with each other has been invaded too much and lost. The home life is disrupted, tension and battles rend the peace of the home every day. It is not wisdom to take on so much that there is no healthy home life left to impart; natural children's God-given right to peace and joy in their own home must not be sacrificed.

Some counselees have had no other experience in the

home than to compete with siblings. Some lie and cheat and steal. Some are seductive both to the parents and/or to siblings. Some are loud and boisterous. Some teach wrong things. Some entice others to immoral, reckless, or inconsiderate actions. Parents must be alert to protect their children—in body, heart, and mind. The struggle can help parents, as their own children see and discuss wrong examples, in training them in right ways. But when and if too many forces impinge on the home, parents must hold their calling to raise their own in security as their absolute first priority.

Not all surrogate parenting is successful, and we need to be sensitive to the guidance of the Lord, directly and through pastor and friends, as He sometimes says, *"Hang in there; you are not a hireling, to flee out"* (see John 10:13), and at other times when He may say, *"Quitting is not flight; it is merely wisdom to admit that this attempt isn't working out."*

As each person in counseling comes closer to the core rottenness and thus to the depth of real, life-changing repentance, he approaches levels of fear heretofore unknown. One pastor friend and his wife entered into a small group with Paula and me. As the Holy Spirit began to reach to the inner core of him, he said, "I don't believe I am going to like what I see." At the depths of us all is a nature so evil it cannot be healed; it can only be slain. One way of viewing the book of Revelation is to see that it can also be a parable of our interior life. Once one confronts his inner depths, he knows that whatever "beast" may be out there, his first battle is with his own inner beast. He takes home to his own heart such scriptures (Rev. 13-21) as a parable of his own interior Armageddon. (This is not to say there is not an exterior "beast," "Armageddon," etc.—only that the wise know the same is in their own hearts.) This pastor saw the beginning depths of the battle, and fled. Subsequently, since he had refused to listen to the kind messenger (the Holy Spirit), a pharasaical, false, holiness teaching took hold of him and his church, and cost him his pastorate. The same flight may happen in spiritual parent-child relationships.

When parents in Christ discern flight mechanisms developing, they need to pray strength into the other (Eph. 3:14) and then to confront the other. Needless to say, tact is paramount, but even without tact, chastising and discipline are wisdom at all times. There is no guarantee a parent will be able to keep a child from fleeing. We could not keep that pastor from fleeing from the depths of himself, though we tried everything we knew to do. Parents need to have "see through" faith for their children in such cases. We need to be able to hold in heart the faith that though our loved one has not chosen the safe road, God will teach him the hard way, and he will come out wiser in the end. It is important to know when to let go—even as we had to learn to let our natural children learn the hard way, as the father of the prodigal son had to let him go.

Re-parenting in Christ is similar to natural parenting save in this one dimension: that in it God is not merely raising a child, as He is in natural homes. He may also be digging to the depth of transformation. There is a depth of transformation that not all Christians enter. Some call it the "wilderness experience," some call it "the long dark night of the soul." We wrote of it in *The Elijah Task*, pages 61-64. Whether or not all are chosen (1 Pet. 2:9, Eph. 1:3-5), only a few respond to enter such depths. Those who do may also be in a re-parenting process. Those children will require the parent to be perceptive and to stand by longer in the process, letting it happen. It is especially important that parents in Christ know when a child in Christ is entering that time of shattering and brokenness reserved for only those whom God receives for fullness. Such children of the Lord will require paradoxically different treatment than other children in Christ. They must not be palliated, over-comforted, helped too much, counseled too much, or expected to perform outwardly as competently as others or even as they themselves previously could. They will not be helped at all by pity or sympathy, and little by empathy. Theirs is a private desert of death, and needs to be so. But paradoxically they will need the parents to stand by more than others who may not be going through such throes. They need precisely and only that—standing by. They need to know, while everything else is in interior flux, that their parents in Christ are *standing*, merely there, not changing, not doing anything but being something of calm permanence which does not change.

Parents then fulfill 1 Cor. 13:7 at its highest. They bear what the one being crucified cannot bear, even as the Father sent an angel to strengthen Jesus in the garden (Luke 22:43). They stand by quietly believing when the other can't believe for himself any more. They hope when the worm in the chrysalis has lost hope. They endure whatever flip-flops and hurts the other goes through, saying nothing. It is important in such situations that parents in Christ know to say nothing, only to be there, for whatever they impart will only postpone that person from entering fullness. Each child must find for himself or the wilderness does not accomplish its full purpose. Parents must know then not to teach and advise as they would another not so engaged. They must only stand and watch, knowing that watching is far from inactive; it is love at its fullest. (We would like to protect ourselves from the suffering of it by getting the other through it faster and easier, but true love knows it must not.)

Sometimes those who are single—never married, widowed or divorced—find themselves called to be parents-in-Christ, sometimes for persons chronologically older than themselves. In the Roman Catholic Church, priests and religious have long been "spiritual directors" (a position much akin to re-parenting). Since it is the Father who accomplishes, and since we have all had experience being raised in natural families, of course the unmarried, even the never married, can raise children in Christ. As no one can know to advise married couples and parents so well as a married parent, it would be far better if the counselor were married and a parent, but lack need not prevent. God can impart wisdom. Not having a mate also leaves the counselor vulnerable, but that also is regularly overcome, for example by fathers and nuns in the Roman Catholic Church. Though we could all point to instances of seduction or failure, so could we in cases of married counselors. In short, though married parents have a natural head start in counseling and in re-parenting, no single person should feel disqualified or second class—it is God who accomplishes.

As love is the cornerstone of re-parenting, transparency is its touchstone. We shall know whether success has been attained not only by the signs of maturity given earlier but primarily by one distinction—has the person reached through to Jesus? Is he closer to Him than he was before (Phil. 3:7-10)? Does he know and cherish Jesus more, or less? Is his walk in Him stronger and freer? Natural maturity is fine, but we want foremost growth in Christ. Is he into the Word more? Does he attend church more faithfully? Has he found a viable ministry in Christ? Is he seeking the Lord more zealously? Is his devotional life more tender and full?

It is the Word of God which causes growth in Christ. "Like newborn babes, long for the pure milk of the word, that by it you may grow in respect to salvation" (1 Pet. 2:2). Counselors and parents in Christ only adjust that growth (Eph. 4:11-12). We do not cause growth. God does, mainly through His Word. We must be careful never to replace God, in attention, affection or whatever is happening. The other must be kept free first to relate to God himself. We stand by. Only that.

Body Ministry and Fellowship

The hand of the Lord was upon me, and He brought me out by the Spirit of the Lord and set me down in the middle of the valley; and it was full of bones. And He caused me to pass among them round about, and behold, there were very many on the surface of the valley; and lo, they were very dry. And He said to me, "Son of man, can these bones live?" And I answered, "O Lord God, Thou knowest." Again He said to me, "Prophesy over these bones, and say to them, 'O dry bones, hear the word of the Lord.' Thus says the Lord God to these bones, 'Behold, I will cause breath to enter you that you may come to life. And I will put sinews on you, make flesh grow back on you, cover you with skin, and put breath in you that you may come alive; and you will know that I am the Lord.' " So I prophesied as I was commanded; and as I prophesied, there was a noise, and behold, a rattling; and the bones came together, bone to its bone. And I looked, and behold, sinews were on them, and flesh grew, and skin covered them; but there was no breath in them. Then He said to me, "Prophesy to the breath, prophesy, son of man, and say to the breath, 'Thus says the Lord God, "Come from the four winds, O breath, and breathe on these slain, that they come to life." ' " So I prophesied as He commanded me, and the breath came into them, and they came to life, and stood on their feet, an exceedingly great army. (Ezek. 37:1-10)

Now there are varieties of gifts, but the same Spirit. And there are varieties of ministries, and the same Lord. And there are varieties of effects, but the same God who works all things in all persons. But to each one is given the manifestation of the Spirit for the common good. *(1 Cor. 12:4-7, italics mine)*

But now God has placed the members, each one of them, in the body, just as He desired. And if they were all one member, where would the body be? But now there are many members, but one body. (1 Cor. 12:18-20)

And if one member suffers, all the members suffer with it; if one member is honored, all the members rejoice with it. Now you are Christ's body, and individually members of it. (1 Cor. 12:26-27)

From whom the whole body, being fitted and held together by that which every joint supplies, according to the proper working of each individual part, causes the growth of the body for the building up of itself in love. *(Eph. 4:16)*

The Body of Christ is not yet fully functioning as a living organism. Right now it more likely resembles a two-year-old's collage—toes stuck gleefully to the head, fingers protruding from the heel, and eyes popping out from the navel. Or, we could be compared to multitudes of fish swimming in the same bowl, largely unaware of relevance or duty to one another. This is true whether we speak of members within one local church, of churches in a denomination, or of independents and denominations in the Body.

That condition will not long remain. The Body will arise like a sleeping giant to stretch in unity and discover its strength.

What remains to be defeated is individualism. Not individualism in itself. We will always need and cherish strong individuals. But the archetype which isolates and idolizes. The archetype of privacy now prevents that depth of sharing which alone can awaken the giant.

Arise, shine; for your light has come,
And the glory of the Lord has risen upon you.
For behold, darkness will cover the earth,
And deep darkness the peoples;
But the Lord will rise upon you,
And His glory will appear upon you.
And nations will come to your light,
And kings to the brightness of your rising.
(Isa. 60:1-3)

The Word will not fail to bring forth (Isa. 55:11). The Church will arise.

In the last days,
The mountain of the house of the Lord
Will be established as the chief of the mountains,
And will be raised above the hills;
And all the nations will stream to it.
And many peoples will come and say,
"Come, let us go up to the mountain of the Lord,
To the house of the God of Jacob;
That he may teach us concerning His ways,
And that we may walk in His paths.
For the law will go forth from Zion.
And the word of the Lord from Jerusalem."
(Isa. 2:2-3)

If Isaiah spoke as we believe in vision of these latter days, and of the Church, then this word prophesies of the new. "Zion" is His gathered and prepared people, and so is "Jerusalem." That means that the "law" which will go forth from Zion is not the Old Testament, nor the Ten Commandments nor the Torah. It is the New, not even the Sermon on the Mount, but the commandment of Jesus, "A new commandment I give unto you, That ye love one another; *as* I have loved you" (John 13:34 KJV, italics mine). How did He love us? By laying down his life for us. "Bear ye one another's burdens, and so fulfill *the law of Christ"* (Gal. 6:2 KJV, italics mine). That is the law which will go forth, not as a law passed by a senate, but a way of life written in the heart and acted among men by every Christian.

> In that day shall the branch of the Lord be beautiful and glorious, and the fruit of the earth shall be excellent and comely for them that are escaped of Israel.
>
> And it shall come to pass, that he that is left in Zion, and he that remaineth in Jerusalem, shall be called holy, even every one that is written among the living in Jerusalem:
>
> When the Lord shall have washed away the filth of the daughters of Zion, and shall have purged the blood of Jerusalem from the midst thereof by the spirit of judgment, and by the spirit of burning.
>
> And the Lord will create upon every dwelling place of mount Zion, and upon her assemblies, a cloud and smoke by day, and the shining of a flaming fire by night: for upon all the glory shall be a defence.
>
> And there shall be a tabernacle for a shadow in the day time from the heat, and a place of refuge, and for a covert from storm and from rain. (Isa. 4:2-6 KJV)

The Shekinah glory of God will again rest over God's people, this time not only over the tabernacle ("her assemblies") as in the wilderness, but "over every dwelling place," meaning over every home of every Christian! Each and every one in the Church will be called holy. When? "When the Lord shall have washed away the filth . . . by the spirit of judgment and by the spirit of burning." That means that the fullness of power waits upon one thing—for the coming of the spirit of judgment and burning. That very thing is prophesied as the task of God's "messenger."

> Behold, I am going to send My messenger, and he will clear the way before Me. And the Lord, whom you seek, will suddenly come to His temple; and the messenger of the covenant, in whom you delight, behold, He is coming, says the Lord of hosts. But who can endure the day of His coming? And who can stand when He appears? For he is like

a refiner's fire and like fullers' soap. And He will sit as a smelter and purifier of silver, and He will purify the sons of Levi and refine them like gold and silver, so that they may present to the Lord offerings in righteousness. Then the offering of Judah and Jerusalem will be pleasing to the Lord, as in the days of old and as in former years. Then I will draw near to you for judgment; and I will be a swift witness against the sorcerers and against the adulterers and against those who swear falsely, and against those who oppress the wage earner in his wages, the widow and the orphan, and those who turn aside the alien, and do not fear Me, says the Lord of hosts. (Mal. 3:1-5)

For behold, the day is coming, burning like a furnace; and all the arrogant and every evildoer will be chaff; and the day that is coming will set them ablaze, says the Lord of hosts, so that it will leave them neither root nor branch. But for you who fear My name the sun of righteousness will rise with healing in its wings; and you will go forth and skip about like calves from the stall. And you will tread down the wicked, for they shall be ashes under the soles of your feet on the day which I am preparing, says the Lord of hosts. Remember the law of Moses My servant, even the statutes and ordinances which I commanded him in Horeb for all Israel. Behold, I am going to send you Elijah the prophet before the coming of the great and terrible day of the Lord. And he will restore the hearts of the fathers to their children, and the hearts of the children to their fathers, lest I come and smite the land with a curse. (Mal. 4:1-6)

The Church does not exist for itself. Its glory is not to bask in God's presence. That is our joy and His joy, to have His sons in fellowship with Him. Its glory is in being that ". . . shadow in the daytime from the heat and for a place of refuge, and for a covert from storm and rain." God does not intend to jerk His own out of the world so He can beat up on everyone who hasn't received Him. It is the exact opposite! He sees the increasing wickedness of mankind and knows the holocausts He must send in reaping for what we have sown. Therefore, "God so hated the world that He pulled the Son out of it"—shame on mankind for ever perverting a proper understanding of God's

Word and of his nature so! No! "God so *loved* the *world* that he *gave* his only begotten Son . . . ." He is still sending the Son, that when men reap the horrible destructions they so richly deserve, His Church may be there, in the midst of tribulation, to spread a canopy of defense, to be an umbrella of protection, a mother hen under which the frightened chicks of the world may run for cover!

God is raising up the Church to stand, prepared and victorious, an army of light in a darkened world. That presages a definitive, learned and achieved life style—a people who have become disciplined to live Christ regularly, as instinctively as breathing, for the welfare of others. What God wants is a transformed people, through whom the sacrificial life of Jesus is as normal as flowers reaching for sunlight.

Many Christians yearn for the life style without paying the price of disciplined effort to learn and achieve: "I accepted Jesus and suddenly my life was changed" is the testimony heard again and again in the Christian media and at inspirational banquets. Such claims need some translation. "Suddenly" Jesus' power *is* available for transformation, but real change is always only sustained by multitudes of subsequent little choices and deliberate acting upon them:

> Even so *consider* yourselves to be dead to sin, but alive to God in Christ Jesus. Therefore do not *let* sin reign in your mortal body that you should obey its lusts, and *do not go on presenting* the members of your body to sin as instruments of unrighteousness; but *present yourselves* to God as those alive from the dead, and your members as instruments of righteousness to God. (Rom. 6:11-13, italics mine)

When we have prayed for and received forgiveness, when we have in prayer brought the power of an old habit structure to death on the cross, the old way has no more *claim* upon us. However, it may have some power to allure and grab us because: (1) we have so long practiced that habitual way of thinking, of feeling, and of acting that it is the easiest way to go, causing us to slide into the familiar groove, without thinking; (2) Satan would love to entice or push us to act out the proverb, "Like a dog that returns to its vomit Is a fool who repeats his folly" (Prov. 26:11). That means that each time we are tempted to act in the sinful way from which we have been set free, we have the power by the presence of Jesus in us to stop, and to make a choice. "I recognize that I am tempted (for instance) to respond with an outburst of temper. Lord, I'd really like to belt that guy! I know where that old habit started (in my childhood). Thank you, Lord, that I *have been* set free by the blood of Jesus. It no longer has the right or power to control and drive me. I renounce that old habit. I *will not* respond in the old way. Come, Lord Jesus, let your living presence within me supply me with a wise and loving answer to the present irritation." Especially when we are newly set free, the choosing of the new way may involve some struggle, but as we persist, the new way will gradually become that which automatically flows from us as a trained-in habit pattern. We will always retain enough of the struggle to keep us aware that without Jesus we can do nothing (John 15:5).

The irritations which trigger our old habit patterns are not always easily recognizable. They are often like sneaky little foxes slipping in to eat our tender grapes.

Catch the foxes for us, The little foxes that are ruining the vineyards, While our vineyards are in blossom. (Song of Sol. 2:15)

In Bible lands, when a field was planted, a hedge was put about that field to protect it from invasion by small, hungry animals. A booth was erected on stilts in the midst of the field and a boy was hired to watch for intruders. Spotting an animal breaking through the hedge, the boy would hurl a stone with his slingshot in an attempt to frighten away the potential attacker. Or he would descend from his high perch to chase away or to catch and throw out the more persistent ones.

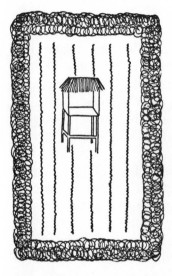

In the same way there are foxes of thought which can creep through our mental and emotional defenses to threaten the development of the new fruit of the garden of our life as it begins to blossom in us. A reformed alcoholic may take just a little nip to relax his nerves before encountering that next, most-important client. A healed homosexual may return to former associates too soon in his zeal to help. A person may indulge in a bit of fantasizing in loneliness and fall prey to an old pattern of self-pity or to the enticement of a relationship which wrongly promises comfort.

Any one of us may indulge in a short flash of anger (because "they deserve it" or "they have to learn not to walk on people") and soon find ourselves overwhelmed and carried away by our emotional outburst. Any acceptance or expression of "just a little won't hurt," when the tender grapes of our new life are still in fragile blossom, leaves us wide open to the taking over of our garden by little foxes who will greedily devour our promises of new life and grow thereby to be big foxes who rule the garden before we have experienced much harvest of fruit in our lives.

It is for this reason that we read such passages from the Scriptures:

> We have not ceased to pray for you and to ask that you may be filled with the knowledge of His will in all spiritual wisdom and understanding, so that you may walk in a manner worthy of the Lord, to please Him in all respects, bearing fruit in every good work and increasing in the knowledge of God; strengthened with all power, according to His glorious might, for the attaining of all steadfastness and patience, joyously giving thanks to the Father, who has qualified us to

share in the inheritance of the saints in light. (Col. 1:9-12, italics mine)

As you therefore have received Christ Jesus the Lord, *so walk in Him*, having been *firmly rooted* and *now being built up* in Him and *established* in your faith, just as you were instructed, and overflowing with gratitude. *See to it* that no one takes you captive through philosophy and empty deception . . . . (Col. 2:6-8, italics mine)

(See also Eph. 4:1, 1 Thess. 2:12, Eph. 2:10)

We are called to live and grow in a healthful balance of *resting* in the Lord with a sure knowledge of the fact that it is not by might, not by power, but by the Lord's Spirit that we accomplish anything (Zech. 4:6), *coupled with very active, moment-by-moment discipline:*

"Conduct yourselves with wisdom . . ." (Col. 4:5).

"Let your speech always be seasoned with grace . . ." (Col. 4:6).

"Let the peace of Christ rule in your hearts . . . *be* thankful" (Col. 3:15).

". . . *do not be* embittered . . ." (Col. 3:19).

". . . *be* obedient" (Col. 3:20).

". . . *do your work heartily* . . ." (Col. 3:23).

". . . *examine* everything carefully . . ." (1 Thess. 5:21).

". . . *abstain* from every form of evil . . ." (1 Thess. 5:22).

"Fight the good fight of faith; *take hold* of the eternal life to which you were called . . ." (1 Tim. 6:12).

"Be diligent to present yourself approved to God as a workman who does not need to be ashamed . . ." (2 Tim. 2:15).

"Refuse foolish and ignorant speculations . . ." (2 Tim. 2:23).

"Continue in the things you have learned" (2 Tim. 3:14).

". . . *endure* hardship" (2 Tim. 4:5).

". . . do not speak against one another . . ." (James 4:11).

". . . do not complain . . ." (James 5:9).

". . . *keep fervent* in your love for one another" (1 Pet. 4:8).

". . . *casting* all your anxiety on Him" (1 Pet. 5:7).

". . . *make* straight paths for your feet . . ." (Heb. 12:13).

"Pursue peace with all men . . ." (Heb. 12:14).

"*See to it* . . . that no root of bitterness springing up causes trouble . . ." (Heb. 12:15).

"*Keep* yourselves in the love of God" (Jude 21).

". . . applying all *diligence*, in your faith supply moral excellence, and in your moral excellence, knowledge, . . . *self-control*, and in your self-control, *perseverance*, and in your perseverance, godliness; and in your godliness, brotherly kindness, and in your brotherly kindness, Christian love" (2 Pet. 1:5-7).

All of these scriptures of discipline possess one basic motif; they are all meant to establish and maintain the life of Jesus in us. That life is His life of giving us to others for their sake. Such a life creates humility, for it so often drives us against the stubborn walls of our yet-undead flesh that we see again and again our continual need of daily death and rebirth. We soon lose our willingness to judge others and feel superior, wondering how they can be gracious when we so often can't.

> Do nothing out of selfish ambition or vain conceit, but in humility consider others better than yourselves. Each of you should look not only to your own interests, but also to the interests of others. (Phil. 2:3-4 NIV)

When self is finally overcome (and what more appropriately than self can Jesus be mentioning as a constant refrain as something that needs to be overcome in Rev. 2:7, 11, 17, 26; 3:5, 12, 21?), then the Body will be one constant light of love poured out for the sake of mankind and all the heavens as God intended.

> Although I am less than the least of all God's people, this grace was given me: to preach to the Gentiles the unsearchable riches of Christ, and to make plain to everyone the administration of this mystery, which for ages past was kept hidden in God, who created all things. His intent was that now, through the church, the manifold wisdom of God should be made known to the rulers and authorities in the

heavenly realms, according to his eternal purpose which he accomplished in Christ Jesus our Lord. (Eph. 3:8-11 NIV)

The end of transformation is not a few scattered individuals who shine as sparks running through the stubble (Isa. 47:14). It is an army of fire blazing a pathway of mercy. No one is fully transformed who does not yet know himself to be one tiniest portion of the Body of Christ. Ephesians 4:16 says that we are to be ". . . fitted and held together by that which every joint supplies, according to the proper working of each individual part. . . ." As each transforming individual contributes that unique glory (1 Cor. 15:41-42) God created him to be, our joining supplies to each of us what we need from one another, as all are held together by love. That supply mutually equips, and the Body upbuilds. We need one another. No man is complete alone.

However significant any man's contribution may be, the warfare is that of an army, and the victory is that of the Lord of hosts (Gen. 32:2, Josh. 5:14, Ps. 103:21).

The fullness of transformation means that we will no longer have to think to remind ourselves that we are an army. We will no longer have to work to establish teamwork. We will no longer have to struggle against the self which isolates, nor have to fear domination and control. Oneness will be our most natural and easy ground (Ps. 133), and blessedness will roll down like a mighty river. The purpose of transformation is to bring us to that point, in which unity of faith has succeeded unity of the Spirit (Eph. 4:3-13), and in which truth sparks responses in love and laughter and all enhance each to fullness—without sweat and strain. The home of each soul is the company of the faithful. And home is the place of rest. We shall know when we are departing from oneness by the recurrence of striving, and shall laughingly and easily return by the door of grace.

Transformation is not the end product. It is the process by which we get there. Transformation proceeds within each individual by the presence and power of the Lord mainly through the company of Christ, but its purpose is not solely to present *individuals* without spot or wrinkle before the Father (Eph. 5:27), but a *Body*, one in all its holy motives and desires. "That he might present it to himself *a glorious church*, not having spot, or wrinkle, or any such thing; that it should be holy and without blemish" (Eph. 5:27 KJV).

Transformation struggles in the beginning by leaps and bounds (and pitfalls) from crag to crag of knowledge and revelation, but it is simple fellowship which walks us in the end across a level plain of rejoicing into the hall of the marriage feast! It is fellowship which graces the heart with possibility for living in heavenly repose and response. It is fellowship which sings a song to tired hearts and sparks resurrection of skills first planted by God and long forgotten by men. It is fellowship which strikes hands and lifts loads far beyond one alone. It is fellowship which finally enables forgetting of what lies behind (Phil. 3:13), and makes possible pressing forward to the mark of the prize of the high calling of God in Christ Jesus (v. 14).

In the end it shall be a chorus, not a solo. And we shall all find a voice which no longer creaks and cracks, and carried in embrace we shall find it easy to stand in judgment, without being fearful.

> By this, love is perfected with us, that we may have confidence in the day of judgment; because as He is, so also are we in this world. There is no fear in love; but perfect love casts out fear, because fear involves punishment, and the one who fears is not perfected in love. We love, because He first loved us. (1 John 4:17-19)

Obeying the command to ". . . remember all the way which the Lord your God has led you in the wilderness these forty years" (Deut. 8:2a) shall no longer be a disgrace but the prelude and vast fount out of which our wisdom arises (Matt. 11:25) to rule the many things over which God places His own in the kingdom (Matt. 25:21-23).

The end of transformation is rule, but not as solitary kings and queens; rather as a company of the faithful, lovingly cherishing what each gives to each.

ELIJAH HOUSE MINISTRY CATALOG

A catalog is available from Elijah House that lists products and resources in the following categories:

I. **COUNSELOR RESOURCES** — *Unique tools of reference for any counseling office.* Audio tapes: Theology of Healing; The Healing Process; Healing Early Experiences; Burnout; Responses and Behaviors; Healing Spiritual Wounds; Healing Sexual Abuse; Chemical Dependency.

II. **MINISTRY TRAINING TOOLS** — *Practical teaching for pastors and church leaders.* Audio tapes and manuals: Divine Doctoring of Small Groups; Prayer Ministry Teams; New Testament Church; Prayer Ministry Teams.

III. **ADULT EDUCATION** — *Terrific curriculum for adult study.* Audio tapes: Life in Christ; Healing the Wounded Spirit; Renewal of the Mind; Twelve Functions of the Prophetic Office; Nurturing the Prophetic; What God Is Saying to the Church.

IV. **PERSONAL STUDY LIBRARY** — *Anyone can benefit from these teachings about marriage, children, and understanding ourselves.* Audio and video tapes: Before You Say 'I Do'; Married Forever; For Men Only; Functions of a Father's Love; Ministering to Youth and Children; Parental Love; Keeping Your Healing; Living a Full Live!' Comfortably Corporate; Garlands for Ashes; How Could It Happen?; Life's Common Sexual Experiences; Homosexuality.

V. **BOOKS** — *Ground-breaking books about inner healing and issues facing the Church today.* The Transformation of the Inner Man, Restoring the Christian Family; Healing the Wounded Spirit; The Elijah Task; Why Some Christians Commit Adultery; Healing Victims of Sexual Abuse; The Renewal of the Mind; Wounded Warriors; Healing Womens' Emotions.

Write to:
Elijah House
1000 S. Richards Road
Post Falls, ID 83854

FOR WOMEN EVERYWHERE

"I have never read a book that speaks so directly to me," one woman wrote. "I feel as if Paula Sandford knows me, and her book is like a personal counseling session. She's in tune with the feelings of women today."

As a wife, mother, teacher and counselor, Paula Sandford writes with compassion, from her heart to yours. Her sensitive and liberating insights will help you to:

- Cope with your feelings
- Deal with grief and sorrow
- Identify your source of pain
- Express your emotions
- Sort through confusing signals
- Experience emotional wholeness

A HANDBOOK FOR FAMILIES

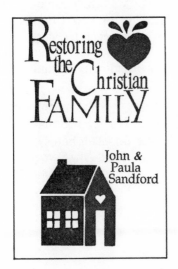

"And He shall turn the heart of the fathers to the children, and the heart of the children to their fathers" (Mal. 4:6). God is restoring families to His original purpose — to be the foundation of society, the seedbed for Christian values. Those who have discovered this treasure chest of teaching report that it has transformed their families. Fresh insights from the Sandfords' teaching and counseling ministry will enable your family to grow and develop according to God's plan.

AVAILABLE AT CHRISTIAN BOOKSTORES EVERYWHERE.

INNER HEALING CLASSIC

This sequel continues in the footsteps of **The Transformation of the Inner Man** by providing new insight and healing salve to such problems as rejection, child abuse, occult involvement and generational sin and depression.

Healing the Wounded Spirit is for everyone who suffers from hidden hurts — past or present. Through this book, God can help you to discern a wounded spirit in yourself and others and, best of all, He will show you how to receive His healing power in your life.

PROPHETIC INSIGHT

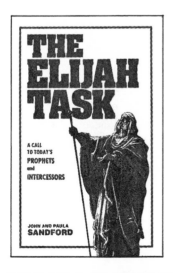

In the **Elijah Task,** John and Paula Sandford give a clear message, a balanced and practical in-depth study of the office of a prophet in the church and world today, the power and ways of intercession, and prophetic listening to God.

TRANSFORMED BY THE RENEWING OF YOUR MIND!

THE RENEWAL OF THE MIND glows with fresh insights and anointing. Its revolutionary approach will still the battleground where carnal thoughts and feelings rage. There is a solution — a process of spiritual transformation by the renewing of your mind. As you read, new peace and life will fill your innermost being.

WHY ADULTERY?

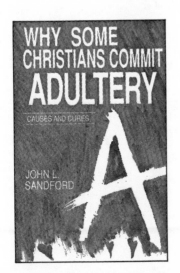

John L. Sandford founder of Elijah House, and author of several books on inner healing, provides answers for all who are concerned about this issue. He explores the personal causes that may lead a Christian into adultery and reveals biblical cures.

The book's main purpose, the author states, "is to provide informed bases for compassion and healing, and keys of knowledge for protection from falling."

AVAILABLE AT CHRISTIAN BOOKSTORES EVERYWHERE.

RESTORATION FOR THE ABUSED

With profound empathy and clear understanding, Paula Sandford ministers healing to all who have been victimized by sexual abuse — the abused child, parents, relatives and friends, as well as the abuser. She has dealt with this problem through many years of counseling and teaching, and this book shows how the victims of sexual abuse can find new life and freedom.

HEALING FOR THE WOUNDS OF STRESS

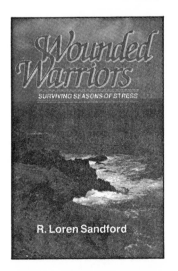

The author of *Wounded Warriors,* Pastor R. Loren Sandford, knows what it's like to be in a stressed out and wounded condition, as he came near to a total breakdown while ministering to others.

His book provides believers with an honest look at stress — its symptoms, causes and effects — and it shows how to deal with this all-too-common problem in effective, lasting ways. For the person who lives with or counsels a wounded warrior, this book imparts empathy and wisdom. For the wounded warrior himself, this book imparts hope, peace and healing.

BOOK ORDER FORM

To order additional books by John and Paula Sandford or Loren Sandford direct from the publisher, please use this order form. Also note that your local bookstore can order titles for you.

Book Title	Price	Quantity	Amount
Healing Womens' Emotions	$10.99	_____	$_____
The Renewal of the Mind	$ 9.99	_____	$_____
Why Some Christians Commit Adultery	$ 9.99	_____	$_____
Healing Victims of Sexual Abuse	$ 8.99	_____	$_____
The Transformation of the Inner Man	$12.99	_____	$_____
Healing the Wounded Spirit	$13.99	_____	$_____
Restoring the Christian Family	$11.99	_____	$_____
The Elijah Task	$ 9.99	_____	$_____
Wounded Warriors (by L. Sandford)	$ 7.99	_____	$_____
Total Book Amount			$_____
Shipping & Handling — Add $2.00 for the **first** book, **plus** $0.50 for **each** additional book			$_____
TOTAL ORDER AMOUNT — Enclose check or money order (No cash or C.O.D.'s)			$_____

Make check or money order payable to: **VICTORY HOUSE, INC.**
Mail order to: **VICTORY HOUSE, INC.**
            P.O. Box 700238
            Tulsa, OK 74170

Please print your name and address **clearly:**

Name _____

Address _____

City _____

State or Province _____

Zip or Postal Code _____

Telephone Number (_____) _____

Foreign orders must be submitted in U.S. dollars. Foreign orders are shipped by uninsured surface mail. We ship all orders within 48 hours of receipt of order.

MasterCard or VISA — For orders totaling **over $20.00** you may use your MasterCard or VISA by completing the following information or for **faster service** call toll-free **1-800-262-2631.**

Card Name _____

Card Number _____

Expiration Date _____

Signature_____
                    (authorized signature)